Dempsey J. Travis

AN AUTOBIOGRAPHY C.

Black Jazz

introduction by Studs Terkel

Library of Congress Cataloging in Publication Data

Travis, Dempsey, 1920–
    Autobiography of Black jazz.

    Bibliography: p.
    Includes index.
    1. Jazz music—Illinois—Chicago—History and criticism. 2. Afro-Ameri-
cans—Illinois—Chicago—Music—History and criticism. 3. Jazz musicians—
Illinois—Chicago. 4. Afro-American musicians—Illinois—Chicago.

I. Title.
ML3508.T7 1983   785.42'08996073077311   83–16899
ISBN 0-941484-03-3

To my mother and late father,
who taught me that
black was beautiful
forty-five years before
the idea became acceptable.

Acknowledgements

Whenever you attempt to introduce from the dais V.I.P.s that are scattered in the audience, you invariably omit someone. Hundreds of very important people helped me to complete this work. I am not going to introduce them because space will not permit it, and I do not want to leave anyone out.

However, there are some V.I.P.s who sit on the dais regularly with me to whom special thanks must be given and they include: Ruby Davis, my senior researcher, who unearthed thousands of valuable papers and documents; Sondra Gair of WBEZ for whose great assistance I will be forever grateful; a special appreciation to the staff of the Vivian Harsh Afro-American Collections of the Carter G. Woodson Library in Chicago; Orville A. Hurt, the illustrator who designed the jacket of this book; Paula King, my administrative assistant, who transcribed hundreds of tapes and deciphered my script with a perpetual smile; Pam Frye, who typeset manuscripts and made silent corrections; Anita Miller, whose aid extended beyond ordinary editing; and Horace Taylor, graphic designer, who worked hard to lay out this entire book page by page and pasted up the final copy. Finally, without the help of my wife Moselynne, this book would not have been written. She understands better than I that you cannot write a book in a crowd.

Dempsey J. Travis
October 1, 1983

In 1965 when he was sixty-six years old, the Pulitzer Prize Music Committee recommended Duke Ellington for a special award. That recommendation was turned down by the full Pulitzer committee and America's most creative jazz composer said:

> Fate is being very kind to me. Fate doesn't
> want me to be too famous too young.

Duke Ellington
1965

Contents

PART TWO: THE VOICES OF JAZZ ARTISTS FROM THE PAST AND PRESENT

Introduction

This is like no other jazz memoir I've read. The author is not a jazz critic nor a jazz artist. He is simply a friend of the heroes and heroines, whose dreams, dark and sweet, he recounts. And whose hard truths he captures. Because he is simply a friend, there are things revealed that might otherwise be forever hidden. Or blown up into myth. No, Dempsey Travis offers us an informal, mostly oral, history of the way it was. That is all one can ask.

As I play, for the millionth time, Earl Hines' "Boogie Woogie on St Louis Blues," I hear that distant voice, ebulliently calling out, "Play it until 1951." I always got a wallop out of Fatha's playing and out of George Dixon's impulsive shout. Now, thanks to Travis, I know more about these artists and the plantation on which they labored.

Oh, yes, I loved all those memories of the Grand Terrace, where Hines and his gifted colleagues held forth. Though I was vaguely aware of Syndicate connections, I had no idea of the power they held over the jazzmen. And of the meager payoff. The Mob, though at times grandly handing out a C note, held the artists in bondage. In reading this work, you come to love the artists even more—for their survival as much as for their gifts.

> "Hey, boy, come here!" Ralph Capone called out as he beckoned toward "Lucky" Millinder, the bandleader in the syndicate who controlled the Cotton Club in Cicero, Illinois. Millinder, who was dressed formally in white tie and tails with a wing-tip shirt, hastily moved in snow-white slippers from the bandstand to the boss's front row table.
>
> "Boy, I like the way you colored people play music and I get a big kick watching your jazzy steps and pearly smiles as you direct that band," said Capone. "My brother, Al, and I decided we're going to keep you boys working regularly, but you can't work for nobody but us."

There are certain things a man tells his friends from high school days that he might neglect to tell the most sophisticated of critics or dedicated of historians. Those long-remembered hurts and humiliations. The little things. Travis and Millinder go back to days, so long ago, of Wendell Phillips High. Did I ever tell you, Dempsey, about the time . . . hence, another revelation.

Listen to this portrait of the most celebrated of all jazz clubs:

> The bandstand at the Harlem Cotton Club was a replica of a Southern mansion, with large white columns and a backdrop painted with weeping willows and slave quarters. The orchestra performed in front of the large double doors to the mansion. Down four steps was the dance floor, which was also used for floor shows. The waiters were dressed in red tuxedos, like butlers in a Southern mansion. . . . The entire scene created a *Gone With the Wind* atmosphere that made every white male feel·like Rhett Butler and every white woman like Scarlet O'Hara. Since the waiters were paid only one dollar a night, they had to hustle like Rochester and hope that Rhett Butler would leave a big tip.

Aside from his boyhood closeness to the jazzmen from Chicago, Dempsey's appreciation of his father's art molded him. Louis Travis was a "piano man." That meant only one thing, during all those hard times, before and after the Depression. It meant the lord of the rent parties. It was the blues, of course: "How Long Blues" and "The Fives." And boogie woogie: exhilaration and delight, as "the little girl with the red dress on" is doing her stuff. And the shot glasses of moonshine are lined up on the ledge of the piano. As tribute to the man making all that music. And all the fried chicken, cole slaw and spaghetti you could eat. And, of course, going a long way in helping pay the rent for the host/hostess at Mecca Flats or the Baby Doll. Those multi-apartment buildings were cities, worlds in themselves. And the piano man was emperor.

Dempsey recalls his mother's pride in her husband's artistry and manner, who was a common laborer six days a week. "Your daddy would assume an air of extraordinary importance as he sat down at the upright piano with his black der-by hat tilted forward and to the right with a ten-cent cigar hanging out of the left side of his mouth . . . the rent party dancers would shout: 'Louie! Louie! Play that thing!' "

Why, he was a mirror image of Willie "The Lion" Smith. Or was he simply a man named Louis Travis living out his dream, smack in the middle of a hard life? He was Meade Lux Lewis, the car washer; Jimmy Yancey, the ballpark grounds-keeper; Albert Ammons, doing what he had to do. He was all these and himself. And a son remembers.

Here are the memories, too, of Milt Hinton, "the Judge", and Franz Jackson and an under-rated old friend, John Young. And the fabled band teacher at DuSable High, Captain Walter Dyett, who taught, and I do mean taught, some of our very best.

As I read these pages, I remember a small white boy standing out in front of Dreamland Ballroom on Chicago's West Side, listening hard to the strains coming from inside, where his older brother was dancing. He was hearing for the first time—this was in the Twenties—a kind of music that caught him and held him for the rest of his life. He was hearing jazz. Oh yeah, memories of Charlie Cook's Band and Lottie Hightower's are made green, in the reading of this book.

Studs Terkel

PHOTO CREDITS

Opal Bernaugh: pp. 110 (top), 115, 119, 178, 209, 210, 213, 215, 216, 267, 271 (lower left), 456, 461. *Ken Blewett:* pp. 74 (lower), 102 (lower right), 103 (top), 152, 153, 154, 155, 156, 163 (right), 165 (top), 166 (left), 170, 171, 174 (top right and lower), 175, 177, 189, 201, 207 (top), 218, 225, 260, 271 (lower right), 326 (left), 427, 472, 495. *Johnny Board:* pp. 209, 210, 213, 215, 216. *William Y. Browne:* pp. 15, 27. *Roy Butler:* pp. 223 (top), 323 (left). *Dr. Jive Cadillac:* p. 101. *Cab Calloway:* pp. 220, 223 (lower), 227, 230, 231, 233. *Floyd Campbell:* pp. 24 (top), 211, 236, 238, 241, 243, 244, 245, 246, 247, 248. *Chicago Historical Society:* pp. 13, 55, 85. *Carol Chilton:* pp. 250, 253, 255, 256, 258, 259 (left). *Charlie Cole:* pp. 422 (bottom), 263 (outer), 271 (top), 497. *Freddie Cole:* pp. 24 (lower), 42, 124, 125, 126, 129, 131, 132, 133 (top right), 135, 136, 137 (top left and lower right), 140, 141, 142, 143, 168, 174 (top left), 312. *Barrett Deems:* pp. 274, 278, 280. *James DeLisa:* pp. 122, 139. *George Dixon:* pp. 38, 40 (top), 44 (right), 47, 48, 53, 67 (lower), 71, 72 (lower), 160 (top), 229, 284, 286, 288, 291, 293, 294, 296, 437, 439, 441, 443, 444, 445 (top), 462. *Eva Wheatly Edwards:* pp. 14 (right), 31 (left), 159 (right and lower), 166 (right). *Marty Faye:* pp. 187, 339, 346 (right). *Henry Fort:* pp. 181, 183, 184, 336. *Edward Gillespie:* pp. 89 (lower), 90–91, 92. *Harry Gray:* p. 44 (inset). *Johnny Griffin:* pp. 350, 355 (right), 356, 357, 362. *Vernon Guider:* pp. 104 (top), 108, 165 (lower), 173. *Finnis Henderson:* pp. 137 (top right), 195 (top), 445 (lower), 447, 471 (lower). *Milt Hinton:* pp. 225, 364, 367, 369, 373, 375, 377, 379. *Art Hodes:* pp. 57 (left), 380. *Joe Hughes:* pp. 169, 182, 301, 335. *Franz Jackson:* pp. 277, 388, 390, 395, 397, 398. *Viola Jefferson:* pp. 102 (left), 400, 403, 405, 407, 408, 410. *Eddie Johnson:* pp. 414, 417, 420, 422 (top). *Johnson Publishing Company:* p. 466. *Gordon Jones:* p. 103 (lower). *Nat Jones:* pp. 367, 421. *Ripley B. Mead, Jr.:* p. 29 (top). *Sy Oliver:* pp. 434, 448. *Anthony Overton:* p. 35. *Tommie Patterson:* p. 315 (left). *Eddie Plique:* pp. 95, 96, 97, 99, 102 (right). *Herman Roberts:* pp. 190, 193, 195 (below), 197, 198, 199, 200. *Lonnie Simmons:* pp. 132 (lower right), 133 (top left and bottom), 137 (lower left), 139 (outer). *Maxine Sullivan:* p. 450. *Theater Historical Society—Chicago Chapter:* pp. 144, 147, 149, 150. *Mittie Travis:* pp. 50, 62, 79, 106, 107. *John Young:* pp. 505, 507, 509. *All other photographs are the property of Urban Research Institute, Inc.*

Part One:

They Survived with Music

The 1893 Columbian Exposition. Above is a north view from Machinery Hall.

Chapter 1

The Incubation of Jazz in the White City

The World's Columbian Exposition of 1893 was known also as "The White City", since the buildings on the Fair grounds were all fashioned from a mixture of hemp and plaster which resembled white marble. But The White City was white in another way. After considerable pressure from black groups led by Ida B. Wells and Frederick Douglass, the Directors of the Fair named August 25, 1893 "Colored People's Day". In actual fact the Columbian Commission appointed only one black man—an alternate from the state of Missouri—and serving on the New York Board of Lady Managers was one black woman, Imogene Howard, who pulled together an Afro-American exhibit for the Woman's Building. However, outside of these, and three blacks who held clerical positions on the administrative staff, black people were employed at the Fair only in relatively menial capacities: as janitors, laborers and porters, and even then in relatively small numbers.

Frederick Douglass, the brilliant former slave and Abolitionist, was invited by the Republic of Haiti to manage its pavilion. Douglass had served as the minister to Haiti from September 1889 to July 1891 during the administration of Benjamin Harrison. Potter Palmer invited Douglass to give a speech at a banquet for the representatives of all nations at the opening of the Exposition. His talk was called by the *Cleveland Plaindealer* "the gem of the occasion" which "gently" hinted "at the great injustice done the Afro-American". The *Plaindealer* called the speech "a pleasing incident", and reproduced it in its columns for May 12, 1893:

> I did not come here to entertain, but to be entertained. I have been finely entertained since coming. here. I am entirely unused to making after-dinner speeches. I am almost unused to dinners anyway. I am certainly unused to such dinners as we have had a specimen of this evening. I believe it is usual on occasions of this kind to make short speeches. I am glad this is so, but I never made a short speech in my life with which I was well satisfied, and I never made a very long speech with which anyone else was very well satisfied. (Laughter.)

After this genial opening, Douglass became somewhat more serious, although not so serious as to jar the mood of the evening.

> I look upon this occasion as yours. I have a very small part or lot in it. This is a day . . . for the Caucasian, not for the Ethiopian. It is the day for Spain, for the Castilian; it is the day for Chicago especially. (Applause.) I look upon this as a continuation of the opening of the World's Columbian Exposition, and one of the most pleasing features of the whole affair. This World's Fair, as it is called, has many sides. It has a side for the aesthetic, the lovers of the beautiful. It has a side for the administration, for the organizer and for the discoverer.
>
> But it has also another side, a moral side, which to me is the most important. If this sin-cursed world of ours is blessed with peace, with brotherly love, with fraternity, with millenial affection, we may well claim for this result the participation of the World's Columbian Exposition. ('Hear! Hear!') It has brought together all nations, countries and people. It has shown to us that while the types of mankind differ like the waves of the sea they are together one, like the sea itself: that a common humanity runs through us all. . . These World's Fairs . . . are instrumental in bringing together the children of men, removing mountains of prejudice, envy, of ill-feeling and bringing us into the common brotherhood. It is this aspect of the Columbian exposition which is most precious to my heart, most consonant with the life that I have lived and the cause to which I have devoted what little energy and ability I possess. (Applause.)

Above: The Haitian Pavillion. Left: Ida B. Wells, civil rights leader. Right: Frederick Douglass, ex-slave, Abolitionist, editor of the North Star *newspaper, and distinguished orator.*

Left: Scott Joplin. Right: Arthur Marshall, Joplin's protégé and collaborator on "Swipsey Cake Walk".

A kind of brotherhood did result for black people from this Fair. Hundreds of black itinerant musicians and entertainers came together from all over the country, searching for work in the heightened atmosphere of the Exposition. It was the Haitian building to which they eventually went, because that building, under Frederick Douglass's management, became a showcase for Negro entertainers—the only one on the Fair grounds. It is described in *The Book of the Fair:*

> Near the German building Hayti [sic] erected a modest pavilion of the Southern Colonial style, with broad piazzas on three of its sides, and surmounted by a central cupola, from the flagstaff of which is displayed the national standard in horizontal stripes of red and blue. Above the main portico is the coat-of-arms, and below it, in gilt letters, the words Republique Haitienne, with the figures 1492, 1892 and 1804, the last referring to the acquisition of independence. Of the interior space a large portion is occupied by a central hall, draped with festoons of color, and in the centre a statue of 'Reverie' by a native artist. Relics are freely displayed, among them the rapier of Toussaint L'Ouverture, while others refer to the Columbian era and to the aboriginal inhabitants, including one of

the anchors lost from Columbus's flag-ship in 1493. . . There are also portraits and busts of prominent men, as of the Haytian liberator, of the first president of the republic, and of Frederick Douglass.

All that Hayti has contributed to the Fair is contained within this pavilion, where first of all are native woods, some polished and others in their natural state, the most massive specimen being a huge block of mahogany. There are also minerals, fibres, needlework, laces, embroideries, and various articles of manufacture, especially in leather, including some highly finished saddlery. Coffee is a feature in the display, and of this there are some two-score varieties, the beverage itself being served in an apartment in the rear of the hall. Of sugar there are numerous samples, these with syrups, liquors, liqueurs, and a few other articles. . .

Among the first to wipe their well-travelled shoes on the welcome mat at the door of the Haitian pavilion were Scott Joplin, Bert Williams, Paul Laurence Dunbar, Dr. W. E. B. DuBois and James Weldon Johnson. Although Scott Joplin had no job at the Fair, his visit there enabled him to discover that black musicians playing in relative isolation in various parts of the country had developed a form

Left: Paul Lawrence Dunbar, poet, the 19th century's best known black writer. Right: W. C. Handy, who appeared at the Exposition with his Mahara Minstrels.

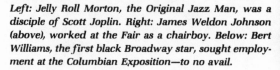

Left: Jelly Roll Morton, the Original Jazz Man, was a disciple of Scott Joplin. Right: James Weldon Johnson (above), worked at the Fair as a chairboy. Below: Bert Williams, the first black Broadway star, sought employment at the Columbian Exposition—to no avail.

of musical expression with common elements. Joplin was overwhelmed with admiration at the technique and style of two of Chicago's most well-known bawdy house piano players: Arthur Marshall and Louis Chauvin. Both men worked in Chicago's red-light district, also known as the Levee—two hundred and sixty licensed houses of prostitution spread out between 18th and 22nd Streets, and running from South Wabash Avenue on the east to Wentworth Avenue on the west.

Also at the Haitian building, Joplin was able to see the Creole Show, a revue in which the black performers discarded the customary blackface minstrel skits and simply sang, danced and played music. The Creole Show gave Joplin the first ray of hope that black music might one day come out of the bawdy house into the concert hall, or at least into the respectable dance hall.

James Weldon Johnson must also have been encouraged by the events at the Haitian building. Johnson was a chairboy at the exposition. He had the opportunity therefore to hear the young Paul Laurence Dunbar read his poetry at the pavilion. Dunbar's work subsequently won the admiration of many whites and inspired blacks with hope. This hope saturates Johnson's best-known poem, "Lift Ev'ry Voice and Sing", which was set to music in 1900 and is now called "the Negro National Anthem". Another impressive presentation at the Haitian pavilion was W. C. Handy's "Mahara's Minstrels" which must certainly have interested both Joplin and Johnson. In this arrangement Handy incorporated elements of both Memphis and Mississippi ragtime for the first time in show tunes.

Joplin stayed in Chicago for nearly a year and worked in bawdy houses and saloons until early 1894, when he went first to St Louis and then to Sedalia, which had one of the largest red light districts in the state of Missouri. In the summer of 1899 he presented John Stark with the manuscript of his revised version of "Maple Leaf Rag". It was an unqualified success: when Joplin moved back to Chicago about this time, and took residence at 2840 Armour Avenue (now the Illinois Institute of Technology campus), he could hear his "Maple Leaf Rag" being played on pianolas in whorehouses up and down State Street, while its twenty-five cent sheet music version was being sold by the thousands in Chicago music stores. Scott Joplin wrote more songs, but by the end of 1905 his creativity seems to have become exhausted.

Seventy-two years later Joplin's work has been internationally acclaimed. In 1974 "The Entertainer", which was originally published in 1902, was used as the theme in the film *The Sting*, and because of this Joplin's music is more popular today than it was in its heyday when more than 100,000 sheet music copies of "Maple Leaf Rag" were sold.

Scott Joplin was the original "Piano Man". Ferdinand "Jelly Roll" Morton, a disciple of Joplin's from New Orleans, bridged the gap between ragtime and jazz. Morton was the most prolific jazz composer in this century. His widow Lottie Joplin has written, "In the early 1900s, Jelly and . . . Porter King were working on a jazz composition when they evidently got stuck and decided to mail it off to Joplin for help. Some months later Joplin completed it and mailed it back. It was not published until years afterward. By then, Scott and Porter were dead, so Jelly named it after his old friend and called it "King Porter Stomp".

It was in Chicago that "King Porter Stomp" was first recorded, by King Oliver in 1924. It was in Chicago that it was made popular by Benny Goodman, playing a Fletcher Henderson arrangement of it in 1936. And of course it had been in Chicago that black musicians had gathered together to share talent and ideas during the Columbian Exposition of 1893—this looked forward to Chicago's Century of Progress Fair of 1933, after which that city became the most fertile ground for jazz, later called "swing". Jazz was not of course conceived in Chicago, but it was most certainly incubated there.

Top: The Frogs, a theatrical association for colored entertainers in the early 1900s. Bert Williams was a member. Below: the Cakewalkers.

Chapter 2

No Seats on the Main Floor

In 1894, the year after the Columbian Exposition, my father's elder brother Otis first set foot—in a size twelve shoe layered with newspapers to keep the wet and cold from its punctured sole—on the turf of the land of Lincoln and was immediately recruited along with several hundred Negroes to break a strike in the stockyards, where the unions were lily-white. In 1900, as another gift of free labor from Georgia to Chicago, my father Louis arrived aboard the Jim Crow car of the New Orleans and Vestibule Limited, wearing a threadbare green box-back suit and a second-hand derby. The youngest brother, Joe "Pretty Boy", arrived in 1904. Like Otis, both Louis and Joe were enrolled instantly upon their arrivals into the profession of strikebreaking. Because the unions wished to keep themselves lily-white, the black man entered the urban job market in the North through a door marked "For strikebreakers only".

The Travis boys were not in the city by the lake very long before they learned that the job market was not the only thing closed off to them. Black leaders in Chicago were upset over the dehumanizing treatment they received whenever they wanted to buy tickets to seats on the main floor or in boxes in theaters outside the Black Belt. Often, indeed, even in theaters in the Black Belt itself Negroes were denied seats on the main floor. My father told me that Chicago Negroes dreamt of a first-class theater of their own where they could sit in dignity wherever they chose.

In 1901 several "top dog" blacks on the South Side came together to open what was to be called Havlin's Theater on a site near 31st and State Streets. Dr George C. Hall, a prominent black physician, was the organizing force behind this plan. He was fed up with the unpleasant treatment he had received at the hands of bigoted box-office clerks, pompous ticket-takers and rude ushers. Hall agreed to invest $20,000 in this theater project and, since there were no university-trained black architects licensed in Illinois, the group hired Saint Suttle, a cakewalk artist, and "Billy" Caldwell of the vaudeville team of Caldwell and Henry, to draw up plans. However the whole venture came to nothing. Dad said, "The idea of a black-owned theater was a hot topic along the Stroll (South State Street) for almost a year and then it evaporated like steam coming out of a teapot."

Three and a half years later the dream of a black-owned theater was to be made reality by a tall, stocky, medium-brown complexioned South Side gambler with a quick smile, named Robert T. Motts, who had come to Chicago from Washington, Iowa, when he was about twenty years old. Motts had learned the gambling and saloon business from Chicago's premier black hustler, John "Mushmouth" Johnson while Motts worked for Johnson at the establishment at 464 South State Street in the First Ward. Motts subsequently opened his own cafe, saloon and gambling operation at 2700 South State. On June 18, 1905 he opened the "Pekin Temple of Music" at that address, at the north end of the building.

According to my father and Uncle Otis, some four hundred well-dressed black people attended the opening of the Pekin Temple, and sat cabaret-style to witness the all-Negro show presented for the first time in the city's history in a theater owned by a black man. Ida B. Wells said later that "the race owed Mr Motts a debt of gratitude for giving us a theater in which we could sit anywhere we chose without any restriction." Attorney Earl B. Dickerson, now ninety-two years old, remembers seeing the perfumed ladies and elegant gentlemen entering the theater. He was thirteen years old at the time, and watched everything from the curb outside the Pekin.

"It was a long and relatively lavish bill," a newspaper critic said. "Many of the acts were typical of the nineties—sentimental, saccharine tear-jerkers. Interspersed between the tears were the new dance acts represented by the cake-walk

Above: Bob Mott's Pekin Theater, 2700 South State Street. Left: The 400 block on South State Street, 1893. Mushmouth Johnson's saloon was here.

Lower Left: The Lafayette Theater in New York, which benefited from the earlier productions at the Pekin.

along with the early ragtime music which had already begun to replace the lush waltztime airs of a period fast ebbing away."

White folks, curious about the Negro theater venture, began to attend the Pekin. The theater's popularity grew, and on April 12, 1906, less than one year after its opening, the Pekin, remodeled, was reopened as the "New Pekin Theater".

The Lafayette and Lincoln theaters of New York have been called the first black dramatic theaters. However, they were both launched almost ten years after the Pekin opened its doors in 1905. It was the Pekin which was the formal cradle of Negro drama in the United States.

Since the Pekin was proof that the Negro community would support theater, white investors began to seek theater sites. Accordingly, in 1909, three theaters were built between 30th and 39th Streets on South State Street: The Grand (3110–12), the Vendome (3145) and the Lincoln (3132).

William Y. Browne, a retired realtor who died recently at the age of eighty-eight, remembered all those theaters.

"As a boy," he said, "I was permitted to go to the theater at six p.m. every Fri-

Earl B. Dickerson

Bill Robinson.

William Y. Browne, a young theatergoer who enjoyed Bert Williams' performances.

day night. My friends and I would always start the evening at the Pekin. Since the shows lasted only one hour, we could go from the Pekin to the Monogram, to the Grand, and then to the Vendome, and be home by eleven o'clock. The entire theater excursion, including candies, would cost each of us less than seventy-five cents. We saw stars like Nettie Lewis singing 'Won't You Be My Teddy Bear?'; Shelton Brooks, who wrote 'Darktown Strutters Ball'; and Bill 'Bojangles' Robinson, the legendary tap dancer who later hit the big time on Broadway. We also saw Clarence Muse, the stage actor who later became the dean of Hollywood black movie stars; and Abbie Mitchell, probably the best actress among the Pekin soubrettes. She distinguished herself later as a star in the stock productions at the Lafayette Theater in New York and received glowing reviews during her many European trips."

This proliferation of theaters in the Black Belt caused no change in the Jim Crow practices at theaters in the Loop. Earl Dickerson says that there were no Jim Crow signs in Chicago Loop theaters saying that blacks had to sit in certain places. That would have been a violation of the Civil Rights Act of 1887. However ushers could readily identify most blacks and those who could not pass for white would automatically be directed to seats in the section unofficially reserved for colored only. On December 12, 1909, the *Chicago Defender* reported:

> On Friday, December 3, 1909, Mr Frank D. Donaldson, one of our enterprising young men, desiring to attend a theatre one evening, selected the Colonial Theatre. . . He . . . bought two tickets for he [sic] and his friend, Mr George A. Wilson. . . . he asked . . . for seats in the balcony, but was told that seats in that part of the house were sold, but he could have two on the main floor. He therefore purchased them. The evening came, he and his friend appeared and presented tickets to an usher who looked at the tickets, then at Mr Donaldson, and . . . whispered to another usher: 'These are niggers; how did they get these tickets?' Mr Donaldson . . . was informed that the tickets were not for that night, but . . . they would seat him in the balcony. This Mr Donaldson objected to and asked for the return of his tickets, stating he would use them on the night for which they were intended, but the usher told him he would do nothing of the sort, and the best thing he could do would be to get out, which Mr Donaldson did, with the intention of suing the company.
>
> He secured the best attorney in Illinois, a black man [named] Edward Morris. The case was tried on Monday, May 9, 1910. The Jury rendered a verdict in favor of the Plaintiff and the Colonial Theater was fined.

In contrast the *Defender*, on January 6, 1912, reported another incident:

> Mrs T. P. Morgan, 3805 South Wabash Avenue and several other ladies went to the Globe Theatre at Wabash Avenue and Peck Court. They expected to occupy the seats which they had bought earlier. However, after their eyes adjusted to the darkness of the theater and after they had removed their wraps, they observed around them only people of the darker hue and suddenly realized that they had been seated in the Jim Crow section. In this instance, the ladies protested vehemently and the manager gave them better seats.

On top of the humiliation black people suffered at theaters downtown, they encountered a brand of "super Jim Crow" in the heart of the Black Belt. The *Defender* said on September 6, 1913:

> The Avenue Theater located at 3108 South Indiana, opened its doors in August, 1913, and from all reports will cater to white people only on the first floor and sell tickets exclusively to colored people for the balcony. Two of our most representative citizens, Mr and Mrs Richard Hill, went to the theatre on Tuesday evening, September 2, 1913, and were told at the box office that 'only balcony seats were available for colored people.'

The *Defender* kept up a drumbeat of headlines about this insulting treatment of "American citizens of color who had fought in all America's wars". On

September 6, 1913, the *Defender* urged all citizens to write Mayor Harrison and Police Chief McSweeny and demand that the license of the Avenue Theater be revoked.

The ultimate contradiction was a black-owned theater which had a "whites only" seating policy. On February 23, 1908, Robert R. Motts, the black owner of the Pekin Theater, opened the old Columbia Theater at Clark and Division Streets with a colored stock company in a show called *Honolulu*. This venture was designed to appeal to white theater-goers—although it remains a question whether Motts would actually have refused to seat black patrons, if any wandered as far afield as Clark and Division, which was in fact about a mile and a half north of the Loop theater district. The white theater-goer had seen Motts' acts—Bob Cole and J. Rosamond and James Weldon Johnson, to say nothing of the great comedy team of Bert Williams and George Walker—in Loop theaters, and had no reason to frequent the Columbia. It died young, therefore, and its demise marked the beginning of the decline of the Pekin as well, which led to that South Side theater's eventual liquidation.

The liquidation of a theater is always sad; it is not necessarily tragic, however.

The Colonial (left), and Illinois (right). Theaters where blacks were not permitted to sit on the main floor.

The destruction of a human being, physically and emotionally, is tragic. And that is what happened to Bert Williams because of the mindless grip of racism on the American theater.

Bert Williams was the most widely acclaimed comedian in America during the first two decades of this century. He started out in Chicago working in the post office and rose to become the only black star of the Ziegfeld Follies. But because he was black, he was treated differently from other stars. Earl Dickerson remembers seeing Bert Williams in the Follies at the Illinois Theater at 65 East Jackson. He says that although Williams was the star of the show, he had to stand one step behind the line of white performers when they all took their curtain calls. "To have done otherwise," Dickerson says, "would have been considered a personal affront to the white audience and a symbolic indication of black equality."

William Y. Browne also saw Bert Williams perform at the Illinois Theater on several occasions. He remembered vividly that blacks were forced to sit only in the balcony during those performances. Browne also remembered Williams' act with his partner George Walker; they billed themselves as "The Two Coons". Browne pointed out that at that time no Negro performer could appear before white audiences without covering his face with heavy black greasepaint. It was, in fact, not until early 1925 that this tradition was discontinued at the Chicago Theater, where Carol Chilton and her partner Earl Partello appeared as a black team without blackface.

Browne saw Ben Vereen's impersonation of Bert Williams on television at the Reagan Inaugural, and he said it was all wrong. Vereen acted the fast-dancing, strutting dandy, a part that Browne said was taken by Williams' partner, George Walker. Bert Williams himself acted the buffoon, with a shambling, shuffling gait that would change at intervals to a grotesque sliding glide that was the essence of comic awkwardness.

White audiences laughed heartily and applauded generously when they saw Williams' blackened face behind the footlights. He played the game according to the American rules that allowed no black man acceptance on the stage unless he was black-faced and funny. Williams was the funniest of them all. The bigoted American could feel pleasantly liberal and tolerant while he was laughing at Williams. But Williams himself was literally a clown with a breaking heart.

He was inked into the Follies in an act so special that he appeared in roles barely related to the rest of the review, and he appeared for the most part alone. He was in the Follies, but he was not allowed to be part of the Follies. The "you ain't there" treatment he received sustained the "separate and unequal" mentality both for the white audience and for the white performers who worked with him, or around him.

W. C. Fields, who was in the *Ziegfeld Follies* with Williams for four years, said

Bert Williams.

A sketch of the handsome Bert Williams (above, and as he appeared in blackface. Right: A scene from Bert's last play Under the Bamboo Tree.

SHUBERT

Studebaker Theatre

"The play's the thing"—Shakespeare

Under the Direction of the Messrs. Shubert
CHICAGO

FIRE NOTICE

Look around now, choose the nearest exit to your seat, and in
case of disturbance of any kind, to avoid the dangers
of panic, WALK (do not run) to that exit.

Matinees Wednesday and Saturday

The Messrs. Shubert

(By Arrangement with A. H. Woods)

Present

BERT WILLIAMS

—In—

UNDER THE BAMBOO TREE

Staged by J. C. Huffman
A MUSICAL COMEDY
Book and Lyrics by Walter DeLeon.
Music by Sigmund Romberg and Will H. Vodery
Dances and Ensemble Numbers by Allan K. Foster and John Lowe

The stagebill from Bert Williams' last play.

Above: Left to right: Joe Schenck, Bert Williams, Gus Van, Eddie Dowling, and Ray Dooley in a scene from the Follies. Left: Bert Williams and Right: Left to Right: George Walker, Bert Williams, and Ada Walker.

Frederick O'Neal, distinguished actor of stage, screen and television, was the first black to be elected president of the Actor's Equity Association.

that Williams "was the funniest man I ever saw and the saddest man I ever knew."

"I'm just relegated," Williams said to Fields. "I don't belong."

He always called Fields "Pops". He said, "Do you know what happened to me on the night of the Actors' Equity Association strike, Pops? I went to the theater as usual, made up and got dressed. Then I came out of my dressing room onto an empty stage, facing a big, dark auditorium. The strike was on, and I didn't know anything about it. No one told me anything. You see, I just didn't belong. . ."

The stress of all this was too much for Williams. In the early 1920's, just after he appeared in *Under the Bamboo Tree* at Chicago's Studebaker Theater, he died, in early middle age. He suffered from heart and blood pressure problems, the result of the abnormal life he had been forced to lead.

In the 1930's Negro performers received somewhat wider acceptance on the American stage—though not, of course, on the American screen—thanks largely to Franklin Roosevelt and the support for the arts given by the WPA. In 1964 Frederick O'Neal, a veteran Negro actor, was elected president of Actors Equity, and he presided over its governing council.

Today, seventy years after the struggles discussed in the *Defender*, blacks can sit physically anywhere they choose in most American theaters. Let us hope that white citizens will some day no longer psychologically relegate blacks to the Nigger Heaven of American life, because of an inbred feeling that they do not belong anywhere else.

A South Side dance floor and bar at the height of the swing era.

Chapter 3

On the Trail of Chicago's Black Belt Ballrooms and Saloons

Between 1890 and 1910, while their population ballooned from 14,271 to 44,000, the majority of black people in Chicago were packed into a narrow corridor on the South Side from 16th Street to 39th Street, and bounded by State Street on the east and the Rock Island Railroad tracks and LaSalle Street on the west.

Until 1900 most black-owned businesses were to be found in that portion of the first ward now known as the South Loop, the site of Dearborn Park. John "Mushmouth" Johnson, after working for several years as a porter in a white gambling house, opened what became a very successful saloon and gambling hall at 464 South State Street in 1890.

Mushmouth's establishment was considered to be one of the most elaborate of its kind in the city. It was ornate in the Gay Nineties style, with glittering incandescent bulbs in rococo chandeliers, bright tile floors and painted stucco walls panelled in places with rich dark wood. On the south wall was a brilliantly illuminated bar made of polished Honduran mahogany, behind which were kept varicolored cut glassware and many brands of wines, liquors and cigars. The gambling tables were in the rear, or west part, of the building. Voluptuous waitresses served the tables, while white-aproned mustachioed men tended bar.

Johnson's attracted gamblers of all colors from every economic and social spectrum: for those with lean purses there was a poor man's game. You could roll the dice or draw a five-card poker hand at the "short-pocket" gambling table for a nickel. It was talk about the nickel games that caught my father's ear on June 5, 1900, soon after he started working as a strikebreaker on a construction job at the northeast corner of State and Madison. The building was to be Mandel's Department Store, now occupied by Wieboldt's.

"I heard the young men from the South talking about Johnson's gambling establishment the way dudes talk about girls," Dad said. "Most of the boys had been to Johnson's place the previous Saturday and they were going again the coming weekend. Saturday was payday. I could hardly wait 'till quitting time to gallop down State Street. . . 'Mushmouth' Johnson had the cheapest action in downtown Chicago. Boy! Where else could a country boy go just ten days out of Georgia and feel like a big time gambler for only a nickel?"

Johnson's white tutor was Michael Cassius McDonald, King of Gamblers, who operated the fabulous "store" at 176 Clark Street, and who was the virtual dictator of City Hall for three decades—with the exception of a brief period of eclipse following the election of Mayor John A. Roche in 1887. McDonald and Harry Varell, who had more than ninety faro dealers and croupiers working for them, turned their noses up at the "chicken feed" which enabled Johnson to amass property worth more than $500,000 in the areas between Harrison and Polk Streets, on South State, Dearborn and Federal Streets. In the late '90s much of Johnson's real estate was sold to railroad companies, and almost one hundred years later these companies in turn sold it to the developers of Dearborn Park.

When Johnson died in 1907 the *Daily News,* on September 14 of that year, estimated his wealth at more than $250,000, while the *Defender* said that it was between half and three-quarters of a million. Johnson's sister Eudora inherited sixty percent, and the balance was divided equally between another sister, Louisa A. Ray, and a brother, Elijah. Johnson's estate was to have a positive effect on Negro banking, real estate and entertainment ventures.

Mushmouth's sister Eudora married Jesse Binga, an ex-Pullman porter from Detroit, who had come to Chicago in 1893 to attend the Columbian Exposition in Jackson Park, liked what he saw in the city by the lake, and decided to make it his

99 YEAR LEASE.—Helmer's form.   NO. 1400.   Printed and for Sale by the Chicago Legal News Co.

This Indenture, Made and entered into this *Sixth*

day of *November* A. D. 19*12*, Between
John B Danis and Eva Danis his wife

of the City of *Denver* County of *Denver* and State
of *Colorado* party of the first part (hereinafter designated Lessor*s*),
and
Elijah H Johnson
of the City of *Chicago* County of *Cook* and State
of *Illinois* party of the second part (hereinafter designated Lessee—),
witnesseth:

First. The first party hereto, the lessor*s*, in consideration of the rents hereinafter reserved and of the covenants and agreements herein expressed on the part of the second party, the lessee—, to be kept, performed and fulfilled, ha*ve* demised and leased and by these presents do— demise and lease unto the lessee— all the following described premises situated and being in the City of *Chicago* County of *Cook* and State of *Illinois*:

Lots Nine (9) Ten (10) and Eleven (11) in Block One
(1) in the Subdivision of Out Lot Seventeen (17) of the
Canal Trustees Subdivision of Section Thirty three (33)
Township Thirty nine (39) North Range Fourteen (14)
East of the Third Principal Meridian

Parties.

Premises.

To Have and to Hold the above described premises, with the rights, privileges, easements and appurtenances thereunto attaching and belonging, unto the lessee— for and during the term of ninety-nine (99) years from and after the first (1st) day of May in the year of our Lord one thousand nine hundred *One hundred and Twelve* (A. D. 19*12*); that is to say, from the first (1st) day of May, in the year of our Lord one thousand nine hundred *and Twelve* (A. D. 19*12*), for and during and until the thirtieth (30th) day of April, in the year of our Lord two thousand and *One hundred Eleven* (A. D. 2*111*), paying rent therefor, and yielding possession thereof as hereinafter provided.

Term/99 years.

Second. The lessee— in consideration of the leasing of the premises aforesaid of the lessor*s* to h*im*, the lessee—, do*th* hereby covenant and agree to and with the lessor*s* to pay rent as follows:

The Lessee Covenant*s* and Agree*s* to pay the lessor*s* as rent for said demised premises during the said demised term of *One hundred and* ninety-nine years, the yearly rent or sum of *Twelve hundred* Dollars ($ *1200 ⁰⁰⁄₁₀₀*), without any deduction or abatement whatever, which rental shall be paid

Rent $*1200* per year; quarterly instalments $*300* each, in gold coin. *Quarterly*

Ninety-nine year lease for the site of the Dreamland Cafe which was located at 3618 South State Street.

home. Binga started out peddling vegetables in the street. Subsequently he went into real estate, and in 1908 he established a private bank at 3637 South State Street. Binga's commercial acumen combined with Johnson's money launched a business empire unparalleled in the black community in Binga's lifetime.

The Binga-Johnson nuptials received national attention: congratulatory telegrams were sent by Mr and Mrs Booker T. Washington from Tuskegee, Alabama, and by other prominent people who lived out of the state. Dr Washington telegraphed his regrets: his health and other conditions prevented his attendance. The *Chicago Defender* on February 24, 1912 described the wedding:

> The marriage of Miss Eudora Johnson to Mr Jesse Binga, on Tuesday evening, February 20th, was the most brilliant ever held in our city. The ceremony was performed in the presence of about sixty friends at their palatial home, 3324 Vernon Avenue, by Rev. E. T. Martin, pastor of Bethesda Baptist Church, assisted by Rev. A. Binga of Richmond, Va., a cousin of the groom. The bride was attended by her sister, Mrs Louise A. Ray, as matron of honor, whose gown was of chiffon, richly ornamented in silver and electric blue palettes; the latter were worked in palm-leaf design. The corsage had a fichu of silver net.
>
> Mr Vance Anderson was best man. The Bride's gown was of Marie Antoinette Gold Brocade Silk cut low and with a bodice of heavy embroidered silver leaves. The train was five yards long, trimmed effectively with silver leaves. The material trimmings were imported from Paris.
>
> The dining room decorations were pink and white. The dining room table was a piece of artistic work with a bridal basket as a centerpiece, with evergreen extending from the four corners of a magnificent dome, formed a perfect ball. Tomaso's Mandolin Orchestra furnished the music for the occasion all during the evening which added to the charming affair. Music, flowers, young and old friends mingled together in one accord of a happy culmination of a happy couple. Mrs Julius N. Avendorph was master of ceremonies assisted by Mr F. B. Waring. Brawley served.

Ten months later, on November 6, 1912, Elijah Johnson, another Mushmouth heir, leased property for ninety-nine years from John B. Davis and Eva Davis of Denver at 3618–20 South State Street, directly across from Binga's private bank and real estate office. On that site, Johnson built the Dreamland Ballroom, which was converted in the 1920s to the Dreamland Cafe, a plush nightclub with a mirrored dance floor. There Louis Armstrong, Ethel Waters, Alberta Hunter and a host of other stars played to a black and white clientele.

The Binga-Johnson fortune played a major part in a story that ran in the *Daily News* on December 14, 1916, about Negro businesses in the Chicago area. There were 731 businesses practicing in sixty-one different trades—among them were thirteen limousine services, four blacksmith shops, three bookstores, twenty-three saloons, eight public halls, five hotels and one movie house. There were

Above: Jesse Binga, real estate entrepreneur and banker. Below: Alberta Hunter, blues singer and comedienne (left), and Ethel Waters (right).

also twenty-one chiropodists. Most of these businesses were on the South Side, on or near State Street. Binga's was the only "colored" bank in the city and, since banks have historically been the centers of commercial activity, Binga was considered by both whites and blacks to be the guiding hand in the successful commercial area between 31st and 39th Streets on South State Street—the area known as "the Stroll". East 35th Street and South State were the black man's Broadway and Wall Street from 1918 to 1928.

Black businesses had to share the area with white businesses. There were more theaters in the 3100 block on South State during that period than there were on Randolph or North State Street. Four of these theaters were owned by whites, but they catered to blacks. One was the Vendome Theater at 3145 South State, where Erskine Tate and his symphonic jazz orchestra played, along with such stars as Teddy Weatherford, who was considered the champ of the ivories until Earl Hines came to town. Across the street at 3104 South State was the Phoenix Theater, next door to the Grand Theater, at 3110 South State.

The Grand was the home of vaudeville acts like Butter Beans and Susie, and such great blues belters of the period as Ethel Waters, Mamie Smith, Bessie Smith and Clara Smith. A few doors south on the same side of the street at 3132 South State was the Lincoln Theater, where great silent westerns were shown, with Tom Mix, Hoot Gibson, William S. Hart and "Bronco Billy" Anderson, the first western cowboy star.

A short four-block walk south from 31st Street would bring you to the corner of 35th and State, which was the heart of the Black Belt and the center of sporting life in Chicago. On the east side of the street, at 3435 South State was the Monogram Theater, a major vaudeville house featuring such stars as Ma Rainey, Sleepy Harris and Stovepipe Johnson. Three doors south of the 35th Street intersection, on the east side of the street, was the State Theater at 3509 South State, which showed dramas starring, for instance, Norma Talmadge and Francis X. Bushman, along with serials like *The Perils of Pauline* and comedy "quickies" made in one day by Mack Sennett. The silence of the films was enlivened by mood music which was usually performed by a pianist and drummer in small houses, and a full orchestra at major theaters in the Loop. The initial appearance on the screen of the villain would be accompanied by a thunderous bass in a minor key, while the good guy would be greeted with an upbeat tune in a major key. The music gave dramatic continuity to the silent film.

At 209 East 35th Street, near Indiana Avenue, was the Entertainer Cafe, where Clarence E. Muse produced shows starring black artists like the beautiful Marion Harrison, supported by Slick White, Shakey Beasley and a dozen other acts. Music was provided by Sammy Stewart and his Knights of Syncopation. Down the street, at 315 East 35th Street, on the southwest corner of Calumet Avenue and 35th Street, was the Sunset Cafe, where Carroll Dickerson and his sixteen-piece

*Above: The Erskine Tate Vendome Symphonic Orchestra. Erksine Tate, second from left. Lower left:
Butter Beans & Susie, and Bessie Smith, right.*

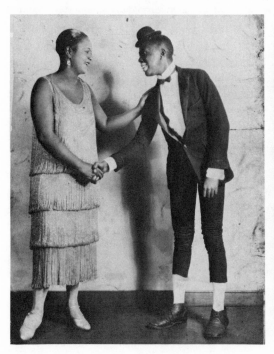

Mamie Smith, blues singer, credited with making the first blues recording. Two members of her 1922 Jazz Hounds became jazz giants: trumpeter Bubba Miley and a sixteen-year-old saxophone player named Coleman Hawkins.

The Carroll Dickerson Band, 1924. Left to right: Honore Dutrey; Tubby Hall (drums); Nattie Dominique; Willie Hightower; James Hall; Earl Hines; Carroll Dickerson; M. Carr; Cecil Irwin; Ralph Brown; Dave Brown. For a period of about ten years, Dickerson fronted some of the finest bands Chicago produced. But only two recorded sides by his group exist.

orchestra played music for an all-star review featuring the diminutive and dynamic Frankie "Half-Pint" Jackson who scatted and cavorted across the stage with the rhythmic background support of ten beautiful "high yellow" chorus girls.

Diagonally west across the street from the Sunset was the Plantation Cafe at 338 East 35th Street, a popular black and tan (black and white) cabaret known for the heavy drinking and all-night dancing that went on there. At daybreak on December 25, 1926, both the Plantation and the Sunset were raided by forty policemen, led by Chief of Detectives Shoemaker and Deputy Chief Stege. Five hundred men and women, both white and black, were doing a dance called "The Black Bottom", which Chief Collins described as an immoral exhibition. "The dance was particularly vicious in its effect upon young white women," the Chief said. "Many college students frequented these cafes on the South Side."

The Black Bottom was mildly sexually suggestive when compared with such dances as the Grind, the Mess Around, Snake Hips, Itch or the Shimmy. Perry Bradford's lyric explicitly describes the Black Bottom:

> Hop down front and then you
>   Doodle back,
> Mooch to the left and then you
>   Mooch to the right,
> Hands on your hips and do the
>   Mess Around
> Break a leg until you're near
>   the ground.
> Now that's the Old Black Bottom
>   Dance!

It was of course the time of Prohibition, and the police said that the black and white Black Bottom dancers had been drinking. Bottles had been found on top of and under the tables. Twenty gallons of liquor and some counterfeit revenue stamps were found at 334 East 35th Street, where the Plantation waiters were said to have obtained liquor for their patrons. The Sunset Cafe was owned by Joseph Glaser, and the Plantation by Edward Fox. Both men gave the same home address—4637 South Drexel Avenue—and both clubs were controlled by the Capone syndicate.

Two doors west of the Plantation Cafe on the second floor, was the Apex Club, an elegant new supper club owned by Julian Black, the sepia policy baron who later became part owner and manager of the world heavyweight champion, Joe Louis. Black was also a close friend of Dan Jackson, the political boss of the South Side. When the Apex opened, its review starred Norah Holt-Ray, a celebrated pianist and the toast of white jazz lovers from Chicago's Gold Coast.

The Apex had formerly been called The Nest. There Earl Hines in earlier years had pushed a miniature piano from table to table; he played tunes requested by patrons from midnight to six in the morning, seven days a week.

During the day, both 35th Street and State Street were beehives of commercial activity, but from dusk to dawn the night spots along the Stroll blazed with neon lights and resounded with loud music and the happy laughter of the dancers and merry-makers.

Jesse Binga did not waste his energies on laughter and all-night dances. He was not particularly jovial as he went about the business of consolidating his South State Street real estate and banking interests in the fashion of Wall Street. Dr Julian Lewis remembers him.

"Binga was a very light sleeper," Dr Lewis said. "He would call me at the most ungodly hours before daybreak just for small talk. At least once a week he would call me to meet him for a golf game before sunrise. One morning he called in a state of distress and asked me to come over to his house right away. I thought to myself that Jesse Binga, the banker, was going to be my patient. When I got to his home, at 5922 South Park, I was rushed up to a second floor bedroom, where I discovered that it was Binga's dog that was sick. That was quite a comedown."

On January 3, 1921, Binga was authorized by the state of Illinois to convert his private bank into a chartered state banking institution. Binga's accomplishments inspired Anthony Overton, the son of an ex-slave, and an extremely competent and competitive neighbor of Binga's, who was president of the Overton Hygienic Manufacturing Company, which produced cosmetics for blacks. Overton also owned the *Half Century Magazine,* the *Ebony* of its day.

In June, 1921, six months after Binga's bank was chartered, Overton began to work on organizing a federally chartered national bank and in July, 1922, the Douglas National Bank opened for business at 3655 South State Street, just a few doors south of Binga's old bank building. Overton's was one of only two national banks in the country owned by Negroes. The other one was in Oklahoma. The existence of two black-controlled banks created an atmosphere of financial stability in the area that encouraged black people to expand their commercial and real estate interests east of State Street to Cottage Grove Avenue and south of 39th Street to 59th Street. A trend was growing.

John B. Stradford, an attorney and hotel developer from Tulsa, Oklahoma, anticipated the trend by buying some vacant land three blocks east of State Street on Indiana Avenue. Stradford, who was the paternal grandfather of the prominent Chicago attorney Jewel Stradford Lafontant, hired an architectural firm to draw plans for a 200 room hotel and ballroom complex on the northwest corner of 36th Street and Indiana Avenue. Jesse Binga, who was a friend of Stradford, initially gave the plan his blessing, but for some reason he backed out of giving it his financial support and the plan never went beyond an architectural rendering

Above: Anthony Overton, pioneer businessman, with his marketing staff in 1912 in front of his building at 5200 South Wabash Avenue. Below left: the commercial department of the Douglas National Bank. Right: the Bank's savings department. The Bank was located in the 3600 block on South State Street.

of the hotel that was printed in the *Tribune* on November 12, 1922.

Mrs Elizabeth Barnett Lewis, an astute businesswoman with an ample build and an infectious smile, was an excellent cook who sold soul food to the theater crowds at her Pullman Cafe on South State Street. She made enough money to quit the Stroll; in November, 1919 she purchased the Vincennes Hotel, a six-story, elevator-equipped, ninety-four room building at 601 East 36th Street. It was the first quality hotel in Chicago to be owned by blacks. Dr W. E. Dubois stayed there in the summer of 1921 and commented: "I stayed at the Vincennes and around me were ghosts of white folks who used to live at this beautiful, quiet and exclusive hotel. Now Negroes own it and it is still beautiful and quiet but, thank heavens, neither exclusive nor dear. Every Negro in the United States ought to take a trip to Chicago just to stop at the Vincennes with his family."

Until 1940 the Vincennes was a social and cultural center for the black community. Sepia ladies in Paris gowns and perfumes graced the beautiful ballrooms and diningrooms of the hotel accompanied by black men in formal attire at festivities sponsored by such exclusive clubs as the Chicago Assembly, the Original Forty Club, the Snakes, and most of the Negro Greek sororities and fraternities.

If one stands quietly on the southeast corner of 36th Street and Vincennes Avenue, where the hotel once stood, one might still hear the moaning of Jimmy Noone's clarinet and the rapid, trumpet-like piano of Earl "Fatha" Hines echoing through the Vincennes lobby from the Platinum Lounge in the basement. "Pops" Lewis, who owned the Lounge, was married to Elizabeth B. Lewis, the owner of the hotel. "Pops" was a major gambling and policy operator on the South Side.

Earl Hines was so fascinated by the lifestyles of gamblers and pimps with big cars and stables of prostitutes that he decided to go into business himself. He thought that would be a fast way to get a Packard or a Pierce-Arrow. In November, 1927, after he finished his engagement at the Sunset Cafe, Louis Armstrong approached Hines and Zutty Singleton about going into the amusement business. Hines and Singleton agreed eagerly. In December Louis signed a one-year lease for the Warwick Hall at 543 East 47th Street. He called his new "dancing school" the Usonia. Less than three months later Louis, Earl and Zutty were forced to recognize the fact that the heart of the Usonia Dancing School was not beating: it was as cold as a Chicago December morning. The venture was a failure, and Louie had to pay the landlord the balance due on the lease.

Armstrong and the boys were reading notes but they were not reading business trends. Three weeks before the collapse of the Usonia, on Thanksgiving Day, the million-dollar Savoy Ballroom had opened its doors—it was only three blocks west of the Warwick Hall. Louie and Zutty obeyed the adage: "If you can't beat 'em, join 'em." The first week in April, 1928, Louie and Zutty were to be found playing at the Savoy with the Carroll Dickerson band.

Above: The Hotel Vincennes was the first modern American hotel owned by a black, Elizabeth Barnett Lewis, who made her fortune operating the Pullman Cafe on South State Street.

Right: Jimmy Noone, the master clarinetist.

The opening of the Savoy Ballroom marked the day that gangrene began to spread through the arteries of the black man's Wall Street and Broadway at the crossroads of 35th and State Streets. By contrast, 47th Street, the black man's new Broadway, would be controlled for the next three decades by white retail merchants and banks.

Above: Duke Ellington and his 1930 Cotton Club orchestra. Lower left: Cab Calloway. Right: The Original Cotton Club, at 142nd and Lenox Avenue in Harlem.

Chapter 4

The Jazz Slave Masters

"Hey, boy, come here!" Ralph Capone called as he beckoned toward Lucius "Lucky" Millinder, the bandleader in the syndicate-controlled Cotton Club in Cicero, Illinois. Millinder, who was dressed formally in white tie and tails with a winged-tip shirt, hastily moved his snow-white slippers from the bandstand to the bosses' front row table.

"Boy, I like the way you colored people play music and I get a big kick watching your jazzy steps and pearly smile as you direct that band," said Capone. "My brother Al and I decided we're going to keep you boys working regularly, but you can't work for nobody but us."

To which Millinder responded, "Boss, I am your man with the band."

Capone said, "Lucky, don't forget. Take this hundred dollar tip and go play my favorite song."

Millinder replied, "Thank you, Mr Capone!" then returned to the bandstand and began leading the orchestra in a gutsy rendition of W. C. Handy's classic "St Louis Blues."

Top: Ed Fox, owner of the Grand Terrace, and manager of Earl Hines. Left: 1925: the Al Capone family home at 7244 South Prairie Avenue. Right: Al "Scarface" Capone.

My old friend, the late Lucky Millinder, a Chicago South Sider and Wendell Phillips High School alumnus, once told me that he did not realize the full implications of Ralph Capone's conversation at that time. Capone's statement became crystal clear during Lucky's first trip to New York in the late 1920s. There he saw the syndicate network unfold through Owney Madden, one of the most notorious of the pre-prohibition bootleggers and a principal owner of Harlem's famous Cotton Club. The mob network was tied together like a musical triad: Madden controlled the East Coast's booze and beer distribution; Al Capone reigned over Chicago and its environs; Johnny Lazia controlled the police, liquor and gambling in Kansas City, Missouri; and the Purple Gang dominated Detroit. Chicago, New York and Kansas City housed a disproportionate percentage of all the great jazz talent in America during the 1920s and 30s. These cities were controlled by the Jazz Slave Masters and some of the very best black musicians were their serfs. Talented jazz musicians were chained to bands and specific night clubs and saloons in the same manner as the ante-bellum Negroes were shackled to plantations. Louis Armstrong, Duke Ellington, Jimmie Lunceford, Cab Calloway, Lena Horne and Earl Hines are a few of the many top artists who were inmates behind the "Cotton Curtain" at various points in their careers. All of the aforementioned stars except Earl Hines had worked at the Cotton Club in New York City, which was the best known entertainment plantation in the country between 1924 and 1936. All blacks other than entertainers, waiters, cooks and the cleaning crew were excluded from the interior of the Jazz Slave Master's New York mansion.

The bandstand at the Harlem Cotton Club was a replica of a Southern mansion, with large white columns and a backdrop painted with weeping willows and slave quarters. The orchestra performed in front of the large double doors to the mansion. Down four steps was the dance floor, which was also used for floor shows. The waiters were dressed in red tuxedos, like butlers in a Southern mansion, and the tables were covered with red and white checked gingham tablecloths. The entire scene created a *Gone with the Wind* atmosphere that made every white male feel like Rhett Butler and every white woman like Scarlet O'Hara. Since the waiters were paid only one dollar a night, they had to hustle like Rochester and hope that Rhett Butler would leave a big tip.

Even the great composer W.C. Handy was barred from the Cotton Club when he went there one night with Gene Buck, the president of ASCAP (American Society of Composers, Authors, and Publishers) to hear his own song "St. Louis Blues" that was being featured in the floor show. The Cotton Club was not the only club smack dab in the middle of Black Harlem that had a Jim Crow policy where Negroes were on the outside looking in. Connie's Inn, the Harlem Uproar House and the Ubangi Club also banned blacks.

Mike DeLisa and Freddie Cole in front of Club DeLisa on the evening of her retirement party, June, 1954.

Classy nightclubs on Chicago's South Side never had a "for whites only" policy as Harlem's Cotton Club did. However, Chicago had a Jim Crow seating policy. During the 1930s and 40s, when I walked into any of our finer night spots, such as the Club DeLisa at 55th and State Streets, I saw white folks hugging the stage, while blacks sat behind them at the outer edges, and in the rear near the entrance.

Young Jim DeLisa said, "The Jim Crow seating policy was not implemented by my father and uncles, but by the eight Negro bouncers, captained by the 300 pound, six-foot-eight-inch Grover 'Big Boy' Chapman. The black bouncers seated you according to the tips they received and not according to your skin pigmentation. 'Big Boy' used to tell my father, 'I like your people'—pointing to my Dad's white skin—'because they give me the most money.' "

Money was what the plantation system was all about. The Grand Terrace in Chicago was the most grandiose plantation in the country. Its appointments were more elaborate than New York's Cotton Club or Chicago's Club DeLisa. Everything and everybody in the club smelled like money except the black entertainers. They all sweated for a pittance, including Earl Hines, the internationally renowned band leader. The band's star trumpet and saxophone player, George Dixon, did not realize how the mob's plantation system worked until he decided to better his lot in life and gave notice of leaving Hines at the Grand Terrace to join Don Redman's band in Detroit. Don Redman was the brilliant former musical director of McKinney's Cotton Pickers. Omer Simeon, Hines' alto sax man, and Billy Franklin, the trombonist, decided to join Dixon in his move to Detroit.

Dixon told me, "The day we left Chicago, Ralph Cooper, the producer of the show at the original Grand Terrace, came out of the club and shook our hands while we were standing near the curb. When I stepped into my little 1929 Ford and said 'Goodbye,' Cooper replied, 'I am not going to say goodbye because you'll be back.'

"I said, 'Not a chance.'

"Shortly after we arrived in Detroit, Don called his first rehearsal at the Graystone Ballroom. Before we could play the first note, Don's manager came up and said, 'Where's the three fellows from Earl Hines' band?'

"We all identified ourselves. Don's manager said, 'Well, I just got a call from New York and I won't be able to use you guys.'

"The three of us yelled in unison, 'Does that mean we have to go back to Earl?'

"The manager replied, 'Yeah, that's what it means.'

"After hearing that bad news, the three of us jumped into my little Ford and came back to Chicago. The mob, through intimidation and organization, had things so well-regulated we couldn't even change jobs."

Above: The new Grand Terrace. Inset: Harry Gray, President of the Musicians' Union. Lower left: The old Grand Terrace. Right: Ralph Cooper, producer of the Grand Terrace shows.

Later Dixon accidentally overheard a conversation between Ed Fox, manager of the Grand Terrace, and Frank "The Enforcer" Nitti, the Capone treasurer, which shed light on what had happened. It seemed that Joe Fusco, Al Capone's superintendent of breweries who was also plantation overseer at the Grand Terrace, had called Owney Madden at the Cotton Club in New York, and told him that Dixon and the boys had to go back to the Grand Terrace. Madden immediately called a member of the Purple Gang in Detroit, and that individual gave the word directly to Don Redman's manager: the boys had to return to Chicago. The "word" was always the final message.

Cab Calloway was once threatened with violence by the Owney Madden mob if he didn't do right. Cab was working and broadcasting from Madden's New York Cotton Club. His popularity was soaring and the mob had arranged to book him into the Paramount Theater for a three-week engagement at a salary of $200 per week. Cab became obstinate about doubling on both gigs for that short bread.

Cab was given the word: "You'd better go into the Paramount on those terms or we'll see to it that you never work again."

With that message ringing in his ears, Cab hi-de-ho'd it to both his midtown gig at the Paramount Theater and his uptown gig at Harlem's Cotton Club for three consecutive weeks and was not late for a single performance.

The New York Jazz Slave Masters had long arms that frequently reached into Chicago to protect their chattel. Duke Ellington recalls an experience when he was scheduled for an engagement at the Paradise Theater on Chicago's West Side. When he arrived at the theater the manager, Sam Fletcher, told Duke that some members of a West Side mob had been there that morning and said that Duke had to send them $500 or he wouldn't leave the theater alive that night.

Duke called Owney Madden at the Cotton Club in New York and told him what had happened. Madden said: "Duke, don't worry about it. I can assure you that you won't have that kind of trouble anymore."

After reassuring Duke, Owney Madden carefully hung up the phone only to grab it again within minutes to call Al Capone in Chicago and tell him about Duke's troubles with the West Side hoodlums. Capone immediately issued the following order: "Duke Ellington is not to be bothered on the West Side or in the Loop." Duke later said, "Those words closed the chapter on the gangster problem for me and the band in Chicago from that day forward."

Al Capone saved Duke Ellington from threats of violence, but chained Earl Hines to a $150 a week contract that was constructed to last forever. Capone, through his Grand Terrace manager, had a contract with Hines that literally would not permit Hines to use his own name if he attempted to leave the Grand Terrace plantation. His contract was perpetual: if Ed Fox died, Hines would become the personal property of Fox's widow, and in the event of her death,

Fox's eldest son would be the heir to the contract for a lifetime. If the oldest son died before Hines, the contract would pass to Fox's youngest son. This chattel contract on Earl Hines was in effect from December 1928 until a 1941 engagement at the Regal Theater in Chicago where Hines collected his music after the last show and told the band:

"I am not working for Ed Fox anymore."

Hines had made this threat before, but this time he apparently intended to keep his word.

Early the following Monday, Hines and George Dixon, his saxophone and trumpet player, went to Harry Gray, the president of Local 208, at 3934 South State Street, which was the headquarters of the colored musicians' union. Earl told Gray the story and Gray called James (Jimmy) C. Petrillo, president of the National Federation of Musicians in New York. Petrillo was also the President of Local 10, which was the Chicago downtown union for white musicians. Petrillo came into town that Wednesday and met Harry Gray, Earl Hines, Charlie Carpenter and George Dixon at the Palmer House.

According to Dixon, Petrillo read the contract and said, "This contract is not worth the paper it is written on. It's too much Ed Fox and not enough Earl Hines, so you go and work anywhere you want for anyone you want and I will protect you."

Dixon remembered that Fox did not give up on Hines even after the powerful Jimmy Petrillo had told Hines he was free. Shortly after his emancipation, Hines took a band into New York's Apollo Theater. Fox immediately procured an injunction through his New York lawyers and tied up the band's weekly salary. When Petrillo got the news he called Jack Shiffman, the manager of the Apollo and told him, "If you don't release the band's payroll, your show will not go on tonight!" Jack Schiffman immediately responded by releasing the payroll.

Fox subsequently enticed Earl Hines to return to Chicago and open at his New Grand Terrace, which was located in the Old Sunset Building on the southwest corner of 35th and Calumet. [The original Grand Terrace which was located at 3955 South Parkway (now King Drive) had been reconverted to a theater and named The Park. It had been known as the Peerless Theater from October 1917 to December 1928.] Earl, the freedman, was now brighter in the ways of business and insisted that Fox put the band's four week's salary up in advance and place it in escrow with a third party. Fox agreed and the band opened. Fox then got an injunction to tie up the money he had placed in escrow. Since Fox owned this plantation, a call from Petrillo did not release the money. This time it was necessary for Petrillo to take Fox to court. The judge rendered a decision in Hines' favor. Hines was "free at last!"

Ralph Fusco, a West Side hoodlum who operated a Chicago version of the New York Cotton Club at 12th Street and Blue Island Avenue, gave Erskine Tate and his entire fifteen-man orchestra their freedom one night. However, he refused to pay the $1,500 weekly salary he owed them and threatened to use his weapon if they attempted to remove their instruments from the premises.

Harry "Fearless" Gray, who was the musicians' business agent, came to their rescue. He described the events that took place: "When I heard what had happened the next day, I jumped in my car and went directly to the Cotton Club to talk to Ralph Fusco. When I walked through the double doors leading to the cabaret, there was a tough-looking guy sitting at the end of the bar shuffling bullets in and out of a large automatic pistol.

"He said to me, 'What do you want?'

"I said I wanted to see Ralph Fusco. About this time Ralph walked out of a back office. His henchman said, 'Here's a crazy guy who wants to take over the joint.'

"Fusco said, 'What do you want?'

"I replied, 'I want the $1,500 due Tate's band and the instruments.'

"Fusco turned around and went back into his office without any further con-

The Earl Hines Band. Billy Eckstine (extreme left); Franz Jackson soloing (center); and George Dixon (standing).

versation and came back with fifteen $100 bills and put the bundle in my hand. His final message was, 'Tell the boys to come back to work tonight and I assure you they won't have any problems.' "

Harry Gray could deal effectively with hoodlums because he was not afraid to die in his quest to free black musicians from the slave masters.

Although jazz is a music known for its free forum, the black people who played it were never free agents. Owney Madden once told Duke Ellington that he would never be free to leave the New York Cotton Club plantation unless he agreed to pay the orchestra that replaced him out of the money he made on the road tours during the entire period his band was absent from the mansion. Duke's leave would vary from two weeks to three months, depending upon the nature of the engagements. Sometimes the gigs were extended theater tours or maybe a fourteen-day movie assignment in Hollywood. Ellington's first replacement was the Missourians, with Cab Calloway fronting the band. Duke paid Cab $200 a week to conduct and act as the master of ceremonies. The actual choice of Cab and the Missourians was made by the Cotton Club mob. The gangsters simply took control of Cab and his band from a white booking agent named Moe

Duke Ellington and his orchestra detraining at LaSalle Street Station in Chicago in 1931.

Gale with pure muscle and threats to the agent's health. The mob closed the deal by kissing Gale on the left cheek and offering him ten percent of Cab Calloway's annual earnings.

The Ellington and Calloway Cotton Club venture was ultimately structured with Duke and Irving Mills, song publisher and booking agent, owning fifty percent of Cab Calloway Enterprises. In addition, Mills owned fifty percent of Duke Ellington Inc. In the post-bellum period, the Jazz Slave Masters permitted some serfs to own at least fifty percent of themselves.

Remember, the Jazz Slave Masters always controlled the cash register, paid the piper and called the tune. The keepers of the cash box were usually Jewish or Italian and, occasionally, they were mob-connected blacks. The creators of jazz music were black. All this had a positive side. Wherever there was a generous segment of Jews, Italians and blacks coexisting within an urban area, the results favored jazz music. A population survey taken between 1927-1930 supports these observations.* The important jazz centers which had the aforementioned population mix were New Orleans, Kansas City, Chicago and New York. Philadelphia was the only major exception: it had the ethnic mix, but never became an important jazz center.

*Selected Ethnic Populations (1927–30)

Percent Black		*Percent Jewish/Italian*
Charleston	47	–
Memphis	38	2
Richmond, VA	32	–
Atlanta	30	2
Washington, D.C.	30	–
New Orleans*	28	4.5
St. Louis	15	1
Indianapolis	12	–
Gary, Ind.	14	–
Kansas City*	10	6
Philadelphia	10	8
Chicago*	8	8
New York*	5	18
Detroit	2	4

Source: World Almanac & Book of Facts, 1927–30
(*Indicates important jazz centers in 1926.)

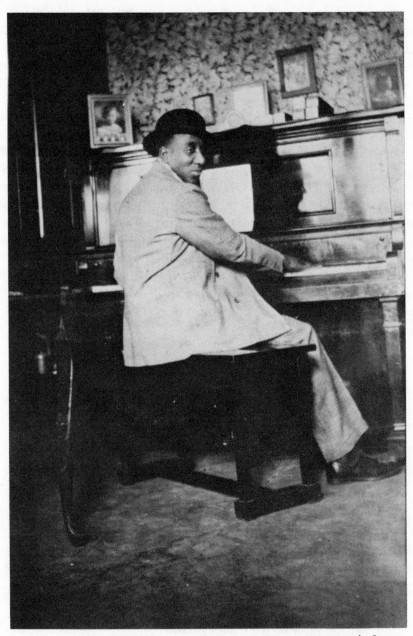

Louis Travis at the piano at home at 3609 South Cottage Grove Avenue, in January, 1926.

Chapter 5

Piano Man

The "Piano Man" is what the bunch called Louis Travis as he made the rounds of Saturday night house-rent parties on the South Side of Chicago. The early 1920s, thanks partly to Prohibition, gave birth to a multitude of self-styled keyboard plunkers who specialized in playing the blues. My father was a blues man and at the height of his glory when anybody called him the "Piano Man." This was particularly true when he was playing one of his two favorite blues tunes, "How Long" or "The Fives," in a buffet apartment in the Mecca flats at 34th and State Streets or in the Baby Doll building at 38th and Vernon. To my father, sitting on a piano stool was like sitting on a royal throne; it transformed him from a six-day-a-week laborer to a self-anointed Saturday night "prince of the blues keyboard."

My mother said: "Your daddy would assume an air of extraordinary importance as he sat down at the upright piano with his black derby hat tilted forward and to the right with a ten-cent cigar hanging out of the left side of his mouth. He would then posture a few seconds before leaning forward to become totally en-twined with the eighty-eight black and white ivory piano keys. The keys were his black and white subjects and he was their king. As your father played, the rent party dancers would shout: 'Louie! Louie! Play that thing!' or 'It's tight like that!' and he would bang his subjects harder and louder."

Shouting emotionally at the piano player while dancing the "Shimmy-She-Wobble" or the "Slow Drag" at a house-rent party was a common practice in the 1920s and early '30s. (Landlords preferred tenants who owned a piano and were tolerant of the piano player because they knew that anyone who owned an up-right 1,000 pound music box was not likely to move out in the middle of the night.) However, it was not until September, 1939, that George Dixon, the trumpet player and saxophonist with the Earl Hines band, immortalized the shout when he let out several unpremeditated screams as Earl Hines played "Boogie-Woogie on the St. Louis Blues" on the stage of the Oriental Theatre in Chicago.

George's first yell occurred within the first thirty seconds of the torrid boogie-woogie number. He hollered, "Put out all the lights and call the law right now!" which could be interpreted to mean that the sensations that George was experi-encing were too good to be legal. Before Earl Hines could get much deeper into his boogie-woogie solo, George shouted again, "Play it until 1951!" meaning he wanted this good feeling to last continuously for eleven straight years. The thought of that possibility caused George Dixon to howl in an ecstasy of joy. And just as Hines was finishing the final notes of this blues, George screeched, "Don't quit now, Jack! Don't quit now!"

George Dixon told me that the compulsion to shout overwhelmed him as he listened to Hines' torrid, rolling boogie bass. The heavy, left-handed boogie beat reminded him of the house-rent parties he had attended in the 1920s and '30s. George's spontaneous blues' shout became a permanent part of the "Boogie Woogie on the St. Louis Blues" arrangement that was recorded by the Earl Hines Orchestra in February, 1940. To this date, it has remained "Fatha" Hines' biggest hit. It sold over one million 78 rpm records. The first recording of boogie-woogie piano was made by Boogie "Pine Top" Smith in March, 1928, in Chicago. The boogie-woogie style had been played by blacks up and down the Mississippi for many decades before Pine Top put it on wax.

My father told me, "The house-rent parties' hip-swayers and floor vibrators did not always have a monopoly on the shout because some piano players could out-holler the belly-floppers."

He cited as a prime example the late Ferdinand "Jelly Roll" Morton, who is still considered one of the greatest pianists and composers of this century.

Dad said: "Jelly Roll with his flamboyant style would take over a house party when he sat down at the piano and throw his head back and shout, 'I am the great

The Earl Hines Orchestra at the Grand Terrace in 1930.

Jelly Roll Morton.' Jelly-Roll would exhibit his crowning glory, which was a glittering diamond in his front tooth, and would then bang the keyboard hard and loud. After tremoring the keyboard powerfully, he would soften his touch on the ivories and shout: 'I am the great Jelly Roll,' and with a rolling left hand in the bass clef, accompanied by a single or double note obligatto with his right in the treble clef, he would scream, 'I invented jazz! Yes, I did! I did that!'" There is a mountain of historical evidence that shows his boast may have been very close to the truth.

A house-rent party was considered a big hit when the dancers were continually buying the piano player drinks. I can remember many times as a child seeing five or six shot glasses of moonshine lined up like tin soldiers in front of my father on the ledge above the piano keyboard. Daddy would prefer not to play at his own house-rent parties if he could get James A. or "Hot Foot" McAfee to do the job for the usual two dollars plus drinks and all the chitterlings, fried chicken, cold slaw, spaghetti and potato salad one could eat. Both James A. and Hot Foot were big eaters and heavy drinkers, as evidenced by their rotundity and heavy breathing. These men were known as real ivory ticklers on the South Side house-rent party circuit.

An ideal circuit would be a bunch of four. This meant that everybody got a shot at making his or her rent money once a month, inasmuch as the parties rotated from flat to flat every Saturday night. I always looked forward to the Saturday night rent parties at our house because I knew the following Sunday I would get an opportunity to go to either the Lyceum Theater at 38th and Cottage Grove or the Pickford on 35th Street near Michigan Avenue. Mother seldom said no because on the top of the dresser on the left side of her bed I would see stacks of dimes, quarters, half-dollars, silver dollars, plus some brick-size yellow and green dollar bills. If mother felt liberal, she would give me fifteen cents—a nickel for the one o'clock Sunday matinee and a dime for candy. However, most of the time she was conservative and I received only one thin dime.

The money made at house-rent parties was not used by my parents for conspicuous consumption. It was needed to pay for basic human necessities, such as food and clothing. My father and most of Chicago's blacks were confined within the boundaries of the Black Belt in vertical shanties where the high rents in many instances were sealed at seventy-five to one hundred percent of their monthly salaries. Lodgers and child labor often provided rent supplements.

"Cooking" moonshine was another activity people engaged in to supplement their incomes. Making "alky" in primitive household stills was common practice among those on our street who were willing to take the risk. In some buildings the smell of sour mash hung over the illegal apartment distillery like a London fog. In addition, making your own table wine and home brew for personal consumption was an acceptable practice in our neighborhood. Dave Young, former tenor sax man with Fletcher Henderson and Roy Eldridge, told me about an incident that took place at a house-rent party.

Dave said, "The piano player was beating out a mean boogie-woogie and the floor was crowded with dancers shouting and having a ball. The sound of seven shots rang out. People ran, screamed and scrambled to get under the table, the bed or the bathtub, if possible. After several minutes of silence, people started getting up from the floor to discover that the sound of the firing gun was nothing more than the tops blowing off bottles of overheated, home-brewed beer in the bootlegger's kitchen pantry."

Children were frequently used by some small-time neighborhood bootleggers to deliver moonshine during those rare periods when the police were enforcing Prohibition. A kid would be given a nickel to carry a gallon kerosene can filled with moonshine to "Mama" Sue's apartment on the second floor at 3710 South Cottage Grove where the Saturday night chitterling stomp was going to take place. In preparation for the delivery, the bootlegger would smear some coal oil on the exterior of the gallon can to give it an obnoxious kerosene odor that would override the smell of the moonshine contents.

Almost nothing could neutralize the stinking smell of boiling chitterlings. My mother tried putting baking soda in the pot and that helped to nullify the odor a

Above: The exterior of the Mecca Building, at 33rd and State Street, Chicago. Below: The Mecca was built in 1891 by Daniel Burnham & George Edbrooke. Its interior court, a glory of glass and iron, was an ideal shelter against Chicago's cold, windy winters. Blacks moved into the building in 1916 and shortly thereafter, the Saturday night house rent party piano pluckers composed the "Mecca Flat Blues".

bit. However, once you got beyond the smell of the cooked small intestines of the pig, there was no delicacy more tasteful than a bite of chitterlings that were thoroughly cleaned and properly prepared with some cold slaw, spaghetti and crackling cornbread on the side. I can remember hearing the party-goers call to my mother, "Landlady! Bring me a yard of chitterlings and a pitcher of moonshine to cut the grease." You could buy a ten-gallon can of chitterlings at Wilson & Company in the Chicago stockyards for a dollar. Blacks created the primary market for the hog bowels the packing companies had considered a total waste.

The rent party-giver paid a dollar for a gallon of moonshine and sold it for fifty cents per cream pitcher. Moonshine parties were as varied as the people who gave them. My folks' activity was restricted to one Saturday night house-rent party a month, but some individuals made a full-time occupation out of giving drinking and eating parties. Some party flats could be categorized as the "poor man's cabaret," while others were simply fronts for houses of prostitution, with some crap shooting and poker playing taking place between the acts.

White houses of prostitution were unofficially dispersed throughout the black community when the 260 bawdy houses in Chicago's red-light district were closed by Mayor Carter Harrison in October, 1912. On August 4, 1928, during Mayor William Hale Thompson's administration, the following statement appeared in the *Chicago Whip:* "For some unexplainable reason a cloak of immunity has been draped around notorious vicious institutions operated by white people for white people in black districts."

Alberta Hunter, the eighty-seven-year-old jazz and blues singer, captured the flavor of Chicago's sporting houses in the lyrics of a song she wrote while working in the Windy City during the 1920s:

> Come on up some night, my castle's rocking,
> You can blow your top, 'cause everything's free.
> On the top floor, second door to the rear, that's where you'll always find me.
> The stuff is there and the chicks fairly romp with glee.
> Don't worry about a thing because I'm laying it on the line for protection,
> Tell them cats downtown that they can let their conscience be.
> Come on up, bring your friends, and we'll start that ball to rolling,
> My castle's rocking, run on by and see.

There is nothing that will draw a crowd of Adams to your castle like a bunch of pretty Eves. Smart party hustlers knew that and they would pass the word a week in advance that "Foxy Eve" and her gang were going to be in attendance at the "belly rub" Saturday night. That kind of promotional gossip would almost guarantee a financially successful rug cutting. "Foxy Eve" and her crew of six would be there "with bells on" for several purposes: to entice Adam to buy the landlady's moonshine and then assist him in its consumption, and, with proper inducement, Eve and some members of her gang were willing to remove their fig leaves if Adam had a desire to bite the apple.

Art Hodes, the Chicago-style jazz piano player, and the late Dave Tough, a highly rated and extremely talented drummer who worked in the Benny Goodman, Tommy Dorsey and Artie Shaw orchestras, were busted in a castle operated by "Pappa" Couch at 48th and State Streets.

Hodes said, "I sent a kid who was hanging around the flat across the street to get some ribs."

Dave Tough, who was greasing his chops in the rib joint, asked the kid, "Where are you going with all them bones?"

The kid replied, "To 'Pappa' Couch's across the street."

Dave, who was three-fourths stoned, got up from the counter and followed the kid across the street. Just before they reached the curb in front of 4830 South State Street, two cops in a squad car observed this unusual scene of a white man in a black neighborhood following a black boy who had both of his arms wrapped around a stack of paper plates that were loaded with smoking ribs. The cops followed them upstairs to the "castle" where they found an ethnically mixed

Art Hodes, renowned stride piano player (left), and his pal, Dave Tough, a favorite drummer with Benny Goodman and Tommy Dorsey.

party drinking and having fun. The cops busted the joint and took everybody to the lockup at 4800 South Wabash.

Art said: "They even put our barbeque in jail. That's where we polished those ribs."

The next day Dave Tough and Art Hodes were taken before an Irish judge at the 11th Street Station.

Art said, "I will never forget what that judge told Dave and me."

The judge said, "Why don't you white fellows learn to stay in your own neighborhood? Case dismissed."

Art said he later thought, "What would have happened to us if Christopher Columbus had stayed in his own neighborhood?"

If Columbus had landed in Chicago and heard the boogie-woogie, he would never have returned to Spain. He would have been enthralled and possibly endowed with some semblance of soul just as many young white musicians were influenced by their fascination with the boogie style during the first forty years of this century—a style loaded with magnetically powerful intensities. Its thunderous drive utilized all eighty-eight keys in the search for new creative expressions. At times the booming boogie bass had been considered too loud, mercurial and threatening by the uninitiated listener. The booming, walking boogie bass could be achieved in many ways. The pianist would rock his left hand up and down the bass clef in octaves as if walking sideways on his fingers. His fourth finger was a substitute for his left foot and the thumb for his right. This distinctive bass treatment is musically powerful.

The chief exponents of the boogie style, which is endemic to Chicago, were the "piano men" who had graduated from the house-rent party circuit. Although their musical objectives were the same, their boogie forms were as varied as the contours of the assorted buttocks on the piano stools. Albert Ammons, a native Chicagoan, played a forceful boogie. Ammons used driving, riff-like figures in the right hand as well as the left, and then he would amplify his boogie theme up to a powerful and intense musical experience. Whenever I listen to Ammons' recordings of "Boogie Stomp" and "Boogie-Woogie Blues," I relive the same exciting experience when I first heard him at Club DeLisa on the South Side of Chicago in 1936. "Cripple" Clarence Lofton, a 1918 Tennessee import, had a boogie style that contrasted greatly with Ammons' in that he used a simple, jump-like touch with his left hand and a brilliant, flickering, moderato offbeat melodic tempo with his right hand. Lofton's recordings of "Early Blues," "South End Boogie" and "The Fives" showcased his style.

Meade Lux Lewis, another native Chicagoan, on his famous recording of the "Honky-Tonk Train Blues," brilliantly captured the boogie rhythm of the elevator trains that rattled by his third floor apartment. Lewis' technique is masterful in the intricate way he mixes blues figures, frills, riffs, tremolos and guitar-like

James P. Johnson, stride piano player.

Cripple Clarence Lofton, piano player.

Albert Ammons.

Meade Lux Lewis.

Jimmy Yancey.

arpeggios in his colorful creation of the railroad sound in his recording of the "Chicago Flyer."

Jimmy Yancey, an ex-rent-party blues man whom I enjoyed hearing many times at the Bee Hive on East 55th Street, was one of Chicago's most talented native sons. His style was folksy and simple: you could hear the keys in the bass clef talking to the treble clef as his hands moved with equal dexterity through such masterpieces as the "How Long, How Long Blues," "Eternal Blues" and the "Yancey Stomp."

The boogie-woogie reached its zenith on December 23, 1938, when both Albert Ammons and Meade Lux Lewis appeared in concert at New York City's Carnegie Hall and drove the audience wild. The boogie fad faded and only small remnants can be found today. Virtually every one of the authentic boogie-woogie stylists is dead and many of the older piano plunkers did not even leave a record or a traceable photograph.

A youthful author in 1938. This photograph was taken at the request of William Samuels, of Associate Artists, who was promoting the Travis Orchestra's Midwest tour. The author comments that this was the last picture taken of him with hair.

Chapter 6

You Are Going to Be More Than Me

My father repeated variations of the following words to me almost every day: "Son, I know that you are going to be more than me one day. I can't let you grow up like a weed, not learning to read and forced to feed a time clock six days a week just to get by, like your Uncle Joe and me." I have often wondered if those were the first words my father spoke to me when I was brought out of the delivery room.

Although he himself had not finished the third grade in his native Atlanta, my father had big plans for his first and only child. Musicians were the "somebodies" in my dad's life; they were the only free spirits in the black community. They could dress well, sleep late, and were generally admired by their audiences. My father's own musical talents had not enabled him to quit his job in the stockyards. He wanted me to learn music early so that I would not get caught in the packinghouse trap. Shortly after my first birthday, he encouraged me to sit beside him, bracing my back with his huge left hand, while he tickled the piano keys with the five nimble ivory pickers of his right hand. When I was thirty-six months old, he began to teach me the keyboard.

Although Louis Travis knew little about written piano music, he had a torrid auditory relationship with boogie-woogie piano, and he felt comfortable about teaching it to me. But he wanted me to learn to read music too. He had been told that I should start with the Matthews Music Primer. My mother came to our rescue by discovering Elmer Simpson, an extraordinary musician who had been choir director for many years at Grant Memorial A.M.E. Church, then located on the southwest corner of 46th Street and Evans Avenue. Mr Simpson agreed to teach me the Matthews piano method for fifty cents a half-hour lesson, plus fourteen cents carfare. I received my first formal lesson from him at our apartment at 3609 South Cottage Grove Avenue on January 5, 1926, just seven weeks before my sixth birthday.

In four months Simpson prepared me to play "Violets Blue" in a children's musical recital at the West Point Baptist Church, still standing on the northwest corner of 36th Street and Cottage Grove Avenue. My parents were ecstatic about my ability to play a simple melodic scale. After the recital Dad conveyed his delusions of grandeur about his son's future. His first words after we left the church were "Jelly Roll Morton, look out, 'cause my boy is coming!"

My mother said, "Sweetheart, you're crazy!"

Dad just looked at her with a smile, and tightened his grip on my hand as we walked home.

His dreams for me were heightened by what he had seen and heard in the music halls and gin joints on South State Street between Polk and 35th Streets in the early years of the century.

He had seen Jelly Roll Morton at the Elite Club at 3030 South State Street, playing his original compositions: "Jelly Roll Blues", "King Porter Stomp", and "Alabama Bound". He considered Jelly Roll's talents to be unequalled. He had also seen Shelton Brooks at the Pekin Theater at 2700 South State Street, conducting the orchestra and playing his own works, which included "Darktown Strutters Ball", "Balling the Jack", "Walking the Dog" and the immortal "Some of These Days," made famous by Sophie Tucker. "Darktown Strutters Ball" was an interpretation, through music and lyrics, of Brooks' observations of black social life on South State Street in the early nineteen hundreds.

All these things my father had seen before my mother came to Chicago in 1916. The bright lights he had seen on South State Street made him believe that he could light another lamp and brighten the road for me.

My father always said, "A man can never be bigger than his dreams." And he

Jelly Roll Morton.

Shelton Brooks.

had mighty big dreams for me!

He never thought of me as his little boy. I was always his little man, and he talked to me as if I were an adult. He described gang fights he had been in as a newcomer to Chicago in 1900. He even described some of the women he had known before he met my mother. In contrast my mother always treated me like her sweet chocolate baby, a habit she has not broken in sixty-three years.

My father was most impressed with the nightclubs he had gone to in the early twenties with my mother or his brother Joe. At that time Louis Armstrong and King Oliver were musical legends. Dad first saw Louis Armstrong in September of 1922, when Armstrong was playing second cornet to King Oliver at the Royal Gardens at 459 East 31st Street. The Royal Gardens was later repainted and renamed The Lincoln Gardens.

Dad said Louis was about five feet seven inches tall and weighed two hundred and twenty-six pounds: he looked as though he were eight months pregnant. His hair was combed into bangs that hung over his oval head like a shiny black umbrella. His eyes were saucer-shaped and sparkling and his large lips parted easily into a smile, revealing his milk-white teeth. As a boy he had been nicknamed "Dippermouth" for obvious reasons. In later years musicians called him "Father Dip" in respect and affection.

Unfortunately, not everyone admired Armstrong's talent. Sammy Stewart, the sophisticated society band leader at the mob-owned Sunset Cafe, at 35th and

Calumet, refused to give him an audition. In fact he dismissed Armstrong without even looking him in the eye. Roy Butler, who was a saxophone player with Stewart's band, told me, "The first time the members of our band saw Armstrong and Oliver at the Lincoln Gardens, we thought they were funny. We didn't know that we were listening to something important. Louis always kept his music on the seat of his chair and stood up and played a second voice to everything that King Oliver blew out of his horn—he never looked at the music. Louis was showing signs of genius but we didn't recognize it at the time. The importance of jazz had not seeped through yet to 'dicty' colored folks. They just made fun of it."

In contrast, white musicians by the dozen would come out nightly, after they finished their one a.m. gigs at the big downtown clubs and hotels, to hear the new jazz being played at the Lincoln Gardens. They were so intent on learning these new sounds that they literally muscled their way through the throngs of black dancers to get near the bandstand. Once they were there, they would hog that area until just before dawn, when the last note was played by Armstrong and Oliver.

Bud Freeman, the legendary tenor saxophone "white hope" for the Coleman Hawkins crown, said about the New Orleans Rhythm Kings, a white group: "Once I heard King Oliver and Louis, I never went back to the Rhythm Kings—because I knew that now I had heard the real thing."

Dad said that, in addition to the music, he liked the atmosphere of the Lincoln Gardens. The room would accommodate about a thousand people, he said, with some tables, chairs and benches along the walls for shy young ladies who came without escorts. It had a balcony because before 1917 it had been a theater. A low false ceiling was decorated with artificial maple leaves attached to criss-crossed chicken wire. Hanging six feet from the ceiling was a huge rotating ball studded with tiny mirrors. It scattered multi-colored dots of light onto the merrymakers. "Boy!" Dad said. "That was a sight to be remembered!" My father told me that in the 1920s and '30s the law required that female monitors be present at all public dances to prevent an overindulgence in "jelly rolling" and "slow grinding".

One of the most elegant nightclubs in the Black Belt was the Dreamland at 3520 South State Street. It was considered the best black and tan club on the South Side. Gangsters owned it, and it was managed by a black man named Bill Bottoms, who became Joe Louis' chef in 1934 and kept that position until Louis' retirement.

The walls of the Dreamland were glazed in the latest art deco colors, and held interesting murals and sconces. One of its innovations was the installation of hundreds of tiny lights which illuminated the area around the dancers' feet. In general, the Dreamland symbolized style to people of all colors, and drew a sophisticated crowd. My father did not have enough money to go there more

Louie Armstrong and his wife, Lil. A great jazz team of the 20s.

Sammy Stewart's Band in November, 1929, just before they opened at the Michigan Theater on East Garfield Boulevard in Chicago.

than twice in a period of two years, but my eighty-six year old mother remembers the Dreamland vividly. "The first night your father took me there," she said, "we were seated near the rear of the club, but we could see Al Jolson, Fanny Brice and Sophie Tucker, the superstars of the '20s, sitting in separate parties at the ringside. I will never forget how excited I was to be there and how flattering it was to be greeted and seated by floor managers in tuxedos."

My mother had no idea that the white stars she saw at the Dreamland were doing what is known in the theatrical world as stealing. Lil Armstrong, an accomplished pianist, arranger, and orchestra leader, who was married to Louis Armstrong from 1924 to 1938, told me, "Many famous white performers came out to seek inspiration at the Dreamland, or so they said. Actually, they were stealing our material. . ."

Alberta Hunter, the South Side's favorite singer during that period, said, "Sophie Tucker came to see me do 'Some Day, Sweetheart' at the Dreamland. Later she sent her maid, Belle, to ask me to come to her dressing room and teach her the songs. I would never go. . ."

Alberta Hunter, one of the hottest blues singers to hit Chicago in 1920.

Jack Johnson directing the band in 1912 in his famous Cabaret D' Champion at 42 West 31st Street, Chicago.

Another nightclub where white musicians came to learn from the enter-tainers was the Cabaret de Champion at 42 West 31st Street which had been opened by the heavyweight champion Jack Johnson in 1912. My father thought the Cabaret was the classiest black and tan public club in the country. Johnson had decorated it with art works and curios that he had picked up in his European travels: several of his favorite Rembrandts hung in the club's foyer. The furniture was solid mahogany. Even the cuspidors were silver with gold ornaments. Nine life-size pictures of Johnson himself in various poses graced the mahogany panels of the Cabaret's main room. This decor naturally stirred a good deal of comment, and black folks who could afford to see it were mighty proud of Johnson's accomplishment. It was a prototype for class cabarets in the Black Belt during the 1920s and '30s.

The night spots were jazz laboratories open to all who wanted to improve their skills in "jazzology." There was a galaxy of talented black instructors such as Jelly Roll Morton, Louis Armstrong, King Oliver, Erskine Tate, Earl Hines, Fletcher Henderson, Buck & Bubbles, Ethel Waters, Mae Alix, Jimmie Noone, Bessie Smith and Sammy Stewart, along with at least a thousand others who practiced their crafts in the theaters, nightclubs and amusement centers on Chicago's South Side.

At the Sunset Cafe, a mob-controlled night spot at 35th and Calumet, the short, stocky doorman, Bill Summers, occasionally greeted young white musicians with: "Good morning! I bet I know why you boys are back here again this morning. You came for another music lesson, didn't you?"

Some would reply, "You're right, Professor." Others would say, "Here's a

The King Oliver Band. Front row, third from left: Darnell Howard. King Oliver is directly behind him.

The Fletcher Henderson Orchestra in 1925. Left to right: Scott; Coleman Hawkins; Louie Armstrong; (?) Dixon; Fletcher Henderson; Marshall; and Buster Bailey.

quarter, Sam. Get yourself a cigar." The more timid ones only nodded, sometimes with a smile.

On stage at the Sunset the teachers were Earl Hines and Louis Armstrong, both featured with the Carroll Dickerson Sunset Syncopated Orchestra. Among their regular pupils were Benny Goodman, Gene Krupa, and Bix Beiderbecke. Others seen at ringside in front of the bandstand from time to time were Tommy Dorsey, Jimmy Dorsey, Dave Tough, Muggsy Spanier, Joe Sullivan, Jess Stacy, Bud Freeman, along with others who learned their music lessons well enough to build financially successful musical careers on a black cornerstone.

The "whites only" tag is still attached to financial success in black music. In 1924 Red McKenzie, a white singer and part-time talent scout for Okeh Records, arranged a recording date for the Austin High School gang, of which Bud Freeman was a member. Freeman says, "The record was later to be called 'Chicago style'. What we were playing was our impression of Louis Armstrong and King Oliver. It was entirely different from the way they actually played, but it became known all over the world. . ."

My Dad used to say, "The white man can write down the black man's musical riffs and chord changes on his shirt cuff but he will never be able to capture the black man's rhythm on paper."

Above: The Carroll Dickerson Band in 1924. Earl Hines at piano. Below: Jimmy Dorsey.

Gene Krupa; Tommy Dorsey and the Edwards Sisters in 1943 backstage at the Chicago Theater.

Dad overlooked one point, and that is that what the white man can't borrow, he will buy. Benny Goodman bought several of the most talented black music arrangers: Jimmy Mundy who came from the Earl Hines band and Fletcher Henderson who abandoned his own orchestra to earn more money working for Goodman, who also hired Mary Lou Williams, a pianist and arranger for the Andy Kirk band, to score hits for Goodman like "Roll 'Em", "Camel Hop" and "Whistle Blues".

Woody Herman hired Zilner T. Randolph, who wrote "Old Man Mose is Dead" with Louis Armstrong, to give his band a black flavor. Randolph also did arrangements for the Ted Weems orchestra. And throughout the '30s Don Redman furnished the black jazz sound through arrangements for Paul Whiteman, Ben Pollack and Isham Jones, and produced 'specially commissioned orchestrations for Bing Crosby. "Deep Purple", a hit for Jimmy Dorsey's band, was done by Don Redman.

Since neither Baby Dodds, the drummer, nor Johnny Dodds, the clarinetist, could put their New Orleans Dixieland style onto paper, Bob Crosby simply imported Dodds' entire band to the Blackhawk Restaurant at 139 North Wabash

Above left: Mary Lou Williams. Right: Bud Freeman. Below: Bandleader Don Redman.

Avenue every morning after they had closed their show. For a small fee the Dodds brothers taught the Bob Cats the Dixieland beat.

Tommy Dorsey's prize was the very talented Sy Oliver, former star trumpet player and arranger for Jimmie Lunceford's orchestra. Sy told me in April, 1982, that he quit the Lunceford band to go to law school. "The Dorsey manager happened to be at Brighton Beach the night I put my notice in to leave the band," Sy said. "He began to call me because Dorsey had been trying for years to get me to write for his band. Finally the manager talked me into going to the Pennsylvania Hotel in midtown Manhattan where the Dorsey band was working. When I walked into the room, without even saying hello, Dorsey said, 'Sy, whatever Lunceford paid you last year for writing and playing, I'll top by $5000.'

"And there went law school right out the window. Back in 1939 that came to quite a lot of money."

Sy Oliver's experience was not typical of black musicians. Their average pay in 1939 was four dollars a night, or about $1248 a year. Postal workers in Chicago then earned $1800 a year, stockyard workers earned $1200, and laundry workers $750. My Dad wanted me to be more than he was, but he never learned that without white power one cannot earn big bucks in the music world.

Since most black musicians never had an opportunity to make any real money, they obviously played music for the love of the art. They had come to Chicago in search of opportunity in the 1890s and Chicago had acted as a catalyst for their work. As a result, in the 1920s the world of jazz music was centered in Chicago. No town or city in the forty-eight states had the talents or the spirit to generate the kind of jazz that caused toe-tapping rhythm to course through the veins and arteries of Chicago, "the city with the big shoulders".

Chapter 7

Jumping at The Savoy

I first heard of the Savoy Ballroom on Christmas Eve in 1927. I went to bed extremely early that night because I wanted Santa Claus to hurry to our house with my Christmas toys. It must have been about eleven o'clock that I was awakened by our jangling doorbell and the sound of someone scrambling up the stairs to our second floor apartment at 3609 South Cottage Grove. I peeped out from under the covers and saw my father quickly open the front door without asking the customary, "Who is it?" Instinctively my father must have known it was someone who needed help because my first cousin, Joe Crawford, who was about seventeen years old, literally fell to the floor in a state of exhaustion after he crossed over the threshold. I jumped out of bed and ran to where Cousin Joe was lying. Although our windows were frosted from the bitter cold weather, Cousin Joe's shirt collar was wide open, his vest and suitcoat unbuttoned and he was sweating profusely.

My father said: "Boy! Where are your overcoat and hat? Are you trying to catch the double consumption?"

After catching his breath and gaining his composure, Cousin Joe looked up at my father with the grin of a Cheshire cat and said: "I left them at the Savoy Ballroom."

"Boy! Have you been smoking some of those crazy cigarettes?" Before my cousin could answer, Dad shouted: "How in the hell did you get here? God Almighty knows, it must be two miles from 47th and South Parkway to 36th and Cottage Grove!"

Cousin Joe nodded his head forward with that silly grin on his face. My mother was standing in her bedroom door wearing a heavy blue cotton nightgown and listening to the conversation with a disturbed expression on her face. After several minutes had passed, she said, "Joe! What kind of trouble are you in this time?"

"Aunt Mittie, the only thing I did wrong was to dance with the wrong fellow's girl too many times," he replied.

My father started laughing hysterically and I joined in without really knowing why.

"This is not funny," Mother retorted.

Dad quickly stopped laughing and then asked, "Who were these fellows?"

Joe answered, "'Big China,' and some members of the 39th Street gang."

Dad rubbed his chin thoughtfully. "You were smart to leave your coat and hat behind because they weren't likely to follow you out into that below zero weather without theirs." Dad chuckled softly before making the following observation: "Joe! You probably ran a half mile before they could get their coats out of that check room. Ha! Ha! Ha!!"

I was enjoying the excitement when mother said: "Boy! You get your little behind back in bed before I put a strap to it."

I scurried back to my room because I knew that action would follow mother's threat. Before slipping back into a deep sleep, I could hear the murmur of Dad and Cousin Joe's voices coming from the living room.

Mother prepared her usual Christmas dinner which consisted of a twenty-five-pound tom turkey filled with cornbread stuffing, cranberries, giblet gravy and rice, green peas and carrots, potato salad, boiled rutabagas, sweet potato pie, coconut cake and hot homemade rolls. (My father's self-image related to the size of the turkey, just as some egos relate to the size of a car.) After we finished stuffing ourselves with mother's delicious dinner, we all felt too heavy to move away from the table. The men had loosened their belts and opened the top two buttons on their trousers and I did the same thing. Since the women ate as much as the men, they must have come to dinner without their corsets.

During the lull around the dinner table Cousin Joe rehashed his experience at

Left: Joe Crawford, the author's cousin and his mother in Washington Park in the summer of 1928. Right: An announcement in the Chicago Defender *offering both chaperone services and romance at the Savoy, America's Smartest Ballroom.*

the Savoy. Aunt Willie and Uncle Howard were as surprised about the incident as my mother had been the night before. My parents had gone to the Grand Inaugural Ball at the Savoy the previous Thanksgiving Eve: the ballroom's official opening had been on Thanksgiving Day. During December mother and dad had attended Savoy dances several times without running into any problems. So my mother found it hard to believe her nephew's story about hoodlums at the new dance palace. The Savoy's public relations people had boasted that the dance hall had excellent security, as well as plenty of mature women chaperones for unescorted young ladies and fifty beautiful dance hostesses for young men who came alone. Although Mother never said it I know she believed that Cousin Joe had created his own mess because of the manner in which he was "Jumping at the Savoy"; she knew he had a penchant for being a bully and starting trouble.

The Savoy Ballroom that my mother described that Christmas afternoon sounded like something out of one of my fairy tale books. She said that although it had been raining on Thanksgiving Eve the fashionably dressed patrons had begun to fill the ballroom as early as six p.m., two hours before the announced opening at eight o'clock.

Dad interrupted her with a description of the stream of cars which were inching both north and south down the congested South Parkway Boulevard past the blazing fireworks on the east parkway in front of the Savoy.

"You would not believe that colored people would own as many big cars as I saw that night," he said solemnly.

"Hush up, sweetheart!" Mother said. "Let me tell them about the pretty things." She described the huge banks of blooming flowers which had filled the lobby and the lounges—especially an immense horseshoe of white roses. "It had 'Good Luck' in gold letters on a satin ribbon across it," she said.

Aunt Willie, who had been listening, finally said something. She spoke with authority because she had worked part-time at the Savoy for two weeks. "Mittie," she said, "I know all about the Savoy. When you leave the outer lobby, you go into a lounge with red plush divans—the latest thing, and comfortable—just like the Drake Hotel." Aunt Willie had worked for a woman who lived in the Drake. "And the Savoy has got a house doctor and a registered nurse on duty at all times. And there are men's and women's lounges on the north side of the building; there's a regular boudoir room for ladies to refresh themselves and redecorate their faces. And there is an ultramodern checkroom on the south side of the lobby, did you see it, Mittie? It can hold 6000 hats and coats—they hung the coats so they wouldn't get crushed. . . ."

Dad laughed. "Willie," he said, "they should have made you manager."

"Louis," Aunt Willie said, "that could have happened if I had been both male and white."

There was a pause. Dad stood up to stuff his shirt tails back into his partially buttoned pants, and muttered through his half-smoked cigar that he thought the Savoy was good for the community. In addition to the bevy of fifty dancing beauties, the owners had hired 150 local colored men and women; these were new jobs. "We don't owe Big Bill Thompson for those jobs," Dad said, referring to the Mayor. "Him and his plantation politics!"

"How did you like the Savoy's two jumping bands?" Cousin Joe asked. "Charles Elgar's orchestra and Clarence Black's band?" Everyone in the room thought those bands were great. "I heard Ethel Waters sing five numbers with Elgar's orchestra the Saturday after Thanksgiving," Joe said. "She was so good they called her back for five encores."

Dad said he thought Ethel Waters was appearing downtown at the Palace Theater on Randolph and Wells.

"She was," Cousin Joe replied. "The Savoy people made an announcement

Ethel Waters.

before she sang that they got her through a special arrangement. I believe she is the best singer and comedienne we've had since Florence Mills passed."

"Now listen, Joe," Aunt Willie said. "Let me finish telling you all about the Savoy. Mr. J. J. Fagin, the white gentleman who manages it, told us that the dance space covers a half acre—6000 people can dance in comfort. And there's a refreshment bar in the northwest corner of the ballroom to serve the tables that go around three sides of the dance floor. You can relax between dances in the plush red chairs and enjoy those refreshments, and watch the dancing. . . ."

"Cut out the cement talk," Mother said. "Let me tell you about the society folks I saw at that Grand Inaugural Ball: there was Mr and Mrs Jesse Binga, the Robert S. Abbots—he's the publisher of the *Chicago Defender*—and Dr George Cleveland Hall and his wife, and Alderman Louis Anderson and his wife, and Mr and Mrs Oscar DePriest, and a whole lot of people from the *Chicago Defender*. That was some evening to remember. Right, sweetheart?"

A military ball at the Parkway Ballroom.

Exterior shot of the Savoy Ballroom in New York City. The Ballroom was on the second floor of the structure, which occupied the entire block at 141st and Lenox.

"Right," Dad said. He poured himself a fourth of a water glass of pure white bootleg moonshine and downed it in one gulp. From his frown you would think he had just swallowed a bottle of my nasty castor oil.

Before the Savoy Ballroom opened, the Mecca of black Chicago was the area between 31st and 35th Streets on State Street. A small syndicate of white New York businessmen had come to Chicago looking for a site so that they could repeat the triumph they had enjoyed in uptown New York with the Savoy Ballroom they had built in Harlem at 598–612 Lenox Avenue. That ballroom was said to be the largest in America, white or colored; it covered the entire block on Lenox from 140th to 141st Streets. The Savoy, later known as "The Home of Happy Feet," opened in March, 1926, and grossed over a million dollars in its first year; that sum represented ten times the initial investment. Since Chicago offered the country's second highest concentration of urban blacks, the Savoy owners naturally decided to build a Midwest Savoy.

The area they investigated was south of the 31st–35th Street district. The site they initially preferred for both the new Savoy and the Regal Theater was owned by Julius Rosenwald, the Sears Roebuck prince of merchandising and great philanthropist for black causes. It was bounded on the south by 47th Street, on the north by 46th Street, and by Wabash Avenue on the west and Michigan Boulevard on the east. Rosenwald had bought the land before the first World War in order to develop low-income housing for the black people who were flocking to Chicago from the South. This site was therefore not available to the syndicate. Their second choice was 47th Street and South Parkway. It was the selection of the South Parkway site that accelerated the movement of Chicago's black Broadway and Wall Street from 35th and State Streets to the spacious former Grand Boulevard at 47th Street.

This movement to the south was not greeted with universal joy. Those people with heavy investments in the 35th Street area were alarmed. Already on July 23, 1927, Jesse Binga, at the same time that he announced the construction of the Binga Arcade Building on the northeast corner of 35th Street, one door south of the Binga State Bank, was quoted in the *Defender* as saying somewhat defensively:

> Many people don't realize it, but practically all of our business institutions and our substantial investments are located on or near 35th Street. Not less than $3,000,000 is invested by our people in commercial property in the area five blocks north and five blocks south of 35th Street between State Street and Cottage Grove Avenue. There is the *Defender* plant, Liberty Life Insurance Company, the YMCA, YWCA, Pythian Temple, our largest undertaking establishment, the Overton interests, our most important hospitals, clubs and the bulk of our residential real estate investments. That condition, coupled with the fact that new investments and new enterprises are being opened by our people in

this neighborhood, means that 35th Street will always be colored Chicago's most important commercial center.

Binga was, however, alarmed enough about the southward movement to attribute it to racist machinations:

> All this movement southward was started by a group of unscrupulous white real estate dealers. It began before the Chicago race riot of 1919, and some of them are still up to their nefarious tricks. This is the way they operate. First, they get all the white owners in a neighborhood to sign up not to sell to colored people and then get them agitated about the black invasion. When the agitation is at its peak, one of the very dealers who has started the propaganda sells to a colored man. The other whites are urged to sell cheaply to a fellow white real estate dealer who in turn sells to another colored man and the white flight is on!

The Binga Arcade cost $400,000: it was a five story Tudor Gothic elevator building with twenty-one stores, forty-eight offices and a ballroom on the top floor. It was an impressive forward step for the community, but it was not enough to turn back the southward movement of blacks to 47th Street and beyond. Harry Engelstein's South Center Department Store had already anchored just east of South Park Boulevard at 417 East 47th Street, and ground-breaking for the Rosenwald Garden Apartments was imminent. With the coming of the Savoy Ballroom in November, 1927, and the Regal Theater in February, 1928, the importance of the new commercial area was no longer a question.

The Savoy provided the stage for Louis Armstrong, who had tuned up his trumpet to high 'C' and was blowing a battle charge for the black brigade. Times were indeed changing: in 1926 the Metropolitan Theater at 4644 South Parkway dropped its all-white admission policy. The management saw the black hand on the face of the white moon. But of course everyone did not see that black hand. In 1927 Dr Green G. Johnson, a physician with offices at 4652 South Parkway, two doors south of the Metropolitan Theater, filed suit against the management of the Trianon Ballroom at 6201 South Cottage Grove Avenue. Dr Johnson had paid one dollar to attend the Sixth Ward Republican dance and rally for William Hale Thompson in January of 1927; Trianon policy prevented him from dancing because of his color. Dr Johnson's attorney was William L. Dawson, then a staunch Republican, but later a powerful Democratic congressman representing the First Congressional District of Illinois. The owners of the Trianon were not abashed by Dr Johnson's suit: they maintained a "whites only" admission policy until early in 1950, four years before their doors closed forever. The Trianon building was demolished in 1967.

First-class dance halls were off-limits to black people on the South Side before

Jesse Binga's Arcade and Bank, on the northwest corner of 35th and State Street.

the second World War, or at least before the Savoy Ballroom. For example, although the White City Ballroom and Casino was located within a stone's throw of black residences in Woodlawn before 1900, blacks were kept out until the early 1940s. And the Pershing Ballroom, in the Pershing Hotel at 64th Street west of Cottage Grove, just across the alley from all-black west Woodlawn, was for whites only until the hotel was leased by blacks in the fall of 1944. At 6350 Cottage Grove Avenue was the Coconut Grove Ballroom which excluded blacks until 1952, when the street traffic in front of the ballroom was ninety-five percent black.

A lawsuit was filed against the Medinah Club, 505 North Michigan Avenue, on January 30, 1939, by Ishmael P. Florey acting for the Joint Council of Dining Car Employees of which he was secretary-treasurer, because the Club cancelled a contract with the Newspaper Guild for the use of the Club on February 15, 1939. The Guild and the Council belonged to the same union, and the Club's action was caused by their discovery that Council members were to be present. The suit was based on a letter signed by E. Edgar Gregory, the Club's resident manager and sent to Graham P. Dolan, a white official of the Guild. The contents of the letter were reprinted in the *Chicago Defender* on February 4, 1939:

> The rule of the Medinah Club of Chicago as administered by the House Committee expressly forbids the entrance of colored people to the Club or the renting of any Club rooms to outside parties where colored people are to be in attendance. . . .
> It is therefore . . . necessary for us to advise you that we are cancelling the renting of the ballroom to the Chicago Newspaper Guild for Wednesday, February 15, 1939, and we are enclosing our check in the amount of $25.00 to cover the deposit which you paid us.

Obviously, these restrictive practices caused a demand within the colored community for white-owned, hand-me-down ballrooms. Among the ballrooms available within the Black Belt south of 39th Street was the Forum Hall at 324 East 43rd Street. The Forum is best remembered as headquarters for Professor Watts' Monday, Wednesday and Friday night dance school. It was also the scene of afternoon high school hops, and unforgettably romantic spotlight dances, where an appropriate theme song would be Lil Green's "In the Dark". On the northwest corner of 43rd and Prairie was the Movement Hall, which attracted workers from the Union Stockyard and from nearby laundries to its Friday and Saturday night dances. The Boulevard Hall, at 366 East 47th Street, was where local tough boys and girls did the Lindy Hop and the Jitterbug Waltz. On the several occasions that my band played dances at the Boulevard Hall, the reefer smoke could have been cut with a knife.

The Warwick Hall at 543 East 47th Street was managed by Charlie Hall, a medium brown-skinned gentleman who brooked no nonsense.

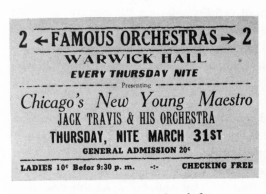

The Jack Travis Orchestra played for dances at the Forum Hall at 43rd and Calumet (above), and the Warwick Hall at 543 East 47th Street.

Since Charlie was an ex-heavyweight boxer who stood six feet four inches tall and weighed two hundred and fifty pounds, he could easily evict any young hoodlums who were foolhardy enough to try to invade the ballroom by prying open a back fire door. Charlie Hall stood guard at the front door to make sure that these ruffians were not sold tickets. In 1934 I started attending the Sunday afternoon "battle of the bands" at the Warwick. The best sessions were between Nat Cole (he was not called "King" until six years later) and his Twelve Royal Dukes and Tony Fambro and his Jungle Rhythm Orchestra. Nat patterned his band after the Earl Hines Orchestra, while Fambro was into the Duke Ellington jungle sounds.

In 1936 my band started playing jam sessions against the King Kolax Orchestra and others at the Thursday night dances sponsored by the Musicians Protective Union, Local 208 of the American Federation of Musicians. On trumpet I had Pee Wee Jackson, who later played with the Earl Hines and Jimmie Lunceford aggregations; Nat Jones on alto sax, who subsequently joined Duke Ellington; John Simmons, who was picked up by Benny Goodman, on bass; and Henry Fort, a former member of Nat Cole's group, also played bass; on trumpet and trombone, Gail and Charlie Brockman, who joined Earl Hines, and later Billy Eckstine's band. These are only a few of the fine musicians I worked with at the Warwick Hall between 1936 and 1939.

There were at least seventy-five small public halls on the South Side that could accommodate one hundred people—Mary Bruce's place at 52nd and South Parkway was one, and the Century Club at 49th and Michigan was another. Then there were some larger ballrooms off the beaten path, like the Alvin Dansant Hall on the northeast corner of 51st and Michigan and the Blue Heaven Ballroom at 6 West Garfield Boulevard—on the former site of the Citizens Bank.

The most popular ballroom owned by blacks was Bacon's Casino on the northeast corner of 49th Street and Wabash Avenue. This was a former garage which had been converted by the Bacon brothers, Robert and Ernest, into a dance palace in June, 1927. (Robert Bacon was the father of Warren Bacon, a former member of the Chicago School Board.) The ballroom, which had two large decorative fountains in the center of the dance floor, was used by hundreds of social and civic clubs for formal and semi-formal dances, concerts and public meetings. Young middle-class and upper middle-class blacks found the Casino very attractive, and always dressed elegantly for the dances. At the spring and summer semi-formals young ladies wore ankle-length chiffon dresses in varying delicate hues, contrasting beautifully with the strong colorant of their faces, which ranged from reddish black to an orangey white. When the young women waltzed they looked like a garden of flowers blown by the wind.

The Bacon brothers, who had worked in 1916 as dance instructors and managers of the old Dreamland Dance Hall at 3618–20 South State Street, ran

Above: The Alvin Dusant Hall at 51st and Michigan.

Below: The Owl Club of Chicago gave a dance at the Dusant Hall on November 9, 1930.

Harrison Studio

Committee of 100
Becons Casino
Feb 28 1941

Function given by the Committee of 100, on February 28, 1941, at Bacon's Casino. Among notables present were: Anthony Overton, John Sengstacke, Lloyd Wheeler, Ernest Rather, and Alderman Benjamin Grant. Bacon's was a center for civic and social activities on the South Side from 1927 to 1945.

their hall efficiently: since they excluded rowdy elements, they had almost a monopoly on private dances until the modern Parkway Ballroom opened at 4457 South Parkway under black ownership in 1940.

Thirty-fifth and State Streets, the "street of streets", died at the height of its glory before the fall of Wall Street on Tuesday, October 29, 1929. What was once

black Chicago's "gay white way" was a shambles by 1931. The Pullman Cafe, the Vendome, and the Grand Theater that had shone in brilliant splendor were now shady ladies with unpainted faces. Rising above the ruins was the Binga Arcade Building, standing on the northwest corner of 35th and State like a giant tombstone in the midst of a commercial graveyard. The crossroads of black America in the first three decades of this century was gone. Not even a ghost of its dynamic energy is left: there is neither plaque nor sign to remind our youth two generations removed that this was once a center of black pride. It was real and it was ours. Today the former parade ground of the sepia giants in our world of commerce is just another thoroughfare.

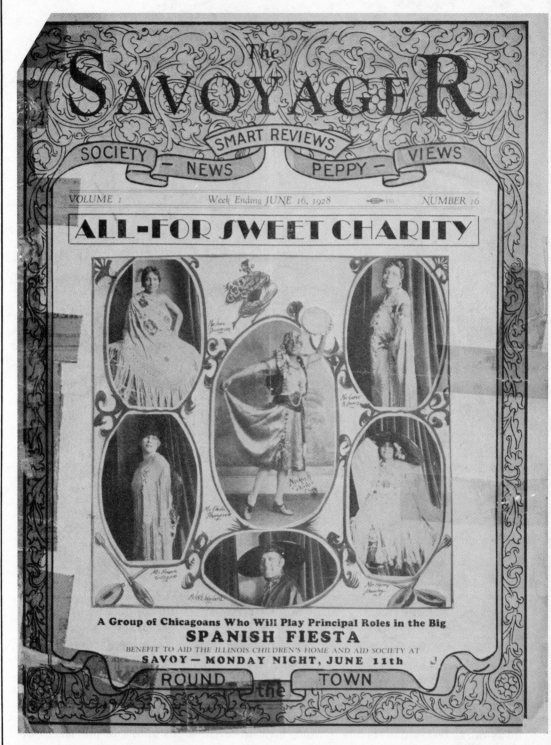

The Savoyager

SMART REVIEWS

SOCIETY — NEWS — PEPPY — VIEWS

VOLUME 1   Week Ending JUNE 16, 1928   NUMBER 16

ALL-FOR SWEET CHARITY

A Group of Chicagoans Who Will Play Principal Roles in the Big
SPANISH FIESTA
BENEFIT TO AID THE ILLINOIS CHILDREN'S HOME AND AID SOCIETY AT
SAVOY — MONDAY NIGHT, JUNE 11th

ROUND the TOWN

The front page of the Savoyager, a 34-page weekly house organ that covered the various activities at the Savoy. In addition to a gossip column about its patrons, the magazine featured sports, fashions and general community news and was supported by ads from local businesses.

Chapter 8

The Many Faces of Lady Savoy 1927 to 1948

The face of the Savoy Ballroom at 47th and South Parkway was like the face of a beautiful woman who applies extra layers of makeup each year to hide the natural aging process. The Lady Savoy I knew as a teenager in 1934 was unlike the one that my parents knew in 1927. Because of the stock market crash in 1929 the Savoy had ceased to be open seven nights a week. From 1927 to 1928 the Savoy was like a little city, with its own newspaper, barber shop, beauty salon, shoeshine parlor, saloon and extensive security system headed by Manager-Director Tom Cross. According to my mother, Mr Cross was very protective of young people, and especially of young women who came to the hall unescorted, as many did in those days.

When I was in the sixth grade at Willard Elementary School at 49th and St Lawrence Avenue, I heard the big boys talking during recess about the good times they had had the previous afternoon at the Savoy Ballroom. They mentioned the great music and the beautiful girls. Some of them acted out a dance with an imaginary girl in their arms. I knew all about the music, because when I was eight years old we lived at 4826 South Evans, and on Sunday afternoons we boys would walk over to the Savoy and stand in front watching the people and listening to the music. In fact, that is how I heard Louis Armstrong for the first time. You could stand on the sidewalk in front of the Savoy and hear Louis' trumpet as clear as a bell. The bandstand was four hundred feet east of the ballroom entrance on South Parkway, where we stood on the curb.

When I was fourteen I went to the Savoy for the first time and gawked at the big boys and girls dancing. I wasn't much of a dancer then. I marvelled at the huge size of the Ballroom and at the red hot music spewing from the horns of the two bands. On my maiden visit the Erskine Tate Orchestra and the Johnny Long Band were playing. I was impressed also by simultaneous indoor and outdoor dancing. The Ballroom was not air conditioned: many people chose to dance under the stars, weather permitting. On those Sundays when I lacked the extra twenty cents to enter the Ballroom, I stood near the fifteen-foot wooden fence of the outdoor pavilion on the South Parkway side and listened to the music. Occasionally the security people would chase me away and I would go and stand near the fence on the alley side of the pavilion.

I remember one face in particular from my early visits to the Savoy. This gentleman was very light, had straight black hair and looked white. He made announcements over the microphone and seemed to me to be in charge of everything. This was Eddie Plique, a native of New Orleans who had spent most of his life in Chicago. Years later I became friendly with Eddie, and this is what he told me about the Savoy:

"I started promoting fights at the Savoy Ballroom in 1927. I was asked to come to work there by a close friend named Jimmy Gentry who told me that the Savoy was not doing well; big bands were costing too much money, and the management wanted to go into some other kind of activity. Jimmy knew that I had successfully promoted fights at the Rainbow Gardens on the Northwest side at Clark and Lawrence. Gentry introduced me to Harry Englestein, the owner of the Ballroom, and we talked for an hour and a half about the possibility of promoting fights at the Savoy. Englestein decided to hire me to promote fights one night a week on a six week trial.

"When the six weeks were up, things did not look too good. Mr Englestein was going to stop the fights but I persuaded him to give me an additional four weeks to see if we could make the venture pay. Luckily after the eighth week attendance at the fights swung dramatically upward, and the bottom line went

Above: Left to right: Eddie Plique (kneeling), Former Heavyweight Champion Jack Johnson (seated center), surrounded by a stable of amateur boxing hopefuls. Below: A patron prepares to enter the Savoy for the Tuesday night boxing match.

Above: Reporters and spectators flank ringside at the Savoy Ballroom. The late anchorman Fahey Flynn (third from front) broadcast the fights live from the ringside. Left: A group of celebrities at Savoy ringside. Third from left is Adolphe Menjou, the movie star, and second from right is Eddie Bracken of TV and films.

A typical Tuesday night boxing scene at the ringside. Below: Third from left: Earl Hines and Stuff Smith. Seventh from left: George Kirby and Red Saunders, who acted as judges for a ladies' hat contest. Contests were held monthly in various categories like beauty, fashion, etc.

from red to black. After that the Savoy promoted fights regularly every Tuesday night for fifteen years, from 1931 through 1946. Two thousand boxing fans could be accommodated inside the Ballroom and in the summer three thousand five hundred could sit in the outdoor dance pavilion. The boxing events became so popular that the late Fahey Flynn used to broadcast them live from the Savoy ringside for WBBM radio."

Lady Savoy became prematurely aged when the economic picture did not improve between the mid-'30s and the early '40s. At the suggestion of Jimmy Davis, the Savoy management decided to add another layer of makeup in 1939, with the introduction of a roller-skating program. Davis convinced Englestein that you could use skates with wooden wheels on the dance floor and not do any damage.

Lady Savoy now had three layers of cosmetics holding her face together. She had dances on Sunday, boxing on Tuesday and roller-skating on Wednesday, Thursday and Friday. Roller-skating was very popular among high school students at that time. Tiny Parham played the organ for the skaters, joined by Joe Williams, who also sang on Tuesday nights before the main boxing event and during the intermission.

The dance program at the Savoy had deteriorated to the point that John Mackie, the general manager, decided to go outside the white community and get some black talent. Mackie had met Dr Jive Cadillac, the assistant to Dave Kellum, the theatre editor of the *Defender;* when Dr. Cadillac stopped by the Savoy office to pick up their advertising and public relations copy for the *Defender,* Mackie asked him to manage the dance programs at the Ballroom.

"You've got to be kidding," Cadillac said.

"No, we're not kidding," Mackie replied. "We want you to take over the ballroom and turn our dance program around. We think you can do it."

Cadillac went with Mackie to Harry Englestein's office in the South Center Building at 417 East 47th Street, where Englestein readily agreed that Cadillac should take on the job. Cadillac said, "Okay, if you gentlemen are serious, I'll take the job. But you're going to have to give me total control of security. I want the right to bring in security people to clean up what I know is a big mess in the Savoy Ballroom."

At that time you could go into the Ballroom on Sunday nights during a dance and find half-pint whiskey bottles strewn by the hundreds all over the place, and the walls of the once beautiful Lady Savoy being defaced. Cadillac told Mr Englestein that he wanted at least four security people of his choice: he wanted four boxers, all at least six foot two and all trained at Eddie Nichols gym at 48th Street, east of South Parkway and directly south of the Savoy outdoor pavilion.

The security personnel were hired and outfitted in red uniforms as Dr Cadillac instructed. It took roughly seven months for Cadillac to clean the hoodlums out of the Ballroom. In 1936 after the big band policy was im-

Roller skating was another of Lady Savoy's many faces. Above: A security guard observes young skaters on the floor. Below: Young skaters prepare to race at the Savoy Roller Rink. Note the architectural details in left background.

The Erskine Hawkins Band on the Savoy bandstand in New York City.

plemented, people began to return to the Savoy Ballroom. That program began with the top big bands of the day: Duke Ellington, Jimmie Lunceford, Andy Kirk, Chick Webb, Tiny Bradshaw, Erskine Hawkins, Fletcher Henderson and Count Basie.

That was Dr Jive Cadillac's name band policy and it was a big hit. He booked Andy Kirk and his Twelve Clouds of Joy into the Savoy shortly after Kirk had recorded a tune called "Until the Real Thing Comes Along", originally known as the "Slave Song", sung by Kirk's vocalist Faye Terrell. When the song hit the jukeboxes across the country, the Andy Kirk Band became an overnight sensation, particulary in Chicago. On the Sunday night that Kirk appeared at the Savoy, you could hardly get near the place. People must have been turned away by the thousands, because I got there around five that evening and there was a long line, four abreast, waiting to get in. The dance was set to start at seven o'clock. It was held inside and it was hot as all get-out because there was no room for any air to stir anyplace. People were jammed in that ballroom like boat people.

The thrill of the evening for everyone occurred when Kirk's band began to play "Until the Real Thing Comes Along" and Faye Terrell opened his mouth and said "I . . ." Everyone went wild. The lyrics ran:

> I've worked for you, I've slaved for you,
> I'd be a beggar or a knave for you.
> If that isn't love it will have to do,
> Until the real thing comes along. . .

The Savoy Chatterbox *reflects the many faces of the Savoy's activities: big band dancing, boxing and roller skating.*

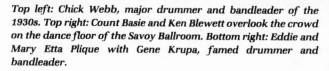

Top left: Chick Webb, major drummer and bandleader of the 1930s. Top right: Count Basie and Ken Blewett overlook the crowd on the dance floor of the Savoy Ballroom. Bottom right: Eddie and Mary Etta Plique with Gene Krupa, famed drummer and bandleader.

Above: The Count Basie Band with Jimmy Rushing at the mike. Below: The Johnny Long Band.
Front row: Seated left to right: Rudy Martin, piano; Nat Jones and Gordon Jones, tenor saxes;
Moses Grant, tenor sax. Standing: Johnny Long, trumpet.

Dr Jive Cadillac

Above: Louis Armstrong and Eddie Hubbard distribute records to young fans at a Sunday afternoon hop at the Savoy Ballroom. Below: The Fletcher Henderson Orchestra in 1936 at the height of the Goodman/ Henderson collaboration. Left to right: Chu Berry and Joe Thomas, trumpet; Horace Henderson, piano; Sidney Culen, drums; Dick Vance, trumpet; Teddy Lewis and Buster Bailey, clarinet; Elmer Williams, tenor; Ed Cuffee, trombone; Roy Eldridge, trumpet; Unknown, bass; Fernando Arbello, trombone; Bob Lassey, guitar; Don Pasquall, tenor; and Fletcher Henderson seated at the piano.

Willie Bryant headed the New York band that opened the partially refurbished Savoy Ballroom in spring of 1938.

Terrell would repeat those bars before going into the bridge of the song in a high falsetto and the girls went mad and so did the men. I've never had an experience like that in my life. When they played tunes like this, the Kirk band could be as smooth and soft as Guy Lombardo and his Royal Canadians. And when they played Mary Lou Williams' arrangements of "Foggy Bottom", and "Little Joe from Chicago", "Moten Swing", and "Walking and Singing", they made Count Basie stand back and look. Mary Lou's arrangements gave the band a real Kansas City beat.

I would say that during that period Andy Kirk's band was much more popular than Count Basie's, although both bands came from Kansas City and played Kansas City sound. The combination of Andy Kirk, Faye Terrell, Mary Lou Williams and the Clouds of Joy drew foot-stomping, cheering audiences from coast to coast. Kirk's Clouds of Joy had a unique sound; the sidemen of that great band were highly talented. Dick Wilson, the tenor man, died young at thirty. He

A night after the ball. Left to right: Harold Washington, current Mayor of Chicago, Marcella Davis, Duke Ellington, Moselynne Travis, and the author.

rivaled Coleman Hawkins, Chu Berry and Ben Webster on the tenor sax. Ben Webster himself played for Andy Kirk, as did Lester Young, Don Byas and Al Sears—all tenor men. Kirk's outstanding brass men included Ted "Muttonleg" Donnelly and Henry Wells on the trombone, and Harold "Shorty" Baker and Earl Thompson on the trumpet.

In 1938 a total facelift was started on Lady Savoy, although it was destined not to be completed. At the same time the management decided they would launch a program of dances four nights a week with live radio broadcasts from the

MUSIC

LOCAL 208, A.

PRESENT THEIR

MAMMOTH JAM SESSION

AN ELABORATE PRESENTATION OF

25 - SWING BANDS - 25

Fletcher Henderson
Jimmie Noone
Freddie Williams
Erskine Tate
Floyd Campbell
Tony Frambo
Tiny Parham
Jack Travis
Eddie Stovall
Count Rich
Robt. Marshall
Mrs. Louis Armstrong

Woode-Anderson
Willie Bryant
Johnny Long
Eddie Cole
Bob Tinsley
Danny Williams
Red Sanders
Les Wilcox
Chatman McIntosh
Fletcher Butler
Roy Eldridge
Johnny Dodds

Chas. Autrey and his Caviliers

SAVOY

BALLROOM

Mon. Night, May 16

Continuous Dancing 'till 4 A. M.

ADMISSION 60c

This billboard advertises the largest jam session of professional bands ever held in the city of Chicago.

Above: Just a small sample of the bands featured at the Savoy during its last days.

ballroom. Every band within a radius of nine hundred miles of Chicago came to audition for that gig. I enlarged my band from ten to sixteen pieces in the hope of getting that job. I felt that this might be my last opportunity to break out as a big-time bandleader: I was already eighteen years old. My band lost to Willie Bryant and his New York Orchestra, followed by the Horace Henderson Band. The only opportunity I got to play at the Savoy that year was in a mammoth jam session with twenty-five bands, on May 16, 1938. I will never forget that date because I had never seen that many professional musicians working in one ballroom before, and I have never seen anything like it in the forty-five years that have passed since then.

Savoy's four-night-a-week dance policy folded within a year. Management returned to Sunday-only dances with an occasional name band. That policy continued for the next ten years until Lady Savoy died and was buried on July 6, 1948.

Above: The finale of a Rhumboogie night-club production. Tiny Bradshaw, (left), and Joe Ziggy Johnson (right), in front line. Right: The Ritz Building at 343 East Garfield Boulevard: the Rhumboogie was on the first floor. Roy Eldridge had an apartment on the third floor.

Chapter 9

Jazz Joints Along East Garfield Boulevard

It was about 2:15 a.m. Sunday, August 23, 1936. The dance was over at Mary Bruce's place at 5228 South Parkway. All the members of my five-piece band were packed and ready to go home, except the drummer. Brad Taylor was sitting on his saxophone case and I was seated on the piano stool waiting for Chauncey Murdock to finish talking with some "chick" and disassemble his drums and cymbals. Sepio West, our trumpet player, and G. W. Harris, the bass player, had started out the door when Brad Taylor yelled, "Wait a minute, fellows! Let's catch the show at Club DeLisa. I hear it's red hot."

Sepio and G. W. stopped dead in their tracks and turned around. Sepio said, "Man, if you guys are going now, okay. If you are talking about sometime in Juvember, forget it!"

Murdock abruptly finished his conversation with the young lady and started putting his bass drum in its case, saying, "Solid! That Club DeLisa suggestion sounds good to me."

Brad Taylor looked at me with his funny, half-crooked grin and said, "What about you, Jack?"

"I promised my mother and old man that I would come directly home after this gig," I said.

Brad put his left hand on his hip and bellowed, "Man! You are a drag! How are you going to learn about the big time unless you dig some big-time scenes?"

After a very brief moment of consideration, I agreed to join the group. My initial reluctance was based upon my fear that they would not admit me to Club DeLisa because I was only sixteen years old. The other fellows in the band had all seen their twenty-first birthdays and more.

I had been gigging in Calumet City and on Chicago's North Side in small white nightclubs without any problems with club owners since I was fourteen. I attributed my good luck to the fact that I was six feet tall, and, too, I had always heard that white folks are poor judges of black folks' ages. Since G. W. lived at 5300 South Parkway, just half a block south of Mary Bruce's small basement dancehall, the fellows decided to leave their instruments at his house and walk the seven blocks to Club DeLisa at 5512 South State Street. A jitney cab ride from South Parkway would have cost us fifteen cents a man, which was enough money to buy seven steins of beer and one hot dog.

It was a hot night and people were sitting out on their front stoops to escape their stuffy apartments. South Parkway between 51st and 55th was very dark. The street lamps were extremely dim. About the only light came from the headlights of the hundreds of jitney cabs which plied South Parkway, hustling dime fares. The restricted operating boundaries for black-owned cabs in the Black Belt was South Parkway between 31st and 65th Streets. On the east side of South Parkway was Washington Park, thick with bushes and trees, which made everything even darker. However, when we got to 54th Street, in front of Burke Elementary School, it was brighter: we could see the shapes of people sleeping in the Park under the full moon.

Garfield Boulevard (55th Street) was brightly lighted. There was a large Standard Oil gas station on the southwest corner of South Parkway and Garfield Boulevard which illuminated both sides of the street, including the block-long Presbyterian Home for aged white men between South Parkway and Calumet, directly across the boulevard on the north side of 55th Street. On hot summer nights the parkway that divided the east and west drives on East Garfield Boulevard looked like a landing ground where hundreds of parachutists had abandoned their chutes. Men, women and children slept on the parkway under, and on top of, blankets and sheets of every color and description; some slept directly on the silky green grass. This was a common sight on summer nights: families had little fear of robbery or attack in those days. There were no bunches of crazies and addicts running loose in the streets. Occasionally you would see a veteran of World War I who had been gassed by the Germans. These people behaved strangely but were usually childlike and harmless.

Most of the nightclubs and lounges along Garfield Boulevard were open twenty-four hours a day, so there was a lot of all-night sidewalk traffic. Neon signs hung in front of the showplaces that were strung like pearls along the Boulevard. Dave's Cafe at 343 East Garfield was a class cabaret where you could light your evening fire and lose your tomorrow. The nightclub section of Dave's was run by Benny Skoller, and Sam "Golf Bag" Hunt operated the gambling section. In fact, "Golf Bag" was the mob's overseer of gambling for the entire South Side. "Golf Bag" Hunt got his nickname during his days as a torpedo for Al Capone: he would track down his prey with his shotgun concealed in a golf bag.

The entertainment at Dave's Cafe took place in the main room at the rear, while "Golf Bag" Hunt's gambling tables were in the front bar, clearly visible from the street to both the public and the police. Dave Young, the former star tenor player with the Roy Eldridge and Fletcher Henderson orchestras, still talks about the night the band and the chorus girls delayed the show for an hour and a half because they all wanted to watch the thousand dollar-a-card blackjack game between Livert "St Louis" Kelly and Sam "Golf Bag" Hunt. Although "St Louis" played with the treasury of the Colored Bartenders and Waiters Union in his pocket, "Golf Bag" won the game. In the end the house always won.

Dave's Cafe was a Caesar's Palace in miniature: it provided excellent entertainment along with the gambling. That night, from the balcony bar—reputed to be the city's only balcony bar—you could watch a stage show produced by Leonard Reed and featuring such stars as George Dewey Washington, the celebrated baritone singer, Arthur "Georgia Boy" Simpkins, the former star singer with the Earl Hines Orchestra at the Grand Terrace, and Billy and Charles, two clever and talented dancers, along with a chorus line of coffee-cream beauties dancing to the music of the Francois Orchestra.

Dave's Cafe had originally been in a building on the northwest corner of 51st and Michigan. Unfortunately, in 1933, the Cafe was destroyed by the mob. Oliver Coleman, drummer with the Ray Nance band, was a witness. "In 1933 the clubs never closed," he said, "and nightlifers, musicians and entertainers would go from club to club after daybreak to jam, drink, talk and party. This particular morning a group of gangsters walked into Dave's and ordered everybody out because they were going to burn the place down. They started pouring gasoline over everything, including my drums. I screamed, 'Man, you can't do that to my drums!' One of the hoods handed me $500 and told me to get my black ass out of there posthaste. They started the fire and jumped into waiting cars and sped away while we stood across the street watching the damn place go up in flames. I learned later that the mob wanted Dave's property for a liquor chain, which they subsequently opened there, and Dave heatedly moved his nightclub to 343 East Garfield Boulevard."

In 1938 Benny Skoller changed the name of Dave's Cafe to Swingland, to cater to current tastes in popular music. Joe Louis, the heavyweight boxing champion, bought the club in 1940; his partner was Charlie Glenn, the sportsman and Cadillac salesman. They changed the name once again: this time to Rhumboogie.

We had not walked more than 200 feet west of Dave's Cafe down Garfield Boulevard when Sepio stopped and pointed at a good-looking man about four feet eleven inches tall, with a conk hairdo, who was standing in front of the drugstore next to the El station. "Hey, man!" Sepio yelled. "Look who's here!" He threw his arm around the little guy's shoulders. "Man," he said, "I haven't seen you since 1927 in Pittsburgh, but I been reading and hearing about you. I'm proud that a homie is making good. Man, what are you doing in Chicago?"

The cat said, "I'm opening at the Three Deuces at 222 North State on September 6th with my own orchestra. I'm using eight pieces now."

"Solid!" Sepio roared. He turned to us. "Fellows," he said, "I want you to meet my boyhood friend from Pittsburgh—the world's baddest trumpet player, Roy Eldridge."

Roy Eldridge had a big perpetual smile and was very jovial. After you talked with him for five minutes, you felt as though you had known him for five years. "Tell me what the hell you been up to," Sepio said to him.

Roy replied, smiling his infectious smile, that he had worked until 1935 with McKinney's Cotton Pickers. Then he had rejoined Teddy Hill's Orchestra at the Savoy Ballroom in New York, where he also made records on the side with Benny Goodman and Teddy Wilson. He recorded with a small band, and Billie Holiday was singing the vocals. At that time, he said, the French Casino wanted Teddy Wilson and four of them to play for them.

The Jackson Park El thundered overhead, interrupting him, and Roy stopped and covered his ears with his hands. After the train had gone by, he said, "We had signed the contracts and were rehearsing to go in the Casino when Teddy Wilson received a threat: if he played the Casino the place would be stinkbombed. I believe to this day that it was some of those darkies at the Savoy. We had such a good combination that they didn't want to lose us. Our leaving would have broken up Teddy Hill's orchestra. When we found out we couldn't play the Casino, I took my first combo to the Famous Door where I played opposite Red Norvo. We had six men apiece at that time. And here I am in Chicago, ready to blow the roof off the Three Deuces."

Roy Eldridge looked at his watch and said, "Come on, you cats! Let's go upstairs and light up. I've got a cigar box full of dynamite stuff and six brand new

Left: Charlie Glenn, Joe Louis' partner at the Rhumboogie, with David Kellum, the originator of "Bud Billiken." Right: The Rhumboogie, the only nightclub in Chicago with a balcony bar.

records that are killers."

"No, man!" Sepio said. "We're on our way to DeLisa. Come along!"

"I would," Eldridge said, "but it's about time for me to take my German police dog out for an airing."

"Then we'll dig you later," Sepio said.

"Cool."

Dave Young played tenor sax in the Roy Eldridge band when it opened at the Three Deuces. Dave recalled those days.

"The other guys in the band," he said, "were Ted Coles on piano, Truck Parham on bass, Zutty Singleton on drums, Scoops Carey on alto sax, and Joe Eldrige, Roy's brother, on violin and alto sax. Art Tatum played piano in the Swing Room downstairs during intermission. Gladys Palmer, the boogie-woogie piano player, worked at the bar upstairs. On payday most of the guys would buy a shoebox full of marijuana. A size thirteen shoebox full of the stuff cost only five dollars.

"The first three nights after payday the guys would be smoking marijuana cigarettes as big as LaPalina cigars. By Wednesday the joints would get smaller, and the night before payday the guys would be sweeping up roaches—that's what they called burnt-out marijuana butts. The cats stayed high while they played the gig. They always played well because they knew their instruments. The boys in the band were well-trained musicians. If they hadn't been we would not have made it to the big times.

"In those days our band broadcast a half hour program from the Three Deuces seven nights a week. The radio network had to clear the popular tunes before they could be played on the air. Many times we did not know whether a tune had been cleared until the night of the broadcast. So Sam Beer, the owner of the Deuces, decided that Roy should make a list of tunes for broadcast for the coming week. So Roy would get high and go home to his forty dollar a month one room kitchenette apartment on the third floor of the Ritz Building at 343 East Garfield Boulevard—Dave's Cafe was on the ground floor of that building. Roy would make up the list of tunes while he was closeted with his tea. He had hallucinations from the pot: he came up with titles for tunes we never heard of.

"One broadcast in particular sticks in my mind. The engineer came to the bandstand and handed Roy the list of tunes we were going to play on the air that night. When Roy gave me the list, I looked at it and I said, 'Roy, what the hell is "Gee Jake, What a Snake"?' He said, 'Don't worry about it. Just play the chords to "Honeysuckle Rose" and I'll put the melody to it and we'll be gone.' We used that system for years and it worked. Roy was good at making up melodies. We would play the basic chords for whatever tune he wanted to play and he would ad lib the melody. 'Drum Boogie' was created that way along with hundreds of other tunes that we played at Three Deuces."

In April, 1941, Roy Eldridge joined Gene Krupa's band as featured soloist and often played drums while Krupa was conducting. During this period Eldridge became a national figure as a result of record hits like "Rocking Chair" and the celebrated duet with Anita O'Day on "Let Me Off Uptown". He was with Artie Shaw's band from October, 1944, to September, 1945.

About 300 feet west of Dave's Cafe was Ciro's, at 317 East Garfield, a very swanky cocktail bar where Billy Ward, the noted pianist and entertainer, appeared nightly. Next door, on the second floor at 309 East Garfield was the Golden Lily, well known for its excellent Chinese and American food. The jazz bands and entertainers who worked that room were top-flight. Coleman Hawkins played his immortal "Body and Soul" there when he returned to Chicago in 1941—by that time the name of the Golden Lily had been changed to White's Emporium: the Chinese owner had sold the club to a black policy baron named White in 1939. I was in White's on that cold February night when the great Hawk opened. The general public could not get near the place for the first week, because every musician in Chicago who could lift a horn or plunk a piano was there every night gawking in amazement at the performance of this genius of the tenor saxophone.

Hawkins did not invent the tenor sax, but he singlehandedly turned it into a jazz solo instrument. He was a formidable technician with a natural talent that he had taken time and pains to develop. There is not a tenor saxophonist living or dead who ever attained the full, rounded power of the great Coleman Hawkins' instrumental tone. He died in New York City on May 19, 1969.

On the southwest corner of Garfield Boulevard and Prairie Avenue, at 231 East Garfield, was the Garfield Hotel. In its basement was the El Rado Cafe, where Jimmy Noone, the legendary New Orleans clarinet player, led the band. Floyd Campbell, the orchestra leader and singing drummer from St Louis, talked to me about the El Rado and its neighborhood.

The legendary Coleman Hawkins.

"When I first came to Chicago, on May 9, 1930," he said, "I took a cab to the Garfield Hotel, which was in the hub of the jazz scene on the South Side. Charlie Farrell's barber shop and poolroom on the ground floor of the hotel stayed open all night. There was a Greek restaurant on the Prairie Avenue side of the hotel, and Jimmy Noone was playing in the El Rado Cafe in the basement. Down the street were the Golden Lily and Dave's Cafe. I went down to the El Rado that first night. A fellow named Wells was playing the drums. He let me sit in for him and play, and I sang with the band. The cats liked the way I played and they asked me to stick around and watch the floor show.

"The show was loaded with talent. I will never forget Helen Warren's torch dance. When she finished her number, the temperature in the room had been raised at least sixty degrees. Anybody who had not seen that woman dance had not seen all that was worth seeing. And there was the chorus: four charming girls who danced and sang and strutted. They were, as the boys say along the Stroll, 'tight' and in their specialties they were 'tighter' if you see what I mean. If you still don't understand what I mean, it means they were 'tight like that'."

Two days later, on May 11, Floyd Campbell was eating in the Greek restaurant at 5508 South Prairie when Freddie Williams, the orchestra leader, tapped him on the shoulder and asked, "Are you the singing drummer from St Louis?"

Floyd replied that he was.

"Would you like to have a job?" Williams asked.

Floyd said that he would.

"Well," Williams said, "I'll pay you forty dollars a week plus tips. I'm playing at an exclusive white nightclub on the Near North Side."

"Well, you'll have to give me time," Floyd said.

"Time?"

"Yes, time to get my drums and get over to the gig," Floyd retorted. "Man!" he told me later. "That was my first job in Chicago!"

Our walk from the Garfield Hotel to Indiana Avenue was uneventful until an attractive lady of the evening stopped us in the middle of the block. "You fellows want to spend some time?" she asked. "I have a daisy chain of girls across the street at the Spencer Hotel."

G. W. looked cool. "How much is it going to cost, baby?" he said. "And what are you going to do?"

The streetwalker replied, "One dollar per man, and I can do everything."

Brad Taylor grabbed G. W. by the sleeve, and said urgently, "Come on, man! You didn't make but two dollars on the gig tonight, plus you owe me a dollar from last week."

The prostitute looked at them with disdain. "Later for you mothers!" she said, and walked swiftly away toward two prospective tricks sitting in a green 1934 Buick.

Production number at the Rhumboogie Nightclub.

"Slow down, Jack!" Sepio said. "Don't walk so goddamned fast. My corns are beginning to hurt."

"Dig that!" Brad pointed across the street. "That's 'Baby Bell', the baddest pimp in the Midwest. Look at him sitting out there on that balcony without a shirt, drinking that cold beer and just waiting for his stable of whores to come home from work. Pimping has got to be better than playing music."

Directly below "Baby Bell's" balcony, in front of Herb "Speedy" Bruce's Lounge at 118 E. Garfield, was a group of pimps, hustlers and potheads. Baby Bell could be heard shouting obscenities at the hustling peons. They obviously en-

Louis Armstrong and Bing Crosby in a scene from the 1936 movie Pennies from Heaven.

joyed getting his attention, because they were laughing.

I had met Louis Armstrong at Herb's place several months earlier when he returned to Chicago from Hollywood after completing the film *Pennies from Heaven* with Bing Crosby. Next door west of Herb's was the Michigan Theater where both the Sammy Stewart and Erskine Tate bands played for several years.

Michigan Boulevard at Garfield was a lively area at night. On the northeast corner was Young's "The Policy Baron's" Drugstore, which had a twenty-four hour lunch counter where musicians would stop after work to eat and shoot the breeze. Directly across the street, in the basement at 5450 South Michigan Boulevard, was the It Club, where John Kirby, the bandleader, and Maxine "Loch

Backstage at the Rhumboogie. Left to right: Walter Fuller, trumpeter; Horace Henderson; Phyllis Smiley, vocalist; and Fletcher Henderson.

Lomond" Sullivan, the internationally known black singer, hung out every morning after they finished their gig at the Pump Room in the Ambassador East Hotel.

Booker Ashford's 65 Club, at 5515 South Michigan, headlined Ann Simmons and her famous swinging Buddies, a floor show produced by Lovey Taylor, and featuring stars like Bob Love, the mellow crooning baritone, and Billy Williams, a beautiful and shapely hip-slinger, who could sizzle your shoe soles off. A few steps south at 5557 S. Michigan was the Speaker's Inn, a watering hole where chorus girls and guys went when they wanted to rest their feet and wet their throats.

By the time we reached Wabash Avenue, Sepio was cursing because his corns were giving him hell. We stopped for several minutes in front of the Four Corners Liquor Store on the southwest corner of Garfield and Wabash to give Sepio's corns a chance to cool off.

"Come on, Sepio," Brad said. "We only have one short block more before we get to Club DeLisa."

A hobbling Sepio trailed along.

The menu cover at the New DeLisa in 1941.

Chapter 10

Club DeLisa

"Feet, we are here at last!" Sepio sighed as he viewed the brightly illuminated neon sign flashing: "Original Club DeLisa."

"Man, I am not going to wait in that long line because my feet are dying a fast death and taking me with them," Sepio wailed.

"Cool it, man," Brad said. "Let me see if I can lay something on the doorman."

Brad walked over to the doorman, whispered something in his ear and slyly mashed something into his hand before he beckoned for us to follow him. Brad led us to the original tavern opened by the DeLisa brothers during the 1933 World's Fair. It was located at 5516 South State Street, one door south of the nightclub. The doorman had wired Grover "Big Boy" Chapman, the floorman, and we were admitted to the main room of Club DeLisa through a private sliding door entrance between the tavern and the club. Although the nightclub was packed as a can of sardines, Big Boy simply picked up a table with one hand from a stack at the rear and carried it directly to the center of the club where he created some space by making the patrons in that area move even more closely together.

The jammed sixty-by-one hundred foot room had very little ventilation. Nothing disturbed the clouds of blue cigarette smoke floating upward to the eleven-foot ceiling except the breeze from the fast movement of the waitress's arm when she presented some party with a check. The joint was so packed that we sat through an entire floor show before the waitress could take our order.

Young Jim DeLisa says, "That was typical service for a Saturday night crowd. There were many instances when patrons sat through three shows on Saturday night and would not get service until the fourth show. The club could accommodate 350 people comfortably, but on Saturday night my Dad and his two brothers would squeeze over 500 people in the room."

Mike, Louie and Jim DeLisa Sr. were all immigrants from Italy. Although Mike and Louie were trained as tailors in the old country and Jim as a carpenter, they all wanted to get into some fast action shortly after they settled in Chicago. In 1923 they went into moonshining. They had "stops" along State Street between 47th and 59th streets where both blacks and Italians distributed moonshine for them on foot and in cars.

Left: Eloise Williams, member of the chorus, with Nat "King" Cole at the DeLisa Bar. Right: Four DeLisa chorines.

Dave Young, who lived in the DeLisa brothers' territory at 5244 South LaSalle Street in the early 1920s says, "The Italians in my neighborhood around 52nd and Federal and LaSalle found cooking alcohol more lucrative than selling ice during Prohibition. They converted the horse stables behind their homes into facilities where they could distill alcohol. I remember when the strong stench of horse manure disappeared from the alleys and the smell of perfume became pervasive. To us, the alcohol smelled like perfume."

Jim DeLisa recalls: "My father and his brothers had about a half dozen locations in the South Federal and LaSalle street areas where they made moonshine for about ten years. They sent more than $600,000 to my grandfather in Italy to build two churches. That money was made in their moonshine operation on the South Side. In April 1933, they opened a beer tavern at 5516 South State two months after the repeal of Prohibition."

Freddie Cole Bates, who was captain of the chorus girls at DeLisa for twenty-one years, received a telegram dated June 5, 1934, which is printed below.

Freddie Cole reminisced: "When I started working at DeLisa on Friday, June 15, 1934, it was a small tavern at 5516 South State. There were only two

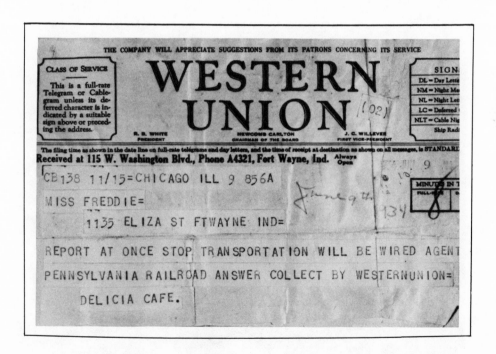

Above: The old Club DeLisa in 1936. Below: Albert Ammons (center), and his Rhythm Kings.

chorus girls in addition to myself. I danced in the chorus and also performed my famous toe-tap and rhumba dances as special features. They paid us ten dollars a week. We worked seven days a week and put on four shows a night. During intermission, every fifteen minutes, we three girls would take turns singing and dancing at the patrons' tables for tips. We did what was known as the 'Ups' in show business. As I danced up to the table I would pull up my dress and pick up the dollar tips from the edge of the table between my thighs. For big tips the girls would pick the dollar bills up with another part of their anatomy and I don't mean their hands. I made so much money from tips doing the 'Ups' I used to forget about payday. For three dollars and fifty cents a week in 1934 I had a private room and bath, plus maid service, at 5512 South Michigan Avenue. I did not have any transportation expense because I was only two blocks from work."

Hap Draper and his Arcadians were furnishing the music for both the floor show and patron dancing. The Draper band was replaced by Albert Ammons and his Rhythm Kings in 1935. Ammons was a short, thickset man with an exceptionally dynamic left hand. I was fascinated by Ammons' boogie piano style. Ammons was a protegé of rent-party pianists Jimmy Yancey and Pine Top Smith, but he learned to play all styles well. As a young musician I was inspired by the professional sound and personal appearance of Ammons and his five sidemen. They were all sharply dressed in black trousers and black shirts with button-down collars, which contrasted well with their white Palm Beach jackets and ties. Guy Kelly played trumpet; young Israel Crosby, bass fiddle; Jimmy Hoskins, who later replaced Chauncey Murdock with my band, was on drums; Del Bright played clarinet and sax; and Ike Perkins, guitar. This group was without a doubt the swingingest small band in the Midwest, and they proved it during their two-year stay at the original Club DeLisa.

"Hey, Jack," Brad called laughingly across the table, "the cat that printed that band sign behind the drummer must have gone to Doolittle Grammar School with you because he couldn't spell 'rhythm.'"

The sign read:

ALBERT AMMONS
AND HIS
RYTHM KINGS

The rhythm section of the Ammons group was driven by the astonishing instrumental virtuosity of Israel Crosby, the seventeen-year-old string bassist. The full deep sound he produced on his instrument complemented Ammons' heavy boogie beat. Crosby's musical talent did not go unnoticed by any musician who had the opportunity to hear him. Our party watched the band like hawks until they played the last number at 6 a.m. Chauncey Murdock, our drummer, sat in with the Ammons group and played the last two sets, including the show that morning.

Jimmy Hoskins, Ammons' drummer, had gotten so high that he fell off the bandstand twice within one hour. When he toppled from that high perch at the rear of the band the last time, he had reached a stage of inebriation that would not permit him to return. Hoskins gigged with my band at various nightclubs and ballrooms on both the South and West Sides of Chicago in 1937 and 1938. He was an excellent drummer but he could not handle the "corn" or the "grape." G. W. Harris, our bass player, sat in for Crosby on the last set. Crosby joined us at our table and I learned that he had played trumpet since the age of five, had changed to trombone and tuba, and at age thirteen was gigging regularly on these instruments. In 1934, he switched to the string bass and gigged around the South Side with the Tony Fambro Band and the Johnny Long Orchestra, both very popular local dance bands.

Fletcher Henderson grabbed Crosby after hearing him play at one of Club DeLisa's Monday morning breakfast dances. Crosby replaced John Kirby, who left Henderson's Grand Terrace Orchestra to organize his own group. After leaving Henderson in 1939, Crosby worked with Raymond Scott at CBS and with Teddy Wilson, Ahmad Jamal, George Shearing and Benny Goodman. He died at age forty-one in Chicago, his birthplace, in the West Side Veterans Administration Hospital, of a blood clot on the heart.

Del Bright, the alto sax player in the Albert Ammons band, was selected to replace Ammons as leader when Earl Partello, the new floor show producer, demanded that he be fired by Mike DeLisa because he could not read or fake the tough musical scores. Drummer Red Saunders joined the Bright aggregation. When Bright decided to go on the road with the Horace Henderson band in 1937, Saunders became the leader. Mike DeLisa provided Partello some first-class musical talents with the Saunders band but he only paid the musicians eighteen dollars and fifty cents a week. In addition to being a hell of a musician and show drummer, Red Saunders and his band made the Club DeLisa crowd jump for twenty-one consecutive years.

When Harry W. Gray was elected president of the Musicians Protective Union (Local 208 of the American Federation of Musicians) in 1937, his first official act was to call Mike DeLisa and demand that he double the pay scale of the Red Saunders Orchestra.

Mike DeLisa responded, "I am going to shoot you in your head if you don't keep your nose out of my business."

Harry Gray retorted, "All right, I'll give you that opportunity. Where do you want to meet me?"

Mike DeLisa said, "In my business office at 5501 South Halsted within one hour!"

Upper left: Chippie Hill, blues singer.
Right: Tommy Powell and his Hi-De-Ho
Boys. Below: Interior shot of the old
DeLisa with whites dominating the ring-
side.

Harry Gray said they assumed that he was going to show up in that lily-white neighborhood with four or five tough darkies to start some trouble. "I fooled them and showed up by myself. When I finished talking to Mike DeLisa and his lawyer, John Comise, they agreed to double the salary for the Saunders orchestra and give each member of the band an additional five dollar weekly bonus. Forty-two dollars a week was good money in those days."

Red Saunders was not making any regular money until the DeLisa gig. One of his first jobs was with Stomp King who played at suburban road houses for tips. He later looked for his extra dough from "Ups" when the female vocalist or dancer would visit tables and sing or dance for tips during intermission. Sometimes a girl would run into the toilet to steal the tip after she had finished making the rounds. Red had a guy in the band who would run right after her to catch the washroom door before she could lock it. He would make her split the dough.

Attorney John Comise was a former bailiff of Judge Barelli. The DeLisa brothers hired him when they first entered legitimate business in 1933. He served as their business administrator and was a political contact who could help them keep their nightclub and gambling operations going twenty-four hours a day without any fear of interference from the police department.

The original Club DeLisa burned down on Tuesday morning, February 11, 1941. The fire started in the checkroom and spread quickly. Hazel Griffin, a sixteen-year-old girl, was injured when she leapt from a second floor apartment in the adjoining building and fell through the roof of the burning nightclub, from which she was later rescued. Six other persons were injured in the fire, and Howard "Smoky" Homer, the porter, was killed. It was fortunate that the club was closed when the fire started; otherwise, the police said, the disaster could have equalled the Rhythm Club conflagration in Natchez, Mississippi, in 1940, where more than a hundred people perished, including Walter Barnes, the popular Chicago band leader. The only side exit from the DeLisa was a secret side door.

I talked about the DeLisa with William "Lefty" Bates, the guitar player with the DeLisa Hi-De-Ho Boys, and with Freddie Cole, his wife.

Lefty said, "Baby 'The Pimp' Bell would come to Club DeLisa every Monday morning to gamble with the other pimps, hustlers and squares in the club's basement. He would always have five or six of his white working girls with him and a big sack full of money. A lot of money was lost down in that basement. The DeLisa brothers made a fortune cutting the games for the house. They had tables for blackjack, poker and dice. The big money was in the card games."

"Lefty, you thought you were a bigtime gambler like those other guys," Freddie Cole said. "I remember that cold morning in February when the Club was burning down and you were gambling in the back with some smalltime hustlers,

Left: The DeLisa burns down: Tuesday, February 11, 1941. Right: Savoy Ballroom jitterbuggers turned professional at the old DeLisa.

cabdrivers, entertainers and musicians. Smoke was pouring out of the top of the building, but I had to come back down into the club two or three times to tell you it was burning down. The only game where men become that single-minded is called 'sex'."

Lefty nodded. "You're right," he said. "My guitar was burned up, and all the instruments that were left in the old locker under the bandstand were messed up. 'Smoky' the porter was trapped in the kitchen and burned to death. . ."

Freddie said, "I will never forget that long black table you fools were gambling on that could have become your coffin. . . That morning was a very dark moment in my life. But," she added, more cheerfully, "I can remember a lot of exciting moments at the old club. Lots of times you would hear a police siren blowing full blast, and a motorcade would pull up outside the club with an entourage of movie stars like Bob Hope, Bing Crosby, Gene Autry, George Raft, Mae West, John Carradine, Paul Robeson, Joe Louis, John Barrymore. . ."

"The police used to come out to the club looking for John Barrymore all the time," Lefty Bates said. "He would miss the curtain at the Blackstone Theater

Upper left: Gene Autrey is greeted by the DeLisa doorman.
Right: John Barrymore, the legendary actor, and Billy
Eckstine standing behind Levertt Kelly (second from right),
and two ladies at the DeLisa bar.

Lower left: Bob Hope and party.
Right: Paul Robeson and Lonnie Simmons

Upper Left: (Left to right): Johnny Ray, Red Saunders, and friend. Right: (From left to right): George Raft and lady friend, with Mike DeLisa. Below: Lonnie Simmons (left) and Pat O'Brien (right).

down on Balboa Drive, and the management would send the police out to find him; they always thought he had been kidnapped. The only kidnapper that ever saw that cat was the shake dancer he used to chase around the club and shack up with whenever he could. Barrymore always managed to catch the last show every morning he was in town."

When John Barrymore was not shacking up he would drink till noon at the Club DeLisa bar with the late Chippie Hill. Chippie was one of the DeLisa's all-time favorite blues and torch singers. Her tough voice was both appropriate and sensuous enough to give the night life crowd the kind of material they wanted to hear. She was loved on New York's Park Avenue in the late forties for the nostalgic songs she had performed for the Chicago South Side bunch at the Apex and Club DeLisa in the 1920s and '30s. She recorded "Trouble in Mind" on Okeh Records in 1926, with Louis Armstrong on trumpet and Richard M. Jones on piano. That single recording reached the 300,000 sales mark. Chippie lived long enough to hit the glory road twice. She was run over by a car in May, 1950.

Club DeLisa was the road to glory for many entertainers, like Big Joe Williams, who was there when Count Basie discovered him, and George Kirby, who worked there as a thirteen dollars a week bus boy until a group of DeLisa entertainers insisted that Mike DeLisa give him a trial up on the stage and the audiences never let him come down. Kirby is the man with a thousand voices. He cleverly imitated old movie star Wallace Beery's pebble voice, sloping coat, drooping trousers and snarling dialogue—to the tobacco-spitting end. He also copied Edward G. Robinson in his familiar movie gangster regalia of floppy hat and well-chewed cigar. Another big hit in his repertoire was a take-off on the song style of Duke Ellington's blues singer, Al Hibbler, in his rendition of "Trees"; the loudest applause came when he mimicked the famed Hibbler's hesitation style while singing the number. The uninitiated might think that Kirby had forgotten the lyrics. Kirby performed that number with all the gusto and emotion of the electrifying Hibbler. When the lyrical chanteuse Sarah Vaughan first heard Kirby imitate her, she exclaimed in delight, "That's me!"

Another star tracker found at the club was Ann Henry, who with her dancing group went on to become a star in the Broadway musical "New Faces." She substituted for Eartha Kitt. "Gatemouth" Moore may be best remembered for his hit blues recording, "I Ain't Mad At You, Pretty Baby, Don't Be Mad At Me," inspired by a street fight between a couple that ended with the husband forgiving his mate for beating him up. Lurlene Hunter, originally hired to sing with the band, became a single at the club and went on to become a top recording artist. The Berry Brothers, the Edwards Sisters and Kitty Murray were also seen and heard at DeLisa. Kitty Murray was at the DeLisa when "Rochester" signed her for

Joe Williams lifting Freddie Cole at her retirement party at Club DeLisa.

his vaudeville tour, and Billy Eckstine was discovered at the DeLisa by Earl Hines in 1939.

When I interviewed Hines in June, 1982, he recalled: "That morning I went to Club DeLisa to look for a dancer to put in the Grand Terrace review. When this good-looking boy came out and sang the opening number, I said to George Dixon, 'Who the hell is that boy with that robust, baritone voice?'"

George Dixon replied, "That's a young man from Pittsburgh named Billy Eckstine."

Hines said, "Goddamn! I'm going to try and steal that boy! He will kill everybody."

"Billy Eckstine was not hard to get because Mike DeLisa was only paying him $25 a week," George Dixon told me.

Hines recalled that Mike DeLisa did not want to let Billy Eckstine leave. "I told Ralph Capone about Billy and he arranged without fanfare to get Eckstine released from his DeLisa gig."

The musical and artistic talent found at Club DeLisa made it the "in" place to go whether you were a native or a visitor to Chicago. To make certain that everybody got into the act, the club furnished souvenir table knockers to every

Top left: Red Saunders. Right: The Dyer-ettes. Lower left: Redd Foxx & DeLisa Chorine. Right: "Gatemouth" Moore with chorus girls.

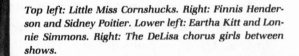

Top left: Little Miss Cornshucks. Right: Finnis Henderson and Sidney Poitier. Lower left: Eartha Kitt and Lonnie Simmons. Right: The DeLisa chorus girls between shows.

patron. Every night at Club DeLisa was a holiday like Christmas or New Year's Eve. The patrons would pound uninhibitedly on the tables with their knockers to show their appreciation for the entertainment. People would wait in long lines on weekends just to get into the club. There was no minimum and no cover charge. All you had to do was pay for your set-up of ice, water, ginger ale or coke. Most people brought their own booze in a brown paper bag.

The New Club DeLisa opened its doors on Sunday afternoon, April 27, 1941, with the Juggs Social Club's annual cocktail party. Nat Jones, the alto sax and clarinet player in the Red Saunders band, said, "The band started playing the first dance set for the Juggs Party at four that Sunday afternoon. Man, we didn't leave that bandstand again except for emergency trips to the toilet and the brief intermissions between shows. They put on six shows between the Sunday afternoon cocktail party at four and the Monday breakfast dance at six a.m.

"In addition, the band played four shows nightly for the other six nights. I worked that grind for six consecutive years with the exception of the six months I spent playing with the Duke Ellington Orchestra in 1943."

Nat said that the breakfast dance at the DeLisa was showtime for entertainers from all the other clubs in town. They all showed up there before daybreak on Monday prepared to party until the sun was shining on both sides of the street.

"Joe Williams used to come to work wearing sport clothes on Sunday afternoon in order to avoid the stares of the day people when he left the club in the middle of the morning," Nat said. "You know it looks stupid for a person to be seen walking down the street in a tuxedo or an evening gown at high noon."

The new Club DeLisa, a modern structure of white glazed brick, was built within three and a half months after the fatal fire, at 5521 South State Street, directly across the street from the old location. As you pass the vacant site of the Original Club DeLisa, you might wonder if all you hear is the moan of the Chicago wind, or whether there is also the faint sound of Chippie Hill bringing that "Wabash Cannonball" home to glory once again.

The new club cost $300,000, seated 1000 people comfortably, and could actually seat 1500 in a pinch. It had a gas-fired furnace and central air conditioning. The lighting was mellow red fluorescent, so mellow that your eyes took a few seconds to adjust to it when you entered the club. The bandstand was at the east end of the room; the dance floor in front of it could be raised hydraulically for shows. The stage area was equipped with vari-colored floodlights. But the brightest and most sustaining light to walk across the stage of the new Club DeLisa was Joe Williams.

When Joe started singing "Every Day", the house literally went wild—screaming, whistling, applauding, and beating on the tables with their souvenir knockers. Joe Williams' rich baritone voice, with its built-in rhythm, can make a room explode like a firecracker on the Fourth of July. The audience would join in

Inset: The three DeLisa brothers, left to right: Louie, Mike and Jim. Marquee of the New Club DeLisa.

with a rhythmic beat when he began to sing:

> Every day, every day I have the blues. . .

Chicks would yell, "Yeah, yeah, yeah!"
Joe sang:

> Nobody loves me, nobody seems to care. . .

A white groupie sitting at ringside jumped up, shouting, "I will take care of you, you sweet black mother!"

The beat continued with the drunks, half-drunks and coke drinkers pounding on the tables with their knockers as Joe wailed:

> Speaking of bad luck and trouble, you know I've had my share. . .

Joe began to shout louder as he did a half "trucking" step across the stage with an empty travel bag in his hand:

Above: The DeLisa staff, including band, chorus girls, waitresses and bartenders, assemble in preparation to attend the funeral of Earl Partello (left) the multi-talented show producer, who died suddenly from appendicitis.

Sammy Dyer (below) was Earl Partello's successor as producer at the Club DeLisa.

1

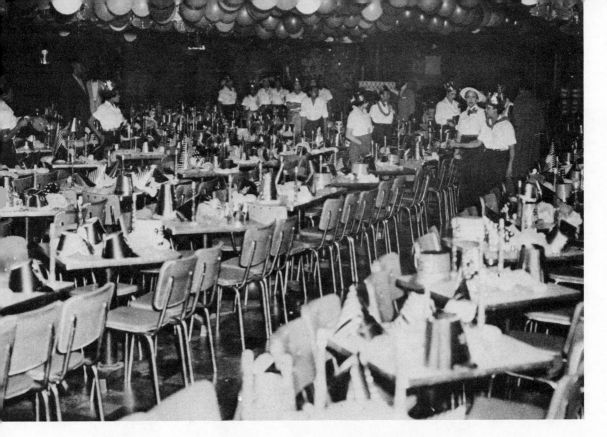

Above: Interior of the New Club DeLisa. Below: The DeLisa chorus girls in action on the new elevated stage.

Louis Armstrong, a frequent visitor at Club DeLisa, works out with chorus line at a Monday morning breakfast show.

> I am going to pack my suitcase
>   and move on down the line,
> Where there ain't nobody worried, and
>   there ain't nobody crying.

Several teasing-brown chicks sitting near the stage exit on the north side of the room yelled, "Oooooooh! Don't leave now, Joe baby, don't leave!"

And with a steady beat the show closed with everybody getting into the act.

The bongo drummer had not missed a beat when the band started playing "Honeysuckle Rose" and the chorus girls returned to the stage doing a dance known in show business as the B.S. Chorus.

According to Freddie Cole, the B.S. Chorus has four basic steps:

The finale of one of the famous DeLisa floor shows.

"Off to Buffalo": a shuffle with one foot crossing and re-crossing in front of the other as the dancer edges sideways, usually toward the exit.

"Falling off a Log": a shuffle like the "Off to Buffalo" shuffle, which includes a leaning pause before the next step.

"Over the Top": the dancer bends forward, springs up and brings each leg, in turn, around from the back and across the front of the other leg in a 'figure 8' pattern that would cause most people to fall on their faces.

"Through the Trenches": long, backward slides on the outside edge of the foot, alternately, while the body is bent forward at the waist, and each arm alternately flails the air.

The girls would perform the B.S. Chorus with increasing vigor with the ascending reputation of the star taking the bow. It is said that some of the chorines thought that the initials "B.S." stood for "Boy Scouts".

The most vigorous dancing was saved till the very end when the top star of the show made his or her final walk-on appearance. Then everyone on the stage who could lift a foot would join the chorus girls in a rip-roaring tap-dance that would bring the house down. Freddie Cole was captain of the chorus, and the last dancer to leave the stage shaking her caboose to the rhythm of the drumbeat.

The Regal Theater in 1928. The four-story marquee above the building was removed in 1931.

Chapter 11

The Regal Theater
That I Remember

April 8, 1928, was a very important day in my life. My cousin Frank and I were both eight years old, and my mother and her sister Willie had promised to take us to the magnificent new Regal Theatre at 4719 South Parkway. (Grand Boulevard was renamed South Parkway in 1926, and Martin Luther King Drive on July 31, 1968.) The Regal had had its official opening on February 4th of that leap year. The week before the opening the South Side was decorated like the Loop at Christmas time: flags flew from 43rd to 51st Streets, and from Indiana Avenue to South Parkway, to announce the coming of "the theater of theaters". The people could hardly wait for the big day to arrive.

The *Chicago Defender* reported on February 11, 1928:

At é:&& a.m. Saturday, February 4th, large crowds began gathering in front of the Regal to welcome the opening of the new million dollar motion-picture and stage show house. At noon, the hour set for the opening, the theater lines stretched south to 48th Street and then east for a very long city block to Vincennes Avenue. The downpour of rain did not dampen the enthusiasm of the throng that was hell-bent to be among the first to set foot in the luxurious playhouse.

Until my eighth birthday six weeks earlier I had worn only short pants. Now I put on a grey suit with long pants that my mother had bought me that Easter, and a new pair of light tan shoes. My cousin Frank was wearing a dark brown suit, also with long pants, and dark brown Buster Brown shoes. My mother and Aunt Willie both looked very pretty in identical light blue flapper-style dresses and shoes and hats to match.

East 47th Street was the Magnificent Mile of Chicago's Black Belt in 1928. On that Sunday it was packed with colored folks all dressed up in their latest finery for the Easter Parade. Everyone was both a participant and an observer. We had a leisurely walk through five crowded city blocks from my aunt's apartment at 4550 South St Lawrence Avenue to the corner of 47th and South Parkway where the Easter Parade was in full bloom, judging by the colorful Easter bonnets worn by the women. People stood eight abreast, packing the wide sidewalks, from Walgreen's Drugstore on the southeast corner to the curb. Nobody was moving because that was the north end of a half-block line of theater-goers waiting for the doors of the Regal to open.

It was high noon and the hot sun was shining directly on us as we stood in line. My new tan shoes were beginning to give me trouble. I shifted from foot to foot, trying to relieve my discomfort. After a wait of about an hour, we finally reached the front of the Regal, the most majestic building I had ever seen. It was built in Spanish baroque style, with heavy Moorish influence. On its roof was an electric sign about four stories high; it could be seen for a mile or more by people driving north or south on South Parkway.

Dazed, I heard the honking of automobile horns. There at the curb stood a gigantic doorman in a light brown military coat with braiding, helping ladies alight from their stylish motorcars.

"Look, Frank!" I exclaimed. "There's a yellow Pierce Arrow! Oh—and there's a four door Moon like Uncle Howard's!"

"I like that two door Stutz and that black Lincoln coach," Frank said. "Dempsey, that looks like cousin Joe in the rumble seat of that Hudson."

"Boy!" I said, "the Packard is the best car made! Ask the man who owns one."

At this point my mother pulled me toward the box office where Mrs Edna Peters and another light-skinned colored lady were busy exchanging ducats for dollars. We took ten steps around the right side of the cashier's cage and found ourselves facing a tall, handsome, medium brown-skinned ticket-taker, who was

The spacious lobby reflected a Moorish architectural influence.

wearing a dashing full-length beige cape and an infectious smile as he punched our tickets. Then we stepped into the lobby.

"Oh!" my mother squealed to Aunt Willie, "this place looks like that palace in the Ben Hur movie!" Then she gasped, and pointed her finger upward. "Look!" she shrieked, "Look at that chandelier with all those precious stones!" Before my aunt could answer, my mother shrieked again. "My God!" she shouted, "Look at those columns! There must be a dozen of them. . . . More than a dozen!"

"Mittie, be quiet!" my aunt said. "People are staring at us."

My mother paused in the middle of the lobby, to try and decide whether we should sit on the main floor or in the mezzanine. (Downtown, a few years earlier we would not have had that choice.) The lobby was almost as large as the average theater of today: it could accommodate 1500 people standing up. It had a center dome made up of 69,000 small crystals that emitted enough dazzling light to illuminate a small park on a dark night.

It was my aunt's turn to gasp. "Look at that beautiful wide marble staircase," she said. "Mittie, it's too pretty to walk on!" The wall above the staircase leading to the balcony was draped with maroon velvet. "I wish I had drapes like that in my living room," my aunt said wistfully.

"Willie," my mother said, "we will never own drapes like those, but Frank and Dempsey might. Come on, let's sit downstairs. We can sit upstairs next time."

I was glad mother had decided to sit downstairs: my new tan shoes were squeezing the little toes on both feet. I didn't want to say anything because the day before in the shoe store I had told mother that those pretty tan shoes felt fine.

From the lobby we passed into a smaller inner lobby through an entrance that was hung with more red velvet. Here there were a checkroom, a candy counter (but no popcorn), a restroom and a ladies' lounge on the north end, along with a smoking lounge and men's restroom on the south end. Both restrooms had full-time attendants, and there were always shoeshine boys in the men's room. The inner lobby also served as a waiting room with attractively arranged upholstered chairs and settees, on which one could lounge and enjoy the works of art, like the statue of Sira, the slave girl, looking at the brand which stigmatized her as a slave.

Finally, we entered the auditorium, with its sea of 3500 red plush seats. The walls were dull gold, which did not compete for attention with the decorations: the stage curtains were studded with rhinestones, which glowed and twinkled in the light of the very large electrically-lighted collet crown above the stage. Overhead was a dome which gave the effect of a palatial tent of brightly striped silk damask through the loose folds and openings of which could be seen glimpses of a simulated sky. The North African architectural style provided an illusion of distance and depth.

All this beauty mesmerized our bunch. We sat in total silence until my mother whispered, "Look at that ceiling! It looks like a midnight blue sky with bright stars shining everywhere. Oh, my goodness, we are under an Arabian tent! See there—it's supported by those two poles on both sides of the stage."

I was immediately attracted to the organ loft and the Barton organ which was on a "twist" elevator. I had been studying the piano for three years. But I was distracted by my painful feet. As soon as the house lights dimmed, and the bottom of the huge stage curtains were brilliantly illuminated by the "curtain warmers", I unlaced my shoes, to get some relief. A spotlight followed the urbane conductor and arranger Dave Peyton as he strolled through the orchestra pit, pausing briefly to bow to the audience when he reached the podium. Then he turned to face the twenty-two men in the symphony orchestra who sat in the pit with their eyes fixed attentively upon him. Peyton raised the baton in his right hand and slowly lowered it as the drummer gave a long roll on the timpani, and the trumpeters lifted their instruments to begin the *William Tell* overture. On the stage was a magnificent replica of a lush green meadow. While the overture was playing, Clarence Tidale, a singing shepherd, led fifty live sheep onto the stage

Above: The Regal Theater and the Savoy Ballroom dominated the entire block on the east side of 47th and South Parkway. Below: The Regal foyer with a statue of Sira, the slave girl.

where Tidale was joined by Mame Moon, a graceful and charming contralto. The show included a dramatic thunderstorm, complete with lightning, and the overture ended with the stage lights illuminating a brilliant rainbow, as the singers completed their duet and led the sheep offstage. Peyton's orchestra and Tidale and Moon received a standing ovation.

During the excitement, I took off both my shoes. Boy, what a relief! Now I could enjoy the rest of the show in comfort.

Cab Calloway, who was then a young and handsome popular singer, introduced the revue, singing "Memphis Blues" in a way that made this black boy's newly emancipated feet tingle. When Cab finished, the curtain ascended about four feet, and the shapely legs and lower torsoes of the Regalettes became visible. As the steel curtain continued its roll to the ceiling, the orchestra wailed an even louder rendition of W. C. Handy's "Memphis Blues", and Fess Williams walked onto the stage, which was large enough to accommodate four hundred people comfortably.

Williams had been imported to Chicago to lead a group of musicians who had

The Regal Auditorium seated 3,500. The overhead dome gave the effect of a palatial Arabian tent of brightly striped silk damask, with glimpses of a simulated sky.

actually been organized by Dave Peyton. The owners of the Regal wanted a band leader who was both flashy and dynamic. Fess Williams filled the bill: his trademark was a shimmery diamond-studded suit, and he had the personality and showmanship to match it. He was a top-flight master of ceremonies with plenty of jive talk for the audience and we loved it. Unlike Peyton, Williams conducted with both arms. He would lean forward facing the band, called the Royal Flush Orchestra, as if he were preparing to dive into Lake Michigan. At the same time he would swing each arm alternately back and forth to the beat of the music. From where I sat, he looked as though he were attempting to swim upstage. Despite his odd style, Williams was a big hit in both New York and Chicago; his band had been selected to open the new Savoy Ballroom in New York City in 1926.

Williams extended himself for this special Easter Sunday show. He introduced two dancers called the Cole Brothers. They could not have been more than four years older than I, but they tied up the show with their fast act. I learned later that the twelve and thirteen-year-old Cole Brothers had played all the major theaters in America. They were billed as royal entertainers, and they were all that the word "royal" implies.

The choreographer of the theater, Percy Venable, had created a dance for the ladies of the ensemble, the Regalettes, called the "Fess Williams' Stomp", in honor of Fess. The girls wore white suits with shiny silk lapels, replicas of the suit Fess Williams had on during the Regal's opening week. They were good dancers, and very pretty. Fifty-four years later, in October, 1982, I interviewed Mrs Lina C. Gray, one of the Regalettes. She said, "I was the only Regalette who worked in the *Shuffle Along* musical with Eubie Blake and Noble Sissle. The other girls were recruited from dancing schools on the South Side of Chicago. Those girls had to be able to do something other than dance. They had to have a good figure, personality, and a generally attractive appearance."

There was one quality the Regalettes had to have which Mrs Gray did not mention, but which was self-evident at the time. They had to be light-skinned, almost white, to qualify for the show. Josephine Baker, who was also a chorus girl in *Shuffle Along*, and a few other teasing brown-skinned girls, like Eva Jones Wheatly, were the exceptions.

Blanche Calloway, the final single act in that Regal review, was a showstopper. She was high yellow, agile and talented. She was Cab Calloway's oldest sister. Blanche could belt out a song like nobody I ever heard. And she was an excellent dancer who seemed to be in perpetual motion. She did the splits back and forth across the stage, and she could sell a song in a style that kept her listeners spellbound.

Earl "Fatha" Hines describes Blanche Calloway in his autobiography, *The World of Earl Hines:*

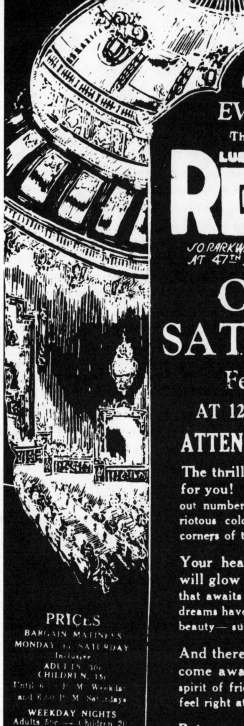

COME ON EVERYBODY!

The Magnificent new

LUBLINER & TRINZ

REGAL THEATRE

SO.PARKWAY AT 47TH ST.

OPENS SATURDAY

February 4th

AT 12 O'CLOCK NOON

ATTEND THE OPENING!

The thrill of a life-time is in store for you! You'll see wonders without number—beauty beyond compare—riotous color—treasures from the four corners of the earth!

Your heart will leap—your eyes will glow at the dazzling spectacle that awaits you. Never in your wildest dreams have you imagined such imposing beauty— such romantic charm.

And there's a cheery, smiling welcome awaiting you Saturday — a spirit of friendliness that will make you feel right at home!

Put everything aside! Come! Attend the Regal opening — a gorgeous sight—A glorious experience you'll never forget!

PRICES

BARGAIN MATINEES
MONDAY to SATURDAY
Inclusive
ADULTS 30c
CHILDREN, 15c
Until 6:30 P. M. Weekdays
and 6:00 P. M. Saturdays

WEEKDAY NIGHTS
Adults 50c — Children 20

**SATURDAY NIGHTS,
SUNDAYS and HOLIDAYS**
Adults 65c—Children 25c

The Greatest Amusement Bargain in Chicago.

No Reserved Seats

This advertisement appeared in the Chicago Defender February 4, 1928.

Blanche Calloway, Cab's sister, had a very good way of entertaining. She was wild and wiry in certain things and very sensitive when it came to balance. To me, she had a better voice than Cab. Although Cab may not say this himself, I think all of his style was hers.

When I interviewed Cab on January 14, 1983, he graciously admitted, with a broad smile, that his sister Blanche had taught him everything he knew about performing.

The remaining portions of the stage review were loaded with style and pace from such acts as the Right Quintet, a vocal aggregation that also doubled on several musical instruments, to Rogers and Lovejoy, two comics who kept the audience in stitches for better than fifteen minutes. The Right Quintet had been imported from New York to open the Regal with Fess Williams. They delivered their repertoire of songs in Mills Brothers fashion and were an instant hit.

Fess Williams lifted his baton for the finale. All the acts returned to the stage, centering around the ten dancing Regalettes, dressed in costumes of baby blue, and tapping their hearts straight through their toe-plated slippers onto the oak-planked floor of the Regal stage.

Then the curtain dropped, and the great screen was illuminated with the handsome face of Douglas Fairbanks, the star of the silent film classic *The Gaucho.*

Dave Peyton, bandleader.

Blanche Calloway, entertainer.

Above and below: The Regalettes, who were the darlings of the South Side theater-goers, were all products of several local dance schools.

Fess Williams, the bandleader (in white suit) was imported from New York to front a group of Chicago musicians for the Regal Theater opening.

The acts in the Fess Williams Revue set the standard for stage shows at the Regal for the next three decades. The Mills Brothers, Duke Ellington, Jimmie Lunceford, Cab Calloway, Louis Armstrong, Lucky Millinder, The Ink Spots. Sugar Chile Robinson, along with hundreds of other fine performers, met the challenge of the Regal audiences in the 1930s, '40s and '50s. However there was never another box office attraction in the Regal's forty-five year history that equalled the popular Fess Williams' fifty-four consecutive weeks of flawless entertainment.

My afternoon at the Regal would have been perfect if it had not been for my brand new tan shoes. When I left that royal theater palace I was in my stocking feet, and I carried a shoe in each hand. My mother was both disgusted and embarrassed when she looked down and discovered that I was shoeless. But I made a vow that day which I have never broken: I would never again wear a pair of shoes that hurt my feet.

Above: Ken "Mr. Regal" Blewett. Below left: A typical crowd scene at the Regal Theater. Right: Blewett at age 18.

Chapter 12

Ken "Mr. Regal" Blewett

Ken Blewett came to Chicago from Bowling Green, Kentucky, on a Jim Crow coach of the Illinois Central Railroad. The year was 1926, and Ken had just celebrated his sixteenth birthday. After he left the 12th Street Station, he took his maiden streetcar ride south along State Street, and the first musical sound to reach his sensitive ears in Chicago were the strains of the gut-bucket "Black Snake Blues" drifting like smoke from a chimney through the open windows of the buffet flats that lined South State Street like holes in a honeycomb.

Young Ken loved the sound of the boogie-woogie piano, but he couldn't play it. He loved the sultry voices of the blues singers, but he couldn't sing. Still, he was drawn to show business. The streetcar passed the Grand Theater on the west side of the 3100 block on South State Street; the Vendome Theater was on the east side of the street, and there were a dozen other vaudeville houses within a three-block span. Ken was mesmerized by the lights and the activity around these buildings: he had not seen that many theaters in his entire life.

The Blewetts had not been settled into their new third floor apartment a 3555 South Indiana Avenue for more than two days when Ken wandered over to the Grand Theater. The sights and sounds he encountered from that stage show were unlike anything he had encountered in his old Kentucky hometown. There were women doing the shimmy and singing "The Heebie Jeebie Blues" right there in front of his eyes. The trumpet's moan seemed to rise from the birth pangs of a music born on the dirt floors of black cotton-pickers' shacks. Ken's dreamy eyes were opened. He was hooked on show business and determined to become part of it.

After the Blewetts had been in Chicago for about a year, they joined the movement of black families southward from the area of 35th Street to 47th Street or beyond. In March of 1926 jazz had moved to the Metropolitan Theater at 46th and Grand Boulevard (renamed South Parkway in that year) with the booking of the Sammy Stewart Orchestra for a seven month gig. In September, 1926, Stewart was replaced at the Metropolitan by the Clarence Jones Orchestra, featuring Louis Armstrong on trumpet, and Stewart then moved farther south to the Willard Theatre at 340 East 51st Street, where he became one of the first victims of the new Regal Theatre, which opened February 4, 1928. In March of that year competition from the Regal caused the owners of the Willard Theater to reduce the size of Stewart's band by half, from twelve men to six, and finally, in May, 1928, the entire group was fired.

Young Ken, a student at Lane Technical High School at the time, watched all these developments with great interest, trying to figure out how he could become a part of the South Parkway action. Although he had studied the violin back home in Bowling Green, he knew he was not good enough to compete with the Clarence Blacks and the Erskine Tates of that period. Finally he decided that if he was not qualified to go through the stage door, he would try his hardest to make it through the front door. In January, 1929, after graduating from Lane Tech, he applied to become an usher at the Regal Theater, and was hired as a trainee on February 11, 1929.

The Regal was making so great an impact on theater business on the South Side that the owners of the Metropolitan and Vendome theaters decided to shift their bands around. Erskine Tate's Vendome Theater symphony orchestra, which was one of the most popular and influential groups on the South Side, was sent to the Met to compete against the Regal's two red-hot orchestras, Dave Peyton's twenty-two piece pit band, and the stage band directed by the great Fess Williams. Clarence Jones and Louis Armstrong were rushed back to the Vendome so that Armstrong's popularity could draw crowds to 31st Street.

None of this worked. Within three or four weeks the Jones group with Louis Armstrong literally died at the Vendome. Shortly after, when Jones' band was

Stage Scene at the Grand Theater in May, 1919. Inset: it was demolished for urban renewal.

Above: The Sammy Stewart Band. Stewart is at the piano. Fifth from left is George Dixon. Below: A recent photograph of the Metropolitan Theater, where the Stewart Band opened in 1926.

reduced from fourteen to four pieces, Armstrong left the group and joined Carroll Dickerson's band at the new Savoy, which was just a couple of doors south of the Regal. The area of State Street around 31st to 35th Streets was commercially dead, although it still refused to be buried.

Ken Blewett, who was handsome and dapper, with a quick wit and an urbane manner, had not been on the Regal staff more than six months before Dave Wallerstein, the district manager, was asking about him. John Balaban, head of the Balaban and Katz thirty-four theater chain, which owned the Regal, was once heard to say that Kenneth Blewett must have fallen into the concrete when the Regal was built, and left a part of himself in the foundation. It almost seemed as though the Regal was a part of Blewett, and Blewett was a part of the Regal.

Blewett moved up through the ranks of the ushers like castor oil through a kid with a cold. Within eighteen months he was promoted to floor captain, and a year after that he became treasurer. In 1935 Balaban and Katz rewarded Blewett for his services by making him a co-assistant manager with Myron Wright, another young fellow who had worked in the theater from its inception. In 1939 Myron Wright was appointed manager of the Savoy Ballroom next door, and Blewett became manager of the Regal—the first black manager in the Balaban and Katz chain. Blewett was at the forefront of the fight to keep live entertainment on the Regal stage: vaudeville was being discontinued at most neighborhood houses because of the Depression.

On Monday, November 23, 1931, Balaban and Katz announced that the front doors of the Regal were going to be locked permanently following the last performance on Friday, November 27. However public outcry was so great that the day before the intended closing the owners posted a sign on the front door of the theater which said that the Regal would stay open indefinitely.

Blewett continued his fight for live entertainment; he insisted that the South Side would support good acts and top bands. The South Side didn't let Blewett down. It supported those acts and bands for the better part of forty years. Blewett became a South Side institution for thirty of those high-stepping years. He left the Regal in February, 1959, to manage the Maryland Theater at 831 East 63rd Street. From the Maryland he was sent to manage the Tivoli at 6329 South Cottage Grove Avenue. From there he was sent downtown to the Roosevelt Theater at 110 North State Street, and finally, his last post before his retirement was at the Michael Todd Theater on North Dearborn Street.

The Regal is gone, the Tivoli is gone, the Roosevelt is gone, but Ken Blewett is here, and through his eyes and mine, we can visit some of the great bands and acts that graced the Regal stage over four decades. I once asked Blewett to name the two orchestras that he considered to be the top attractions during his tenure. He said that Duke Ellington and Count Basie consistently drew the biggest crowds. However the top one-week attraction of all time, he said, was Sugar Chile

Robinson, with his boogie-woogie piano and lilting voice. Sugar Chile broke the all-time one week box office record.

I asked Ken to rate comedians, and he said that Dusty Fletcher was the greatest comic that he had ever seen. I certainly agree with Ken that Dusty was a very funny man. I remember vividly one of Dusty's acts: he played a drunk trying to climb into his window from a stepladder after he had lost his housekeys. His roommate, Richard, had fallen asleep after dead-bolting the front and back doors. Fletcher would stand in the middle of the Regal Theater stage looking up at an imaginary window and yell, "Open the door, Richard! Open the door and let me in!" After numerous appeals to Richard, involving a good many pratfalls, he would employ the stepladder, from which he fell, repeatedly. He would then sit looking forlornly from the window to the audience, before he emitted his final bellow: "Open the goddamed door, Richard!"

After this he would shuffle off the stage amid thunderous applause, dragging his ladder after him. Dusty always wore oversized white dress gloves, pants that were too short, shoes that were ten sizes too long, a coat that was too big and a black top hat to cover a head that was nine months pregnant with an enormous comedic talent.

Ken and I agreed that Moms Mabley was one of the best stand-up female comedians in the country. I remember the first time I saw Moms was at the Regal with Cab Calloway. She always presented herself as a pathetically comic person in sloppy clothes, with a toothless grin, radar eyes beaming an innocent look, and a gravel voice with an operatic range. Cab Calloway sometimes acted as her straight man when she joked about liking pretty yellow men with straight hair. Moms frequently said, "If you say I only love young men, I am guilty and I am going to become guiltier. Can't no old man do nothin' for me but die. I used to have an old man and he got out of breath lifting his fork to his mouth. Girls! An old man can't do nothing for me but show me where I can find a young one." The audience would always crack up behind Moms' jokes.

Ken and I also agreed that Dick Gregory was probably the greatest political and social satirist of this century. Dick would come out on the Regal stage carrying a newspaper and remark, "Isn't this the most fascinating country in the world? Where else could I be required to ride on the back of the bus, have a choice of going to the worst schools, eating in the worst restaurants, living in the worst neighborhoods, and average $5000 a week just talking about it?"

I remember another occasion when Dick Gregory came on and said, "I understand there are a good many Southerners in the theater tonight. I know the South very well. I spent twenty years there one night. It's dangerous for me to go back there. You see, when I drink, I think I am Polish. One night I got drunk and I moved out of my neighborhood.

"The last time I was down South, I walked into this restaurant and the white waitress came up to me and said, 'We don't serve colored people here.' I said, 'That's all right. I don't eat colored people. Bring me a whole fried chicken.'

"About that time three cousins came in. You know the ones I mean: Ku, Klux and Klan. They said, 'Boy, we're giving you a warning. Anything you do to that chicken, we're going to do to you.'

"About then the waitress brought me my chicken. 'Remember, boy,' they said, 'anything you do to that chicken, we're going to do to you.'

"So I put down my knife and fork, and I picked up that chicken and kissed it."

Dick Gregory could keep an audience in stitches all evening.

Ken said that he thought Sammy Davis Jr was the greatest all-around entertainer of this century.

Oddly enough, Blewett said that whenever he really wanted to see show business at its best, he went to the Indiana Theater at 219 East 43rd Street. It was known as a theater for entertainers who wanted to be entertained. Every Saturday following the evening's last regular performance, a "Midnight Ramble" was held, where comedians, singers and dancers put on their "bluest" jokes, their "special material" songs, and their most revealing dance routines for the midnight audience at the Indiana. Occasionally the dancing would get so wild that

Cab Calloway.

Moms Mabley.

Above: A rare photo of the historic Vendome Theater. Below: Erskine Tate's Vendome Symphony Orchestra in 1925.

Above: The Regal ushers in 1929. Third from left is Ken Blewett. Below: Display cards of coming attractions at the Regal.

the police would stop the show and warn the performers to turn down the burner.

"When you are playing a Ramble, you've really got to be on the ball," said Butterbeans of the famous comedy team of Butterbeans and Susie. "You've got to be careful of the gags and blackouts you use because you can never tell whether the comedian you stole the joke from is sitting out there looking you dead in the mouth."

Ken remembers that, back in the '30s and '40s, nightclubs held "celebrity nights", when entertainers from the Regal would be guest celebrities. Since Joe Hughes, the owner of Joe's Deluxe Nightclub at 63rd and South Parkway, was a good friend of Ken Blewett's, entertainers like Duke Ellington, Cab Calloway, Nat "King" Cole, Earl Hines and others would visit Joe's Deluxe on Monday nights after they had finished their last show. I can remember going to various clubs, and particularly to Joe's Deluxe, to see the celebrities. In those days there was no television, of course, so you could not see entertainers as you can today. And these people were heard infrequently on the radio. So Monday celebrity nights still jog my noggin with a lot of pleasant memories.

Ken Blewett first saw Duke Ellington downtown at the Oriental Theater in 1928.

Sammy Davis, Jr.

Butter Beans & Susie.

"I was impressed with Duke's polished manner, his clothes, and overwhelmed by his music," Ken recalls.

The next contact that Ken had with Ellington was backstage at the Regal in 1930, after Ken had become an usher. Ken caught Duke one evening as he was walking off the bandstand and said, "Mr. Ellington, that is a beautiful suit that you have on."

Duke replied: "Thanks, young man."

Every time Ken got an opportunity to go backstage he would stand in the wings and peep at the clothes that the very elegant Mr. Ellington was wearing. On Thursday, which was closing night, Duke sent for Ken to come backstage to his dressing room. Ken went backstage and the Duke said with a broad smile on his face: "Young man, I want to make you a present of that suit that you liked so well."

Ken recalls: "When Duke handed me that iridescent blue gabardine suit, I almost fainted before I could thank him. I will never forget that moment."

The Mills Brothers—Harry, Donald, Herbert and John—were a fine group of singers. They were the first big time quartet of color to make it to the top. They were successful on radio, in the movies and on the stage. I remember they were in the middle of an engagement at the Regal Theater in 1936 when John Jr., the youngest of the four brothers, became very sick. They wanted to send him to a good doctor because they didn't know what was causing his apparently sudden illness. I suggested Dr. L. D. Morrison in the South Center Building at 4709 South Parkway. Upon Dr. Morrison's recommendation, the Mills Brothers canceled their engagement.

John Mills Jr. subsequently died of tuberculosis. He was replaced by John Mills Sr., a former light-opera singer and the father of the four boys. That was some group. They have never been equalled. Harry Mills once told me the brothers were lucky because they started right at the top. Radio then was like television now in terms of the tremendous exposure it afforded. The Mills Brothers were on radio over WLW in Cincinnati for almost three years before they were permitted to sing under their own name. The sponsors of their early radio shows did not want the audience to know that they were black, so they sang under such names as "The Steamboat Four," "Will, Willie, Wilbur and William," and the "Tasty Yeast Jester." Every sponsor gave them a different name.

Count Basie, Joe "Ziggy" Johnson, and I were great buddies. Count Basie had a standing gift for Ken Blewett every time he worked the Regal Theater: a two week trip to the west coast by train. Count would charter two railroad cars and he would stop at Kansas City to pick up some of the other fellows en route to California. Boy, we would have a ball. Some of the guys would gamble all the way across the Great Plains. Others would hold "Kansas City jam sessions" all night and all day. My wife and I had a jolly good time. When we reached Los Angeles, we were

The Four Mills Brothers.

always the house guests of Mr. and Mrs. Eddie "Rochester" Anderson, the movie star and radio comedian with the Jack Benny show. When Rochester was at his zenith, he always played the Regal at least once annually. Those were some great people and some great times.

Ken was with Lionel Hampton backstage at the Regal when Joe Glaser, Louis Armstrong's manager, told Lionel about a friend of his named Joe Sherman who owned a lounge downtown called the Garrick. Sherman employed a washroom girl who kept coming out of the washroom trying to sing with the band. Walter Fuller, the ex-Hines trumpet player, had a six-piece group working on that gig. Joe Glaser took Ken and Hamp down to the Garrick one night and Joe Sherman had the washroom girl come out and sing a couple of blues numbers. Hamp was so fascinated with the young lady that he told her, "I am working at the Regal. Come on out and sing with my band tomorrow."

The first number that she sang on the Regal stage was "Evil Gal Blues." She tore up the house. Hamp told the girl right after her performance that she was hired if she would change her name from Ruth Jones to Dinah Washington. Ms. Jones replied, "I don't care what you call me, just give me a job."

Joe Williams, who was the backstage doorman at the Regal at that time, said to Lionel Hampton: "I didn't know you wanted a singer. I am a singer. Give me a chance."

Hampton let Joe sing in the next show. Joe Williams sang, "Everyday." However Joe wanted to be a ballad singer with the band and Hamp did not need one at that time. Hamp sent for Joe several months later when his ballad singer left the band at the Tick Tock Club in Boston.

Joe Hughes greets Eddie "Rochester" Anderson on celebrity night at Joe's DeLuxe Club. Center is Ken Blewett. Right rear: Harold Youngblood, bandleader.

Erskine Hawkins, bandleader.

Tiny Bradshaw, bandleader.

Pigmeat Markham, comedian.

Dusty Fletcher, comedian.

Backstage at the Regal: Standing left to right: Joe "Ziggy" Johnson; Baby Lawrence and his wife; Dusty Fletcher; Nelson Sykes; Savannah Churchill; Unknown; Count Basie; Jimmy Rushing; and Arthur Prysock. Kneeling: Unknown (left) and Ken Blewett.

Tony Bennett takes a camera shot of Duke Ellington backstage at the Regal Theater.

Ken Blewett said it is mandatory for a stage show to be balanced. He recalled an incident when Dinah Washington and The Ravens were on a bill at the Regal along with a young blues singer named Jimmy Witherspoon. After the first show, Dinah went to Ken Blewett and said that the show was not balanced because there was just too much blues singing. To achieve balance, Ken cut Jimmy Witherspoon out of the show at Dinah's request. Some years later after Witherspoon began to enjoy some fame, he had an opportunity to play another bill at the Regal with Dinah Washington and on that occasion he told Ken Blewett that he had never forgotten that incident. Jimmy said that being dropped from the show was the worst hurt and disappointment that he had ever suffered in his whole life.

Daddy-O Daylie, the radio personality, said: "I've never seen anyone balance a stage jazz package as well as "Mr. Regal" Blewett. In the fall of 1958, Ken Blewett called and asked if I would be interested in acting as the master of ceremonies for a jazz package that he was bringing in for a week. I agreed because although I had been promoting jazz on three radio shows simultaneously during the period, I had not had an opportunity to act as master of ceremonies for some of the big time artists. I considered Ken's offer a rare opportunity, especially since he agreed to pay me $1,000 for a week's work."

The jazz package included Count Basie and his orchestra; the Miles Davis Quintet, which included Cannonball Adderley and John Coltrane on saxophone, Paul Chambers on bass, Jimmy Cobb on drums, Kelly on piano, and the mighty Miles on trumpet. Dakota Staton was also in that show, along with Nipsey Russell and Sonny Stitt, who did a solo spot with the accompaniment of the Basie band.

"Since everybody was a star in his or her own right, nobody wanted to go on first, so I figured I had better lay down the ground rules early before I got into any difficulties," recalls Daddy-O. "I had heard that Miles Davis was a disgruntled type of person, and was notorious for swinging on people. He used to train and would go to the gym and box, and he would go upside your head in a minute. I didn't want any problems, so I went up to Miles and asked him if he would go on first.

"Miles said: 'Hey, Daddy-O, no problem. Me and you.'

"Miles and I got along beautifully the entire week. In fact, Miles was one of the nicest dudes on that show.

"Sonny Stitt was just kicking the habit at that time, and you know when you give up something you have to replace it with something else, so he gave up drugs and started drinking gin and vodka. The thing that stands out vividly in my mind is the first day I went back to Sonny's dressing room. He had two fifths of vodka and two fifths of gin sitting on a small table. He was drinking that stuff the way most people drink water, and before every show he would actually kill a fifth of vodka or gin by himself. I had occasion to check Sonny's dressing room before leaving the theater on the last night of the show. I found three cases filled with empty fifth bottles stacked in the corner of his dressing room. Considering the way Sonny abused his health, I think he lived a long time.

"Ken really put together the right mix in that show. Everybody who came to that theater got something out of it. For example, Miles had his fans and his cheerleaders went wild everytime he soloed. Cannonball received the same kind of adulation. Then there were Sonny Stitt and Dakota Staton fans. Everybody apparently loved Basie. It was a perfect mix for jazz lovers.

"Nipsey Russell was the only one in the group who never quite adjusted, because Nipsey thought that he was going to be M.C. When Ken told him up front that that was what I was being paid for, Nipsey never got his attitude together. Nipsey Russell is a brilliant entertainer and M.C. In fact, I've only seen two real masters of ceremonies in my life, and the first on that list would certainly be the great and late Duke Ellington. Second to him would be Nipsey Russell. I don't think anyone can M.C. any better than Brother Russell. You might recall that he was the producer and master of ceremonies at the Baby Grand nightclub in

Left: Sugar Chile, the piano genius sharing the keyboard with Hamp. Right: The Regal coming attraction display.

Sammy Dyer, show producer.

A Sunday afternoon crowd scene at the Regal.

Left to right: *Arthur Prysock, Ken Blewett, and Big Joe Turner in the lobby of the Regal.*

Nat "King" Cole.

Cab Calloway and Leroy Wimbush.

Bill Kenny, of the Ink Spots, Joe "Ziggy" Johnson, and companion (center).

Patterson & Jackson, dancers.

Joe Louis and Leonard Reed on stage at the Regal.

Harlem for over thirty years.

"I brought Jimmy Smith, the organ player, to Ken Blewett's attention. A fellow named Babs Gonzales out of New York called me collect and I refused to accept the call. So he called back about ten minutes later, paying for the call himself, and said: 'Hey, man, there is a cat here in the "Apple" named Jimmy Smith that is playing more organ than you have ever heard.'

"I thought that if Babs, whom I called a world gypsy because he never had any money and was always free-loading, would spend his change to tell me about Jimmy Smith, then Jimmy Smith must really be into something. I went to Morry's Record Shop, which was at 58th Street and the 'L' and asked if they had anything by Jimmy Smith, and they did. They had two Blue Note LPs which I listened to and couldn't believe. This guy was so fast on the organ that I thought it was a dub. He was just a fantastic musician. So I began playing Jimmy Smith's LPs on my radio show and, at my suggestion, Ken Blewett brought Jimmy into the Regal for the first time. Jimmy Smith stole the show and was an absolute sensation in Chicago. As I recall, Little Johnny Griffin was fronting the band for that show. The Regal was the launching pad for Jimmy Smith into the big time."

Dizzy Gillespie recalls a gig at the Regal with Dinah Washington in 1961 (two years after Blewett's departure). The late Al Benson, Chicago's foremost rhythm and blues disc jockey, was the promoter and producer of the show for S.B. Fuller, the first black owner of the Regal-South Center building complex. Diz had a big sixteen-piece band but was allotted only twenty minutes for each show.

Diz said: "When I got to 'Manteca,' which was about ten minutes long, I would have to go overtime. Al Benson personally asked me to limit myself to twenty minutes. The next time I played overtime on the show I received a telegram from Al Benson that said I had no regard for the wishes of the management of the Regal Theater and that my contract called for me to play to the policy of the house.

"He later said that the telegram was a clear request for me not to do more than twenty minutes of entertaining for the remainder of my engagement at the Regal and if any changes were to be made in the length of time that I was to perform, the management would notify me in writing of that change before each show. That's what the old swing master, Al Benson, thought about jazz. He gave me twenty minutes with a big band after I had already performed all over the world for people who never seem to get enough of our music."

The Regal and many of the stars that graced its stage have gone on to a higher platform. However, the magic of the edifice and the greatness of the talent that made the Regal live still haunts the territory of 47th and South Parkway. The gallery of pictures on the preceding pages should rekindle fond memories for the old, and introduce the young to a jazz scene that should not be forgotten.

Above: Red Saunders, orchestra leader, discussing the shape of Dizzy's trumpet in his dressing room backstage at the Regal. Below: Ken Blewett under the marquee of the Tivoli Theater, his last South Side assignment.

Nat "King" Cole at piano.

Chapter 13

Nat "King" Cole Remembered

In January of 1934, Henry Fort, a young bass player and childhood friend of Nat Cole's, received a telephone call from Cole asking him to join a teenaged band he was organizing. Henry went to the first rehearsal of the new twelve-piece band in the home of Nat's parents, the Reverend Edward and Mrs Perlina Cole in the 4200 block on South Prairie Avenue in Chicago. Cole had called together four saxophone players, three trumpet players, a trombone player and a full rhythm section including guitar, bass, drums and piano.

"Nat seemed much older than seventeen," Fort says. "He was serious and so intense and nervous that he bit his fingernails. He was authoritative without being dictatorial, and he was able to whip a bunch of undisciplined teenagers into a music unit in less than sixty days. His objective was to make us sound like Earl 'Fatha' Hines' band; Earl was Nat's idol.

"Nat lived within four blocks of the old Grand Terrace where Hines' orchestra played and Nat used to hang out in the gangway next to the Terrace and listen to Hines. Nat's musical memory was almost perfect. He could hear something and repeat it note by note without a mistake. This was a great asset to our young group. Nat lifted so much of the Hines material intact that at first he called our group the Rogues of Rhythm.

"Nat's father objected to young Cole's intense interest in jazz piano. But his mother, Perlina, had a different opinion. Finally the family reached a compromise: Nat could play jazz on Sunday afternoons as long as he played organ for the morning service at his father's True Light Baptist Church. Nat's mother made our first uniforms, Cossack shirts, to give the band a professional look.

"Malcolm Smith made an arrangement for us to play at the Warwick Hall on East 47th Street every Sunday afternoon. Consequently we began to get a lot of press, especially when we did a battle of the bands with Tony Fambro and his Jungle Rhythm Orchestra, another teenaged group. By early 1935, the band had become so popular among South Side youth that Malcolm Smith arranged a tour of Illinois for us. I recall our first trip took us down to Aurora, Joliet and then Kankakee, where we suffered our first casualty. A trumpet player named Rail became caught in the undertow while he was swimming in the Kankakee River, and was never seen again. That incident disturbed Nat's mother so that she decided that Nat's eldest brother, Eddie, should leave Noble Sissle's band, one of the top bands of the period, and come back to Chicago to give Nat the benefit of his mature wisdom. Nat had three brothers and one sister, Evelyn, and Eddie was a good ten years older than Nat. He was one of the best musicians Chicago produced: a master bass player, but he could play any number of instruments, including the piano. All the Cole boys were proficient piano players, but none was as proficient as Eddie. On the other hand, none had the style of Nat "King" Cole. Nat played like Earl Hines and sat at the piano like Earl Hines, but he bore himself like Duke Ellington. Nat was proud. Even when he couldn't afford a new suit, he was always neat and he was always professional on the stage. It was just in him, and in his whole family.

"Nat could sit down at a piano, from the very beginning, and tell the horn player to play a B-flat here or a C there and believe it or not, it came out perfect. But I never saw Nat read a piece of music the whole time I was with him. If he heard something once, he could play it as if he had been playing it all his life. If someone hummed a tune around Nat, before the last sixteen bars were finished, he would pick up the tune and play it as if it were his own. He could play anything he heard. At rehearsal when the band played a number Nat hadn't heard yet, he usually got up and directed. Then he could sit down at the piano and play that number a second time around as if he had written the arrangement, which was phenomenal. I'm certain that Nat couldn't read music during

The King Cole Trio. Left to right: Oscar Miller, Nat, and Wesley Prince.

our early years, but I'm equally certain that he must have learned how to read later on after I left the band.

"In 1936 after Nat finished a six-month engagement at the Panama Cafe at 58th and Prairie in Chicago, he organized a big band to go on the road with Miller and Lyles, the producers of a show called *Shuffle Along*. Our first stops were in Michigan, where we toured five cities, including Ann Arbor. We played the University auditorium there, and Nat got married to a chorus girl in the show named Nadine Robinson. I was his best man.

"After we completed the Michigan tour we headed West, our final destination being Los Angeles. When we reached Long Beach, California, we found out that the show had to fold because it was running out of money. We decided to go on strike in Los Angeles. But Miller and Lyles got to the union before we did. The union consequently would not permit a strike and ordered us to work, even though we were not going to get paid. At that point some of the guys decided to return to Chicago, but several of us agreed to stay on the West Coast with Nat and form a smaller group.

"We used an old Chicago trick to get a job. Six or seven of us went separately into a nightclub. Of course Nat was a star attraction, and the bandleader asked him to come up and play a number on the piano. Nat did that, and after about ten or fifteen minutes I went up and told the bass player that I would relieve him. A

Left to right: Nat, daughter Natalie, and wife Maria dine at Morris' Eat Shop, 410 East 47th Street, between stage shows at the Regal Theater in Chicago.

little later somebody else from our group relieved the sax man, and before the set was over the entire Cole ensemble was on the bandstand. We outplayed the house band. Management approached us and offered us the job if we would work below scale. Scale at that time was thirty-five to forty dollars in California, but they offered us twenty-five dollars. We obviously couldn't accept that offer and remain in the union, so at that point I left Nat.

"Nat decided that he would stay on the West Coast and work as a single. Bob Lewis of Swanee Inn suggested that Nat add a bass guitar and a drum. The first person Nat contacted was Oscar Miller, a guitarist, who jumped at the chance to get a steady job. Next he called bassist Wesley Prince and then a drummer, who did not show up for the first night. The drummer was not needed on the second night because the King Cole Trio had been born. It had been accepted overwhelmingly by the clientele of the Swanee Inn.

Eddie Cole, Nat's oldest brother, and his orchestra.

"The years changed Nat. You know he was divorced from Nadine Robinson and married Maria Ellington and some people blamed the change in him on his new marriage. I recall in 1958 I took my family to Hawaii and stopped off in Los Angeles. I called Nat and left a message with his answering service, but he never called me back. Shortly after I got back to Chicago I received a call from Ralph Edwards, of the television show *This Is Your Life.* Nat had told him that I was one of the original members of his band, and Edwards wanted me to come back to California and appear on the show for Nat. My first inclination was to refuse, because Nat had not returned my call. But we all did appear on the show in 1958."

Marty Faye, Chicago TV and radio star, remembers that Nat always used to stay at the Ambassador East Hotel whenever he was in town.

"Nat made the transition from 42nd and Prairie to the Gold Coast without any sweat," Faye said. "He was comfortable with opulence. He was very smooth and warm and very businesslike. He always knew what he was doing, how he was doing it and when he was doing it. He always demanded the best.

"Nat was the only celebrity ever to appear on my TV show who would not perform there. I could interview him, and that was all. He was such a perfectionist that he never wanted to do anything unless he was absolutely certain that it was right in every detail. He had to be sure the piano was tuned, that the acoustics were good in the room or the studio and that the lighting was properly

Top left: Ralph Edwards' This Is Your Life Show, featuring Nat Cole. Left to right seated: Collis Gastel, Nat "King" Cole, Maria, Natalie, and Cookie. Standing: Ralph Edwards, Wesley Prince, Henry Fort, Rev. Cole, Russell Shores, Unknown, Nat's sister Babes, Goon Gardner, Eddie Cole, Charles Gray, Unknown. Top right: Ralph Edwards, Nat, and Henry Fort. Below: Eddie Cole, Charles Gray, Goon Gardner, Nat Cole, Russell Shores, Henry Fort and Ralph Edwards.

adjusted. Only his people could set things up for him, otherwise he would not perform. I was satisfied just to interview him because he was very amusing. He could tell funny stories and he was glib. He was a great human being."

Baldwin "Sparky" Tavares was hired as a valet by Nat Cole at the Blue Note in Chicago in 1949.

"I had met Nat earlier in New York through my brother-in-law Ervin Ashby, who played bass for Nat," Sparky Tavares said. "The valet work was actually too much for one man because Nat always carried big trunks filled with a full wardrobe, so he had to hire an ex-railroad man to help me. If Nat was going to do six shows a day, he would have nine or ten changes of clothing. That meant everyone in the trio had to have nine uniforms. They were all single or double-breasted suits, not one tuxedo. Nat was a perfectionist and a slavemaster. He worked the hell out of me. By the time I got to California several months later, I had dropped from one hundred twenty-seven to one hundred nine pounds. But I was stuck, I was his man. Around strangers he was very shy and quiet, but with his friends he acted like just another one of the cats. He liked to sit around and have a taste, argue sports and joke. He loved comedy and had a great sense of humor. He had the loudest laugh I have ever heard.

"He could laugh at himself. I remember one afternoon in Chicago we were coming out of the stage door of the Regal Theater and found ourselves facing a big group of kids in the alley. I asked them what they wanted, an autograph? One kid said no, he wanted a hat. Another kid said, 'I want to see the show and you better let me in that door. I am Nat Cole's brother.'

"I said, 'What's your name?'

"He said, 'My name is Charcoal.'

"Nat laughed louder than anyone in that alley. The boy apologized to Nat when he recognized him. And Nat said, 'Come on over here, son, and tell me your name.' When the kid told him his name, Nat told him not to tell lies like that again. Then he said to me, 'Take those kids out front and tell Ken Blewett to give them good seats.'

"A good way to wipe the smile off Nat's face was to mention the NAACP. The only time I've seen Nat really upset was after he sent a telegram to Roy Wilkins of the NAACP which read:

> I will not join the NAACP in speech making, but I am willing to do everything within my efforts in any way I can to further our cause.

"Wilkins immediately issued a press release paraphrasing the telegram and implying that Nat had refused to join the NAACP. A legal official of that organization phoned and had the nerve to call Nat a sort of handkerchief-head. The son-of-a-bitch that called him wasn't even married to a black woman. One ironic

The Huddlers. From left: Johnny Hartman, Nat Cole, Billy Eckstine, and Sarah Vaughan.

thing about the whole episode was that Nat had been doing benefits for the NAACP since Day One—probably as many if not more than most entertainers—and yet he was being publicly insulted just because he didn't want to make speeches or be a card-carrying member. The thing came to a head in Detroit when civic leaders there asked Nat why he wouldn't join the NAACP.

"Nat said, 'I have done more benefits for you people than anyone else you have mentioned.'

"The Detroit officials said, 'Well, join anyway.'

"Nat finally joined on his wife's advice and the advice of his manager Collis Gastell and others he respected. But that incident really hurt him and he carried the bruise to his grave.

"He was hurt again in 1950 when we played the Thunderbird Hotel in Las Vegas. We had a congo player at the time named Jack Coustanza, an Italian boy from Chicago. He was working for Nat, but since he was white he could get a room in the Thunderbird and Nat and the rest of us couldn't: we had to stay at Mrs Shaw's on the west side of town, known as Darkie City. On top of that, although our name was on the marquee, we had to enter the hotel through a side door and stay in our dressing rooms until we went on stage, and our food was brought up and served buffet style every night. We refused to eat it. We did the show, returned to the dressing rooms to change our clothes and then left, because there was nothing they could do for us. When Nat finished that engage-

Nat Cole and Mahalia Jackson with Marty Faye in Chicago at Fritzell's Restaurant on North State Street promoting Nat's recording of "St Louis Blues".

ment, he told Collis, 'I don't want to play this town anymore until I can walk through the front door.' Collis agreed.

"We did not go back to Vegas again until 1953, when we played a place called El Rancho Vegas. It was managed by Jack Entrotter, former head man of the Copacabana in New York. He had an unwritten rule that all facilities must be open to all entertainers who worked in the hotel. Nat was given a large cabin and I also had a cabin. They told Nat he could use all facilities and they meant it. Nat was the first to break the color barrier for black entertainers in Las Vegas and for colored people in general there. Shortly afterward the Sands Hotel brought in Lena Horne and opened the entire place up to her. She could have guests and do whatever she pleased.

"We had a strange experience at the Sahara Hotel. Bill Miller, the manager from New York, called Nat and invited our group over to see the show, and we were treated royally. We had good food and drinks, and everything was beautiful. The next night we decided to go back on our own and see the show. But when we got to the Sahara, the security man stopped us at the door. Nat got on the telephone and called Miller who said he was sorry but his hands were tied and he couldn't do a thing about it. We were their guests one night and turned away from the door the next. Strange things happen in America.

"Life is full of peaks and valleys and one of the peaks for Nat occurred at the Brown Derby in Hollywood. We were sitting around having drinks and talking, when Hoagy Carmichael came over and joined us. After a few minutes of general conversation Hoagy said to Nat, 'You know, the prettiest vocal version I ever heard of my song "Stardust" was by you. I have felt more honored by your version than by any other I know.' Nat bubbled for the rest of the evening; 'Stardust' was one of his favorite songs, but he had no idea that Hoagy felt that way about his version.

"Nat's mother was the leader of that family. She had an incredibly strong influence over her daughter and her sons. They all respected her. Although she was not educated, she was articulate and she spoke as crisply and distinctly as Nat sang. She treated all her children equally, and made no bigger fuss over one that was a star than over the others. When she died, it hit Nat hard. He fainted at the funeral services, which were held at a church pastored by the Reverend Rawls, Lou Rawls' uncle, at 42nd and Indiana.

"In October, 1964, we were working a club in Lake Tahoe, doing two shows a night and flying to Hollywood every day to do a picture called *Cat Ballou* with Lee Marvin. One evening after we returned from Hollywood, we napped for an hour and went over to the club for dinner. While we were sitting around, I noticed that one of Nat's valets was making extra holes in Nat's belt. I asked him what the hell he was doing. He told me that the belt had gotten too large for Nat.

"I turned to Nat and said, 'What's wrong?'

" 'I'm losing weight,' Nat said. He never weighed more than one hundred seventy-four pounds.

"I looked at him and said, 'Yeah, I guess you are losing a little weight, Dick.' I always called him Dick. When I handed him his clothes that night I asked him when he had started losing weight.

" 'I don't know,' he said. 'Maybe I've been working too hard. I should probably take a few days off. I seem to stay tired.'

"After we left Lake Tahoe we went to Vegas to play an engagement at The Sands and one night Nat got dizzy there, and that's when he knew he was really sick and it was more than just fatigue. We called a doctor and they sent us a 'Feel Good' doctor who gave him a shot and said he would be all right. The doctors down there will do anything to stay in good with the hotels. They come in and treat entertainers, but the treatment mostly consists of making the entertainers feel good.

"In November of 1963 Nat saw a doctor in Chicago and that's when he found out he had lung cancer. He had no idea before that that there was anything seriously wrong with him. We finished an engagement at the Fairmont Hotel in San Francisco on December tenth and on the twelfth Nat went back to Los Angeles and checked into a hospital. While we were driving to the hospital, Nat leaned

Nat Cole. The picture in the mirror...

over to me in the car and asked me for a cigarette.

"On the morning of February fifteenth, 1965, when I was in Miami Beach working with Nancy Wilson at the Diplomat Hotel, the clerk called me and asked me if I had heard the news that morning. I hadn't. 'Nat Cole is dead,' he said. I called Nancy and told her I had to go home. I took a flight back to Los Angeles and went directly to the funeral parlor. When I saw Nat's body lying there on a table I walked up and lifted him and held him in my arms. He was as cold as an ice cube, but I just had to hold him."

The creation of Roberts Show Club. Top left: Roberts Cab Company garage which was converted into a nightclub. Top right: Eddie Plique and Herman Roberts discuss plans for expanding the garage into a club. Bottom left: Left to right: Joe Louis, Herman Roberts and Count Basie observe a crane in operation. Bottom right: Roberts Original Lounge and Liquors.

Chapter 14

Roberts Show Club

In August, 1959, Dick Gregory called Roberts Show Club the biggest Negro-owned nightclub in America. All the top Negro acts played Roberts: Sarah Vaughan, Count Basie, Sammy Davis, Jr, Billy Eckstine, Nipsey Russell and Dinah Washington. Red Saunders directed the house band. There was an eight-girl chorus line and more than one thousand seats for people who liked to be entertained in this spacious, well-appointed club. Gregory said, "When I stood on that electrically-powered stage and introduced the acts and gave the coming attractions, I felt like a top Negro act too."

The power behind Roberts Show Club was Herman Roberts, an energetic entrepreneur who found that owning fifty-five taxicabs did not occupy enough of his time. He opened the Lucky Spot, a small nightclub on 605 East 71st Street. Later when he decided to sponsor a seven-girl social club he changed the name of the Lucky Spot to The Roberettes. The members of the club brought their friends there on Friday and Saturday nights, and business thrived. Herman Roberts owned a garage at 6222 South Parkway which was too small for his fleet of cabs, so he moved the cabs to a larger garage at 610 East 61st Street and remodeled the South Parkway garage into a dance hall. People had so much fun there they wanted to come every night. Roberts responded by improving the interior and naming the place Roberts Lounge and Liquor. He told me at the time he never intended to own a nightclub. He had intended only to provide a place for the members of the Roberettes Social Club to bring their friends to drink, dance, and listen to a small band. Then out of the clear blue sky people began providing their own entertainment. One person would get up and sing with the band and another would do a tap solo and it became obvious to Roberts that there was a need for low budget entertainment for young middle-class South Siders.

"The Club DeLisa was very successful with low budget shows," Roberts said. "Mike DeLisa never paid big money to any of his stars, but he always had a good show. I didn't want to duplicate what DeLisa was doing. I wanted to do something better, to bring in top-notch acts, and when you start thinking in those terms, obviously you need space. You have to have a room large enough to accommodate enough people to make the economics feasible. You cannot afford to pay Duke Ellington, Count Basie or Sammy Davis Jr to perform in a room that will accommodate only a hundred people. So I began thinking about expanding my place to seat a thousand or more."

Roberts sold his cab franchises in 1957 to devote full time to being a nightclub entrepreneur. He made his Roberts Show Club the headquarters for the Mambo and the Cha-cha-cha. While the owners of competing nightclubs were crying, Herman Roberts, who was only thirty-two years old, was jumping for joy. He offered free dancing lessons at the club twice a week. Every night he had some kind of activity: a dance contest, a talent show, a fashion show. His club was filled to the rafters even on Monday nights, a traditional off-night for nightclubs.

During the mid-'50s there were more than two thousand social clubs on the South Side of Chicago. Roberts worked hard to get them to bring all their activities into his club. Consequently Roberts' Club was booked months in advance on Sunday afternoons for the traditional fashion shows and cocktail parties given by the social clubs. Every cocktail party or fashion show that I attended at Roberts was a huge success.

In 1957 Herman Roberts adopted a big name policy for his club. He brought in a Chicago favorite, Dinah Washington, who was so popular with the patrons that she was booked into the club at least three times a year.

"Dinah Washington was a very complex person," Herman said. "You don't really get to know a person until you have money or business dealings with him or her. I had to deal with Dinah in those areas and I got to know her quite well. She didn't like taking suggestions from me or anyone else. If I made a comment

Above: Herman Roberts and some fans greet Dinah Washington at her opening. Below: The expanded Roberts Show Club which seated one thousand patrons and booked name talent.

about her show and she knew it wasn't her idea, she would automatically reject it. She wanted to be the creator of everything she did.

"She was both vain and insecure. She was the first entertainer to appear at my club in a multi-colored wig, ankle-length mink coat and tight, skin-fitting dress. She wore that regalia to get attention and yet when customers commented about her clothes to one another, she became annoyed and suspicious. She would stop in the middle of a song and say, 'What are you bitches talking about?' She might go further than that and cuss them out without really knowing whether they were saying something derogatory or whether they were complimenting her. She was unpredictable. I remember times when people would come into the club and order a drink and she would walk over to the end of the stage and say to them, 'Dammit, don't order no goddamned drinks while I'm singing.' You never knew what bag Dinah was coming out of.

"She exhibited her insecurity with Brook Benton, a great singer. She and Benton made several successful recordings together. They could have made a fortune, but Dinah would not work with him after those hit records. And whenever Benton came into the club she created a disturbance in order to avoid having to deal with him as a fellow artist. Personally I loved Dinah, but her psychological problems continually prevented her from becoming one of the great singers of our time."

In 1959 Herman Roberts booked his friend Sammy Davis Jr into the club for five nights at three thousand dollars a night, and additional charges for the large band that traveled with Davis. Sammy attracted a predominantly white audience every evening for the first show. All the seats down front were occupied by white people. Herman Roberts told me that on the second evening one of his regular customers came up to him and said, "Hey, man, I thought you said Sammy was coming out here to work for his people?"

Roberts retorted, "Have you forgotten that Sammy turned Jewish a few years ago?"

Sammy Davis Jr drew large crowds because he was the number one entertainer in America and his religious persuasion was irrelevant.

Because of Sammy Davis' appearance at his club Herman Roberts went into the hotel-motel business. "I wanted Sammy to stay on the South Side near the Club," Roberts said. "I didn't want to send him all the way downtown and then have to pick him up everyday. In addition a lot of my customers came from out of town and had no place to stay. The only hotels on the South Side near the Club were the Southway, the Evans and the Pershing and I considered them hand-me-down dumps. The decent hotels in South Shore and Hyde Park wouldn't accept blacks. So the first time Sammy appeared at the Club I went out and rented a nearby house for him. But I was determined that when he came back the second time I would have a motel. And in 1960 I completed the first newly constructed

Above: The "Rat Pack" arrives in Chicago. Left to right: Peter Lawford, Sammy Davis Jr, Finnis Henderson. Rear left: Frank Sinatra, Joey Bishop and friend. Below: Brook Benton (left) with Herman Roberts.

motel owned by a black in the city of Chicago—directly across from Roberts Show Club at 6633 South King Drive."

In the next decade Herman Roberts built more than one thousand rooms in six different locations in Chicago. He also bult a two hundred room motel in Gary, Indiana, and a hundred room motel in Okmulgee, Oklahoma.

"Dick Gregory started working for me in the fall of 1959 at twenty-five dollars a night or seventy-five dollars for a weekend," Roberts said. "His act was different from most comedy acts. He was intellectual, scholarly. You might even call him serious. His material included racial incidents. Since my audience was black and white, I told Dick to cool it because I didn't want to run the white folks away. But Dick wouldn't alter his material at all. He stuck by his guns because of his philosophy about life in our times.

"Show business is cold-blooded. Most entertainers don't want to offer a hand to the guy or gal trying to climb up the ladder. I brought in several name acts during the period that Dick Gregory was my M.C. and—would you believe it?—they didn't want Gregory to be in the show in any way. One comedian actually told me to kick him out. He didn't want Gregory spoiling his jokes. A singer told me, 'I don't even want him to call my name.' And yet in the end Dick Gregory was the guy that made it possible for all of them. He opened up doors for them that had never been opened before, and to this day I've never met anyone who said that Dick Gregory was not accessible. In other words, success didn't turn Dick Gregory's head.

"A lot of people thought I was prejudiced. I hired yellow bartenders with pretty hair and girls who looked like that too, because I thought it was good business. Today I might get run out of town for that kind of nonsense. However, I still maintain that I'd rather look at a pretty girl than an ugly one. We eventually hired darker Negro girls in the Club. I also hired white bartenders and white girls to greet people at the door and serve drinks. I felt that their presence would make my white clients feel more comfortable, but the fact that whites worked for me made many people in the community think that I didn't really own the Club—that I was fronting for white owners.

"For example, Marty Faye, the radio man, was one of my best friends, and I used to advertise heavily on his show. Marty told me that blacks said to him, 'Marty, why are you advertising for Roberts? You must own a piece of the action.' No, he didn't own a piece of the action but if he said on his show that he went out to Roberts the night before with his wife and had a good time, whites who heard that were going to think that as long as Marty Faye thought it was all right, then it was all right with them. I was trying to develop a business without hurting anyone, and I don't think I hurt anyone. I hired Redd Foxx when he was big and making big money. I used to hear people say, 'That ain't Roberts' place. When you go there they got all those Mafia people standing at the door watching you. I can't

Top left: Quintard Miller and Mantan Mooreland. Top right: At Roberts, Eddie Plique introduces Sugar Ray Robinson on the night he won his third championship. Also included are Joe Louie and Herman Roberts. Below, left to right: Johnny Hartman, Godfrey Cambridge, Herman Roberts, Cordie King, Al Hibler and Duke Ellington.

Top: *Herman Roberts, black tie, and Dinah Washington, white gown, with fans in front of Roberts Show Club. Below left: Louie Jordan and Dolly Smith. Lower right: Billy Eckstine always worked a standing-room-only crowd at Roberts.*

Top left: Herman Roberts and Ramsey Lewis. Top right: Herman with Irv Kupcinet. Below left: Roberts, Cassius Clay and Earl Grant. Bottom right: Roy Hamilton on stage at Roberts.

*Above: Archie Moore and Nipsey Russell. Below: Joe
Louis at the bar in Roberts Show Lounge.*

deal with that.' The guys they were talking about were actually people I knew who worked at the bank I used and others worked at an automobile dealership where I had bought my cabs.

"Back in the 1960s I wouldn't think of booking B. B. King or Muddy Waters in-to my place, because middle-class blacks had not begun to accept the blues as an original art form. I had to think about it seriously more than once before I booked Ray Charles into the Club the first time. Fortunately for me, his engage-ment turned out to be very, very successful.

"I was offered a Johnny Mathis package for $175 a week and I refused it because I didn't think he would sell on the South Side. And today you probably couldn't get him for ten thousand dollars a night. But you win some and lose some."

Herman Roberts has phased himself out of the nightclub business, and out of the hotel and taxicab businesses as well. His latest project is oil drilling and cattle ranching on his 2600 acre ranch in Oklahoma. As Dinah Washington would say, "What a difference a day makes."

Dusty Fletcher performing his famous "Open the Door, Richard" act.

Part Two:

The Voices of Jazz Artists from the Past and Present

Johnny Board

"Working with Coleman Hawkins was like working for a doctoral degree."

Johnny Board

BIRTHDATE: December 8, 1919
BIRTHPLACE: Chicago, Illinois
INSTRUMENT: Tenor and Alto Saxophone
OCCUPATION: Tenor Saxophonist, Composer, and Arranger
PERFORMED WITH: Count Basie, Coleman Hawkins, Woody Herman, Red Saunders, Johnny Long, B. B. King, Jesse Miller, Bobby Blue Bland, and Ruth Brown.

I was born at home at 4337 South Dearborn Street. In 1932 I entered Wendell Phillips High School at 244 East Pershing Road, now called 39th Street. In the spring of my freshman year at Phillips, I read in the *Phillipsite*, the school newspaper, that Captain Walter Dyett, the school bandmaster, was looking for talent for a musical. I auditioned because I thought I could sing and dance. Captain Dyett put me in the show but not to sing or dance. He wanted me to imitate Ted

Lewis, the famous white bandleader.

Dyett hired Joe "Ziggy" Johnson, a former student, to come back to school and help him put the show together. Ziggy taught me a few softshoe dance steps, and how to twirl a tophat Ted Lewis style. Since Lewis was a musician, I was given an instrument to hold onstage while a young lady actually played over a microphone backstage. The audience believed I was really playing. After the first show I asked Captain Dyett what that instrument was that I was supposed to be playing. He said it was a clarinet. I said I wanted to learn how to play the clarinet. He told me to sign up for it next semester.

For the next three years I studied clarinet and saxophone with Captain Dyett. In June, 1936, I graduated from high school—the name of Wendell Phillips had been changed to DuSable that year—and looked forward to playing in a professional band.

However we were in the heart of the Great Depression. I couldn't find a salaried job playing music or doing anything else. But after a lot of convincing I was able to wangle a job as a delivery boy at Walgreen's Drug Store at 43rd and Indiana Avenue. I did not get a salary, but I was to be paid five cents for each delivery I made. Word of this got around the neighborhood and people started calling Walgreen's to have everything delivered. The five cent fees mounted so fast that the manager decided it was cheaper to pay me a flat salary of ten dollars a week.

In 1939 several fellows in the neighborhood asked me to join a small band they had organized. Then they made me bandleader, and the group was called Johnny Board and his Twelve Rocking Planks. We got dressed up super sharp every Sunday, as if we were going on a gig, but actually we were only going to rehearse in a vacant garage behind 45th and Calumet Streets. After about two months of rehearsing, we began to attract attention in the neighborhood, as well as some good musicians. We had Melvin Moore on trumpet, Earl Phillips on drums, Johnny Young on piano, Dick Davis on tenor saxophone, Gene Ammons on tenor sax and Benny Green on trombone—guys who were destined to become master musicians. However at that time we were able to get only an occasional gig at social clubs. So I had plenty of opportunity to play gigs with other bands.

Johnny Long, who was an established Chicago bandleader, called me to go on a job with him to Lansing, Michigan. And after that Long got a regular job for the band playing at Squares Lounge on East 51st Street, near Michigan Boulevard. That was my first regular job in show business. I was lucky: that gig gave me the chance to work with real fine musicians. In addition to Johnny Long on trumpet, we had Cleo Napier on piano and Charlie Norris on guitar. The owners of the Squares were known for bringing in good musical acts. Lonnie Johnson, the famous blues-singing guitar player, had just closed at Squares the night we opened. We were keeping some pretty fast company.

Above: Joe "Ziggy" Johnson, dancer and show producer. Below: Lonnie Simmons, famed guitarist and blues singer. Simmons was a legend in his own time.

DuSable High School (above) produced more jazz musicians in the late '30s and '40s under the direction of Captain Walter L. Dyett (below) than any other institution in the country.

In 1941 Coleman Hawkins came through Chicago en route to Cedar Rapids, Iowa, looking for an alto player. Someone recommended me. I was absolutely floored at the opportunity to work with the great Hawk. We worked the Cedar Rapids nightclub six nights a week, and when we finished playing the last set on Sunday morning, Hawk would head back to Chicago because he said he didn't want to spend a weekend in a hick town. He and I would travel back alone; the other fellows wanted to stay over. Hawk always drove a brand-new Cadillac, and we would glide along, sipping his Seagrams Seven and talking. The roads were narrow in those days, and Hawk drove between eighty and a hundred miles an hour. But for some reason, with Hawk behind the wheel, I didn't worry about anything happening.

Hawkins did not write out a musical score for the band. He brought in an alto part one night, a piano part the next and so on, until everyone had a part. I couldn't figure out how he could remember the part he had written the day before or the day before that. Ordinarily an arranger will write a score and then he can see at a glance exactly who is playing what note at any given time, but to write it in segments as Hawk did is remarkable.

It was an education to watch Hawk work out nightly. He made tenor sax playing seem effortless—that is, if you weren't aware of his tremendous musical training and discipline. Although I was playing alto, I was influenced greatly by what he was doing with his tenor. I guess everyone has somebody that they would like

Second from left: Johnny Board. Extreme right: the legendary Coleman Hawkins in Cedar Rapids, Iowa. Note the black ball by Jesse Price's name in background.

Above: On stage at the Garrick Lounge. Left to right: Jesse Miller, trumpet; Rail Wilson, bass; Johnny Board, alto; Hilliard Brown, drums and Aragon "Dense" Thornton, piano. Below: Exterior of Garrick Lounge at Clark and Randolph Streets in Chicago.

Red Allen, the trumpet star of the 1920s and '30s was probably the most underrated musician of that period. His choruses on "Ride Red Ride", "Pardon My Southern Accent" and "Bundles of Blue" were imitated by all aspiring young trumpet players. In fact there were only two schools: the Red Allen school and the Louie Armstrong school.

to sound like. I know many saxophone players made a real effort to imitate Louis Armstrong's trumpet style on their reed instruments. Well, I wanted to sound like Hawk. If you compare working with him to academic training, you could say that a year with Hawk was like working four years in a doctoral program in one of the best universities in the world.

That nightclub we worked in Cedar Rapids had what was called a "blackball" system. On a white wall behind the bandstand they had a chart listing the name of every bandleader who had ever appeared there. If the band had performed well, the bandleader would get a single black star; if the performance was unusually good, he would get two stars; if the performance was poor a black ball would appear beside his name, and that meant he had no chance to be engaged at that club again.

My next significant engagement was in 1944 at the Garrick Theater Lounge in Chicago, next door to the Garrick Theater on West Randolph Street, just west of Clark. I worked there with the late Jesse Miller, a fellow DuSablite and a great trumpet player. We worked upstairs on the stage behind the bar from two in the afternoon until eight in the evening. Red Allen, the trumpet player, had a group working downstairs in the Downbeat Room. Allen's band had Don Stovall on alto and J. C. Higginbotham on trombone. Stuff Smith also had a trio downstairs, with Jimmy Jones on piano and John Levy on bass: John Levy is currently manager for both Nancy Wilson and Joe Williams. Both the Garrick Theater Lounge and the Downbeat Room operated twenty-four hours a day. It was wartime and the sailors and soldiers were in and out of that place like flies on a honeycomb.

Joe Sherman, who managed and owned the clubs, was a prejudiced man. He stood outside the place like a barker and hollered, "Showtime coming up! Showtime coming up!" If black people came up and wanted to come in, he told them it was crowded. If they insisted on coming in anyway, he let them in, but they would be made to feel unwelcome.

On Thursday night when Red Allen's group was off, we would double. The band members were not allowed to circulate among the bar patrons; we had to go directly to our dressing rooms after each set. We played upstairs from two to eight and then downstairs until two in the morning. For a while Ben Webster was working with Red Allen, and Ben would come down and work Thursday nights with us. He was an absolute gas. He had been influenced by Hawk, as many great tenor players were then. But while Hawk's lyrics were a bit punchy, Ben Webster played in a smooth, silky way. Some night there would be three of us on the saxophone—Eddie Johnson, Ben Webster and me—and we would have a ball. Playing with Webster would make you want to go to the woodshed—that is, he made you want to practice.

Betty "Be-Bop" Carter and I joined the Lionel Hampton Band at the same time in 1948. I'll never forget Betty. She was a very aggressive singer who quickly

In the Circle: Hamp urges Johnny Board to blow one more chorus.

earned recognition in the Hampton group. The second song she did with them was "Lady Be Good" in her own vocal style, different from Ella Fitzgerald. Betty's favorite scat syllable was "Shoo-be-do." In fact, she "shoo-be-dooed" so much we nicknamed her "Shoo-be-do." Ella was just the opposite of Betty: she was a non-aggressive singer, low-keyed and even-tempered, who seldom complained about anything. When I worked with Ella with the Basie band she was so pleased with the way we played her music that she gave us a party at the end of the engagement.

I worked with Count Basie for about nine months. I had to leave his band because I fell down a flight of steps and chipped a bone in my ankle while we were playing a Caribbean cruise—an accident that I attribute to racism. It was an English ship and East Indians and Englishmen were waiters: the Englishmen served the patrons on the upper deck and the Indians served those on the lower deck. The Indians never came upstairs, and the Englishmen never went downstairs. One night the Indians were having a dance and we had to go down to play for them. The ship's elevator went about three-fourths of the way down and then you had to walk the rest of the way down a steep flight of steps. That was where I had my accident, and that marked the end of my tour with the great Count Basie.

After my ankle healed I put together a house band for McKee Fitzhugh at his Disc Jockey Lounge in Chicago on 63rd and Cottage Grove. McKee booked a different solo artist into the joint each week, and our trio was the backup. That was an exciting gig. My two favorite artists at McKee's were Sonny Stitt and Gene Ammons. Whenever they came, together or separately, to jam for a week at the Disc Jockey Lounge, we would always be fighting for blood. They would go after me as if I were Coleman Hawkins or Ben Webster.

I remember visiting Gene and Sonny some years later at Cadillac Bob's at 71st and Stony Island. It was my off night, and I just wanted to go out and relax and listen to the cats blow. The first thing Sonny said when I walked in the door was, "Man, where is your horn?"

Gene chimed in, "Yeah, man! Where is your horn? Come on and blow some!"

I said, "Naw, man, I just want to listen to you guys."

"Man!" Sonny said, "You've got to go and get your horn. This might be the last time the three of us play together."

I got a funny feeling when Sonny said that. I got right up and drove to my house and got my horn. I played with them until we blew the house down. Would you believe it? That was the last time that the three of us ever played together because Gene died very shortly after that. Sonny died recently.

I was the musical director for Johnny Ace, who was one of the biggest blues singers in the country in the early '50s. Johnny, who came from Houston, Texas, was so big that the booking agent insisted that you buy B. B. King and Bobby Blue

Above: McKee's Disc Jockey Show Lounge was the site for some of the hottest jazz jam sessions on the South Side of Chicago. Johnny Board is standing in the foreground. Below: Second from left: Gene Ammons. Center: Johnny Board. Extreme right: Sonny Stitt checks out the horn before going to battle.

B. B. King at the mike with his musical director Johnny Board at his right.

Bland as a package if you wanted Johnny Ace. King and Bland were just coming into their own at that time. Things were going well for Johnny, but he did not know how to handle his money. He always acted like a kid. He bought a gun in Florida and treated it like a toy. He and I were the only ones who could drive his car and when we stopped on the road sometimes to relieve ourselves in a field, he would take out the gun and shoot in the air like a child with a cap pistol.

On Christmas night, 1954, we were playing the Auditorium Hotel in Houston and there was a piano player who worked at a tavern across the street. He was running back and forth during intermissions to talk to Johnny in his dressing room, which was full of people drinking and having a good time. Suddenly this fellow said to Johnny, "Man, you've been clicking that gun on everybody. Why don't you click it on yourself?"

Johnny took the gun out and clicked it, and the bullet blew his brains out. We all went back to Memphis with his body and buried him there. I came back to Chicago where I worked during 1955 with a fellow named Al Smith, who was the A & R man for Vee-Jay Records.

In January, 1956, B. B. King called me and asked me to join him. I was delighted, and I worked as his musical director for four years, from 1956 to 1960. B. B. King was a phenomenal musician: he had no formal training but his ear was uncanny, unlike anything I've ever seen. At that time a lot of guitar players used what they called a bar. They changed from one key to another by moving the bar up or down without changing the picking position on the guitar. King never did that. He could go from one key to another effortlessly without a bar. He just used his musical ear. He had a perfect ear for keys and was a natural singer and master of his instrument. The standard key for blues could be B-flat, G, F, E, or E-flat. King played on a lot of sharp keys, like A-natural, B-natural, F-sharp and C-sharp. If you listen to him closely you'll notice that on some numbers his voice is higher and on some it's lower. He may begin a number in B-flat and decide to raise it to E-flat or A-natural and he will modulate into the new key with a voice change to create a certain blues effect. It was all very easy for B. B. He was unlike any musician I have ever worked with. In addition to being talented, he was very nice and gentle. He deserves all the good things that have happened to him.

While I've been travelling around the country, playing various theaters and ballrooms, I've noticed that the size and shape of a room can affect the musicians' performance. I'm thinking of theaters like the Regal in Chicago, the Howard in Washington D.C., the Apollo in New York and the Royal in Baltimore. I always found the Regal the hardest to play because the people in Chicago didn't applaud easily. They were polite and obviously enjoyed what they heard but it was hard to get them to clap. I would give Chicago a rating of ten for being difficult. I think this came from the distance between the band and the audience. The Regal was a much larger theater than the Howard, the Royal or the Apollo, and it had an orchestra pit which pushed the audience at least twenty rows back from the stage. The Apollo, on the other hand, was so tight that you were practically sitting in the audience. You could reach out and touch the patrons. The Apollo crowd was warm and responded—positively, if they liked you. If they didn't like you, you had to watch out for the boos and the rotten eggs that might collide with your head.

Today I'm playing the Gaslight Club in Chicago where I've worked for some years and I find that very comfortable. It's a small stage and people are sitting around you on all sides. There is good eye contact which enables you to stay in touch with the audience. Without a barometer an entertainer may never touch base.

Cab Calloway

"We could not eat or sleep where we played."

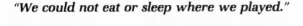

Cab Calloway

BIRTHDATE: December 25, 1907
BIRTHPLACE: Rochester, New York
OCCUPATION: Bandleader and Vocalist

My family moved from Rochester, New York, to Baltimore, Maryland, in 1919. We stayed with my father's mother, who lived at 1017 Druid Hill Avenue in the all-colored section of Baltimore. Grandma Calloway was the most rigid woman I have ever met. She wouldn't let us do anything. We weren't allowed to play on the streets with other kids or even play in the house. It was like being in a prison. Therefore, by the time I reached my fourteenth birthday, I had become one of the most rebellious, stubborn, unrelenting black sons-of-bitches you've ever wanted to meet. I played hooky from school and hung out on the streets where I hustled money and was always in trouble. In fact, I was so incorrigible that my folks sent me off to Downington Industrial and Agricultural School in Downingtown, Pennsylvania. It was a Baptist-church-run boarding school managed by my grand-uncle who pastored a church in Philadelphia, Pennsylvania. They called it an industrial school, but it was really a reform school for bad boys like myself.

My mother was a teacher in the Baltimore public schools, and my father was a lawyer, and I guess having a son like me around was an embarrassement because I spent more time at the racetrack than I spent in the schoolroom. I used to hang out at the Pimlico Race Track which was just outside of Baltimore; hustling and playing the races. The racehorse fever is still in my blood some sixty years later. How I succeeded in life is a mystery. However, I did succeed and I have to attribute a great deal of my success to my sister, Blanche, who was six years older than I, and a natural gifted entertainer. I was stubborn and in the crevices of my mind, I felt maybe I could do it better. That was a tall order by any measure.

It was in the summer of 1927 that Blanche came back to Baltimore in a musical called *The Plantation Days.* The show was at the Royal Theater down on Pennsylvania Avenue and I went down everyday to watch her and of course admire her singing, dancing, and that personality-plus that she always put into selling a song.

The Plantation Days was one of the biggest hits of the 1920s. While hanging around the theater I got to know everybody in the show, roughly about twenty-five people, in addition to the sixteen-piece house orchestra. Because Blanche was one of the *Plantation Days* stars, I felt that I should be a part, although I had had no real show experience. I knew I had some vocal and dancing talents, but nothing that I had ever attempted to sell professionally.

Blanche Calloway with her baby brother, Cab.

During the second week, while the show was in Baltimore a member of the quartet became ill. They were looking for a replacement. So I approached Blanche and told her that she had to do whatever was necessary to get me that part. Blanche discouraged me: she said that show business was a bad life and no way for a person to live. She said it required an extensive amount of traveling and it could be bad for my health. Her sage advice didn't deter me one bit. I became more determined to be a part of show business, and I pleaded with Blanche to give me some assistance. Blanche finally relented and said, "OK, Cab. I think it's a dumb thing for a kid as smart as you to go into this lousy show business, but I'll get you an audition if you promise me that when the show reaches Chicago, you'll enroll in college."

Well, the idea of my getting into the show and going to Chicago was mind-boggling, and for that opportunity, I would promise anything. I promised her that I would enroll in school as soon as we got to Chicago. Blanche got the audition for me and I won the part. I was given the juvenile position of high tenor in the quartet.

The show arrived in Chicago in August of 1927 and we opened at the Grand Theater, which was located at 3110 South State Street. The crowds were absolutely incredible. I had never seen such enthusiastic theater crowds as those at the Grand Theater. The people would jump up and down, scream, stomp their feet, and just generally have a good time. The performers reacted in kind by giving them their best performances. After two weeks, the show closed and Blanche took me down to Crane College and helped me enroll. The curriculum was pretty heavy, but I was determined to make it in college, so for the first three or four months I literally buried myself in books and forgot everything else. In January, 1928, I asked Watly, who was the hustler my sister Blanche lived with, where I could get a part-time job singing. Blanche reminded me that I had promised her that I would make good in school. I assured her that I felt I could successfully handle a part-time singing job along with my studies. Watly took me to a place at 3518 South State Street called the Dreamland Cafe. That was where I got my first gig in Chicago. The Dreamland at that time was managed by a fellow named Bill Bottoms, who subsequently became a chef for Joe Louis during his championship years.

I was very agile and athletic so I joined the basketball team at Crane College. While at Crane I heard that the Harlem Globetrotters were looking for some players so a friend of mine named Toots Wright and I went over to the gym and practiced with the Trotters. Abe Sapperstein, the owner of the team, watched us play for about an hour and then offered both of us a job. When I told Blanche that I had an opportunity to travel with the Globetrotters, she argued that there was no way in the world I could travel with the Trotters and also go to college. So I scrapped the idea of becoming a professional basketball player. However, I have remained an active baseball and basketball player throughout the years. I think that there is a definite relationship between the energy that I'm able to exert on the stage and my continuous program of exercise.

After I had worked about four or five months at the Dreamland, Watly told me he could get me into the Sunset Cafe, which was located at 35th and Calumet. That was some class joint. The Sunset was the most popular club on the South Side. There were several black and tan clubs within the same block on East 35th Street. The Plantation was right across the street, and next to the Plantation was the Nest, which was located on the second floor over a candy shop. It was a small, intimate nightclub with a lot of class.

The Sunset, like the Cotton Club in New York, had first-class entertainment with beautiful chorus girls, a ten-piece band, comedians, and solo tap dancers. At that time, Carroll Dickerson had the band and Louis Armstrong was the featured trumpet player and Earl Hines was on the piano. I was the house singer. It was at that Sunset gig that I first became intimately acquainted with Louis Armstrong. I had been one of his fans for years. I dug his singing; it always got to me. I have often wondered how one man could have so many talents and still have his feet on the ground. Louie was the kind of guy that you could talk to. In fact, anybody could talk to Louis. He was just that kind of person. A real solid human being. Louie was certainly one of the main influences in my career. I used to hear Louie play his favorite songs, "Muskrat Ramble", "Gut Bucket Blues", "You're Next", and the "Oriental Strut". In addition to that, Louis would sing, and everything he did was full of rhythm and fire. He was a scat singer even before scat singing was popular. I guess Louie was the fellow who originated scat singing. I subsequently put his scat material in my own act when I started to work at the Cotton Club a year or so later, with all the hi-de-hoing. It was Louis Armstrong's creative scat-singing that freed us all from straight lyrics.

In May of 1929, I left Chicago with a band called the Alabamians and went on the road. We worked various cities throughout the Midwest, but our destination was New York City, where we arrived in November, 1929, and opened at the Savoy Ballroom. I'll never forget that our opening was approximately one month after the big stock market crash of October, 1929, where investors had lost something in excess of forty billion dollars, and more than six million people were out of work, 5,000 banks had failed, 32,000 businesses had gone bankrupt. There were bread lines everywhere and near-riots in New York because of hunger. It seems that everybody in the country was mad at dear old Herbert Hoover, the man who said that "prosperity was just around the corner". But it's a funny thing that during depressions and recessions, the entertainment business, particularly at certain levels, seems to thrive. In 1929, the entertainment business in New York City and in Chicago was actually booming: just as in our recent depressions of the middle

Louis Armstrong.

The Alabamians, 1927. Left to right: Ralph Anderson, Marion Hardy (alto and leader), Warner Seals, Lawrence Harrison (front man) Artie Starks Red (banjo), Jimmy McHendrick (drums), Eddie Mallory, Elisha Herbert, Charlie Turner (tuba), Henry Clark. The Alabamians in late 1928 featured Cab Calloway as front man and migrated to New York to play the Savoy Ballroom, there opposing the Missourians. Calloway later quit the Alabamians to front the Missourians.

'70s, when although many people were out of work, entertainers were actually doing well in cities like Chicago, Los Angeles, Las Vegas, New York, and Washington, D.C. I guess when things are bad, people want to be entertained.

I thought that the Alabamians and I were pretty hot stuff when we hit New York City, and were booked into the Savoy Ballroom. However, they had a two-band policy at the Savoy. Cecil Scott was the band playing opposite us. Cecil Scott was a saxophone player. He and his brother, Lloyd, were from Springfield, Ohio. Those Scott boys were a bitch, to say the least. They were the most exciting, fiery, horn-blowing guys in Harlem, and of course when you compared what they were doing to what we were doing, we sounded like a Mickey Mouse band. In fact, we were so bad that on our first night, Charlie Buchanan came up to us with a scowl on his face and said, "I'm sorry, fellows, but you've had your chance. You've got to go." We had a two-week contract and on our first night we got our two-week notice. We were just terrible.

I was so furious I was livid. I started screaming and hollering at the members of the band, "Dammit, I told you guys that you couldn't come into New York play-ing that jive music! This ain't Toledo or Mendota. This is New York, and in New York, you've got to swing! After this gig, I'm splitting. I just can't stay with you guys any longer. You can go back to Chicago or whatever you want to do, but as far as I'm concerned, it's all over."

The Savoy Ballroom management was in a dilemma. They had a two-week contract with our Mickey Mouse band. Charlie Buchanan came up with a brilliant idea to start trying to develop some business during our two-week stay so he staged what was called a battle of the bands: the Alabamians, which I was direc-ting, were to battle the Missourians, who were a group of fine musicians. They were not in the same class with Chick Webb, King Oliver, Duke Ellington or Jim-mie Lunceford, but they too ran us off the bandstand. The Missourians made the Alabamians look like the Mickey Mouses that we truly were. But I was singing and running up and down the bandstand getting audience participation and behaving like a character on the stage, while I was directing the band. It was my clowning and my ability to get the audience involved that enabled our group to win the battle of the bands. I know deep in my heart that our winning had nothing to do with what we were doing musically. It was what I was doing as an entertainer.

After that last night, the Alabamians left town and I was stuck in New York without a job, like millions of other guys across the country. I had enough dough to get along for awhile, but I needed some work. I went to see Louis Armstrong, who was doubling on two jobs at that time in New York City. He was playing with Connie's *Hot Chocolates* down on Broadway at the Hudson Theater, and then also playing out at Connie's Inn. I went to Louis and said: "Pops, maybe I can do a little jazz singing or something up here to help you keep the crowd while you are down at the Hudson Theater." Louie replied, "Kid, I don't think I can do that because the show at Connie's Inn is all set." But the very next words out of his mouth were, "Hey, they need a singer for *Hot Chocolates.*"

Connie's *Hot Chocolates* was one of the biggest all-colored revues ever to hit Broadway. It was like *Blackbirds* and *Shuffle-Along*. It had been running at the Hudson Theater for almost a year when I joined the show. I replaced a fellow named Paul Bass. He was a juvenile lead and the songs that I sang in the show were "Ain't Misbehavin", "Sweet Savannah Sue", "Goddess of Rain", and "Rhythm Man". Man, was I happy. *Plantation Days* had been small potatoes compared to Connie's *Hot Chocolates*. All of a sudden I was making $100 a week and hitting the boards on the street of the bright lights . . . Broadway!

After I was with the *Hot Chocolates* about a month, the show went on the road, and our first stop was Philadelphia, and from there we went to Boston, where we played the Tremont Theater. I was at the Tremont when Charlie

The Benny Moten band in Kansas City, Missouri. Count Basie (seated left), Jimmy Rushing (center), and Benny Moten (right).

Buchanan, the manager of the Savoy, came up from New York and asked me to leave the show and come back to the Savoy Ballroom to lead the Missourians. The Missourians had been heavily influenced by Benny Moten, a native of Kansas City, a real giant, and one of the least recognized pianists and composers of the '20s and the early '30s. He attracted stars to his band like Hot Lips Page, Joe Keys, Eddie Bearfield, Howlin Leonard, Walter Page, and Eddie Durham; and Count Basie was his second piano player. In fact, the Basie band was an outgrowth of the Moten band after Moten's death in 1935. The Missourians had definitely been exposed to that Kansas City environment and you could feel that Kansas City drive in the rhythm section, and the way those cats blew their horns.

When I returned to New York, I found that instead of going straight into the Savoy, "The Home of Happy Feet", with the Missourians, we were scheduled to open up a beautiful new club in Harlem called the Plantation Club. The Plantation Club, at 126th Street near Lenox Avenue, had been set up to compete with the Cotton Club, which was located a little further uptown at 142nd and Lenox Avenue.

The Plantation was to be a fine place. It had a seating capacity of 500 people, the same as the Cotton Club. It was designed to look like an old Southern Plantation with slave log cabins and so forth, exactly like the Cotton Club. The show was to be a big revue. The Plantation people really intended to get their share of some of those big dollars from the people downtown who were coming uptown to enjoy the Harlem moon and get their kicks. We rehearsed and worked like dogs to get that act down pat.

On Saturday afternoon after we finished rehearsing, we went home to await the opening that night at nine o'clock. When we returned to the club that evening, we found it in shreds. Everything had been torn up. All of the music was torn up, along with the costumes, and the place was a total wreck. Even the dance floor was chopped up. The Cotton Club mob, which also owned Connie's Inn, had decided that they didn't want any competition coming up there and elbowing in on their action, so they ran the other gang out. That was a fine club in Harlem that never opened.

So we went back to the Savoy Ballroom and played for a week or so until a fellow by the name of Moggie L. Wilson got us a gig down on the east side of New York around 2nd Avenue. After that gig we went to play in another club called the Krazy Kat down on 48th and Broadway in the basement under McGuinesses Restaurant. We had been playing in this club for about three weeks when one night after our last show, the head waiter came over to me and said: "There are some fellows over there who want to talk to you."

"Who in the hell are they?" I asked. "I'm beat, man. I don't want to see nobody tonight."

Cab and Lena.

"You'd better see them, Cab," he said. His tone of voice indicated that he was serious.

I walked across the room to a table in the corner where four guys were standing, all wearing long coats, and big white brimmed hats. One of them had on shades. I could tell from their appearance that they had to be part of the mob. I was cool outside but I was scared as hell inside. I said to myself as I walked across the floor, What the hell have I done this time?

The guy wearing the shades said, "Sit down!"

I sat down.

"Who's booking you?" he asked.

I replied, "Moe Gale."

"Yeah, well, you tell Moe Gale that we want you and your band up in Harlem at the Cotton Club."

I said, "You've got to be kidding."

The one guy with a snarl on his face said: "We ain't kidding, Cabbie boy. We want you at the Cotton Club."

"But Duke Ellington is at the Cotton Club," I said.

He said, "Look, Dukie is going on the road and he's going to make a film in Hollywood while he's on tour. We need a replacement and you are it. Be up at the Cotton Club tomorrow afternoon to start rehearsal."

"But I can't leave this gig. I've got a contract. The whole band is under contract. You've got to talk to my manager, Moe Gale, about this. This is his obligation. I can't do anything."

The four guys stood up and I said to myself, Gee, these are some rough looking dudes. The guy with the shades said, "We'll talk to Moe Gale. Just you and your band be up at the Cotton Club at two o'clock tomorrow afternoon to rehearse the show. That's all you've got to worry about." Then they left. They walked past me without saying another word.

Moe Gale came into my dressing room before I had an opportunity to tell the boys in the band what had happened. I could tell from the expression on his face that the boys from the Cotton Club had already talked to him.

He said: "Cab, the Cotton Club boys want you. I guess you'd better tell the other men in the band to be up at the Cotton Club tomorrow afternoon."

I had never seen Moe Gale look so bad and inwardly I had never felt so good. I didn't ask any questions. I knew better. The Cotton Club mob had just bought my contract and the Missourians' contract the easy way. Pure muscle. I subsequently learned that they had not cut Moe out entirely. Out of the goodness of their hearts, they had let him keep ten percent of my contract at the Cotton Club until they learned the following week that Moe had me under a personal contract for $100 a week for ten years. They said to hell with that, tore up Moe Gale's contract and gave me an instant raise to $200.

Above: Duke Ellington's 1929 Cotton Club Band. First left: Tricky Sam Nanton, standing: third from left, Sonny Greer (drummer), Ellington, Fred Guy, Welman Broad. Seated second from right: Johnny Hodges. Seated third from right: Otto Hardwick. Below: Cab Calloway's 1930 Cotton Club Band.

Cab Calloway.

Cab and Duke.

I had seen some fantastic shows in Chicago, but nothing to compare with the Cotton Club revue. The club ran two revues a year. One opened in September and the other in April. There was usually a month's break in March to prepare for the spring show, and a month's break in August to prepare for the fall show. The opening night for both shows were comparable to a Hollywood or Broadway premiere. Unfortunately, the brothers and sisters of Harlem were never to witness anything other than a curb-stone revue, where they watched the Cadillacs, Rolls Royces, Dusenbergs, and other long luxury cars, roll up to the front door of the Cotton Club with fancy-dressed ladies and formally attired men from midtown Manhattan.

Some of the finest Negro musicians in the country played at the Cotton Club, and accepted their Jim Crow policies. The money was good, the audience and owners respected us and our music. I can assure you that I didn't condone the clubs' racist policies, but what else could I do against the existing social order of that day? I doubt seriously that jazz could have survived if black musicians hadn't gone along with the racial practices of the Cotton Club, Connie's Inn, the Grand

Joe Louis and Cab.   *A young Calloway in 1930.*

Terrace in Chicago, and many other clubs througout America that entertained white patrons with black jazz artists.

I felt with the Cotton Club engagement that I was at the height of my career. I was only twenty-two years old, and Ellington at the time was thirty. I was so impressed with Duke that I literally felt like a kid beside him. I had the greatest admiration for him. He had made it big the hard way. He had the top band in the country without any doubt. There was no competition to Duke Ellington. I remember the first words Duke spoke to me. He came over where I was standing and said, "How are you doing, man?" And all I could say was, "Fine, man, fine." Duke's next words were, "Glad you could make the change. You've got a nice little band."

He told me that if I did a good job they might add some more pieces to my band. He felt that my band should be increased from ten to sixteen piees.

From that point on, my relationship with Duke was strictly business. Duke was scheduled to spend the summer of 1930 in Hollywood doing the Amos and Andy film *Check and Double Check.*

Duke Ellington's Orchestra originally came to the Cotton Club in December, 1927, as a replacement of the King Oliver band from Chicago. In fact, the entire original Cotton Club staff, including the band, was imported from Chicago. The late Jack Johnson, the world's former heavyweight champion, opened the nightery as the Club Deluxe in 1926. The name was subsequently changed to the Cotton Club when the mob took over and bought Johnson out. Before the Cotton Club gig, Duke Ellington and his Washingtonians, as they were called at that time, had been gigging at a place called Club Barron's in Harlem, and earlier, they played at a night spot known as the Kentucky Club down in midtown Manhattan. However, from the first night Duke struck up his jungle rhythm on the stage of the Cotton Club, that club was never the same. He blew it away. He set a standard of music and musicianship with a harmonic quality that has not been equalled by any band up to this day. Duke Ellington's Cotton Club Band included such stars as Sonny Greer on drums, Charlie Irvis on trombone, Elmer Snowden on banjo, Otto Hardwich and Johnny Hodges on saxes, Tricky Sam Nanton and Juan Tizol on trombones, Cootie Williams on trumpet, Fred Guy on guitar, and Wellman Braud on bass. Man! Those were some heavy cats and that was a bad band.

Ellington's reputation started soaring shortly after he commenced his Cotton Club engagement, because the two new radio networks, NBC and CBS, began to carry his half hour show live over national hookup, and people all over the country used to tune in nightly to dig this new jungle sound coming out of New York City—and created by the fabulous Duke Ellington.

We were fortunate that the same networks carried my band's broadcast live nightly from the Cotton Club and it was only a relatively short time before the Calloway Orchestra began to get requests to go on the road making appearances at theaters, dance halls, and nightclubs throughout the country. By late 1933, both Ellington and Calloway bands were in such demand nationally and internationally, that a third orchestral replacement was brought into the Cotton Club. In January, 1934, the fine band of Jimmie Lunceford was brought into the Cotton Club, because Duke and I were continually on the road.

Those road trips were only for the young and pure in heart. We moved around the country from town to town by bus over bumpy roads, and usually in the dead of the night, looking for someplace to sleep until we opened at our next gig. In those days, we weren't allowed to stay in any of the main hotels in the cities and towns in which we played, so everywhere we went, we had a list of Negro families that would rent us rooms. If we had a theater engagement and were going to be in town for a week, sometimes we would have to spread out all over town with these beautiful black folks who let us have lodging and fed us delicious soul food for as little as ten dollars a week. I can still taste those greens and black-eye peas. They were some of the best-cooked meals I had ever tasted in my life. Traveling on the road for black musicians and entertainers would have been impossible if it hadn't been for the graciousness and hospitality of those lovely people who opened their homes to us and made us comfortable. I have always appreciated the kind of treatment that black people gave Negro musicians and entertainers who were on the road. Thousands of families in the Midwest and South opened their homes to thousands of musicians, singers, dancers, comedians and made it possible for us to entertain America. We couldn't have done those road shows if it hadn't been for such warm, loving, gentle folk who treated us like family whenever we were in their town. That practice existed up until the 1950s when some of the lily-white hotels began to admit Negroes.

I remember the first time we played a hotel in Las Vegas in the 1930s. There were only three hotels there at the time, and we were playing at the Last Frontier Hotel. They wouldn't permit us to enter the front door, so we had to come in the back through the kitchen. When we got off the bandstand and finished for the night, we had to go back out through the kitchen and to the colored section of town which was across the railroad tracks. I remember once in 1948 or '49, when we were playing the Sahara Hotel, there was a motor home for "Colored Entertainers Only" in back of the Sahara where we had to eat, drink and spend our time during intermission after we had played our sets. Again we would have to go through the kitchen to the bar, because I was doing lounge work with a smaller band at that time. The big band era had ended.

A funny thing happened to us as a result of Jim Crow practices during that stay in Las Vegas. Remember, our motor home was used as a dressing room, waiting room, dining room and any other function you can think of. We weren't permitted to order any food at the hotel. So if we wanted to eat between shows,

The 1941 Cab Calloway Band. (Front row): Calloway, leader/vocalist; Jerry Blake, clarinet/baritone sax; Hilton Jefferson, alto; Andy Brown, alto; Walter "Foots" Thomas, tenor; (Second row): Danny Barker, guitar; Keg Johnson, Tyree Glenn, Quentin "Butter" Jackson, trombones; (Back row): Dizzy Gillespie, Lamar Wright, Jonah Jones, trumpets.

we had to travel all the way back across town to the colored section to get carry-outs. There was a soul brother who worked at the Sahara who pushed the food cart by our motor home each evening enroute to the dining room and the lounge. Every night, he would stop and load us up with chops, steaks, salads and some of the finest side dishes you ever wanted to eat. The brother gave it to us for nothing, simply because he resented the fact that the white folks would not let us eat in the hotel where we worked.

On another occasion, we were playing a dance down in Ft Lauderdale, Florida. In the south, we played a white dance one night and a colored dance the next night. If we played white and colored on the same night, they would put a rope down the middle of the warehouse. They used to have dances in tobacco warehouses at that time, and there would be as many as 5000 people out on the warehouse floor. Blacks on one side of the floor and whites on the other side, divided by a rope. On this particular occasion in Ft Lauderdale, there was a white girl in the audience who must have been juiced or something, but she wanted to get to me. Now remember, in addition to the rope being down the center of the warehouse, they also roped off the band, because the band was colored and had to be quarantined too.

Somehow this gal got up on the bandstand. I don't know how in the hell she got up there, but she walked right up to me and kissed me in front of 5000 people. You've never heard such angry screaming and moaning from that audience, both blacks and whites, as I heard that night. Well, man, I nearly died! I said, "Lord, have mercy." I knew that that was the end for me. Those crackers were not going to let me get out of there alive. Luck was on my side because there was a trap door on the stage that led to an alley. The manager rushed us through that underground passageway below the trap door and we made it back to the bus for a fast exit out of town. Hey, the man up there let me escape from those mothers in Ft Lauderdale because he knew I had a lot of Hi-de-Hoing to do. I have been both the King of Hi-de-Ho, and Sporting Life.

Back in the late '30s and early '40s, people used to say I had forty suits and forty pairs of shoes. They were wrong. I had fifty suits and fifty pairs of shoes with fifty pairs of pearl gray gloves to match. Man, they said I had lost millions of dollars. They were right. However, the counting hasn't stopped yet. Travis, I have done it all. Women, horses, cars and clothes. Do you know what that's called? It's called living.

People should grab a hold on life and live it to the hilt. Now if you ain't got it, you'd better get it. Find a girl and don't you quit it. Keep on balling cause you got to get to getting while the getting is good. Life is a fleeting and old age is a creeping. You got to get to getting while the getting is good. When you get old and the gals get cold, what can you do? You can't love like you should, therefore, you better get to getting while the getting's good.

The author and Cab Calloway in the home of Mr. & Mrs. Charles Collins in January, 1983.

AUTHOR'S NOTE

Cab Calloway became one of my musical heroes when I was eleven years old and first heard him broadcasting from the New York City Cotton Club in 1931. I finally got an opportunity to meet Cab in 1936 at Local 208 of the Musicians' Union. I was sixteen years old. Since Cab hired some of the best musicians in the business, he directed bands that were always in the top ten in earnings and popularity.

Cab considers the highlights of his career to be the gig at the Cotton Club, his starring role in the 1943 movie *Stormy Weather,* and his 1950s role as "Sporting Life" in *Porgy and Bess.* In my opinion, *Hello Dolly* did not come alive until the Pearl Bailey and Cab Calloway rendition of it hit the boards on Broadway.

Floyd Campbell

"I was the first male to record the blues."

Floyd Campbell

BIRTHDATE: **September 17, 1901**
BIRTHPLACE: **Helena, Arkansas**
INSTRUMENT PLAYED: **Drums**
OCCUPATION: **Bandleader**
FEATURED WITH: **Jabbo Smith, Louis Armstrong, Charlie Creath,
Fate Marable and Al Trent**

The summer that I finished high school, in 1917, I went to St Louis and worked as a dining car waiter on the Pennsylvania Railroad. When I returned to Little Rock, I entered Philander Smith College. That was my annual routine until 1922.

My father owned a barber shop and pool hall around the corner from the Dixie Drug Store, which was owned by a white man named Jack Greenfield. In Prohibition days drug stores with soda fountains were meeting places for people with dry throats. Greenfield sold them medicine that was ninety percent alcohol. He called his medicine "Jamaica Ginger" and "Orange Peel". You could get as high

Mr. Jack Greenfield

Jack Greenfield (white slacks, in front of truck), owner of the Dixie Drug Company which specialized in a potent drink called "Jamaica Ginger". Floyd Campbell (second from left on truck), was hired to drum up the trade, while Zilner T. Randolph (third from left) manned the saxophone.

as a kite on just a small bottle of that stuff. Greenfield was selling so much of his concoction on Friday, Saturday and Sunday nights that he hired a piano player and drummer to entertain the customers while they were waiting to be served. Since I had become known as a pretty good singer in high school, and I had always been attracted to music, I would slip away from my dad's place on Saturday nights to sing a few songs in Greenfield's Drug Store. Customers, both drunk and sober, seemed to like my singing. And the owner was impressed.

In 1922 my mother died. I was getting ready to return to St Louis to continue working as a railroad waiter when Mr Greenfield said that if I would stay in Helena, he would send to Memphis, Tennessee, for a set of drums for me and pay me five dollars a night while I was learning to play them. This sounded good to me.

The regular drummer with the duet, a guy called Slick, got so drunk by ten o'clock that he couldn't find his drums. So the piano player asked me to get behind the drums and just keep time. In a couple of weeks I had reached such proficiency on the drums that Mr Greenfield felt comfortable enough with me to fire Slick after rousing him from one of his drunken stupors. I was determined not to rest on my laurels. So I looked for new ideas from every minstrel show, circus and carnival that came to town. Then along came Zilner T. Randolph, who taught me to read drum music. I sent off to St Louis and Chicago for drum books. Then I practiced the lessons out of the books and more or less taught myself from that point on.

Greenfield's "Jamaica Ginger" was selling so well that in 1923 he let me enlarge the drugstore band to five pieces. Z. T. Randolph joined us, playing the alto sax. Randolph later switched to the trumpet, and he also wrote "Ol Man Mose is Dead" with Louis Armstrong. We also had Cranston Hamilton on the piano and Peter Patterson on the banjo. There were other players whose names escape me now. When I left the drugstore gig in late 1923, my place was taken by Louis Jordan, another Arkansas boy, who became famous in the late '30s as the leader of the Tympany Five.

I jobbed around Memphis for several months and then went to St Louis in 1924 where I got the opportunity to play in Charlie Creath's band. In 1924 and '25 the band recorded for the Okeh Recording Company. On one of the recording dates in 1924 I sang "The Market Street Blues" and made history as the first male ever recorded singing the blues. Stars like Mamie Smith, Clara Smith, Bessie Smith, Ma Rainey, Ida Cox, Sarah Martin and other women had recorded the blues, but no man. White bands had not yet started playing blues. In 1925 I recorded "I Woke up Cold in Hand", "My Daddy Rocks Me with One Steady Roll", and "Every Man that Wears Bell-Bottom Britches (Ain't No Monkey Man)", which I wrote myself, for Okeh Records. The players on those record dates were Charlie Creath and Leonard Davis on trumpet, Charles Lawson on trombone, William Blue, William Rollins and Sammy Long on saxes, Peter Patterson on banjo, Pops Foster on bass, and me on the drums and the vocal.

In 1926 I joined Fate Marable's band on the steamer *St Paul,* an excursion boat. Louis Armstrong had played on the *St Paul* with Marable a few years earlier. I always enjoyed hearing the cats in the band talk about the time Louis got fired at Burlington, Iowa, for fighting on the boat. They said that Louis Armstrong was a pitiful sight sitting on a box waiting for the train to come and take him home. Louis was crying rain drops and wailing, "What will I do now?" Even then a better trumpeter than Louis could not be found. He had not been back in New Orleans a week when Joe Oliver heard he was available and sent for him to join his band at the Royal Gardens in Chicago.

In the fall of 1927 I organized Floyd Campbell's Singing Synco Seven Orchestra. The following spring I got a gig playing a battle of music against Al Trent's band on the *St Paul*. Jesse Johnson, the dance promoter, hired Armstrong, who was playing with the Carroll Dickerson Orchestra at the Savoy Ballroom in Chicago, to come to St Louis to front my band for $100 a night for two nights, plus travel and living expenses. That was an unheard of figure to pay a colored musician for a gig in those days.

"Louis Armstrong versus Al Trent in a Battle of the Bands" was a financial success but a public relations failure. The promoter made no attempt to limit the number of tickets he sold, and five thousand people crowded aboard the steamer, dangerously overloading it. The captain was afraid the boat would capsize and he returned abruptly to St Louis, angering the crowd but possibly saving the lives of thousands of jazz lovers.

After Louis Armstrong returned to Chicago, he wrote me several letters thanking me for the food and companionship in St Louis. He had told me while he was in St Louis that if things did not work out for me there, I should come to Chicago, and he would try to get me a good gig. When I finally came to Chicago on May 9, 1930, there was plenty of work for musicians. It was much better than St Louis. I used to say that there were at least one hundred and ten full-time musicians working at salaries of up to seventy-five dollars a week within a one block radius of 47th Street and South Parkway. There were two bands at the Regal Theater and three large orchestras working at the Savoy Ballroom. Bud Byron's ten-piece band was working at Chin Chow's Restaurant on the second floor at 4709 South Parkway, and across the boulevard at the Metropolitan Theater there was Erskine Tate's large pit symphony orchestra. Chicago was a musicians' town. I was there only two days when I got a job for forty dollars a week, plus tips, playing with the Freddie Williams Orchestra at an exclusive North Side nightspot. That gig lasted about two months. The next job, which lasted six months, was just a couple of blocks away at a speakeasy called Club Max, at 11 East Pearson Street. Louis Armstrong was playing downtown at a place called the Showboat at Lake and Dearborn. It was a major Loop syndicate-controlled bookie operation during the day and a speakeasy at night. Louie's contract was about to expire, and Sam Beers, the owner, wanted to get another trumpet player to head the band that replaced him. Louis told Beers that the fellow who played most like him was Jabbo Smith.

"Where can I find this fellow Smith?" Beers asked.

Louis told Beers that Smith was working in a nightclub called the Wisconsin Roof Garden in Milwaukee. Beers went to Milwaukee, heard Jabbo, and came back and told Louis, "That's my man!"

After Beers hired Jabbo Smith, Louie told him there was a drummer in town he would like to see working. Louie said his name was Floyd Campbell and he was from St Louis. That's how Jabbo and I got together. Jabbo was an excellent

A letter from Louis Armstrong to Floyd Campbell, expressing gratitude for two $100 a night gigs in St. Louis.

trumpet player, but he had no head for business. He turned all the business of running the band over to me. We worked together at the Showboat for almost a year. Every night that we worked, I compared Jabbo with Louis. I decided that although Jabbo was not as creative as Louis, he could play anything on the trumpet that Louie played. I remember one night at the Savoy Louie was blowing his heart out when Jabbo asked Louie if he could use his horn. Everybody looked at Jabbo as if to say, "What's that fool doing asking the great Louis Armstrong for his horn?" You may not remember, but the most difficult thing Louis ever played was the introduction to "West End Blues." Jabbo played that entire song, note for note, just like Louie. Everybody except me was amazed. After that night nobody doubted Jabbo's musical ability. Jabbo was nonchalant, but he could play the trombone as well as he could play the trumpet. And he was good on the piano too.

Jabbo had gotten his musical training at the Jenkins Orphanage in Charleston, South Carolina, where he had been placed when he was six years old.They taught him trumpet, trombone and piano, and he toured with the orphanage band when he was ten. At sixteen he left the orphanage a "cracker jack" musician.

Roy Eldridge was influenced heavily by Jabbo's fast technique in the high note register. After we closed at the Showboat I went to Milwaukee with Jabbo to work his old gig at the Wisconsin Roof Garden. Roy Eldridge was in Milwaukee with a group called Johnny Neal's Midnight Ramblers, and Roy and Jabbo would get together after work and jam until the next afternoon. Roy really grew up in those sessions. It was in Milwaukee that Roy started playing those high B-flats and A's rapidly like Jabbo Smith, who was a true technician.

In January, 1933, Jabbo and I went back to Chicago looking for work. A fellow named Ben Tolliver, from Gary, Indiana, had opened a bookie joint at 307 East 58th Street. When Prohibition was repealed in February, 1933, Tolliver converted the book into a nightclub which he called the Panama Cafe. We worked there for two years.

Dave Young, the former tenor sax player with both the Roy Eldridge and Fletcher Henderson bands, still tells how he replaced Floyd Campbell's tenor sax man, Bud Johnson, at the Panama for one night. He had never heard Jabbo Smith, but he thought Smith acted arrogant, and he wanted to teach him a lesson.

"I played my six best choruses of 'Lady Be Good'," Young says. "And finally Jabbo touched me on the shoulder and said, 'When you finish, give me eight bars.' I am here to tell you that Jabbo Smith played more music in those eight bars than I played all night!"

Eddie Cole's band, featuring his younger brother Nat "King" Cole on piano, followed my aggregation into the Panama in 1935. That same year I married LaBertha Roberts, Johnnie Dunne's sister. She was a piano player and led a band

Above: Freddie Williams, bandleader, second from left; Floyd Campbell, center; and Louie. Below: Left to right: Gideon Honore; Bud Johnson; Floyd Campbell; and Jabbo Smith in 1933 at the Panama Cafe in Chicago.

that was very popular with the South Side social club set. After our marriage we merged our bands, and the result was called the Roberts/Campbell Orchestra. Her brother Johnnie had played with the W. C. Handy Orchestra from 1916 to 1920, and was among the first to popularize the jazz trumpet. He recorded the famous "Sugar Blues" trumpet solo with Mamie Smith's Jazz Hounds. When my wife died in 1939 I continued to play our social clubs with the Floyd Campbell Orchestra.

The late 1930s and early '40s were the heyday of club dances in Chicago. We played four and five club gigs a week at places like Bacon's Casino, Savoy Ballroom, Warwick Hall, Forum Hall, the Binga Arcade Ballroom, the Vincennes Hotel Grand Ballroom and Blue Heaven Hall. On March 9, 1940, we opened the new Parkway Ballroom at 4557 South Parkway.

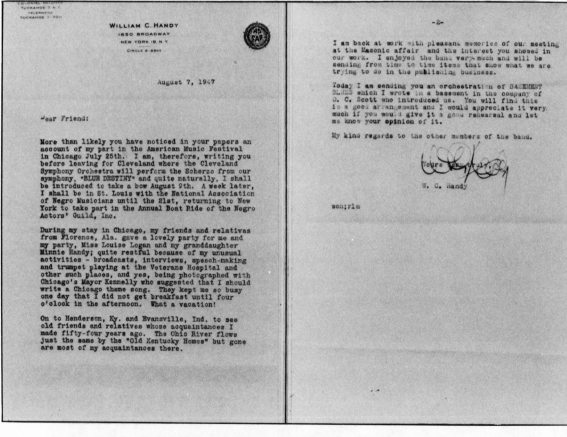

A letter from W. C. Handy to Floyd Campbell after visiting Campbell in Chicago.

Walter Dyett used to accuse me of sleeping at the Parkway because we played there so regularly. For example, we would move our instruments into the Parkway on Christmas Eve and they would stay there until after New Year's Day. One formal dance after another was given by clubs like the Chicago Assembly, the Original Forty Club, the Snakes, the Druids, the Frogs, the AKAs, the Alphas, the Kappas, the Green Donkeys, the Juggs and hundreds of others. I would estimate that there were at least 2500 social clubs on the South Side during that period. There were post office clubs, bartenders clubs, Campbell Soup clubs, U. S. Steel clubs and Packinghouse Workers clubs.

December, 1941, marked another high spot in my career. My band was engaged for a ten city tour with the Ink Spots, who were earning $7000 a week at that time. They were very popular and among the highest paid acts in the country. The entire Duke Ellington Orchestra did not earn fifty percent of what the Ink Spots got. On February 13, 1942, we did our final week with the Ink Spots at the Regal Theater in Chicago. The six other acts in the show included "The Three Loose Nuts" headed by Eddie Cole, Nat's big brother. The entire bill was fantastic, and I will never forget that wonderful experience.

The Floyd Campbell Band at Bacon's Casino. Left to right: Lurlene Hunter; Louis Acerhart; Gordon Jones; Floyd Campbell; Scoops Carey; Adolphus Deem; Al Washington; and Moral Young.

In the spring of 1946 we opened at Joe Louis' Rhumboogie Club, 343 East Garfield Boulevard. Several weeks after we opened, Sarah Vaughan was brought in at $300 a week. Before Sarah played the Boogie, we got our paychecks on Friday with instructions not to cash them until Monday. The place was barely making it. But Sarah Vaughan packed the place every night. They had to send out for extra chairs to accommodate the patrons. George Treadwell, Sarah's husband, wanted the club managers, Leonard Reed and Pat Brooks, Joe Louis' half brother, to raise Sarah's salary to $800 a week. At first they refused. Then Ziggy Johnson, the show's producer, and I threatened to pull the band out if they didn't agree. They did give her the raise and they doubled the length of her engagement from four to eight weeks. Dave Garroway came to the show every night after he got off the air. It was his radio show that publicized Sarah's great talents. He called her "The Divine Sarah."

The Four Ink Spots.

At Joe Louis' Rhumboogie in Chicago. Left to right: Leonard Reed, the show producer; Floyd Campbell; and World Champion Joe Louis.

My band was playing at the Rhumboogie in April, 1947, when the Internal Revenue Service padlocked the doors because the club owed $10,000 for liquor taxes. Some of Joe Louis' close advisors told him not to pay the taxes. Sixty people who worked at the club were consequently thrown out into the street. The Rhumboogie never opened again as a seven-night-a-week club; on August 12, 1949, it reopened as the Premier Studio on a three-night-a-week basis. The Premier Club was the brainchild of the ten black bus drivers newly employed by the Chicago Motor Coach Company in an equal opportunity experiment. Buddy Hiles, a full-time motor coach driver and part-time musician, spearheaded the idea. Sterling Burks, Chester Lewis, George Johnson, Roscoe Cotton, Joe Dixon, William Rose, Frank Washington, Jesse Arbor and Abraham Holt chipped in their money and made the Premier Studio a reality.

Buddy Hiles and the bus drivers organized a fifteen-piece orchestra for the floor show and dancing. Skylark Ketchum, a former member of Lucky Millinder's band, was the singing star in the revue. He had a full repertoire of sweet and blues tunes. Ralph Brown doubled as master of ceremonies and tap dancer. Other entertainers in the show that almost rekindled nightlife on Garfield Boulevard were the Three Classy Misses, a terrific tap-dancing trio; "La Tanya" in the shake dance department; and Lou and Blue, a comedy team with a book full of tomfoolery. Tommye Patterson headed a six-girl chorus line known as the Premierettes. The Premier Studio lasted for about fifteen months before the last light was turned off on what had been a glittering street of lights for almost three decades.

The reed and brass section of the Floyd Campbell Band. Left to right: Herman Barker, Sax Mallard, and Al Washington (clarinets). Second row, left to right: Louis Acerhart, Al Wynn and Louis Ogletree.

Since I retired, I have had a lot of time to think about the musicians who worked with me for over fifty years. The best trumpet player was Louis Armstrong, followed closely by Jabbo Smith. On trombones, I would select Al Wynn and Nat Story. On saxes, George "Scoops" Carry and Oelt "Sax" Mallard on alto, and Budd Johnson and Al Washington on tenor. For piano I would select Moral Young, the former musical director for the "I Love Lucy" TV show, and on bass, Milton "The Judge" Hinton.

AUTHOR'S NOTE

When I interviewed Zilner T. Randolph and Floyd Campbell together on April 14, 1982, I learned that Louis Armstrong had developed from a poor to an ex-

Floyd Campbell (left) and Zilner T. Randolph discuss old times.

cellent music reader between 1928 and 1931. Floyd Campbell said that when Louis Armstrong came to St Louis in 1928 to play a two-night gig with his band, Louie could not accurately read a stock arrangement of "Buffalo Rhythm". But Randolph, who became Armstrong's musical director in March, 1931, said that in January, 1931, he gave Louis a very complex tune he had written called "I Don't Care What You Do" backstage at the Regal Theater, and was amazed to hear the man sightread this difficult tune at perfect tempo in his first effort. The three of us decided that Lil Armstrong, Louis' second wife and an excellent musician, must have taken Louis to the musical woodshed frequently between 1928 and 1931.

Jabbo Smith, incidentally, last appeared in Chicago at the Blackstone Theater in 1981 in a show entitled *One Mo' Time*.

Carol Chilton

"My husband, Maceo Thomas, and I were the first American act to play a command performance before the King and Queen of England at the London Palladium on May 22, 1930."

Carol Chilton

BIRTHDATE: December 13, 1907
BIRTHPLACE: Chicago, Illinois
INSTRUMENT PLAYED: Piano
OCCUPATION: Dancer, Singer, Pianist and Composer
WORKED WITH: Al Jolson, Kate Smith, Eddie Cantor, Jimmy Durante, George Burns and Gracie Allen, Eubie Blake, Duke Ellington, Don Redman, Noble Sissle, The Whitman Sisters, Mills Brothers, Bill Robinson, Milton Berle, and Mae West

On December 21, 1907, when I was two weeks old, my mother, Ethel Blackburn, and my grandmother took me to the adoption courtroom and handed me over to Lucille Bacon Chilton, a probation officer in Judge Tuthill's courtroom in Chicago. Officer Chilton asked my mother, "Are you sure you don't want this baby?" My mother and grandmother said, "No," and that was the last time I saw them until January 27, 1938, when they appeared at the stagedoor of the Paramount Theater in Los Angeles where I had star billing.

I was never adopted by my foster parents, Lucille and Tex Chilton. However, they treated me like their own child. They had a son, but they had lost their young daughter in a swimming accident a year or so earlier. I became the substitute for their little girl.

Lucille Bacon Chilton had a lovely voice and sang in the choir at Quinn Chapel A.M.E. Church, at 2401 South Wabash. Her cousin, Roberta Bacon, played piano for silent films; first at the Atlas Theater, at 4715 South State Street, and then at the Kiawatha Theater at 5452 South State. Both of these women were very musical and they certainly inspired me. Mother Chilton took me to the Monogram Theater at 3440 South State to see my first stage show when I was about three years old. I remember vividly the act of Butterbeans and Susie. They were comedians, singers and dancers. Their act climaxed to the tune of "Heebie Jeebies". Susie sang the lyrics and Butterbeans did a dance called the "Itch", which required some eccentric foot-work. Ethel Waters was on the same bill. In those days, she danced and sang. Seeing Ethel Waters perform ignited a fire in me: I wanted to be an entertainer. From that moment on, I never dreamed of doing anything else but singing and dancing on a theater stage.

Shortly after my fifth birthday I got my first opportunity to fulfill that dream of being on stage. Cousin Roberta told Mother, "That kid is always singing around the house. She'll sing at the drop of a hat, so why don't you let her come around to the Kiawatha Theater and sing one number, and I'll accompany her?" Mother was pushing me in that direction anyway so she agreed immediately. I'll never forget, I stood in the spotlight on the stage of the Kiawatha Theater and sang a song called "Mother". Since I was the only act on the bill, I got what my mother considered a respectful response.

Several weeks after my debut at the Kiawatha, my mother took me down to Warwick Hall, at 543 East 47th Street, where I sang "Pretty Baby" and "China Doll", and danced. I was received well, considering that I had had no formal singing or dancing lessons. Mother Chilton decided then that I had enough talent to go to dancing school, and I was accepted by Hazel Thompson Davis, who was one of the top all-around tap instructors in Chicago. Within two years I had absorbed Mrs Davis' instruction like a sponge absorbs water. In the meanwhile mother had been taking me around and letting me dance at club parties and in amateur shows. At this time she met Sherman Dudley, who was one of the top dancing comedians in the country, along with stars like Ernest Hogan and Tom McIntosh. Dudley was working at the Owl Theater, 4653 South State. Clarence Jones was the musical director for Dudley's act, which included a mule.

Sherman Dudley had a seven or eight year old son named Bill, whom Mother allowed to come to our house and practice dancing with me. Through Mr

Dudley's connections, Bill and I were given a one week engagement at the Owl. That marked my formal entry into show business. I sang "Everybody's Doing the Vamp" and Bill and I did a dance routine together. We went over extremely well. My first dance partnership was broken up when Sherman and Bill Dudley moved to Washington, D.C., where Sherman shortly retired from show business and became a realtor, buying and leasing theaters. He became a spirited member of the Theater Owners' Booking Association (T.O.B.A.), nicknamed "Toby" or "Tough on Black Artists".

Although the public liked my performances, Mother thought I needed more class and grace, so she sent me downtown to take ballet lessons from Nicholas Tsouklas, a teacher of Russian ballet who was considered both an excellent dancer and a superior instructor. His small studio was located at Randolph and State. I studied with him until I was thirteen years old, when Mother decided I was good enough to start my own dance studio. She made arrangements with a woman named McKinley for me to teach dance at her settlement house at 30th

Carol Chilton and Maceo Thomas at the Chicago Theater.

and Wabash. My aggressive mother actually recruited all the students for my class. All the students were poor: Mother was collecting something like ten and fifteen cents a lesson and I was teaching more than one hundred students a week. When I was seventeen I gave my first dance recital with one hundred pupils on Sunday, July 13, 1924, at the Grand Theater at 3110 South State Street. By amateur standards, it was a success. I produced some excellent students from that class. Some of them later did some fantastic things: several joined the Regalettes at the Regal Theater, others went on to dance at the Sunset and Dreamland nightclubs. And some went to New York and got into big time show business.

Earl Partello was one of my students. He was so good that he was picked up by the Whitman Sisters—Mabel, Essie, Alberta and Alice—who were by far the greatest incubators of Negro talent from 1900 to 1943, on or off the T.O.B.A. While Partello was on the road with the Whitmans he met a white woman who liked his dancing. In addition to being an all-around talented performer, Earl was into Adagio and Russian dances. This woman told Earl she would like to use him but she preferred a twosome. He told her he had just the person she wanted, and when he came back to Chicago he told Mother Chilton that he could get me into big time show business as his partner. My mother did not resist this idea. We auditioned downtown at a place on Lake Street near Clark. Earl's female agent said we did well and she booked us into a one week engagement at the Chicago Theater in February, 1925. Obviously we were not the stars of the show, but it was a major breakthrough: we were the first Negroes to appear on the Chicago Theater stage without blackface makeup. That engagement marked the end of my high school education. I was in my sophomore year when I dropped out to enter show business full time.

Earl and I did so well at the Chicago that we were booked to play the Balaban and Katz circuit. At the last appearance on our first tour, at the Palace Theater in Cleveland, we introduced the Charleston. There was also a Charleston contest at the Palace and the winner of the first prize was Maceo Thomas, whom I was later to marry. After he met Mother and me, when he won the prize, he wrote and asked whether he could pay us a visit in Chicago, where he was coming to attend a medical convention with his father, who was a doctor. Mother agreed. While Maceo was in Chicago, visiting us at our home at 5121 South Dearborn, we began to work up some dance routines. After we had polished the routines we went down to the McVickers Theater at Madison near State to audition for Paul Ash, a major bandleader of the period. We went onstage at the McVickers as Act No. 40. Paul Ash liked us, and we were signed up for a week at the McVickers. Incidentally, Bing Crosby was at the theater the day we tried out, waiting for his turn to be auditioned. He had just broken up with a trio that he had been performing with at the Tivoli at 63rd and Cottage Grove. I had first seen him there with the Paul

Carol Chilton. In 1925 her black dance team was the first to appear without blackface on the stage of the Chicago Theater.

Whiteman Orchestra. No one could have predicted that he would rise to the heights which he ultimately achieved.

After the McVickers engagement, Balaban and Katz executives gave the new team of Chilton and Thomas an $800-a-week contract to work their chain and their affiliated theaters. We worked fifty weeks a year and by 1929 our reputation had grown so that we received top billing on marquees with the best white acts in the country.

Europe beckoned to us and we went. The William Morris Agency of New York arranged our tour. We captivated Paris. We made Monte Carlo forget its games. We became the toast of Vienna. We danced and sang to thunderous applause through Italy, Germany and Switzerland, and capped the trip by being the first American act to give a command performance before the King and Queen of England, at the Palladium on May 22, 1930. We were given a royal farewell when we left England for Egypt, where we performed in Cairo and Alexandria. From Egypt we went to Australia where we were welcomed at a time when Australians were not putting out the welcome mat for black folks. Throughout the '30s

Left: Carol Chilton and Maceo Thomas in Chicago in 1935 after a successful European tour. Right: Carol introduced the Charleston in Cleveland, Ohio.

Europe became our playground, and as late as 1938 we did ten weeks for the Tivoli circuit in Australia and seventeen weeks in England: eight weeks at the London Palladium, and then nine weeks touring the provinces from Bristol to Manchester.

We returned to America in the midst of the Depression in 1932, to find that the thirst for our dance act had not diminished here. Al Jolson featured us in his Wunder Bar at Nora Bay's Roof in New York. We followed the Jolson tour with an extended engagement in the Eddie Cantor Revue. We worked for Billy Rose, the premier promoter of show business, at his Diamond Horseshoe in New York and we went from there into Lew Leslie's *Blackbirds of 1934.*

We must have worked with more than a thousand theatrical stars throughout our career. I will never forget many of them. Al Jolson was one of the top stars of that period. Many people have asked me if Jolson was a racist, and my answer has always been an emphatic No. He and his wife Ruby Keeler, the movie star, always treated Maceo and me with the utmost respect. During the entire time that I worked with Jolson in his Wunder Bar we had only one racial incident. The show was being taken down South, and a New York reporter, who had seen our act and liked it, wrote in his column that Chilton and Thomas were the most sepia-looking dancers he had ever seen. When Jolson saw the article he became uneasy because he did not know how the South would interpret that item. "Sepia" meant that we were black and, although we never tried to hide our racial identity, we both had fair skin and many people did not realize that we were black. So Jolson came to us and said, "Hey, Maceo, can't you put on a wig when you go down South and Carol, will you wear dark makeup?"

I said, "We don't use blackface makeup."

And that was that. Although Jolson was running scared throughout the Southern tour, we had no trouble.

This story reminds me of an experience we had on a train going through the South with a USO show in the early 1940s. That was the last show we did before we retired from show business. The show was headed by Butterbeans and Susie, and music was by the Eubie Blake Orchestra. When we pulled into the station in Birmingham, Alabama, the conductor came back and said, "All of you people will have to move up front."

Maceo turned and said, "Man, I'm not going to move any place. I've been sitting here since we crossed the Mason & Dixon Line."

Butterbeans and Susie almost turned from jet black to snow white because they were really scared. The only white in our group was the road manager. And he was scared too.

Butterbeans said, "Look, man, you've got to move or else you're just going to get us all hung!"

My husband said, "Well, man, we're just going to have to hang together because I'm not moving."

The white manager said, "Man, you can't do this to us! You're going to get us all killed!"

Everybody moved except us, and that ended the discussion. Most people would say well, you didn't have any problems because both you and your husband were mulattoes and not obviously black. That's not true. We are light-skinned but discernably black to other black people.

Another great entertainer who I'll never forget is Bill "Bojangles" Robinson. We must have worked with him one thousand and one times and he was always good. He was the smoothest tap dancer that I've ever seen. There were no kicks, no nothing. All of his tap work was on the floor. His taps were always plain, clear and understandable. He had a personality like nobody else in my book. He would joke as he danced and would sometimes put the audience in stitches. It was the Bill Robinson staircase dance that gave Maceo and me the idea of creating a

Maceo Thomas and Carol Chilton with a fellow entertainer at the Diamond Horse Shoe in New York.

Left: The Nicholas Brothers and their sister and mother with Carol Chilton and Maceo Thomas in London. Right: Bill Robinson.

pedestal dance. We created three pedestals that were all graduated in height. The pedestal dance was the high point of our act, and we have always given Bill Robinson credit for giving us the idea. He was the father of stairstep dancing.

We worked with the Nicholas Brothers in England. They were excellent dancers, but not original. Their style was actually a copy of the Berry Brothers, who in my opinion, were the greatest dance team of all time, both in this country and Europe. Wherever they appeared, they were terrific. They were what you would call show-stoppers. The Berry Brothers learned from Buck & Bubbles and particularly John Bubbles. John Bubbles was the greatest tap dancer of this century. In fact, Bill Robinson, as great as he was, could not do the kind of tap steps that Bubbles did. This takes nothing away from Bill Robinson, but they were not in the same class when it came to raw tap dancing. The Berry Brothers, as I said, copied Bubbles. The Nicholas Brothers copied John Bubbles and the Berry Brothers.

We traveled on the vaudeville circuit with Mae West, may God rest her soul. Mae West is the only entertainer that I ever worked with that was shorter than I, and I'm four-eleven. Mae West must have been about four feet, ten inches tall and always gave the illusion of being a tall woman because she wore custom made

The Berry Brothers, considered one of the world's greatest dance teams (standing). Jay McShann at piano.

shoes unlike any I have ever seen. I often wondered how she managed to walk. She was a real personality and a lovely person to work with.

George Burns and Gracie Allen were one of the finest couples we had the pleasure of working with. Both George and Gracie were very quiet people. They were never seen galavanting around with the other people in the show. They stayed in their dressing room and always had their meals sent up to their room between shows. When the last show was over, they went home. They were a sweet and lovable couple. Grace, in my opinion, was George Burn's mentor. He was her straight man. She was as funny as she could be: a very clever comedian. Gracie and George Burns always got top billing and they deserved it.

Milton Berle and his mother reminded me very much of Mother Chilton and myself. Miltie's mother wouldn't let girls get near him. She would not permit women to visit or come back stage to talk to him. I recall a number of occasions we were working with Milton on a tour where he was the master of ceremonies.

His mother would stand in the wings, and about midway in the show, she would go out into the audience and Milton would ask her a question in his funny way. She would stand up in the audience and give the appropriate answer. She was part of his act. She was his heart and he was hers, up until the day she died. Milton didn't marry until after his mother passed. She idolized him just as my mother idolized me. She didn't want me ever to marry. There was no question that Milton's mother and my mother were stage door mothers.

I have no regrets about show business. However, sometimes I think back and feel a bit remorseful that we were so underpaid: we never made more than $900 a week. White acts with less talent were getting two and three times as much as we were. I used to argue about it all the time but my husband Maceo was satisfied and did not want to rock the boat. Although we made a couple of movies, one being *Love and Hisses,* back in the '30s, I feel cheated every time I see Gene Kelly on the late movie in *Singin' in the Rain.* I wrote a song called "Raindrops" while we were in England, and right behind it came the American picture *Singin' in the Rain.* I feel that somebody had stolen our material. I felt that my "Raindrops" was the inspiration for *Singin' in the Rain.* I will never forget the lyrics to that song as long as I live. They went as follows:

> Last night, I looked out of my window pane,
>   and as I looked out, it began to rain,
> And the raindrops fell upon the ground, and
>   made a funny, pitter, patter sound.
> They went pit, pat, pit, pat,—Listen to the rain
>   Drip, drop, drip, drop, drip, drop on the window pane,
> It sounds like music as it falls
>   the kind of music that enthralls
>   those April showers, they bring me flowers,
> Drip, drop, drip, drop, listen to them
>   syncopate,
> Pit, pat, pit, pat—Listen to the rain.

Daddy-O Daylie today.

A young and slim Daddy-O Daylie.

"Look, I don't want you to leave here acting strange, so watch me closely while I count your change."

Holmes "Daddy-O" Daylie

BIRTHDATE: May 15, 1920
BIRTHPLACE: Covington, Tennessee
OCCUPATION: Jazz Impresario

My parents had twelve kids. I was the last because my mother died giving birth to me. Shortly before my mother died, she made my oldest brother, Clint, promise to take care of me and my sister Lucille, if my dad couldn't manage. Dad was having it rough trying to raise twelve kids on five dollars a week in Covington, Tennessee. Covington is roughly thirty-nine miles from Memphis. Things got so bad in 1923 that Clint was called upon by my father to fulfill his commitment to mother. Clint sent for Lucille and me to come to Chicago to live with him and his wife, Joanna. The day I left Covington for Chicago was the last time I saw my dad. Several years later when I was in second grade the family received a letter telling us that Holmes Daylie had died.

The world at that time was so empty for me that I couldn't feel any more sorrow. I just regretted that I had never had an opportunity to know what my folks were like. As I grew up, I began to notice the difference between other children and me. Other kids had skates and bikes and I had none. "We can't afford to buy you toys," is what Clint and Joanna said when I asked for them. Not owning anything made me become a master make-doer. I fixed up old discarded roller skates and scooters that I found and gained a lot of pleasure from putting things together.

There is one thing that happened to me in my childhood for which I can't forgive my brother and sister-in-law. I was seven years old and it was Christmas Eve. Lucille and I were playing around the old pot-bellied, wood-burning stove and wondering out loud what Santa Claus would bring us in the morning.

"I'll bet he gives me a new dress," said Lucille, who was fourteen years old.

"Oh, I know what he's going to bring me—a new baseball glove with Babe Ruth's name engraved on it, because I wrote and asked for it," I said.

Like all youngsters my age, I still believed in Santa Claus. It was practically the only thing I did believe in. No one had ever given me a party for my birthday, so I was really looking forward to Christmas.

Lucille and I went over to the window to see if we could see Santa Claus coming. It was then that my brother yelled at me: "You might as well get away from that window, boy, because there is no Santa Claus. I'm Santa Claus, and I'm not going to spend one hard-earned cent of my money to buy you toys just so you can break them. You might as well go to bed because Santa ain't coming tonight or never!"

It seemed as though someone had just pulled the earth from under my feet. I started crying and couldn't stop. Lucille led me up to our bedroom and told me not to worry too much about what Clint had said. "Just you wait, Holmes, you'll see, there is a Santa Claus." But she couldn't comfort me. I hated Clint and Joanna and felt so alone, I couldn't stop crying.

Grade school came and went. If it hadn't been for my older sister Lucille, I might have had to wear the same pair of raggedy pants to high school that I had worn through grade school. By the time I entered high school I was so ashamed of my poverty and raggedy clothes that I had become almost a bully at school. I figured the kids wouldn't dare laugh at me if I was mean enough. Whenever there was a group gathered around a table during lunch hour, I would go over and entertain them with jokes that I had heard on the radio, thinking that if they would laugh with me, they might not laugh at me. I would sometimes rhyme the information that I had read or heard on the radio to keep them laughing. In fact, I got so good at this rhyming business that I started writing a gossip column for the community newspaper in Morgan Park. The column was a huge success, but I was a failure. As a matter of fact, I got fired. It wasn't the way I rhymed, but what

I rhymed that got the neighborhood up in arms. I learned a lesson in good taste that I haven't forgotten.

I was the first black to make the Morgan Park High basketball team. By the time I reached my junior year, I had become proficient playing both forward and guard positions. After I graduated from high school, I left home to forget my troubles. Clint and Joanna never really cared anything about me and I felt that the farther away from them I got, the better off I'd be. So I went on the road playing professional basketball with a team called the Chicago Grenadiers, and later I played with the Ohio Fleetwings. But I soon grew tired of being the black boy on the team and came back to Chicago after I had saved enough money. I got a job as a bartender in an exclusive club in Morgan Park called Club Kuttawa. The Club was located at 11749 South Vincennes. It was at Club Kuttawa that I met Charlie Cole, the owner of the DuSable Lounge.

The Club was sort of a hideaway for businessmen from the South Side of Chicago. They would come out to Morgan Park, which in those days was a long way, and sort of get "lost." Charlie Cole used to enjoy seeing me flipping the ice while mixing drinks. I employed my basketball skills and gimmicks with my bartending. I would take a cube of ice and flip it and catch it in a glass, throw it behind my back, over my shoulder, and things like that. I would even sometimes pour four glasses of beer simultaneously. I constantly kept a rhyme going as I performed the tricks.

For example, if a guy came into the club and said that he wanted a scotch and soda, I would find out the brand of scotch, and then I would say, "Do you want to be great and drink it straight, or you want to see me operate? You want me to mix it, or you want to fix it," and things like that.

And when I would give the customers their change, I would say something like, "Look, I don't want you to leave here acting strange, so watch me closely while I count your change." Charlie Cole liked my rhyming and acrobatic timing so well that he asked me to come and work for him at the DuSable Bar and Lounge. Both the lounge and bar were located in the basement of the DuSable Hotel at 764 East Oakwood Boulevard.

Floyd Smith and his trio furnished the music in the bar. Floyd Smith was very famous at that time. He had written "Floyd's Guitar Blues" when he was with the Andy Kirk Band. In the lounge, a piano player named Wilbur Hobbs entertained the diners. Fats Waller, who was playing downtown at the Sherman Hotel, maintained a room at the DuSable. Some mornings Fats would come in from his Loop gig and literally take over Wilbur Hobb's piano duties. I remember that one morning Duke Ellington came down to the lounge. He and his band were working at the Regal, and Art Tatum came up from the Three Deuces downtown, and the three of them got into a piano jam session in the lounge that lasted from three a.m. until after one-thirty the next afternoon. I never went to bed that night. How could I with all the electrifying musical excitement permeating the entire hotel?

Although there was always something going on at the DuSable Lounge, the most memorable event was the morning that Ben Webster, Chu Berry and Roy Eldridge got fired up on their horns. I will never forget Ben "The Brute" Webster playing "All Too Soon" and "Cotton-Tail," and sending the joint into a musical high. Ben Webster was called "The Brute" because he was always looking for a rumble, and he walked around talking about it. But, inwardly, he was a very soft-hearted, sensitive man. How else could he have played "All Too Soon," in such a hypnotic, tender fashion. Gene "Jug" Ammons, Claude McLinn, and Tom Archer, who were the young musical tenor sax "Turks" in Chicago at that time, would sit at Webster's feet and drink up his solos with their minds and eyes.

Most of the out-of-town artists stayed at the DuSable Hotel whenever they had a gig in Chicago. Remember, they played downtown but Jim Crow policies would not permit them to stay downtown.

Fats Waller had a suite in the DuSable that was always available to him whenever he came to town. That was Suite 501 and 502. Eddie Flagg, the manager of the DuSable Hotel, would always have an organ in the suite for Fats Waller whenever he was in residence. Fats Waller loved flowers and when you entered the lobby downstairs, you could smell the fragrance from Suite 501 and 502. His fans, who were mostly white, knew that he loved flowers and they sent him forty or fifty bouquets of fresh flowers everyday. His suite was literally a bank of flowers.

Many times Fats Waller would invite me up to his room just to listen to him play. He could entertain one or one thousand individuals. That was just the kind of person he was. As his bartender, I would pour him gin by the water glass, with no chasers. Fats would sometimes have me put a little ice and lemon in the glass to make it look like lemonade. He obviously had an elephantine capacity for gin, because I never saw him drunk, or even inebriated. With his glass of gin, he would sit at the organ and play, compose, create and entertain, and take several mouthfuls of gin between tunes. His organ music could be heard throughout the hotel in the wee hours of the morning, but no one ever complained. Who could? Would you stop a genius at work?

Louis Armstrong and his wife were guests at the DuSable Hotel whenever they played Chi-town. The first time Louis walked into the bar and asked me to fix him a drink, I was inwardly awed, but I had to act cool. At the same time I wanted his autograph so bad I could taste it. You see, asking for his autograph would have blown my "hip and flip" bartender image.

One morning, Armstrong came into the bar and three ladies were sitting there and one of them said: "Mr. Armstrong, may I have your autograph?"

Pops said, "Yes," and he took out his pen and gave each of the ladies his autograph. Now I'm standing there drooling, but I was afraid to say anything. So

Daddy-O Daylie (left), with Billie Holiday at a veterans' benefit.

Louie turned to me and said: "What about you? Do you want my autograph?"

I said, "Yes, if you're going to put it on a twenty dollar bill."

He laughed and went to join his wife, Lucille, who was sitting in the back of the lounge having breakfast. The night before Louie was to check out of the hotel, he came down to the bar and said, "Hey, young fellow, I want you to have my autograph."

He gave me a twenty dollar bill with his autograph on it, and I said to him, "I'm going to keep this, Pops. I'm never going to use it."

He replied, "You're going to spend it."

I said, "No, I'm not."

He said, "Well, everytime I come in, if you have this twenty dollar bill, I'm going to give you another one."

So what did I do? I took it up to my room in the DuSable Hotel, and I scotch-taped it up in the ceiling. And everytime Pops came in, I would take him up and show it to him and, believe it or not, he would always give me a twenty dollar bill.

I will never forget that cat. Both he and his wife, Lucille, were beautiful people.

The first time that I met Billie Holiday, I was tending bar at the DuSable Lounge. I believe every black jazz artist in the world came to the DuSable Lounge at some time or another. One morning about four o'clock I told Lady Day while she was sitting at the bar getting a "taste" before she went to waste that I was taking a show out to Hines Hospital to do a benefit.

Lady Day said, "Daddy-O, I don't do benefits because they are all so crooked, but I will do it for you, baby, because I think you are a straight dude."

Duke Ellington also agreed to go along with Billie Holiday on that benefit. Mike DeLisa volunteered the entire Club DeLisa show, which included Slim Gaillard and Timmy Rogers. The troupe didn't arrive at the hospital until about three p.m. but I started trying to get Duke ready around noon. Duke Ellington would give you a heart attack with any attempt to get him up and out of the bed. I succeeded in getting him up without resuscitation and Duke played the piano accompaniment for Billie Holiday sans his orchestra. When I called for Billie Holiday to come out to the mike and do her number, she stepped up there with her little dog, and said: "Daddy-O, what is that thing up there?"

I looked up and it was the sun.

She said, "I'm never up this early in the day." And all of the veterans rolled over laughing.

Billie went on, "I'm going to do one tune, because it's too early for anybody to be singing and you got me way out here in Hines, Illinois, which is a thousand miles from nowhere."

The vets showed so much enthusiasm and warmth for her singing that she actually sang forty minutes after that first number and I had to ask her to come off because there were other acts that had to go on. But from that time on, Billie and I became very fast friends. The last time I saw Billie was in early 1959, shortly before she became desperately ill. She came to Chicago and called me and suggested that we have a three p.m. breakfast and talk. I took her up to my place after we finished eating and we listened to records. I attempted to play her records but she wouldn't let me. She was very critical of her own work. She would always say she didn't want to hear herself, she wanted to hear "Pres." She loved Lester Young. As you know, Lester Young was the one who named her "Lady Day," and she, in turn, called him the "President," which was ultimately abbreviated to "Pres."

For some reason, Lester and Billie had a terrible falling out and everybody tried unsuccessfully to get them to patch it up. Pres died March 15, 1959. Billie became terminally ill. About the same time, Billie's Chicago friends called me and said: "Dad, you know Lady Day is very, very sick." I started telling my radio fans to write Lady Day because she had given us all of these beautiful years of entertainment, and now she needs us, so while she's still here, send her flowers and cards. I had no idea what kind of response she would receive. Lady Day passed away on July 17, 1959, almost four months to the day after Pres left us. One week after she died, some fellow whom I didn't know came to radio station WAAF while I was on the air and handed me a pair of rhinestone sunglasses. He said, "Lady Day wanted you to have these." The fellow said before he left, "Lady Day told me to thank you, because she received bags and bags of Chicago mail in that New York hospital as a result of your request on the air." The shaded green sunglasses had a cracked left lens. I will always keep them as a constant reminder of the great Lady Day.

Lester Young and I were tight. I remember he didn't like noise, anger or violence. However, when he went to the war something happened to him because when he came back, he was never the same. I recall that in the late '40s Pres worked at the Bee-Hive Lounge on East 55th Street. We would sit around over breakfast after he had finished working and talk about what music was doing to him. He said he would go into clubs to work, and they wouldn't treat him as a star. In fact, they wouldn't even treat him as a professional musician. The pianos in some places were almost keyless. He was not permitted to bring in his own rhythm section; hence, he had to play with some "ham-fats" who really didn't understand what the hell was going on. In fact, when Lester talked about his working conditions, he was actually tearful. Many times he played gigs with tears in his eyes because he needed the money.

During that same period, 1947 to 1949, I became good friends with Charlie "Yardbird" Parker. I always admired "The Bird" as a musician. There is no question but that he was brilliant. He was respected by everybody, particularly musicians. Charlie Parker, the man, was self-destructive. I've watched narcotics and dope pushers work on him. They worked on him like vultures over a dead horse. Can you imagine, Bird would come to a gig and play a set, and then leave with the pushers. Many times, he would not come back. He became so undependable in his last days that no one would hire him. I saw so many great talents destroyed by dope. I remember a blind musician who brought a large band into Herman Roberts' Show Lounge at 65th Street and South Parkway. This fellow was considered a genius. I actually saw this blind man fighting flies because he was at the mercy of the pushers. He was hooked. Dope is a powerful instrument of destruction.

The radio is also powerful. I used the radio to help Gene Ammons, "The Jug." As you know, Jug was not a pusher, but a user of drugs, and if he had been any other color, he wouldn't have had to do the kind of time in jail that he did. After he had been refused parole twice, I started a campaign, and I asked my fans to write Governor Ogilvie on Jug's behalf. Sometime later I was at Black Expo, handling an exposition for the Rev. Jesse Jackson, when he said to Governor Ogilvie, "Do you know Daddy-O Daylie?"

And the Governor said, "Of course, everybody knows Daddy-O. Mr. Ammons should be forever grateful to Daddy-O, because he was personally responsible for over 10,000 cards and letters coming across my desk on his behalf." And that's how Governor Ogilvie remembered and knew me.

In the fall of 1944, Charlie Cole and Harry Fields, who were partners at the DuSable, leased the El Grotto Supper Club in the basement of the Pershing Hotel at 64th and Cottage Grove. They offered me the opportunity to go into the new club as bartender and I gladly accepted. I worked all night at the Grotto Tuesday through Sunday. Monday was my night off, and that's when I first had an opportunity to hear Dave Garroway's jazz radio show. Garroway raved about Sarah Vaughan's beautiful inflections so that you salivated to see and hear her. In fact, it was Dave Garroway who must be credited with pushing Sarah's records to the top.

One night at the El Grotto, a group of white fellows from the University of Chicago were standing near the bar drinking. This was not an uncommon sight, because the supper show at the El Grotto was usually ninety percent white. Therefore, I paid no particular attention to these fellows. One of them came over to me and said: "Hey, guy, you are clever. You ought to be in radio, not mixing drinks."

I had a cocktail shaker in each hand, and I flippantly said in a rhyming tone, "What do you pay in radio, money?"

And of course he replied, "That's why I work."

I retorted, "What do you think I work for here, peanuts?"

So he picked up his drink and went back to the group.

George Treadwell, Sarah Vaughan's husband, was standing at the bar and said to me, "Don't you know who that is? That's Dave Garroway!"

I said, "Oh, I didn't know." See, I had let my lips overload my ears and, of course, I am the first to admit that.

A couple of weeks later I was busy working the side bar and I suddenly turned around because I felt someone looking at me. You know how it is, you can always feel somebody's eyes on you. Sure enough, that somebody was Dave Garroway, who said: "I see you don't have any ambition. You are still tending bar."

Well, this time, my mental lights went on, and I said to myself, this man didn't have to come back and say that to me again. He evidently must think I have some talent.

There was another disc jockey that used to come into the El Grotto. He was a bit queer and unusual to say the least. He wore white suits and shoes in the winter, and he dressed like the colors of the beer that he was sponsoring. I said to myself, "Hey, I'm better than this dude who wears white all the time, because I got a peep at his attitude when he came in to drink with me. He was abusive and always drunk and slurring his words. I know I'm better than he is and I'm not

Everyone has a good time at the El Grotto Supper Club: Seated clockwise: Mrs. Petty; George Petty, creator of the famous Petty Girl; Unknown; the Petty's daughter (The Petty Girl); Mr. and Mrs. Eddie "Rochester" Anderson; Nate Gross, Town Tattler columnist; Phil Harris, famous bandleader and movie star; his lovely wife Alice Faye; and a group of their friends. Standing at the head of the table, left to right: Harry Fields, Unknown, and Charlie Cole. Fields and Cole were the owners of the club.

FROM

El Grotto

Chicago's Most Exclusive Supper Club
6412 COTTAGE GROVE AVE.
CHICAGO ===== ILLINOIS

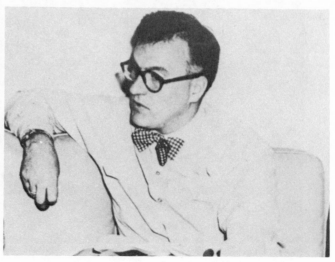

Dave Garroway.

Sarah Vaughan with her husband, George Treadwell.

even in the radio business. Garroway was the positive and the guy in the white suit was the negative. That realization really got me to thinking seriously about going into radio.

My next step was to find someone who might be interested in sponsoring me on the radio show. I went to my boss, Charlie Cole, and told him I was interested in becoming a radio disc jockey and he told me that if I was really sincere, I should go back to school and learn how to be a disc jockey and he would then buy radio time for me. I went back to school and I learned something about radio, and I came back to Mr. Cole and told him I was ready. He told me to go out and find a station that would sell me some time. I found the station and the sales representative came out to the El Grotto from radio station WAIT to talk to Mr. Cole who told him that he wanted to buy a half hour for Blatz Brewéry, and that I would be the disc jockey for the time slot. I was on.

Radio is an exciting business, and one that has enabled me to meet and greet most of the "greats" in the entertainment world, both living and dead. The Duke, the Count, Earl, Ella, and the Divine One—you name them and I know them. It has been a golden opportunity for me to promote America's only original music and that is black jazz.

AUTHOR'S NOTE

Daddy-O, who is a very young and energetic 63, says he is semi-retired, but if you turn on the box, you'll find him still burning the air waves every Sunday on radio station WJPC (AM 95); and every night, Monday through Friday, over WXFM (FM 106) in Chicago.

Barrett Deems

"Louis Armstrong was the best jazz entertainer in the world."

Barrett Deems

BIRTHDATE: March 1, 1914
BIRTHPLACE: Springfield, Illinois
INSTRUMENT PLAYED: Drums
OCCUPATION: Drummer and Bandleader
PERFORMED WITH: Paul Ash, Joe Venuti, Jimmy Dorsey, Tommy Dorsey, Charlie Barnett, Woody Herman, Red Norvo, Muggsy Spanier, Louis Armstrong, Jack Teagarden and The Dukes of Dixieland

I always knew I was going to be a drummer. My father was a movie projectionist for the Tivoli Theater in Springfield, Illinois, and on his day off he would sit in the orchestra pit and play the piano accompaniment for the silent films. Dad couldn't read a note as large as the Hancock Building but he enjoyed playing the piano and I couldn't have been more than twelve years old when he let me come down in the pit with him and play drums. I had a ball playing for the Pearl White movies and the comedies starring Fatty Arbuckle and Charlie Chaplin. When Dad was working in the projection booth the theater owner used a nickelodeon for musical accompaniment: it had its own drums, piano and accordion, and all you had to do to make it play was push a button.

When I was fourteen I won a drumming contest at the Orpheum Theater in Springfield. The prize was a bottle of imported champagne. To this day I have never had a drink, so I gave the champagne to my father, who wasn't a drinker either. He gave it to a friend. My teachers all told me I would never amount to anything because all I cared about were those drums. They were right about my caring about the drums, but I was determined to make them eat their words about my future accomplishments.

I hated school with a passion. I only went to Hay Edwards Elementary School

Barrett Deems, the World's Oldest Teenager, works out.

so I could play drums in the school band. When I was fifteen, I dropped out of Springfield High School in my second year and joined the Musicians Union, Local 19. The union officials liked my drumming well enough to lower their age requirement for a union card from sixteen to fifteen for me.

At sixteen I left Springfield to join the famous Paul Ash band at the Oriental Theater in Chicago. Paul Ash had heard me play with the school band while he was working in Springfield and he hired me. I still remember how scared I was on the first day I played the Oriental. I had never seen a bandstand that moved up and down like an elevator. That was some theater. It was a palace, unlike anything I had ever seen. Unfortunately today the Chicago Theater is the only relic of that age left standing, to remind us of what has been.

When Paul Ash's band closed at the Oriental we went on the road. Our final destination was New York City, but I had been in the "Big Apple" only a month when I got homesick, resigned from the band and returned to Springfield. However after I had been home a short while, Joe Venuti asked me to join him and tour the East Coast. "Man," I told him, "I just came back from New York and I don't want to go back on the road."

But Joe was persistent: he kept calling and writing notes to me and to my Dad. Finally, after two months in Springfield, I decided that I would go back to New York with Joe Venuti. And on 52nd Street I did meet some really fantastic musicians: Roy Eldridge, Louis Armstrong, Red Norvo, Mildred Bailey, Benny Goodman, Dave Tough, and a host of other cats. It was a whole new world for me, and different from my earlier trip with Paul Ash. Now I was meeting the cats who really made things happen. I came under the influence of Gene Krupa and

Barrett (at drums), in concert at the Blackstone Hotel. Standing left are Franz Jackson and Roy Eldridge.

Left to right: Barrett Deems, the world's fastest drummer, with Gene Krupa and Buddy Rich.

Chick Webb. I liked them both and at that time, in the 1930s, they were the hottest thing around.

On the other hand there was Dave Tough. He was with the Tommy Dorsey Orchestra and was a different kind of drummer from either Gene Krupa or Chick Web. Dave couldn't play a solo, but he was a solid drummer who made the band swing, while Krupa and Webb could solo and make the band swing as well. Krupa, who I think had more showmanship than any other drummer on the scene, became my best show business friend. I was pallbearer at his funeral in 1973.

I worked with Joe Venuti from 1937 to 1944 when I formed my own quartet and played at the Sherman Hotel in Chicago for two years. Then in late 1945 I joined the Jimmy Dorsey Orchestra. Jimmy was a nice guy to work for and although I know there was a lot of publicity about fights in the band, I thought the musicians were great guys. There was conflict and rivalry between the Dorsey Brothers because Jimmy and Tommy each thought he had the better band.

Once I remember we were on a train enroute to California and Jimmy's valet came to my berth to tell me that the old man wanted to see me. He knew I loved fried chicken, and when I went to his Pullman compartment he had what looked like a pan full of drumsticks and wings. So we sat in his compartment and ate chicken and talked all night long. I will always remember him, and how I enjoyed my friendship with him: he was a nice man and a great musician. I stayed with him for less than a year before I joined his brother Tommy. After that I went to Charlie Barnett and then with Woody Herman. I was changing bands like some of the movie stars change wives. Regularly.

The finest man I ever worked for was Louie Armstrong. He was a beautiful cat. We got together because his manager Joe Glaser called me and asked me if I was working. I told him yes, I had my own band.

"Well," he said, "fire the whole band."

I told him I couldn't do that.

"Louis wants you to join his orchestra next week," he said.

"I can't do that on a week's notice! The contract I have on this job down in Steiger, Illinois, has two weeks to go."

"That doesn't make any difference," Glaser said. "How much are the musicians making?"

"Three hundred a week," I said.

"Okay," Glaser snapped. "I'll send you a check. Pay them all off."

He sent me a check for $1200 for four guys, and I paid them off and left Steiger. The man who owned the joint was mad enough to kill me, but how often do you get an opportunity to work with the world's greatest trumpet player? I felt doubly honored that Louie had asked me because he had worked for some of the best black jazz drummers of all times—Zutty Singleton, Cozy Cole, and "Big Sid" Catlett. For a while I was really worried about whether I was good enough to sit in the drummer's chair behind that stellar group of skin men.

I remember the second night I was with Louie, I said to him, "Jesus, playing with you is like being in another world. It's a natural ball!"

"I'm glad you're aboard," Louie said. "I enjoy your playing. You do a nice job with those skins."

The Red Norvo Band. Barrett Deems (right), and Red on vibes.

I told Louie I enjoyed playing with him because he had been my idol since I was a kid. Louie said he hoped we'd get along, and he smiled that big smile. We got along very well: I stayed with Louie for eight years.

When I joined his group he had some of the best musicians in the country. There was Orville Young on bass, Trummie Young on trombone, Billy Kyles on piano and Barney Bigard on clarinet. Velma Middleton was the female vocalist. I was holding down the drums, and Louie was blasting through the roof tops. That was some operation. Everybody's dead now, except Trummie Young and Orville Shaw—and me, of course.

On my first trip abroad with Louie we went to England and Germany, then to Ghana in West Africa, and on to Europe. Our reception in England was great. The airport was packed, the concert was oversold. People just wanted to hear the big man in person because he had not been to England for twenty years. But we almost blew the Ghana trip during a stopover in Germany: we were booked for a two hour concert in Frankfurt. At the last minute the flight schedule was changed, and we had to cut the concert by half an hour to get to the airport on time. When we started to pack up our instruments, all hell broke loose. More than five thousand people had paid for a two-hour concert, and they wanted their money's worth. They went absolutely crazy. They destroyed Orville Shaw's bass, bent up Trummie Young's trombone, tore up my drums, and threatened Louis with bodily harm. The German cops had to play water hoses on the mob to protect us. And then we had to go through an underground tunnel with police escort to escape from the concert hall. To say that those Germans were serious about jazz is an understatement.

When we got to Ghana there were more than one hundred thousand people waiting at the airport. I have never seen a reception like that in my life. You talk about the Beatles today—you should have seen Louie twenty-eight years ago. You would have thought he was a god. People just swept him off his feet. They loved him. It was a hysterical encounter, just as it had been in England. Both the Africans and the English had heard his records. In my opinion Louie Armstrong was the biggest man in show business, and the best jazz entertainer who ever lived.

We were in Ghana for almost three weeks. The Ghanaians gave us all presents: they gave Louie's wife jewelry and the boys in the band various gifts. They made me a couple of drums of goatskin. Boy, they still sound good! We were guests of the Prime Minister at the palace. We ate and slept there and just generally enjoyed ourselves. Edward R. Murrow, the famous TV newsman, made an hour-and-a-half long documentary called *Satchmo the Great.* That was in 1955. A camera crew followed us everywhere—every day, through Switzerland, Sweden and France where we went after leaving Ghana. The film played theaters in the States for about two weeks and then it was taken off the market. I don't know what happened, but Joe Glaser, Louie's manager, always wanted a lot of money and if he didn't get his right cut, nothing flew. So I assume that Glaser had something to do with that movie disappearing.

When we left Ghana we did ninety-seven straight one-nighters. I thought I was going to die. I complained to Glaser because Louie never did. Joe told me and other exhausted members of the band that when we got home we were going to be able to take it easy. I said, "Phooey!" Glaser always travelled three or four days ahead of the band, so when we got back to New York he met us at the airport. He said he had good news.

"We're expected at the MGM studios in Hollywood at seven o'clock Monday morning to start working on a pictue called *High Society,*" Joe said.

"Hey, man!" I said. "Where is our vacation?"

He told me we would get it when we finished the picture.

Working on *High Society* was a gas, despite our weariness, because we were able to work with Bing Crosby and Frank Sinatra. But I resented Joe Glaser's attitude. He treated us like we were his money machine. He just would not let us stop. It was all work and no play. He was always consistently greedy about money. We didn't get a vacation when we finished the movie; we were booked in-

Barrett works out for Public Radio at the Windy City Jazz Live *program broadcast from Rick's Cafe Americain.*

to Las Vegas for four solid weeks. And that Las Vegas experience still sticks in my craw.

They wouldn't let Louie gamble in the casino, or Nat Cole, either, who was working out there at the same time. As a white man, I could not understand how they could pay stars like Louie and Cole big sums of money to perform and then refuse to let them use public facilities. It was really stupid. My wife and the wife of Edmund Hall, the clarinet player in the band, had the same experience at Lake Tahoe in the mid-50s. They went out during the show to play the slot machines in the casino and they were approached by a security guard who said he was sorry, but they couldn't play out there. My wife asked why, and the answer was that black people were not allowed to gamble in the casino. What that really meant was that blacks working in Las Vegas and Lake Tahoe were literally prisoners, locked in their rooms until it was time to come out and entertain "Mr Charlie".

We played the Dunes Hotel in Las Vegas with Billie Holiday, who I thought was one of the greatest singers of all time. She was a beautiful person on her good days, but she could be as evil as anybody I ever met, and very difficult to work with on her bad days, which were frequent. I remember once she was playing the slot machines in the casino—this was shortly after blacks were allowed to come into the casino. I was watching her play when she turned and said, "Don't you stand and watch me. You're bugging me! Get away!" She went on to use some language I won't repeat and of course I walked away. I always felt she was a good lady, but all mixed up.

I used to hate to go down South with Louis. I always felt sorry for him. Thirty years ago they just wouldn't treat him right down there. The manager and I were the only two white guys in the organization, and here's Louis with five or ten grand in his pocket, his wife with a twenty thousand dollar mink coat, and they both had to sleep in a gymnasium in North Carolina because they couldn't find any accommodations. That was a killer. It takes the heart out of a man. I used to ask Joe Glaser why he booked us down South. He never answered, but I knew the answer: he wanted the money, and Louie Armstrong never complained.

AUTHOR'S NOTES

Today, Barrett Deems is still billed as the world's fastest drummer. He gigs extensively throughout the country and is in great demand to perform at concerts both here and in Europe. Dick Buckley, the radio personality, calls Barrett "The World's Oldest Teenager". I agree with Buckley, insofar as Deems has as much energy as anyone one-third his age. He has the ability to put a real hurt on the drumheads. He is a Deem.

George Dixon

"Put out the lights and call the law, right now!"

George Dixon

BIRTHDATE: April 8, 1909
BIRTHPLACE: New Orleans, Louisiana
INSTRUMENT(S) PLAYED: Violin, Trumpet, and Saxophone
OCCUPATION: Instrumentalist and Bandleader
FEATURED WITH: Sammy Stewart, Earl Hines, Floyd Campbell
and Eddie King.

My father was a Methodist minister but I was taught the violin by Sister Gerald, a Catholic nun, in the 1920s when my father was pastoring a church in Natchez, Mississippi. I cannot give Sister Gerald enough credit; she helped to build my solid musical foundation.

In 1925 at Arkansas State College I began to double on the alto saxophone and violin and in 1926 I became leader of the College dance band. By this time I had learned the trumpet and I wanted to leave school long enough to earn money playing music so that I could put myself through medical school. Obviously I got

George Dixon (left), with members of the Sammy Stewart Band in Columbus, Ohio.

caught up in a life of music and never got to medical school.

My first job in the North was in Gary, Indiana, where I gigged for a short period before moving to Chicago in 1927. I tried out there for various amateur contests. In the late twenties most theaters had some form of live entertainment and they held an amateur night once a week. They gave cash prizes, like ten dollars for the first place, five dollars for the second and two dollars and fifty cents for the third. I would play violin in one contest, saxophone in another and trumpet in a third. On several occasions I won all three prizes.

In 1928 I auditioned for Sammy Stewart's band in Chicago and got the job because I could play three instruments. I was considered unique because sax and trumpet require two entirely different lipping techniques. My first job with the Stewart Orchestra was in the Metropolitan Theater at 4644 South Grand Boulevard, now King Drive. After several months at the "Met" we accepted an offer to open a new theater in Columbus, Ohio, on Thanksgiving Day, 1928. Columbus was Sammy Stewart's home town. We stayed on that theater engagement for three months and then we were booked into the Black Cat nightclub, a white club, in Columbus, where we stayed for nine months and then we went to New York to open at the Savoy "Home of Happy Feet" Ballroom.

Chu Berry, the tenor saxophonist, was with the band when we left Columbus for New York. Horace Henderson, Fletcher's younger brother, replaced Alex Hill at the piano. Walter Fuller and I had not been in New York very long before we decided we wanted to go back to Chicago. We both returned to the Windy City and joined the Earl Hines twelve-piece band in May, 1930, at the Grand Terrace at 3955 South Parkway Boulevard.

By 1930 the day of radio for big bands had arrived. In Chicago there were nightly live broadcasts direct from such spots as the Grand Terrace, the Trianon Ballroom at 6201 South Cottage Grove Avenue, the Aragon Ballroom at 1100 West Lawrence Avenue, the Edgewater Beach Hotel at 5152 North Sheridan Road, the Panther Room of the Sherman Hotel at Randolph and Clark and the Blackhawk restaurant at 139 North Wabash Avenue.

Our theme song for our broadcast from the Grand Terrace was "Deep Forest", composed by Earl Hines and Reginald Forsythe. Forsythe said to Hines, "Since Duke Ellington is having so much success with his jungle style recordings, let's write something with jungle and hymn."

Hines replied, "I'll write the hymn if you do the jungle."

These nightly broadcasts caused a demand for us to appear throughout the forty-eight states and Canada. Man, my behind remembers every road in this country from those bumpy bus rides. We must have played every theater in America that had a ballroom or theater that could accommodate a big band. We even played the Mardi Gras in New Orleans, the Kentucky Derby at Louisville and a presidential inauguration. As a young man I thought it was glamorous to travel

Earl Hines Orchestra, 1930.

on the road with a famous band. But my first trip disillusioned me. To the young people of this generation it would seem like something out of Ripley's *Believe It or Not* if I described the horrible, degrading experiences inflicted on black musicians and entertainers who criss-crossed the forty-eight states on buses and trains during the first sixty years of this century.

I will never forget that morning in Greenville, North Carolina. We had been riding the bus for an unusually long time that night when we pulled into the gas station at daybreak. The fellows got out of the bus to stretch. The filling station had those old-fashioned hand gas-pumps. Milton Fletcher, one of the energetic trumpet players, walked over to this white fellow who was pumping gas with a large .45 Colt strapped to his side. Milton watched him pumping for a while, and said, "Let me pump that gas. I've been riding all night and I'd like the exercise."

The white fellow drawled, "Sure. But you ought to have been around here an hour ago, and you would have gotten plenty of exercise."

"How's that?" Fletcher asked.

Hines Band at the Regal Theater in 1932.

"I just killed a nigger about your size," the redneck said.

Fletcher laughed. "You're kidding!" he said.

"Naw," the cracker said. He looked Fletcher straight in the eye. "Naw I ain't," he said. He pointed a long, greasy finger toward a spot behind the filling station. "The dead nigger is over there in that ditch," he said.

We walked over there with him and sure enough, there was a dead colored man lying in a ditch within eighteen feet of the station. We got back on the bus in a hurry and headed for Jacksonville, Florida, where I met a colored gentleman who was connected with the local branch of the NAACP. I reported the incident to him. A week later when we were returning from Miami through Jacksonville I asked the NAACP man if he had investigated the Greenville murder. He said he had, but he could not find any witnesses. It was just another lynching.

In Miami there was a city ordinance that a black band could not play for a white audience. So black bands had to play for their white Miami fans in Fort Lauderdale, twenty-three miles north of Miami. Whites who wanted to dance to black music had to make the forty-six mile round trip between Fort Lauderdale and Miami. In West Palm Beach the police would not permit white bus drivers or white managers to accompany black bands into the city.

In Chicago in 1929 I was playing my first gig at the Congress Hotel on South Michigan Boulevard. I started to enter the hotel through the Michigan Avenue entrance, but the doorman told me I had to use the freight entrance and the freight elevator. Teddy Wilson, a member of the Benny Goodman Trio, was the first black to use the passenger elevator at the Congress in 1935 when John Hammond, Goodman's brother-in-law, insisted that the hotel management let Wilson use the front door and elevator as long as he was a member of the Benny Goodman aggregation.

One night we played a dance in a little coal-mining town called Corbin, in Kentucky. When our bus pulled up in front of the hall, we saw people by the hundreds pouring inside. The office in New York had told us to collect our money in front from that particular dance promoter. I got off the bus and went up to the promoter, whose name was Will Saunders, and told him that our booking agent, Harry Squire, had told us we had to collect the money in front.

"Aw," Saunders said, "you'll get your money."

"You've had a lot of advance sales," I said. "Look at all those people in the hall. We've been instructed to get our money in advance."

"I know," he snapped. "I'll check everything out with you at intermission. I can't do it now."

I went to the bandstand and told Earl about it, and he said the valet should start loading the instruments back onto the bus. Then Earl made an announcement over the loudspeaker that there would be no dance that night. The people started raising hell. We all climbed back onto the bus and had travelled about ten slow miles through those curving roads in the Kentucky mountains when two patrol cars flagged us to a halt. A red-faced Kentucky trooper jumped out of his car, and walked over to the bus and said, "You have got to turn this bus around."

Earl asked him what he meant.

"I mean you are going back to that dance hall," the trooper said.

Earl got up out of his seat and said, "No, sir. We're supposed to get our money up front and the promoter didn't have it."

The trooper grabbed Earl by the sleeve, and said, "Listen, those niggers down here have been preparing for this dance for four months. Now you niggers are going to turn this bus around and go back and play for them."

We turned the bus around and went back and played the dance. The promoter paid us as he had promised during the first intermission.

George Dixon.

During the mid-'30s we had a singer in the band named Arthur Lee Simpkins. Everybody called him "Georgia Boy". He had a beautiful tenor voice and he could sing in eight languages. The Jews loved him because he could sing in Yiddish. One night, during the floor show at the Grand Terrace, "Georgia Boy" was singing in his full dress suit and white bow tie when a middleaged white man walked on-to the dance floor and said, "Arthur, what are you doing with that suit on? Come on, you are going back to Georgia with me."

Arthur Lee tried to talk to the man, but we were right in the middle of the floor show. The bouncers tried to pull the man away but he wouldn't turn Arthur Lee loose. So they slugged him in the head and started to drag him across the dance floor. Arthur Lee started crying and begging, "Don't hurt him! Don't hurt him! That's Mr Finnessey from Augusta, Georgia. My people still live down there. Don't hurt him, please don't hurt Mr Finnessey!"

We found out later that Arthur Lee had worked as a porter in a bank in Augusta and Mr Finnessey had been his boss. Finnessey had heard Arthur singing on the radio broadcast from the Grand Terrace and had decided then and there to come to Chicago to get Arthur Lee and carry him back to Georgia. But Mr Finnessey returned to Chicago just like he had come. Alone.

In 1940 Rudy Taylor, our drummer, Pee-Wee Jackson, the trumpet player, Leroy Harris, alto saxman, and I were walking down the street in El Dorado, Arkansas, looking for a movie theater that would admit colored patrons. A white policeman walked up to Rudy and without saying a word hit him in the face so hard that Rudy was knocked to the pavement. Then the policeman said, "If the rest of you niggers don't want the same you better get your black asses back down to niggertown!"

In the fall of 1940 I went down to Champaign, Illinois, to see the homecoming game with Herbert and Harry Mills of the famous Mills Brothers Quartet. When we reached Champaign-Urbana we decided to eat in the train station because we had heard that was the only place blacks could eat except for a grease shack on the other side of the tracks. We sat down at the counter and the counterman told us to move over to the other side. We asked him what was wrong with the side where we were sitting. He pointed to a sign that read: "Railroad Employees". That was the Illinois code for "Whites Only".

I will never forget Friday, May third, 1935. It was two a.m. Our bus was eight miles northwest of Nevada, Iowa, when it collided with a corn truck. Cecil Irwin, our tenor sax man, was killed instantly. He died without ever knowing what had hit him because he had been asleep with his head against the window. I commandeered a car and rushed Trummie Young, our trombone player, to the hospital. Walter Fuller, trumpet, Billy Franklin, trombone, Louis Taylor, trombone, Omer Simeon, alto sax, and Bobbie Frazier, an entertainer travelling with the band, were all slightly injured and were taken to the hospital by ambulance and released. Our battered band opened that night in bandages at the Orpheum Theater in Des Moines. When Kathryn Perry did her rendition of the closing song, "I Never Had a Chance", the entire house was moved to tears.

The music business, like life, had its share of tears and sorrow, but it also had joyous moments. These came from seeing people's appreciation of our performance. And from the many lifelong friends I made in my trips around the forty-eight states. It was at the Apollo Theater in New York that we met and hired an eighteen-year-old singer named Sarah Vaughan. During my years with Hines I met countless great personalities from stage and screen: Duke Ellington, Martha Raye, Clark Gable, Count Basie, Dizzy Gillespie, Fats Waller, Lester Young, Charlie "Yardbird" Parker, Tommy and Jimmy Dorsey and Chick Webb are just a few of

An Earl Hines Band reunion at the Braddock Hotel in New York in 1942.

the many giants of the industry.

Chick Webb had a good band and he didn't mind telling you how good it was. He was crazy about me because I agreed with everything he said. He would tell me about different members of his band, and then he would ask, "George, have you ever heard anyone lay alto sax like Hilton Jefferson?"

I'd say, "No, Chick," and he would chuckle and say, "Yeah, man."

Then he would say, "How about Elmer Williams with that big tone on tenor? You don't know anybody who can do that, do you?"

I'd say, "No, Chick." And he would say, "That's great."

One day Chick came by the Apollo Theater and said, "Dixon, when you get off tonight, make sure to come up to the Savoy. I am going to run old Duke Ellington out of there."

Left to right: Roy Eldridge; Mouse Burroughs; Lotus Perkins; Rozelle Claxton; and George Dixon at Circle Inn, 63rd and Cottage Grove Avenue.

I went up to the Savoy that night and Chick, who was just over four feet tall, was strutting ten feet in the air and looking as proud as a peacock. Chick's band had already set up on the double bandstand when the Ellington band walked into the Ballroom. While the Ellington band were unpacking their instruments on the shadowy side of the bandstand, the lights went up on the Chick Webb Orchestra which began to shower down some terrific arrangements. Chick's band really wailed and the crowd was stomping and applauding when they finished their first dance segment. Then the lights dimmed on the Chick Webb Band and brightened on the Ellington aggregation. Ellington opened his set with Chick Webb's theme song, "Let's Get Together", in jungle rhythm. Duke had that place rocking before he finished the first number. You know, Duke had the greatest band and then the worst band when they didn't want to play. But that night they really showered down.

Later Chick came over to my table and said, "I can't do nothing with him. He's too tough for me."

Another time I was in the Savoy Ballroom in New York having drinks with

Right: Fletcher Henderson, pianist and pioneer jazz arranger extraodinaire. Below: A fan greets Sgt. Joe Louis and George Dixon at the Rhumboogie Nightclub in 1943.

A 1936 Hines Orchestra. Hines is seated at the piano and George Dixon sits at the right.

Fletcher Henderson, Louis Russell, Chick Webb and Artie Shaw. I asked Fletcher, "How's everything?"

"Terrible," he said.

"What's wrong?"

"You know Coleman Hawkins is leaving the band," he said.

"Leaving?" I said. "Well, where's he going?"

"To join the Jack Hylton Orchestra in London," Fletcher said. "In London, England."

"I've got just the man for you," I said. "Read this letter."

I had just received an airmail special delivery letter that day from Lester Young telling me that if I could find anything for him he would be willing to leave Kansas City, Missouri. We went right to the phone and I got Lester on the line to talk to Fletcher. Fletcher made arrangements for Lester to meet him in Detroit at the Greystone Hotel the following Saturday, March 31, 1934.

The guys in the Fletcher Henderson Band did not like Lester Young. They were accustomed to Hawkins' big broad tone and they couldn't get used to

Lester's style. Finally Lester left the band in disgust and went to Count Basie. I had first met Lester Young in 1932 when he, George Hudson and I got into a jam session at a place called the Subway in Kansas City. That session lasted from two a.m. until nine-thirty the next morning.

AUTHOR'S NOTE

Although George Dixon is one of America's most talented musicians, he will be immortalized for shouting, "Put out the lights and call the law right now!" on the 1940 recording of "Boogie Woogie on the St Louis Blues" with the Earl Hines Orchestra.

When I interviewed Earl Hines in July, 1982, he called Dixon his friend, and said that he considered him the backbone of the Hines orchestra for the many years that they worked together between 1930 and 1942. Whenever Hines came to Chicago, until he died in the spring of 1983, he stopped by to visit with Dixon and go over Dixon's scrapbook, which offers overwhelming proof that the Hines Band was one of the best in the land in the 1930s and '40s. The clippings have turned yellow with age, but Dixon's memories of the good old days are fresh and new. "I was the only one in the band to keep a scrapbook," he says. "Whenever I look at it I am jolted into remembering how much I enjoyed the business of playing music."

Dorothy Donegan

"Europeans love blacks who play jazz."

Dorothy Donegan

BIRTHDATE: April 26, 1922
BIRTHPLACE: Chicago, Illinois
INSTRUMENT PLAYED: Piano
OCCUPATION: Jazz Artist
FEATURED IN: Movies, Television, Nightclubs, Broadway Plays and
Concert Halls.

I was born in Cook County Hospital on the West Side of Chicago in 1922. My
parents were living on the South Side at 4801 South Evans at that time. My
mother worked as a domestic and my father worked as a chef on the Chicago
Burlington and Quincy Railroad. They called my Dad "Bad Foot" Donegan. He had
real bad feet but he could bake his buns off.

My folks started me taking piano lessons in 1928, the same year I enrolled in
Willard Elementary School at 4915 South St Lawrence Avenue. My first music

teacher was Mr Alfred Simms, whose music studio was located in his second floor apartment at 5301 South Calumet Avenue. Mr Simms was an excellent teacher. He had me playing well enough after two years to do recital work, and before I reached the age of eleven he had brought me along far enough to do professional work as an organist and pianist in churches, lodges and house parties around the neighborhood. At the suggestion of my cousin, Addison Mosley, I left Mr Simms and started studying with E. Sterling Todd, who was a pianist and organist at the Savoy Ballroom. He introduced me to the three B's: Bach, Beethoven, and Brahms. I devoured the classics at such a rapid pace that Mr Todd suggested that I go downtown and study at the Chicago Conservatory of Music under Lillian Brown, who had a reputation of being one of the best classical teachers in the city of Chicago. By the time I graduated from elementary school in 1935, I was considered both an excellent classical pianist and a very good jazz piano player. Therefore, when I entered DuSable High School at 49th and Wabash, I had no problems qualifying for Captain Walter Dyett's Booster orchestra. Thomas Rigsby, Dyett's favorite piano player, was graduating and the Captain was looking for replacements. The competition was stiff for that piano seat because there was Rudy Martin, who was a tall, good-looking, yellow fellow who played pretty good piano. Then there was Martha Davis, who came in from Kansas City, playing like both Count Basie and Fats Waller. Entering the door of the band room was John "The Terrible" Young, the Earl Hines protege. The DuSable piano field was crowded with talent but I managed to share that piano seat with John Young and the others over the four year period that I was at DuSable High. Nat "King" Cole dropped out of DuSable two months after I arrived to take his first band on the road.

Captain Dyett was an excellent musician and a hard taskmaster. He would always say, "When you're right, you can afford to keep quiet." But he also made you very conscious of being a good musician. He could hear a mosquito urinate on a bale of cotton. His musical ear was that sensitive. Sometimes we could make Captain Dyett so mad, that he would call us all kinds of S.O.B.'s and M.F.'s, and he would say to me, "Hit it! It's a B-flat chord." And I would say, "Oh, it's still a B-flat chord." He would retort, "You've got to hit that B-flat, C-7th and F-7th." And sometimes I would cuss back at him and Dyett never liked it. He had such a terrific ear. Out of a 150 piece concert band, he could tell exactly which instrument had made the mistake, and you would know it because he would stare at you with that one good eye and make you feel smaller than a snail. On the other hand, he had a good band and he always produced an excellent *Hi Jinks* show from the student talent at DuSable.

Dyett had to use the proceeds from the annual *Hi Jinks* affair to buy instruments for the band because the Board of Education would never furnish instruments for the students. Dyett gave each member of the booster orchestra

Left to right: Dorothy Donegan; Unknown; Ted; Joe Hughes; and Nat King Cole. The occasion was celebrity night at Joe Hughes' Deluxe Cafe.

one dollar per night for the four nights that we played the *Hi Jinks*. After my first semester in the DuSable booster orchestra, my mother sent me away that summer to stay with my aunt in Flint, Michigan, because she couldn't control me. People around the school and on the streets were telling me that I played a lot of piano, and I would drink a little wine and whip that piano some more. Staying up late and drinking wine on gigs was not the kind of behavior my mother was able to handle. When I returned to Chicago in September of 1935, I had my act together. I decided that I was going to stay in the house and practice as my mother had wanted me to, and she would in turn give me a pass on doing housework and washing dishes. That was an arrangement that we both found satisfactory.

Participants in DuSable's 1939 Hi Jinks. *Left inset: Dorothy Donegan. Center: Redd Foxx kneeling on tub. Right lower inset: Savannah Strong.*

In 1939, at the age of seventeen, I was playing piano with the Bob Tinsley Band. The nightclub where we were working closed down three weeks after we opened. However, I was at the club long enough to be noticed by a promoter named Phil Shelley, who helped to open some new doors of opportunity for me, both in the Loop and on the Far North Side.

Phil Shelley got me my first big break in 1940, when I was eighteen. He got me a job playing solo downtown at Costello's Grill, at 118 North Dearborn. That was considered a big thing, because in Chicago in those days, Jim Crow was just as common in downtown restaurants, hotels and nightclubs as it was in Jackson, Mississippi. I worked at Costello's for four months before I got fired for insulting one of the boys. As you know, I've always had a rapid tongue and I did not appreciate being hit on by a member of the Costello family. Fortunately my mother chaperoned me during those days, and she would go down to Costello's with me every night and she was the one who actually picked up my paycheck which was the grand sum of thirty-five dollars per week.

After I left Costello's, I went to work at the Bar of Music up on Howard Street. A lot of fine jazz artists like Una Mae Carlisle had worked there. Una Mae composed "Walking By the River" and "I See a Million People". The saloon was actually run by a Madam named Kay Jarrett. She paid me seventy-five dollars a week, which was a very good salary at that time. Also working there was a group called the Three Sharps and Flats; a talented group of musicians. However they complained about me to the union because I jammed a religious song called

Left: Captain Walter Dyett. Right: Una Mae Carlisle, pianist and composer.

"Somebody's Child". Harry Gray, the President of Local 208, fined me for playing religious music in a nightclub. That kind of music belonged in church, to be sung by people like Mahalia Jackson and Sister Rosetta Thorpe.

From the Bar of Music I came back downtown to a place known as Elmer's Cocktail Lounge on the west side of State Street between Randolph and Lake Streets, directly across from the Chicago Theater. That was considered the real big time back in the early '40s. The Capital Lounge was on the east side of State in the same block right next door to the Chicago Theater. Maurice Rocco was playing stand-up piano there and creating a sensation. Louie Jordan's Tympany Five later played the same room. During my stay at Elmer's Cocktail Lounge, I got a fantastic amount of publicity from *Time, Look,* and *Downbeat* magazines. All were saying the same thing. I was a genius. They also said that I had irrepressible lead-ins, formidable technique, and I could do things like the classical people and also play jazz, so I was the original two-way girl. I could go either way, physically and mentally. With that kind of publicity, the Garrick Stage Bar, on Randolph and Clark next door to the Garrick Theater, bid for my talents, offering me the phenomenal sum of more than $200 a week, which was an unheard-of amount at that time. I accepted their offer without reluctance. Working at the Garrick was a real gas. Red Allen, the great trumpet player, was on the gig and there was an old lady who worked there who sang the blues. Her name was Alberta Hunter. She used to wear big diamond rings on all of her fingers. She always told me to save my money and wear big diamonds. I remember she used to sing a song with lyrics that went as follows: "I want an intelligent man." And the musicians in the band would say, "That's me, baby!" Then she would say, "I want a handsome man!" And the musicians would shout. "Look at me, baby!" Then she would say, "I want a man who can use his head!" And then everybody got quiet. She was some entertainer. I saw her in New York recently and she was still going strong at age eighty-eight, and still giving girls the same advice about diamonds and men.

It was during the early forties that I met Billie Holiday, who used to come around to see me both at Elmer's and then later at the Garrick. It appeared that we were going to become very fast friends, and then one night after work we decided to go out to the Club DeLisa to catch the Monday morning breakfast dance. After we were seated in Club DeLisa, Billie lit up a reefer, and I told her I didn't think she should do that.

She said, "Well, if you don't like it, go home!"

I said, "Well, bye!"

I loved Billie, but I just didn't like that habit. I always thought that she should have spent more money on buying clothes instead of pot. Billie used to give me advice about men, and I learned a lot from her. I remember one thing in particular she told me.

She said, "Never give a man twenty-five percent of your money unless he's sleeping with you."

So I told her I didn't intend to give any away if I could help it. Billie had some hip street ideas which I guess she must have picked up early in life.

I befriended a washroom attendant named Ruth Jones while I was working at the Garrick Stage Bar. Her name was subsequently changed to Dinah Washington. She had a glorious voice and I just loved to hear her sing. In fact, we initially had a mutual admiration society. Dinah always raved about my musical ability. But for some reason she resented me as a person. She was very competitive. I remember I got a mink coat and Dinah went out and got one too, but what she didn't know is that I was borrowing mine from the stores. They would let me wear a coat for two or three days and sometimes a week before I had to return it.

Once, Dinah was working at a club and I walked in wearing a full length chinchilla and she almost had a stroke.

She was singing and she saw all the heads turning toward me and she stopped singing and said, "Sit down, bitch! We've all seen it."

I strutted across the floor and said, "A little-bitty act, huh? A little-bitty act!"

"Night-train" Lane, her husband, told me later he had to give her some smell-

Dorothy Donegan.

ing salts when she got back to the dressing room. She had almost collapsed because she knew that with me wearing that full length chinchilla, she could only top it with a sable.

Dinah would fix dinner for my husband, John T. McClain, but she wouldn't invite me. Dinah was opening at the Regal with Buddy Rich, the drummer. Rich cancelled out at the last minute and Ken Blewett called me at home and asked me to come to his office.

I asked him, "For what? Do I owe you any money?"

He said, "Naw, just come to my office."

I went to his office and he said, "Can you open tomorrow in Buddy Rich's place?"

I told him I was available.

Ken Blewett didn't realize that he had selected a musician to play for Dinah whom she couldn't stand personally.

Dinah had a reputation of being an excellent cook. She could put on some pots. She would cook dinner backstage at the Regal and invite everybody but me. I remember one of her cronies came back to my dressing room and brought me some of her food.

I said, "If you don't get that stuff out of here, I'll throw it up against the wall. If she is going to ignore me, then just keep it. I didn't ask her for any food."

Dinah was not consistent. A short time after that, maybe within a half hour, she came poking around my dressing room to try to see what I would wear for the next show. I would always keep my clothes covered up because I had better taste than she did and I was not about to give her any clues.

I remember on another occasion, she was playing Roberts Show Lounge and I walked into the place and right in the middle of her song, she stopped and said: "Sit down, Nut!"

I replied, "Okay, slut!"

It's unfortunate that Dinah and I didn't get along, because I really liked her. However in the end, I don't believe she liked herself.

In the spring of 1942, Joe Sherman, the owner of the Garrick Stage Bar, decided to present me in concert at Orchestra Hall. His friends told him he was crazy to want to put a black woman on the same stage where Vladimir Horowitz had been presented earlier that year. Joe Sherman ignored his friends' advice and the concert was a sellout. At the age of twenty, I was the first jazz pianist, black or white, ever to be presented at Orchestra Hall. My concert was mixed. The first half was classical, and the second half was pure jazz and boogie-woogie. Claudia Cassidy, the music critic for the *Chicago Tribune*, gave me a rave review.

The Orchestra Hall Concert brought my talents to the attention of Louis B. Mayer, Chairman of the Board of United Artists. Mr Mayer came up to Elmhurst, Illinois, to hear me play. My manager Burt Gerbis goofed when he did not let me

Erroll Garner.

accept a twenty year $750-a-week contract. Gerbis opted for a one-shot deal: I appeared in a movie called *Sensations of 1945* with Eleanor Powell, Glenn Ford, Sophie Tucker, Cab Calloway and Woody Herman. I'll never forget that the director made me put on some very dark makeup in order to lower my skin tone so the public wouldn't mistake me for something other than a black woman, and I played the piano back to back with a white male pianist. After the picture was finished, the studio insisted that I go to New York for the opening at Loew's State

Dorothy Donegan and the author in July, 1983.

Theater. For some reason, I was afraid to play a New York theater. I guess I was timid and tired at that time. But they told me if I didn't open with the movie, they would blackball me from ever playing any theater in America again. Therefore I went.

I met Cab Calloway while I was doing the movie, and when he heard that I was coming to New York for the premiere, he invited me to open with him at the Zanzibar Night Club on Broadway. The New York trip turned out to be a good deal because I had a double gig. Travis, I remember you came backstage to see me at the Zanzibar on the opening night. Seeing you made my eyes glad because I hadn't seen any of my old DuSable buddies in a long, long time. Travis, I decided a long time ago that the friends that you had when you were nobody, you should keep when you are somebody. There is no use in meeting any new people. It's best to keep the people you already know. Don't swap the devil for the witch. I've always been kind of skeptical of new people. I like walking down 47th Street seeing people that I knew from DuSable, like Allen the wino or our good buddy Finnis Henderson.

Europeans love blacks who play jazz. They give us full credit for creating jazz music. They don't want us to play too many classical numbers. In fact, they would prefer we didn't do any. They want us to do jazz, blues and boogie-woogie. They are crazy about musicians like Memphis Slim, Muddy Waters and B. B. King. They prefer them to Billy Eckstine or Johnny Hartman. They want you to look black too. They don't like fair-skinned Negroes.

AUTHOR'S NOTE

Dorothy Donegan is one of the very best jazz pianists America has ever produced. Art Tatum is the only piano player I have ever heard with better technique. Dorothy can hold her own playing any style. I saw Donegan invite Erroll Garner to sit in on her gig at Embers in New York City in 1968. That act alone would be a no-no for most pianists, but not for Dorothy. In 1979, I witnessed her performance at a piano concert with eight other top flight pianists at the Newport Jazz Festival at Carnegie Hall in New York City. She stopped the show. Dorothy Donegan is indeed the master of boogie-woogie blues and contemporary jazz. She is technically better today than she ever was. Since she dropped the wiggle and finger popping from her act, she is also very polished.

Billy Eckstine

"Give me Sinatra's money, and I will give him my voice."

Billy Eckstine

BIRTHDATE: July 8, 1914
BIRTHPLACE: Pittsburgh, Pennsylvania
INSTRUMENT(S) PLAYED: Trumpet, Valve Trombone and Guitar
OCCUPATION: Vocalist, Songwriter and Bandleader
FEATURED WITH: Tommy Myles and Earl Hines.

After finishing Armstrong High School in Washington, D.C., I entered Howard University in 1934 where I studied for two semesters before deciding to drop out and try my hand at show business. My first professional job as a singer and master of ceremonies was with the Tommy Myles Band in Washington. Tommy had a good little band and some excellent musicians. Trummie Young and Tyree Glenn were with the band. Elton Hill was the trumpet player. Elton later wrote some fine numbers for Gene Krupa, such as "Let Me Off Uptown". Many of the

Billy Eckstine with a friend on East Garfield Boulevard in Chicago in 1938.

numbers that Jimmy Mundy did for Earl Hines and Benny Goodman were written for us by Elton Hill when we were working at the Crystal Cavern in
Washington, D.C.; numbers like "Cavernism", "In Mad Time", and "Swingtime in
the Rockies", which was a big hit for Benny Goodman. We played the same tune
earlier in D.C. and called it "C-Sharp".

I gigged around Washington throughout the cold Depression year of 1935,
and went to Pittsburgh in 1936, moving to Buffalo, New York later that year. I
stayed in Buffalo for most of 1937 and then went to Detroit, where I stayed only
two weeks before moving to Chicago in 1938. I got a job at Club DeLisa, where I
worked for approximately a year and a half before I left in 1939 to go with the
Earl Hines Orchestra. Hines did not have a hard time getting me to agree to join
his band because he agreed to pay me fifty dollars per week and I was only making twenty-five dollars at the DeLisa.

I remember the night I told Mike DeLisa that I wanted to leave after eighteen
months and go with Earl Hines. He looked at me as if he thought I had lost my
mind. Entertainers left Club DeLisa only by request and Mike thought I was doing
a good job; the patrons liked me. At the same time Earl Hines wanted me, and
behind Hines was Joe Fusco of the Capone gang and Ed Fox, the owner of the
Grand Terrace. I think the boys from the mob must have said something to Mike
which helped him decide to release me from my contract. I say that because I
know that when the DeLisa brothers didn't want you to go, they would take you
downstairs and walk you into the icebox and do a number on you. Since I was
spared that treatment, I knew that somebody up there with an iron fist in kidskin
gloves was giving me an awful lot of help. I told Mike before I left that if I didn't
make good with the Hines band I would come back to his Club and he said I
would always be welcome. And, in fact, when Hines broke up with his manager
Ed Fox after my first road trip with them, I was without a job and I did return to
the Club DeLisa and I was welcomed with open arms by the three brothers and
all the entertainers.

"Gate", short for "Gatemouth", is what the band members called Earl Hines.
After he broke with Ed Fox, Gate decided that he would do a single and open his
own club. So he opened the Studio Club in Chicago, which did not last seven
months because in October, 1940, he had re-established residence in California
and reorganized his band there. I'll never forget recording "Jelly, Jelly" in the Victor studios in Hollywood on December 2, 1940. We had finished a tune called "I'm
Falling for You" and we had a side open, and the A & R man, Harry Myerson, said,
"Earl, can't you think of something else? You have an hour left. Why don't you
play some kind of blues? They sell down South."

Earl turned to me and told me to go to an outer room and write some lyrics
while he and Bud Johnson worked out a head arrangement for the band. We put
the whole thing together in about twelve mintues and we didn't think too much

Seated left to right: Teddy Wilson; Eddie Haywood; Erroll Garner and Earl "Fatha" Hines.

of it because on the road I had been singing blues songs—the kind of thing that Big Joe Turner and Eddie "Cleanhead" Vincent were doing. To me, "Jelly, Jelly" was just another blues song. It was not until we reached New York City that we learned that "Jelly" had been released and that it was a national hit. Every place we went, up and down 7th Avenue and across 125th Street, we could hear the vendors playing "Jelly, Jelly". It turned out to be a springboard to popularity for the new Earl Hines Orchestra.

The power of the blues—and "Jelly, Jelly" specifically—is unbelievable. My son Edward, who manages Quincy Jones, came to me one day about two years ago and said, "Daddy, you're going to make some heavy money, baby."

I said, "What do you mean?"

He said, "The Allman Brothers have recorded 'Jelly, Jelly.' "

I didn't know who the hell the Allman Brothers were, but of course the kids did. Three months after he told me that, I checked with the recording company—Robbins, Feist and Mellow, owned by Warner Brothers—to find out what sales they had had on "Jelly, Jelly" because every two years I check with the companies to find out what kind of royalties I can expect.

The guy told me, "Hey, we have a check down here for seventeen thousand dollars."

In other words, in three months, as a result of the Allman Brothers release of "Jelly, Jelly", I had earned that much in royalties. So I told Earl, "Man, I just got a check for seventeen thousand dollars from 'Jelly, Jelly.' "

He said, "What the hell do you mean? I just got a check for a dollar forty-eight."

I said, "Man, you've got to be crazy!"

But he showed it to me and I said, "Gate, something is wrong. Who sent you the check?"

He said, "The Advance Music Company."

I said, "Man, the Advance Music Company has ben out of business for over twenty years."

In fact it had been owned by Moe Gale, a band promoter who had been out of business for thirty years.

"Gate," I said, "you should call Robbins, Feist and Mellow and see if they haven't got a check for you."

Gate was never one for taking care of business.

Two days later I called him and asked him if he had checked with the company. He said he hadn't, but he would. The next time I called him, he had contacted them and they had sent him a check for twenty-two thousand dollars. Between the two of us, we picked up thirty-nine thousand dollars in royalties for a

Left: Billy Eckstine on the golf course with his partner, Jimmy Jordan. Right: Lena Horne and Billy.

song that had been written forty years ago in twelve minutes. All this bread just ninety days after "Jelly" was released by a popular white rock group. Of course we had never been popular with white audiences. That's what's wrong with the music business. White folks listen to white people sing black tunes, but they won't listen to black people sing the same tunes, or pay them to do it. If they do, the money is always funny.

Blues tunes have been good for me, but I know that white folks want to label all Negroes as blues singers. For example, when Norman Granz takes a group of black musicians to Europe, he doesn't bring black ballad singers but black blues singers like Muddy Waters, Lightnin' Hopkins and Big Joe Turner. I love them all, but I know that they are being used. The white man thinks that blues is all a black man should sing. He doesn't want you to do romantic stuff. When we had nightly broadcasts from the Grand Terrace, white song pluggers used to come in and insist that ballads be plugged without vocals. Of course Hines resisted that kind of nonsense. He always told the pluggers, "If we plug any ballads, my singer Billy is going to have to do the vocal."

That's how I got the opportunity to do hits like "Skylark", "You Don't Know What Love Is" and many other beautiful ballads. Hines was not going to accept that kind of racism. Some of those dudes would try to give us the bullshit that people couldn't understand us because we had Southern accents. I said, "Shit, man, I'm from Pittsburgh! What Southern accent are you talking about? The only South I know is the South Side of Pittsburgh."

They had to back off the B.S. because I've never had a Southern accent and people of both races have been able to understand my lyrics easily. But for some reason the white man does not want the black man to have a romantic image.

Another time I was making a movie in Hollywood called *Skirts Ahoy* with Esther Williams. The director came up and asked me what I was going to wear for the nightclub scene. I asked him what people ordinarily wore for nightclub scenes, and he said he was thinking about white tails. I said, "You've got another thought coming. That's Cab Calloway, that's not me, and I'm not going to wear them."

They had this stereotype thing that they wanted us all to look alike and I've always rebelled against that kind of bullshit. If being a rebel is the only way I can be a man, then I'll be a rebel.

In 1943 I discovered by accident what I consider to be the female voice of the century. I stopped by the Apollo Theater in New York to cash a check and I heard a girl singing at an amateur show. She was on key, and not many singers are. I would guess that she wasn't a day over eighteen at the time, and she was incredible. I rushed backstage to congratulate her and fortunately she won the contest. I think the first prize was ten dollars. I told her I certainly would like her to become a member of the Earl Hines Band. I don't think she quite grasped it; I

Billy discovered Sarah Vaughan singing in an amateur contest at the Apollo Theater when she was eighteen years old.

doubt if she had made twenty-five dollars a week in her life. Her name was Sarah Vaughan, and I got Hines to hire her as our female vocalist for the grand salary of sixty-five dollars a week. She and I became a vocal duo and the rest is history. Sarah's voice cannot be described or categorized. Dave Garroway aptly called her "The Divine Sarah".

In late 1943 I left Earl Hines to do a solo act. I got a gig on 52nd Street in New York. It was an interim job for me because in those days the only way a singer could go over big was to be with a band, his own or somebody else's. A fellow named Willie Shaw, who ran the band department at the William Morris Agency, said that there was a band in St Louis that he wanted me to hear and check out with George Hudson down there. I went to St Louis to hear them and the band sounded good but they weren't doing anything original. When I got back to New York, Dizzie Gillespie, who was also working on 52nd Street, asked me how they sounded. I said, "Well, it's a good band, but they aren't saying anything."

So I went back to Shaw at the booking agency and told him I wanted to make up my band from scratch. He told me to go ahead, and I enlisted Dizzy as musical director. Dizzy would be considered the co-founder and Charlie "Bird" Parker joined us shortly after that. The band, under Dizzy's direction, went to St Louis and when our trumpet player, Buddy Anderson, became ill, he was replaced by a teenager from East St Louis named Miles Davis. Miles had been waiting in St Louis to hear the band because he wanted to dig Charlie Parker.

From St Louis we brought the band into Chicago for a week's engagement at the Regal Theater. We had some line-up. In the reed section, we had Parker, Gene Ammons, Lucky Thompson and Leo Parker. We had John Malachi on piano and Connie Wainwright on guitar. On bass we had Tommy Potter, and of course Sarah Vaughan and I were the vocalists. Shadow Wilson was on drums. In the brass section we had Howard McGee, Fats Navarro, Miles Davis and Freddie

Take five! The Earl Hines Band lights up between dance sets. Left to right starting with third from left: Pee Wee Jackson, Bud Johnson, Willie Randall, Leroy Harris, George Dixon, Madeline Green, Earl Hines, Billy Eckstine, Scoops Carey, Unknown, Streamline Ewing, Unknown, Hurley Ramey, Truck Parham, Unknown, and Franz Jackson.

Webster. Tadd Dameron was the arranger and sometimes he doubled on the piano. Subsequently over the years we picked up Bud Johnson, John Jackson, Dexter Gordon, Waddell Gray, Rudy Rutherford, Frank West, Cecil Payne and Sonny Stitt. We had the Who's Who of be-bop, although they were unknown then. They were just dedicated musicians looking for a new art form.

I kept that band from 1944 to 1947. People stood and listened: every dance hall we played in became a concert hall. We were not making any money but people still talk today about that legendary Billy Eckstine band. Man! The legendary Billy Eckstine was about to starve with that motherfucker, so I decided to break it up and do singles with MGM Records, which was starting a new label. I was the second singer to sign; the first was Art Lund. The contract with the recording company was with or without the band. I decided to go without the band and do my own thing. I gave all the guys a month's notice and I gave Dizzy every goddamned thing we had in the band: the music, the stands—everything. I said, "I don't ever want to see this shit again." That was the nucleus of my good friend Dizzy's band; he subsequently recorded a lot of music from the old Eckstine aggregation.

Dizzy and I were good friends because we had lived in the same apartment house at 2040 Seventh Avenue in New York in 1940. Dizzy lived in the apartment above me. He was constantly working out things on an old piano he had. I respected and admired him because he was serious and persistent, always looking for new concepts. When I met him, I couldn't read a note as big as the Sears Tower. Dizzy, Willie Randall, Bud Johnson and many of the other fellows in the Earl Hines Band put their arms around me and taught me what I know about

Billy Eckstine and the author.

music. I loved the sound of be-bop although at that early period we didn't have a name for it. There was a different sound in the chords and things that Dizzy was playing that actually perfected the way I was singing. I tried to sing the chord changes rather than the straight melody. Some of our earlier things, like "Skylark", were built off chord changes. I worked out the ending of "Skylark".

I don't regret dropping the big orchestra because following my be-bop kick, I made a string of successful ballad hits: "Everything I Have is Yours", "Prisoner of Love", "Fools Rush In" and "I Apologize". When I became popular, I changed the way I dressed. The cats on the main stem were wearing "Mr B" roll-collared shirts and jackets that draped like the clothes I wore on stage. When Duke Ellington and I were on the same bill, we did not wear the same outfit twice. We were both known to change suits for four shows a day for three consecutive weeks without repeating any garment—including shoes, socks and shorts. People bought tickets for the same show every week just to see what the two clothes-horses were wearing.

AUTHOR'S NOTES

In the spring of 1983, "Mr B" was still the essence of casual hip. He was in splendid voice at a recent appearance at Rick's Cafe Americain in Chicago. His voice does not seem to have changed in forty-five years. The women are still flocking to see and hear him. He is a living legend. I told Eckstine that Sinatra would pay five million dollars to keep his voice the way it was forty-five years ago. "Mr B" replied, "Give me Sinatra's money and I will give him my voice." The "Mr B" shirts have faded away, but Eckstine's talent is still shiny new.

Bud Freeman at the mike with his tenor sax.

*"I learned my music from great black jazz players like King Oliver
and Louis Armstrong."*

Bud Freeman

BIRTHDATE: April 13, 1906
BIRTHPLACE: Chicago, Illinois
INSTRUMENTS: Tenor Saxophone, Clarinet
OCCUPATION: Tenor Saxophonist, Composer and Bandleader
PERFORMED WITH: Husk O'Hare Wolverines, Ben Pollack, Red
Nichols, Meyer Davis, Tommy Dorsey, Benny Goodman, and
Eddie Condon.

My house was always full of music because my mother played piano, and she had
five sisters and two brothers who took pride in picking the white and black keys
on a regular basis. Since we were the only ones in the family who owned a piano,
our house was a rendezvous for every member who had an urge to play the
piano. Therefore, not a day passed when someone was not sitting down playing
the old upright.

My father served in the Spanish-American War, and he owned a pair of drumsticks that he got from the Army. That's possibly as close as he ever got to becoming a musician. I used to use his old drumsticks to beat on chairs as an accompaniment to the in-house piano players. I never had a desire to be a drummer or a piano player; however, I always had a very good feeling about rhythm and music. I was about ten years old when my Dad brought a wonderful record home, recorded by Noble Sissle and Eubie Blake. The record was called "Railroad Blues". I was fascinated by Eubie Blake's piano playing because it was so different from the piano style I had heard around the house or on any of our Victrola recordings. It was a fascinating, wonderful music, and I listened to it intensely. I didn't care much for Noble Sissle's vocals, but he was telling a story in this song about a man being killed attempting to rob a railroad. The story-line of the lyric caught my ear, and Blake's piano playing was mind-boggling, even to a ten year old. I remember some years later, maybe forty years later, I had the opportunity of meeting Eubie Blake at a party given by the *Ebony Magazine* staff in New York City. On that occasion, I told Blake that I had heard him play a song entitled "Railroad Blues" when I was ten years old back in 1916. Blake responded, looking me straight in the eye, "If you heard me play 'Railroad Blues' when you were ten years old, it was because I started playing piano when I was six months old." We both laughed.

I hated going to school. I absolutely resented it, and rebelled at every opportunity. In fact, my interest was in three things: music, movies and sports. By the time I reached the age of thirteen, I had become so incorrigible that it appeared that I wasn't likely to graduate from elementary school. It was not because I didn't have the ability, but because I didn't care. As a result of my interest in sports, I entered an all-city track meet and won in all the events. The Principal wrote my father a letter suggesting that my athletic talents were not ordinary. On the strength of my track ability, I was graduated from grammar school and accepted for enrollment at Austin High School, where I met Jimmy McPartland, his brother Richard, and another fellow named Jim Lanigan. They were all musicians, and I just loved hanging out with them. Another fellow who was attracted to our small group was Dave Tough, who didn't go to Austin High, but would come there frequently to meet his girlfriend. I was odd man out since I was the only one in the group who didn't play an instrument or even think about owning a horn.

The McPartland Brothers, who had already begun to play professionally, invited me to a street dance. I will never forget that afternoon, because I had just received my first long pants suit. I couldn't dance and had no desire to dance. I just wanted to listen to the McPartlands play music. There was a kid in the band playing clarinet. He had a very beautiful tone for such a young kid. His technique and sound reminded me of some things that I had heard at home on my Victrola.

Left: Eubie Blake in 1924. Right: Benny Goodman.

His name was Benny Goodman. He was a pleasant little fellow who I'm sure didn't have the faintest idea that he possessed a great talent. Although I was inspired by what the McPartlands were doing musically and specifically by Goodman, I still had not decided that I wanted to be a musician. It was almost two years later that the McPartlands, who had a great influence on me, were able to persuade my father to buy me a C-melody saxophone. It was a brass-colored instrument, and I treated it like it was gold. I was almost afraid to play it for fear that I would damage it. Jimmy McPartland's father gave me my first lessons. I didn't like them because they reminded me of school. Somehow, I expected the saxophone to play by itself. All I wanted to do was simply hold it and look like a musician. I had a lot of musical ideas in my head as a result of listening to records at home, to my relatives play the piano, and to the school band on Friday afternoon at the Austin High School gym. Hip Dick McPartland taught me the chords and I tried to play. I had the ideas in my head, but I wasn't technically capable of fingering them on the instrument. I ended up being a one-note-Johnny: I would get on one note since I couldn't really go to the next, and just play that note in various rhythmic patterns. Some time passed before I was able to play my first full melody.

Dave Tough, (the drummer who was later to become famous), gave me my first professional job. It was at a roadhouse in Sheboygan, Wisconsin, for the summer season. Dave liked me so much personally that he overlooked my ineptitude as a musician. Dave told the owner of the roadhouse that I was the best C-melody sax man in the land, and that a man with my credentials and credibility certainly should not have to audition. Dave knew that if I had had to audition, I would have been an absolute disaster. The owner of the roadhouse was an ex-piano playing vaudevillian who recognized after hearing me for fifteen minutes on the bandstand, that I couldn't cut it. So he told Dave that first night that I would have to go, and Dave told him if I went, he was going. He liked Dave well enough to let me stay on. But in the end, he put so much pressure on Dave, that Dave just had to quit. The night that Dave and I left the roadhouse, the piano player jumped up and grabbed me by the throat and screamed, "You son-of-a-bitch! If you don't get out of town in one hour, I'm going to kill you!" I owe Dave something up and beyond the call of duty and friendship for giving me that opportunity. The job paid forty dollars a week and my room and board was only three dollars and fifty cents a week, so I made out pretty well, considering the fact that that gig offered me some real on-the-job training.

After I returned to Chicago, I joined a group called the Blue Friars. They worked as the Red Dragons under the management of Husk O'Hare. Mr O'Hare managed to get the group a broadcasting spot on WHT. When the original Wolverines disbanded, O'Hare had us work as Husk O'Hare's Wolverines. He got us a good gig in the ballroom at the White City Amusement Park at 6300 South Park. This was pretty good for a kid who had not thought about becoming a professional musician until relatively late in life—and I consider seventeen years old late for a guy to enter the musical profession. That is particularly true when you consider that most great jazz musicians have reached their peak by the time they are twenty-five years old.

I feel that I owe a great debt to black people because it was through the music of Louis Armstrong and King Oliver that I really got some of my best inspiration and direction. I didn't learn anything from just ordinary black musicians. It was the geniuses of jazz music who really gave me my music lessons. My teachers were King Oliver, Louis Armstrong, Earl Hines and Bessie Smith. When you heard Bessie Smith sing, you heard a whole symphony of jazz in one song. I remember one night, Dave Tough and I went to see Bessie Smith out on the South Side, and Dave got so carried away with this woman's talent, that he gave her all the money he had in his pocket as a tip. If I hadn't had any money, we would have had to walk back to the Northwest Side of Chicago. Musically sensitive whites who had an opportunity to hear jazz were usually deeply affected by it. Some years later, I got an opportunity to meet Lil Armstrong and she told me that she remembered seeing us white boys at the Lincoln Garden up on 31st Street, and she often wondered why we were in the audience staring at them. What she didn't realize was that they were making history, and the music that they were playing meant a

Louis Armstrong and his Hot Five, Chicago, 1925. Left to right: Johnny St. Cyr; Johnny Dodds; Kid Ory, and Lil Hardin.

great deal to us as listeners. It was food for our souls, and our artistic develop-ment. If it hadn't been for their genius in developing jazz music, I would never have become a musician. I would probably have become an artist of some sort, or just a maverick.

I've learned black music not by listening only to black musicians, but by also listening to the rhythm of black tap dancers. There is no drummer who can create the rhythmic beat of a Baby Lawrence, a John Bubbles or a Bill "Bojangles" Robinson. Drummers just cannot cut that rhythm the way a dancer does. A dancer tells a story in perfect time with the tapping of his toes.

Bix Beiderbecke, the late great trumpet player, was the first white person I ever knew who felt and understood the black man's rhythm. When I say the black man's rhythm, I'm talking about black dancers, black singers and black musicians. Bix had this wonderful feeling for what they were doing, and he was way ahead of any white man of his time. Listening to Bix's records, it would be hard for you to hear the kind of feeling and understanding that this man pos-sessed, because he was always surrounded by studio or session musicians who didn't have his kind of feeling for black music. Bix took me out on the South Side one night to hear the Jimmy Noone band. I had never heard Jimmy Noone in my life. Noone had a style that must have influenced Goodman and many other clarinet players. Bix listened to that music with great intensity, and became

Left: Baby Lawrence, tap dancer par excellence. Right: Bix Beiderbecke, the legendary trumpeter.

drunk, both on liquor and on song. He was so out of it that he went completely out of his mind. The music had that kind of power over this sensitive man. It was just too bad that he had to go before he fulfilled his musical mission.

I accepted an offer to go with Ben Pollack's band in New York City and I dropped around to see my old friend, Don Redman, who was playing with Fletcher Henderson at the Roseland Ballroom. Don said, "I'm surprised to see you in New York." I asked why and he said, "You won't like it." I asked, "Why not?" He said, "The cats here don't swing!" I said, "You mean nobody swings?" He said "Nobody downtown swings." The exceptions to that statement were the great piano players like Willie "The Lion" Smith, James P. Johnson, Fats Waller, and the singers and dancers up in Harlem who were doing a different kind of thing. Even Coleman Hawkins was still slap-sticking his saxophone. He didn't really get his shoes on until he heard the great Louis Armstrong.

It's been said that New Orleans is the cradle of jazz. I say that's nonsense. Louie and Joe Oliver were the most talented men to come out of New Orleans,

Tommy Dorsey (left), and Bunny Berrigan blowing one of his famous solos.

and they didn't really get their style together until they came into Chicago and started playing what we call show-tunes. It was then that they developed a new style and of course Louie had the creative genius to make this kind of music both palatable and jazzy. Jazz was being played in Chicago long before it was being played in New York and long before it was being played in the South and on the West Coast. In fact, the musicians from Kansas City used to come to Chicago to learn the Chicago sound. Count Basie actually worked in Chicago as an organist and piano player before going to Kansas City. If you just think about some of the great swingers, even those in Harlem, like Willie "The Lion" Smith, Fats Waller, Eubie Blake, James P. Johnson, Lucky Roberts—none of those guys ever saw the inside of the state of Louisiana, and yet we continue to want to give New Orleans the credit when the credit belongs to Chicago. Chicago is where jazz was developed and where it actually happened. I'm not making a Chicago Chamber of Commerce statement. I am simply relating a fact.

When I said earlier that I found Coleman Hawkins in New York City slapping his saxophone I didn't mean to be disrespectful. I got my first in-depth lesson on

Left: Bud Freeman at WBEZ's Windy City Jazz Live broadcast. Right: Bud Freeman solos at Rick's Cafe Americain for the WBEZ jazz program.

the tenor saxophone listening to Coleman Hawkins play at the Graystone Ballroom in Detroit. Hawkins' lessons were what I needed to develop a tenor style of my own. The man was a great musician and probably one of the most schooled musicians around, black or white. He had a degree in music, he played the piano, violin and cello, but he didn't get his jazz wings, in my opinion, until he listened to Louis Armstrong. Hawkins was a great melody man. He could take a song like "Body and Soul", which was written and put together by a wonderful musician, and put his talent to that construction, and develop a masterpiece. In fact, if you listen to Hawk, you'll find him doing his greatest work when he sticks very, very close to the melody. Lester Young also loved melody. He just had a different sound and a different way of expressing how he felt about it. Lester was a quiet, soft, gentle man, while Hawkins was very robust, outspoken, and in many

instances, a very angry man. Ben Webster was also a very soft man, although when he got drunk, he could be very vicious and cruel. But he was a lovely fellow if you knew him, and I knew him as a sober guy. Webster and I became very, very close friends.

Ben Webster was very strongly influenced by Coleman Hawkins. He was a melody man and would not go too far out harmonically speaking. If you listen to his records, you'll see that his best songs were those with strong melody lines, and near the end of his life, the last five years, most, if not all, of the things that he recorded were lovely melodies with strong lines. He wasn't strong on improvisation. It's almost a contradiction when you think about it. The song that really made him famous was "Cotton Tail" which he recorded when he was with Duke Ellington, and "Cotton Tail" is not melodic, but a take-off on the chord structure of an upbeat standard called "I've Got Rhythm."

I owe a big debt for my jazz credentials to the great black jazz master, Louis Armstrong. As a debtor in the jazz arena, I don't stand alone, because there has not been a single soloist in jazz music who developed within the past fifty-five years who was not influenced by the great Louie. I'm not talking about hacks. I'm talking about fellow musicians who have developed into master musicians during later periods. The late and great Bunny Berrigan was certainly influenced by Louis Armstrog. All one has to do is listen to his solo on the recording of "Marie" with the Tommy Dorsey band and you can definitely hear the Louis Armstrong influence. In fact, the entire Dorsey arrangement of "Marie" was lifted from a black band at the Nixon Theater in Philadelphia. I know, because I was there with the Dorsey band when it happened. I can't think of a trumpet player who has put an instrument to his lips, who shouldn't credit Louie for the power and the creativity that he's brought to that instrument, and I'm thinking of greats such as "Hot Lips" Page, Charlie Shavers, Buck Clayton, Harry James, and Rex Stewart. In fact, Rex Stewart imitated Louie so closely that he even went out and bought a pair of shoes like Louie's. Louie was known for wearing big, high-top, oversized shoes. Rex thought that perhaps if he wore those kind of shoes and walked like

Left to right: Bud Freeman being interviewed at Rick's Cafe by Linda Prince, producer of Public Radio's Windy City Jazz Live *program.*

Louie, he would be able to play like Louie. That's the kind of influence Louie had on his fellow musicians. Bobby Hackett is a great soloist, very melodic and very soft, but you can hear the Armstrong influence throughout his work. Billy Butterfield, whom I consider one of the best ballad players in the world, plays like Louie. There is no doubt about the Armstrong influence on stars like Dizzy Gillespie, Miles Davis and Roy Eldridge. Dizzy would probably say he was more influenced by Roy, once removed, from Louie. But then since Roy was influenced by Louie, and Dizzy is influenced by Roy, Dizzy is playing Louie's stuff. Louie had an extremely long musical arm. He could reach across the ocean, and he did. The great legendary Coleman Hawkins changed his style as a result of listening to Louis Armstrong. The Armstrong beat and rhythm can be found in Lester Young's choruses. Earl Hines, Fats Waller, Jess Stacey, Ralph Sutton, Joe Bushkin, Art Tatum, Teddy Wilson, Count Basie, and Duke Ellington have spent untold hours listening and learning from the creative genius of the great Louis Armstrong. We physically lost the most powerful voice in American music when Louis Armstrong left us twelve years ago. Musically, Armstrong's voice will be heard as long as man pursues America's only original art form. Jazz.

John Birkes "Dizzy" Gillespie

"When I think of artistry and music, I always have to remember Paul Robeson, whom I loved."

John Birkes "Dizzy" Gillespie

BIRTHDATE: October 21, 1917
BIRTHPLACE: Cheraw, South Carolina
INSTRUMENT PLAYED: Trumpet
OCCUPATON: Instrumentalist, Composer, Vocalist, Band Leader
FEATURED WITH: Cab Calloway, Lucky Millinder, Charlie Barnett, Fletcher Henderson, Benny Carter, Earl Hines, Duke Ellington, John Kirby, Billy Eckstine.

My father was a brick mason. As a young man he had been a musician. In fact, the first bass fiddle I ever saw belonged to my father. He played several other instruments, including the clarinet, the mandolin and piano. However, back in my hometown of Cheraw, South Carolina, a man with nine kids could not very well support a family on the kind of money that an itinerant musician made during that period.

My father died when I was nine years old. He had made an effort to get my older sisters and brothers interested in music. He failed. The only thing they were interested in doing was getting away from home because my father was what you might call an extreme authoritarian. He was the epitome of that breed of parent who believed in meting out heavy discipline on his children, even when they had not done anything wrong. As a matter of fact, every Sunday that God sent, my father would give me and my brother a beating. I can hear his voice now. I guess I was only about five or six when he began meting out punishment every Sunday. He would say, "John Wesley! Come on, get me the strap!" Dad would beat us every Sunday afternoon—rain or shine, snow or sleet, high or low water. And the funny thing about it, we hadn't done anything. He just beat us to have something to do on Sunday—at least that's what I thought.

I remember the day my father died. My older brother had left the house to pick blackberries that day, and then suddenly turned around after he got about halfway to the field and came back home, as though he had had a premonition of some sort. My brother and I were in the house when my father died of a heart attack. Dad had suffered with a severe case of asthma most of his adult life and was only forty-two years old when he died. I'm not ashamed to say that I didn't cry. In fact, I didn't cry until I found that razor strap and a razor to cut that strap into a million pieces, and then I felt sorry for the old man. But until I destroyed that strap, I felt no pity about his dying.

My mother was just the opposite in temperament. I guess I could best describe her as having the milk of human kindness. Looking back, my father may have had more insight into my character and personality than my mother. I say that because I was a devil when I was a little guy and a strong devil. I could whip all the guys my size and bigger in the neighborhood. In fact, when some of the larger boys in Cheraw saw me coming down the street, they actually crossed over to the other side of the street in order to avoid a possible whipping. Sometimes I would sneak up on them and start a fight or hit them in the stomach as I passed. In the country, if you were losing a fight, you would usually pick up a stick and defend yourself. I never really hurt anyone but I always felt a need for combat. My father's harsh methods of punishment might have set that spirit in motion.

My interest in music began at Robert Small Elementary School in Cheraw when the state purchased instruments for distribution to various elementary and high schools throughout the state. I was one of the first ones to get in line in an effort to obtain an instrument from the teacher, but he passed me by in favor of some of the larger boys in the class. I was only about twelve years old then. After

Left to right: Ted Weems, Joe Hughes, Sarah Vaughan, Dizzy Gillespie, and Joe "Ziggy" Johnson at a Mon-day night celebrity party in Joe's Deluxe Cafe in Chicago.

the teacher had passed out all the instruments, there was only one left and that was a trombone. He said, "John Birkes, you can take this one."

My arms were too short to get down to the last position on the trombone, but I still wanted to get in the band, so I decided I would mess around with that horn until I could do better. My next door neighbor, James Harrington, also attended Small Elementary School. His father bought him one of those long trumpets. One day I asked Jimmie if he would let me practice on his horn and he said, "Why not? We can practice together."

I literally lived over at his house because I was in love with his horn. In a relatively short period I became pretty good at playing the trumpet. Since I was showing that kind of development without any practical training on the instrument, the school gave me a trumpet to play in the band. I remember that all the songs we played in the Small Elementary School Band were in the key of B-flat. Frankly, I thought that was the only key on the scale.

Left to right: The author, Marthann Campbell, Dizzy, and Noor Halani, Manager of Rick's Cafe Americain, Chicago.

I never had a trumpet of my own until I was seventeen years old. I moved to Philadelphia, Pennsylvania, following my mother and brother who had moved there a year earlier. They left me behind, thinking that I could finish high school and then come to Philadelphia, but I just couldn't get my mind on books. My primary interest was music and, specifically, the trumpet. My brother-in-law bought my first horn from a pawn shop. He didn't purchase a case for the horn, so I carried it around in a paper bag and that's when the guys started calling me "Dizzy." First, I was the dizzy trumpet player with the paper bag, and later they shortened it to Trumpet Dizzy, and then to Diz. Now there are at least four or five guys around who say they gave me that nickname. To this day, I'm not exactly sure which one of the four should get credit, but the name has stuck with me for almost fifty years.

I didn't make the ninety-mile trip from Philadelphia to New York, the Big Apple, until 1937. My first big job there was with Teddy Hill's band at the Savoy Ballroom. The other band there at the Savoy was headed by Chick Webb. Chick had an excellent first trumpet man named Mario Bauza, who was fond of me and would let me sit in Taft Jordan's place and take the solos. I had heard Teddy Hill's orchestra on the radio, broadcasting from the Savoy in 1935, and I listened especially to Roy Eldridge. When I joined Teddy Hill's band myself and sat in Roy's chair, I could play all of Roy's solos exactly as he had played them. There is no question that he was my musical father: Roy Eldridge influenced me more than any other single trumpet player on the scene. People often ask whether Louis Armstrong had any influence on my playing style. We all know that Louis Armstrong is the father of the jazz trumpet, and there is a definite connection between Louis and myself, but in between there is Roy Eldridge.

It's difficult to explain how one's style evolves. You start out as a rule playing like somebody else, and then your style evolves and you play less and less like the guy that you started imitating. . . You build on what you have learned from him into something unique to you.

In 1939 my friend Mario, who was then playing with Cab Calloway, suggested that I come over and visit him at the Cotton Club because they were looking for a solo trumpet player. About a week after my visit, Mario called and said he wasn't feeling well. He asked me to go down to the Cotton Club and sit in his chair. He said I should let LaMar Wright take all the first trumpet parts and then when the time came for a solo I should really show my stuff. Cab Calloway didn't know me. In fact, I didn't even formally report that night. I just put on the uniform and went up and sat in Mario's chair. I wasn't afraid of Cab Calloway's famous band because at the country music school I had attended in Cheraw, South Carolina, I had been taught how to read a speck on a fly swatter. I could read anything in the Calloway book. While I was with Teddy Hill's band I had polished my playing and sharpened my reading. So when I took a solo at the Cotton Club that night in 1939 everyone's head turned toward me, as if to say "Who the hell is that playing?" Back in those days whenever a tap dancer like Bill Robinson did his number, he was always backed up by trumpet. I stood up and blew the accompaniment for Bill Robinson and all the musicians and entertainers in the Club that night were flabbergasted at my technique as well as my tone.

Despite all that, the only thing that came out of that evening was an increase in my self-confidence. I felt I could play with ease with the best of them. Cab at that time had one of the best bands in the country.

Several weeks later my wife Lorraine, who was a chorus girl playing too many shows, decided she was too tired to go on working. She had a friend named Rudolph who was Cab Calloway's valet, and she asked him if he could do something to help me get a job. A couple of weeks after that I was working a one week gig at the Apollo Theatre and Rudolph called me and said, "Hey look, man, I think you should come on down to the Cotton Club."

"Yeah?" I said. "What for?"

"Man, come on down. Don't be no fool and bring your horn."

I went down to the Cotton Club that night. I had not yet met Cab Calloway, but there was a vacant chair in the trumpet section. I was ecstatic over the chance to play with Calloway's Cotton Club orchestra. There were some difficult numbers in Cab's book, and that night he threw me "Cuban Nightmare", which was particularly hard. I ate up that song like a whale eating a minnow. Cab liked the way I handled that complex tune, and that was the beginning of a two year association for me with Cab's band. And during those two years he let me do a lot of soloing. That was a real break when you consider how tightly the Cab Calloway arrangements were written. There was not much solo work for anybody besides Cab. After all he was the star.

I left Cab's band because somebody threw a spitball on the stage during a performance at the State Theater in Boston. I was accused of doing it, but I did not plead the Fifth.

My early work with Cab reflected Roy Eldridge's influence. He remained the main influence on me, although later I was certainly influenced by Charlie Parker, and the work of Art Tatum, Coleman Hawkins and Benny Carter also had some effect on my work.

I am often asked about bebop. Actually we were playing around with bebop ideas in New York at Menton's on 7th Avenue back in the late '30s and early '40s, but the whole thing came together when I was in the Earl Hines band, which I joined in 1943. Billy Eckstine was vocalist, Shadow Wilson was on drums, Scoops Carey and Goon Gardner on alto, Thomas Crump on tenor sax and Johnny Williams on baritone. Although Earl did not need another saxophone player, he hired Charlie Parker because Charlie was unique. Charlie was an alto man, but Earl bought him a tenor as a companion to Crump. So we had two tenors, two altos and a baritone. And it was there in the Hines band in 1943 that the whole bebop movement took shape. In 1943 the Hines band was doing things that were ahead of their time. I don't think people realize the kind of contribution Earl Hines made, not just to piano-playing, but to music in general. Hines would have gotten more credit for his work if there had not been a union ban on instrumental recording from 1943 to December, 1948. Some things were done musically during that period that are now lost forever.

The Hines band was the incubator of the bebop school and its leading exponent until 1944. Men from the Hines band formed the nucleus of Billy Eckstine's bebop band. I was in the first Eckstine band with Charlie Parker, Gail Brockman, Miles Davis, Fats Navarro and some other bebop players. I would say that Charlie Parker stands head and shoulders above everybody else as the prime mover among instrumentalists of the bebop style. He played the same notes everybody else played but his unique style contributed to the development and acceptance of bebop in no small way.

I first met Charlie Parker in Kansas City in 1940, and he was no short stop then. A trumpet player by the name of Buddy Anderson brought the "Yard Bird" by my room in the Booker T. Washington Hotel. The young cat pulled out his alto

Dizzy does a dance number with Marty Faye on Faye's television show. In rear at the piano is Joe Williams.

sax and started blowing ideas and concepts that I couldn't believe. "Bird" would be playing one song and go right into another with the same chord structure, perfectly. Man, I could not believe my ears.

Let me tell you a little story about *To Be Or Not To Bop,* which is the title of my latest book. I was in London staying at the Mayfair Hotel. I took a walk one day in Hyde Park and you know they have all these quaint boutiques with paintings, sculptures, books and everything handsomely displayed. I stopped at a little shop to browse and saw all of these little paintings about two inches in diameter. The object that caught my eye was a painting of Shakespeare. Just above was one of those little English hats with a small question mark protruding out of the top, resembling an ornament, and under the bottom was the phrase: "To Be Or Not To Be." I told the saleslady I had an idea. "If you will change the last word for me on that sign, I will buy all of those ornaments that you have on that shelf."

She said, "You come back in half an hour and I believe I can fulfill your wishes. How do you want it changed?"

I said I wanted it to read: "To be or not to Bop."

So when I came back she had changed the last word to "Bop" in very tiny writing. Of course I kept my promise and bought all the trinkets on that particular shelf and that is how my book got its title, *To Be Or Not to Bop.* I took the idea to the editors and publishers but they didn't look on this title too kindly. They had another in mind and wanted to call it *The Movement* or something like that. Another editor wanted to call it *Gillespie—A Legend in His Own Time.* But I said without blinking an eye that I wouldn't accept anything except *To Be Or Not To Bop.* I wanted "To" printed small, a large "Be," and then further down a small "not to," and a huge "Bop," so that when you look at the book cover it says, "Be-Bop," but when you look closer you see the full title. I thought it was a clever idea. However, the book has not sold well.

Whenever I travel abroad, I try to keep my eyes and ears open and I have found more jazz in some parts of Europe than you could find anywhere in the United States. I attribute that to the fact that our country is culturally young and we are not up to the European standard because we deal in commercialism and they look upon jazz as an art form. Of course, Europeans love our artistry and our music. When I think of artistry and music, I always remember Paul Robeson, whom I loved. Paul traveled throughout Europe and the Soviet Union giving concerts and spreading the good word. At the same time that Robeson was idolized in Europe, he was crucified in his own country.

In late 1949 or early 1950, I was playing at the Apollo Theater and received a telegram from Paul Robeson that read: "I enjoyed your performance, but I didn't want to create any heat or anything on you so I didn't come backstage."

I called Paul and asked what he meant. "You are me, man," I told him. I sincerely meant that. Paul Robeson was a great human being. It's too bad that there were those among us who did not appreciate the contribution that this great citizen of the world made to mankind.

On another occasion, when we were touring the Far East, a human tragedy took place in Japan. When we arrived in Japan, Sonny Stitt who had been in trouble earlier with the law, was not permitted to enter the country. He had to stay in a room at the airport, and we had to use a Japanese fellow named Sleepy Motzumoto to replace Sonny. Although Sleepy was a good saxophonist, it was unfortunate that Sonny had traveled such a great distance thinking he would be able to work. It appears to me that when he had applied for his visa and passport, they should have informed him of the problem and thereby avoided the problem. I remember on another occasion when I went through customs, there was a Japanese fellow who searched my bags frantically, looking through underwear, socks and everything. I simply tapped him on the shoulder and said, "Look, man, if you tell me what you are looking for, maybe I can help you find it," and that's the way I left it.

The Japanese are very interested in jazz. Their love for jazz almost equals the Europeans'. One Japanese fellow said to me, "You are a very fast trumpet player, the fastest."

That's not true. There have been many fast trumpet players. I am thinking of Rex Stewart, who played with Duke for many years and, of course, of my mentor, Roy Eldridge. There were also Fats Navarro, Clifford Brown, Lee Morgan and many others that you have never heard of who are equally fast.

I believe my harmonic knowledge of the piano has always helped me with the horn. In fact, I am a piano nut. I cannot pass a piano without touching it, so when someone writes something for me, or when writing myself, it's as though I am writing for a symphony. In other words, someone might elect to write a melody for trumpet in B-flat, but I tell him to write for me as if it were a concert.

When I open my ears, I hear a concert; I don't only hear a single note. As I explained to this Japanese fellow, in analyzing style and what one hears, one can hear not only a certain amount of creativity, but also training and experience. My style did not develop as a sudden flash of genius but was the result of an accumulation of hard-earned ideas from many artists. To mention a few, I would say Thelonius Monk, Lester Young, Buck Clatyon and my close friend and partner, Charlie Parker. We all spent a lot of time down at Minton's in New York City during our formative years.

One misconception is that bop employs whole tone scales. That's true. But it also extends the chords in an unorthodox manner, which gives it its totally different sound. Often these are substitute chords, such as a minor 7th with an associated minor 9th, or occasionally an augmented or diminished 11th. There is no definite pattern to the chord structures I use. I use them as I feel them and that is probably where the difference comes in. I advocate every musician learn as much about the piano as he or she can. I found that all good singers know something about piano. Carmen McRae is an excellent pianist and Dinah Washington could sit down and play piano as well as most people who do it for a living. Sarah Vaughan does that too, and Ella Fitzgerald is not a slouch at the piano. That also applies to trumpet players, saxophone players, trombonists, bass players, guitar players—the more familiar they are with the piano, the better they perform on their respective instruments.

Speaking of performers, Duke Ellington once told me, and I will never forget it: "Birkes, you should never have let them name your music bebop. You should have insisted on it being known as Gillesienna," he said, "because you are dated with a name like bebop, and you shouldn't date yourself at any time. I hope my music will always be remembered as Ellingtonian."

Travis, I think your idea of writing about our music is important. The time for blacks to write about their own music is long past due. It's time for us to do it ourselves and tell it like it is. Whites have given a whitewashed look to our music. Naturally, they are going to ooze off as much as they can to other whites. That is why it is so important to document our own history for the black generations to come.

Dick Gregory

"I never got hungry while I was running."

Dick Gregory

BIRTHDATE: October 12, 1932
BIRTHPLACE: St Louis, Missouri
INSTRUMENT: Drums and Voice
OCCUPATION: Comedian and Civil Rights Activist

I don't think I would have finished high school if I hadn't been running. Track kept me going from day to day. It was a reason to get up in the morning. I would run three hours non-stop around the track every day, rain, sleet or snow. It never got too hot or too cold for me to run. I could talk to myself while I was running and I told myself little stories: "My Favorite Daddy" and "What I Would Do with a Million Dollars". No one looked at me while I was running and talking to myself and said I was crazy. They just looked at me with admiration and said "He's training." The funny thing is that I never got hungry while I was running, even though many mornings we had no breakfast at home, and I didn't always have lunch money either.

In a manner of speaking I ran all the way to Chicago, and stopped running when I hit the Esquire Show Lounge on the South Side at 95th and Wentworth around 1957. The Esquire was a large rectangular room filled with chrome tables and chairs with red plastic seats and backs. I considered it my home and stadium.

I trained for my comedy routines just as I had trained for track meets. Every day during the week I worked out, listening to people, going to libraries, digging into old humor books. I went to parties and created clownish situations and if something got a good response I marked it down in the back of my mind as something I should repeat.

I learned a lot about people while I was working at the Esquire Lounge and I made rules which I follow to this day. I never go to a man's table if I think his woman is making eyes at me. I owe him respect. He has to feel comfortable with me and his lady and, after all, he is picking up the check. I remember that at the Esquire they would throw more money on the stage some nights than I made in a week but I never stooped to pick it up. I wanted to create a certain kind of image, and I couldn't do that if I stooped to pick up that kind of money.

I learned while I was working in small clubs that an entertainer gets the same kind of respect from working-class people that he gets in a big hotel or down-town nightclub. He is the biggest entertainer they know and maybe the biggest they will ever know. There is an atmosphere of glamour around entertainers; even those on the bottom of the pile, and they will get respect if they give respect to their audiences. That's why I always try to dress well and stay clean, both mentally and physically.

Back in the Esquire days the height of my ambition was to work in Roberts Show Lounge. Every night as soon as I got off I would make a bee-line to Roberts to see what was happening. They had acts like Dinah Washington, Count Basie, Duke Ellington, Nipsey Russell, Sarah Vaughan and Sammy Davis Jr. Roberts was the apex of black-owned nightclubs in this country.

I was so impressed with Roberts Show Lounge that I decided to become an entrepreneur myself. I wanted to be my own boss, be respected as an owner and performer, and develop new talent, pay good salaries and create an atmosphere for good comedy. I wanted to make everyone happy. So I borrowed eight hundred dollars from my girlfriend, Lillian Smith, to rent the old Apex Nightclub in Robbins, Illinois, in January, 1959. The *Farmers Almanac* didn't predict it but the winter I went into business was one of the worst in the city's history. My first weekend was fantastic. We had an almost full house on Friday and Saturday nights. It looked like I was really going to be a big-time nightclub owner.

Then the following Friday we got thirteen inches of snow and three customers. On Saturday we got five more inches and twenty people braved the

Dick Gregory visits with Sammy Davis Jr backstage at Roberts Show Club.

bad highways to show up. Sunday brought two more inches and twenty more people. From that point, it was all downhill. The Apex Club gave up the ghost in the summer of 1959.

Luckily for me, I got my old job back at the Esquire in August for ten dollars a night. At the same time I tried to persuade Herman Roberts to hire me. I asked him to come out to the Esquire to see my act, but he wouldn't do it. So I decided that if Herman wouldn't come to the mountain, the mountain would have to be brought to Herman. That year the Pan American Games were being held in Chicago, and I knew a lot of the athletes. I borrowed some money from a friend and rented Roberts Show Lounge for one night for a party for the team. Naturally it was a one man show: me. Herman saw me perform that night, and he asked me

how much I wanted, to be master of ceremonies at his club. I said one hundred and twenty-five dollars a week. He almost dropped his teeth, because he had expected it to be more.

Herman Roberts was a decent fellow and an excellent businessman. My real big break while I was working for him came when he brought in Sammy Davis Jr, Count Basie, Sarah Vaughan and Nipsey Russell; they attracted a lot of whites from the Loop. I was told I wouldn't be needed the week Nipsey Russell was playing. I complained to Herman, and he said, "I didn't tell that guy to get rid of you, but really we don't need you this week."

"Look, Herman," I said. "This is my job, I am the house M.C. and nobody is go-

Dick Gregory and Marty Faye sent 20,000 turkeys to Mississippi for Christmas.

ing to run me off my stage."

"I don't have any problem with that," Herman said. But he explained that Nipsey was a comic and you can't have two comics on the stage at once.

"I'm the house M.C.," I said, "and that's all I am."

I knew that once I got that mike in my hand, whether it was for two hours or two minutes, I was in total control and I could put myself across.

I prayed that the night Nipsey opened something would go wrong: that the piano would break down or the piano player would break his fingers—anything that would give me a chance to stay on stage a few extra minutes because Hugh Hefner and all the money people were in the audience that night. Miraculously, the curtain didn't go up on time, because somebody wasn't ready. So I had the opportunity to lay my rap. Hefner and everyone in the audience loved it.

Irwin Corey, the comedian, was working for Hugh Hefner at the Playboy Club. He wanted to take Sunday off, so they sent for me to take his place. I had not been downtown very often. I had a quarter in my pocket, and they offered to pay me fifty dollars. I didn't know there was that much money in the world for a one-night gig.

On Sunday night there was a blizzard and not knowing much about the Loop, I got off at the wrong stop. Man, I was cold and scared and I knew I had to be there on time and I didn't want to be late, so I started running. The snow was beating against my face and I prayed, God, I've got to get there. I can't be late for that gig. To show you the power of God, I got there on time.

But when I came in, Victor Lownes, who was vice-president of Playboy Enterprises, was standing on the stairs. He said, "Gregory, you don't have to go on. We've made a mistake. We sold this room out to a Southern frozen food delegation." There was a large convention of Southern gentlemen in Chicago and they had rented that room for the evening. Lownes said, "You don't have to work, but we will send you the money." Getting paid for not working may be a good shot, but not for me.

I said, "Man, you get out of my way. I've come through a blizzard, I got off at the wrong stop, and I'm tired. I'm here and I'm going to perform. That snow has made my face feel like it's full of blisters. And there's no way in the world that I'm not going to perform tonight."

I pushed past him and walked into the room, went up on the stage, introduced myself and started my act and three hours later I was still doing it. After I had been on for two hours non-stop Victor phoned Hefner at the Mansion and told him to get out of bed and come see this comedian that was just tearing the house up. Hefner came and he was floored. They couldn't believe that I could work three hours straight, telling Southerners about themselves, and the Southerners loved every damn minute of it.

I went home that morning feeling good. My gig at Roberts didn't last long because Playboy hired me almost immediately and brought me back downtown. *Jet* Magazine carried an article about me and I received a call from a representative of Jack Paar, who was a power in television at that time, asking me to be a guest on his show. I refused, although I liked the Paar show; I had watched it every night for five straight years. But I refused because Billy Eckstine had pointed out to me at the Roberts bar that blacks never sat on the couch on the Paar show. They performed and then left. Whites performed and then sat on the couch and chatted with Jack. Jack's contact man called me back and asked me why I didn't want to go on the show. I told him I had never seen a Negro sit down on that couch. Then I hung up and started crying. Before I could explain to my wife why I was crying, Jack Paar called. He said that Sammy Davis had sat down on the couch.

I said, "He sat down on Monday night when you were off. I saw the show."

He told me to come on in and he would take care of me.

I went on the show and I sat down and I was amazed at the kind of mail I got from white folks. It was the first time they had ever heard a black person dicussing his family. The only black entertainer they had seen was Satchmo blowing his horn; he had never sat down and talked. That show made me an instant success. Within three weeks my salary went from two hundred and fifty a week to five

Counter-clockwise: the author, George O'Hare, John Bellamy, and Dick Gregory.

thousand. The largest salary I've ever drawn was twenty-five thousand in one week. I did very well in nightclubs working on a percentage. I'd go into Washington, D.C., for example, for six grand a week plus eighty-five percent of the gate after the first six thousand. It's incredible the amount of money you can walk away with under those arrangements. In early 1973 I decided I wasn't going to work nightclubs period because of alcohol.

I made so much money as a nightclub comedian that I was able to devote myself to the civil rights movement. I put up twenty-five thousand dollars reward for the apprehension of the person or persons responsible for killing those three students in Mississippi. During that same period I agreed to march every day in Chicago with Al Raby until we got rid of Ben Willis, the Superintendent of Schools.

Hugh Hefner said to me, "Man, whenever you come out here we really get over." I told him, "I promise I will march every day until we get what we want, even though I have to fly back and forth every day from San Francisco to Chicago." It fascinated people back here that somebody had that kind of money. There are people in Chicago, black and white, who dream of going to Kansas City and they are never able to make it. And here's someone flying back and forth to

California every day. It got to be a game. The press asked, "How long can he keep it up?" They interviewed doctors who said I wouldn't be able to go on doing it. I'll be honest with you: during the last two days, I was almost a zombie. I was just that tired, but the thrill of that countdown kept me on my feet. It got to the point where thousands upon thousands of whites downtown would come to their windows and wave to us as we marched by. It had nothing to do with civil rights. It was, "There he is again. That's the one who's flying back and forth every day." The newspapers printed the number of miles it was, and how much it cost.

A very important court action came out of that march. In the first year class at Harvard Law School they read "Dick Gregory versus the City of Chicago." We marched to Mayor Daley's house and we were arrested. The lower courts held that municipal officials had two lives: a public and a private one, and that the public could march around their offices, but not around their houses. That case went all the way to the Supreme Court. The lower court decision was reversed. The Constitution gives the right to peaceful protest and picketing, but it does not map out any area. But the Supreme Court did, and that is why to this day you will no longer hear the cliche, "A man's home is his castle." Today you can march anywhere you please.

I learned a lot in Chicago. I like that city. We laid the groundwork there for the future. One of the highlights of my time in Chicago was my campaign for mayor against Daley. The arrogance, they said, of a comedian running against a white official! They thought no black would dare run against Daley, for political reasons and for reasons of personal safety. I think once you go inside the gorilla's den and the gorilla manhandles you, if you walk out in one piece you can walk back in again without fear. Harold Washington did.

"Europeans would never graffiti-ize the jazz art form the way Americans have done."

Johnny Griffin

BIRTHDATE: April 24, 1928
BIRTHPLACE: Chicago, Illinois
INSTRUMENTS: Tenor Saxophone and Clarinet
OCCUPATION: Bandleader, Tenor Saxophonist, Composer and Arranger
PERFORMED WITH: Lionel Hampton, The Jazz Messengers, Thelonious Monk, Gene Ammons, Lester Young, Walter Dyett, T-Bone Walker, and Dallas Bartley.

I've been around music all of my life because my mother and most of the family on her side of the tree were all regular church goers. Mother was a regular member of the choir at St John's Baptist Church, which is located at 48th and Michigan. In addition to singing in the choir, my mother played the piano and did solo work for church teas and various other religious events. Mother and Dad were divorced when I was four years old, so I never got to know him real well.

But I learned later that he had been a coronet player.

In addition to listening to my mother play the piano, I listened to records when I was four years old. I remember standing up in the chair to wind up the old Victrola to make the record turn. I have always been fascinated by the sound of music. I can't remember all of the artists I listened to back in those early years, but I know that what influenced me the most at that early age were Duke Ellington's recordings.

I took my first piano lessons with my great aunt's husband, Pace, when I was six years old. Pace later founded the Old Ship of Zion publishing company in Pittsburgh. He was heavily into religious music and was an excellent teacher. Within several months after he started giving me music lessons, Uncle Pace moved to Pittsburgh. My next music teacher was a fellow named Sterling Todd, who was the organist at the Savoy Ballroom. At the same time I was studying piano with Mr Todd, I started taking Hawaiian guitar lessons from a Mr Burns, who lived right down the street on East 45th Street near South Park Boulevard. Mr Burns was an excellent teacher. In fact, he had me playing church music on the guitar, and in the '30s, I also played all of the popular Bing Crosby numbers, like "Sweet Lilani", and tunes like that. I played the piano for Sunday school and for church teas, and I was into numbers like "Old Black Joe" and "Swanee River," along with some light jazz tunes.

At age ten, I was looking for an additional instrument to play, because I had been influenced by my Aunt Rose, on my father's side. She was a dancer with Nat King Cole's *Shuffle Along* show, and her husband was a saxophone player. They lived at 46th and Calumet, and I used to go over and visit with her and I would hold her husband's horn. He would let me touch it, but he wouldn't permit me to play it. This cat's horn intrigued me, but at the age of ten, I certainly couldn't afford to buy one of my own.

When I graduated from Forestville Grammar School in June, 1941, the class had a party at the Parkway Ballroom. King Kolax and his band played. Gene Ammons, a DuSable High alumnus, was his star tenor sax man. When I heard Ammons play that saxophone, I knew that I was going to become a saxophone player. There was no doubt in my mind about it.

When I entered DuSable High School in September of that year, I went immediately to Captain Dyett, the band master who was Gene Ammons' former teacher, and asked him to enroll me in the band class. He said he would, and asked me what instrument I was interested in playing. When I told him I was greatly interested in the saxophone, he said, "No son, you can't play the saxophone. You must learn to play the clarinet first." I wanted to play saxophone, because I wanted to be like Ammons, but the first six months I played clarinet in the beginners band, and the second semester I went into the concert band. Dyett took me through a series of changes. Even in my sophomore year, he refused to

Above: The King Kolax Orchestra. Left: Prentice McCarey on piano; King Kolax, and Richard Davis on tenor. Below: Walter Dyett's Booster Band in 1944.

let me play a saxophone. He shifted me from a B-flat clarinet to an alto clarinet and finally, a bass clarinet. Next he insisted that I join the ROTC band and play the piccolo. The oboist in the concert band was graduating, so he decided to switch me to oboe. Someone else graduated who had been the English horn player. He didn't have a replacement, so he made me double on the English horn. Dyett instilled me with a lot of music and a hell of a lot of discipline, because he was still withholding the saxophone from me.

I decided that Dyett would never allow me to play the saxophone, so I bought one outside, and actually started playing little gigs around in the park and on street corners with George Freeman, Wilbur Campbell, James Higgins, Leroy Jackson, and other young musicians. In fact, the police would chase us off the corners and El stops, where we were hustling tips in return for playing requests. I recall the first professional gig I had. It was a picnic for the Elks, and they paid us seventy-five cents per man. I really thought I was a big shot then. Dyett at that point had discovered that I was playing saxophone outside the school band so he let me in the booster band. The booster dance band played the school dances for graduations, proms, and special school assemblies. I felt that I was moving up. When I was fourteen, I got into the union. I am talking about 1942 during World War II. The union lowered the age to let young guys like me in, because the old guys were all being inducted into the Army.

At age fifteen, I was playing with T-Bone Walker's band, and his brother had a twelve-piece orchestra. We played the off nights at the Rhumboogie, the El Grotto and Club DeLisa. I was going to school during the day, and gigging almost every night. In fact, I took Johnny Board's place a couple of times with the Dallas Bartley Orchestra out at Joe's DeLuxe Cafe, which was located at 63rd and South Park.

After I joined the union, McKee Fitzhugh organized a group of young musicians into what became known as the Baby Band. Fitzhugh used to promote the dances down at the Parkway, Pershing, Trianon, and the White City Ballrooms at 63rd and South Park. He was one of the leading dance promoters around town during that period. I will never forget that he put a giant-sized picture of me on the exterior wall of Nick & Angels, a school store on the 49th Street side of DuSable High School. I was only four feet six inches tall, and weighed about 105, but this picture on the wall made me look like a giant. You could look right out of the DuSable bandroom window and see that picture. Dyett got on my case because of it. He would say to me, "Comb your hair, star," or "Star, play this," or, "Star, play that." He was giving me a hard time, but it was his way of keeping me from getting a big head.

Dyett was a beautiful person. I always said that he was a mind reader. He could see through all your foolishness. One of his favorite sayings was, "You'll be missed no longer than the door has closed behind you if you think you're a big

Above: T-Bone Walker, renowned blues guitarist and singer. Right: Johnny Griffin at fifteen in the Baby Band.

shot." He was a tough disciplinarian, but I believed that that was necessary. Although Dyett finally relented and let me play the saxophone, he wouldn't let me play a tenor sax because he said it was too big. He said I should play an alto because I was so short and small. If you look at my old school picture, you will see that when I sat in my chair in the school band, my feet didn't touch the floor. Even worse—I sat next to Bill Atkins, who was so big that he made me look even smaller.

I was playing alto in a tenor style, because musicians during that period were trying to imitate Ben Webster, and on slower tempos, I would play like Johnny Hodges, not realizing at that time that both Webster and Hodges played the same way, only one played alto and the other, tenor. But their styles were more or less the same.

In the spring of 1945 when Lionel Hampton and Milt Buckner came to

The Lionel Hampton Band, starring Johnny Griffin (left), and Arnette Cobb (right), in a sax duo.

DuSable High School, Dyett selected a few members of the booster orchestra to have a jam session with Hamp, and I was one of the musicians he chose. When I graduated in June, 1945, Jay Peters, who had been the tenor player in Hamp's band, was drafted into the Navy. Hamp rememberd me from the jam session, came back to DuSable and asked me to join his orchestra. I joined Hamp's band immediately after graduation and three days later, on June 28, 1945, I was play-ing the Regal Theater. We went to Toledo, Ohio, and the first day there, I walked on the stage and Gladys Hampton, Hamp's wife, stopped me and asked me where my tenor saxophone was. This was the first I'd heard that I was supposed to play the tenor sax. She said, "You have to play a tenor sax in this band." What had hap-pened was that the tenor sax man, Maurice Simon, was leaving and I was to replace him, instead of Jay Peters. They wanted me to play tenor saxophone in a duet with Arnette Cobbs. So I started playing tenor sax. I had to play "Flying Home" with Cobbs and of course Cobbs had a huge sound. Hamp's band con-sisted of all of these fellows from Texas with loads of experience, so it took me a couple of months to get my sound together and feel like I was in competition with Cobbs. They used to call us Big Red and Little Red. Cobbs weighed two hun-dred and thirty pounds, and I weighed ninety-five pounds in my overcoat, soak-ing wet. At four feet ten, I was shorter than Milt Buckner, Hamp's piano player, and I didn't think anyone could be any shorter than Milt Buckner.

I worked off and on with Lionel Hampton from June, 1945, until mid-1946, and then I left. Arnette Cobbs, who had been the mainstay in Hamp's band, left in March of 1947 and Hamp called me back, and I worked with him again from March, 1947, until May, and then I quit for good. I quit playing with Hamp because I got tired of playing the same tunes. I had heard new music that I wanted to play besides "Flying Home" and Hamp's "Boogie Woogie". I was listening to other musicians like Charlie Parker and Dizzy Gillespie. They were into some interesting things, and I felt I couldn't learn to play those things sitting on the bandstand playing "Flying Home" year in and year out.

Joe Morris, the trumpet player in Hamp's band, left at the same time I did, and we came back to Chicago together and formed a sextet with a group of Chicago musicians. We had Emmett Dailey, Wilmus Reeves, and George Freeman on guitar. That band broke up in less than a year and we organized a new group of musicians, mostly east coast guys. We had Philly Joe Jones, Percy Heath,

Hampton in background (dark suit), motivates three tenor saxophone players with his heavy hand-beat.

Left: Charlie Parker, creator of progressive jazz (be-bop). Right: Lester Young and Jo Jones with Count Basie in 1937.

Nelson Boyd, Elmore Hope, and Matthew Gee, and Lucky Thompson joined the band for a short period of time. That second band lasted for almost two years.

In late 1949 after the East Coast group broke up, I joined up with Joe Jones, the former Count Basie drummer. We worked together for about four or five months, and then I left him and joined Arnette Cobbs, who had formed a new band. Cobbs insisted that I play baritone sax in his orchestra. He let me play one tune on the tenor and that was it. He told me I could play as much baritone as I wanted, but he didn't want me to play tenor, and he really wasn't too particular about my playing baritone once I secured a good mouthpiece and was able to get some good sounds.

Because of the Korean War I was drafted out of the Cobbs' band in 1951. I played in the 164th Army band in Hawaii from 1951 to October, 1953. After the war, I joined Art Blakey and his Jazz Messengers for a brief period in 1955. I re-joined them on a regular basis in 1957, and stayed with them for approximately six months. Art Blakey was a heck of a nice guy to work for. He was from Pittsburgh—off the same hill that produced Mary Lou Williams, Ahmad Jamal, Billy Eckstine, Billy Strayhorn, Erroll Garner, Roy Eldridge and Earl Hines. In fact, Art Blakey was initially a piano player. He and Erroll Garner were contemporaries. They had a small band in Pittsburgh. When Erroll Garner decided that he was going to play piano, Blakey's career as a piano player was ended with that outfit, and he switched to drums.

One evening, in 1955, I was in Chicago visiting with my mother and watching television. The telephone rang. It was Wilbur Ware. "Come on over to the Bee

Hive, man," he said. "We need a horn player." The cats on the gig were Thelonius Monk, Wilbur Campbell, Ware and of course myself. That night, I got a real music lesson working out with Monk. He played differently from any musician I had ever heard. It would be an understatement to say his approach to jazz was unique. During the intermission, he said, "Man, you know I can make those runs just like Art Tatum." I said, "Come on, man, who are you kidding?" He sat down and actually made runs just like Art Tatum and equally fast. The guys would say that Thelonius had no technique, simply because he might play two notes to a bar, which was his way of expressing that particular tune. He always said you didn't have to play a lot of notes to express yourself. He could take two or three notes and make a total statement, simply by using different accents, which of course was a Monk trademark. When everybody else was swinging on two and four, Monk's tunes were always on one and three, which made musicians think what he was doing was either difficult or non-technical, because everyone thought that in jazz the feeling was on two and four. Monk proved you could get it on one and three, just as when you were playing "Turkey in the Straw" or any other kind of country song. I think that Monk's recording of "Smoke Gets in Your Eyes" is a perfect example of his unique style. After Monk left Chicago, I didn't work with him again until 1958, when we were together at a place called the Fire Spot in New York City. I admired Monk because he had an awesome presence. He was like Jomo Kenyatta. People were actually afraid to speak to him and yet he had a great sense of humor. We would be in a joint working and everyone around him would be talking music gossip, and Monk wouldn't say a word. He would just sit there, stroking his Van Dyke beard. And maybe after an hour he might say a few words and break up the whole conversation. He could destroy you and yet he was subtle.

Monk carried himself like a nobleman. I remember the Italian owners of the club where we were working would ask me to ask him to go back and play the second set. They were afraid that if they spoke to him, they might offend him. Monk would come to work late every night. We were supposed to start at nine-thirty and Monk would walk in at eleven. People would be standing outside in the rain, and he would come in as if he was in a hurry, pushing everyone aside, and go straight to the piano and start playing, and would play for as much as an hour or an hour and a half non-stop, without even taking off his hat. Monk was another genius we lost before he had an opportunity to make his closing statement.

Another lesson that I learned while I was in New York came from Sonny Stitt. Sonny Stitt was driving me crazy all the time. He was prolific on his instrument and a fantastic musician. I would be sitting in my hotel room in New York, and Stitt would come by and say, "Play me something." I would play something, and he would say, "That's good. Give me your horn." And he would start playing and of course he knew every cliché, every riff and every tune. I would feel devastated. In fact, I felt so devastated many times after he left, that I wanted to throw my horn out of the window. I never went that far because the Walter Dyett discipline always came to the surface, and I would go back to the woodshed. In other words, I would go back and start practicing. Later, after I felt that I really had my game together, I would invite Stitt up on the bandstand to play with me, and I felt that I was holding my own. There has always been a friendly competition between musicians like Don Byas, Ben Webster, Coleman Hawkins, Dizzy, Fats Navarro, Miles Davis, Charlie Shavers, and Roy Eldridge. Competition is really a learning and teaching process, because if you listen and practice, you're going to improve.

In 1957 I started gigging with Gene Ammons and Lester Young in Chicago at the Stage Door and the Crown Propellor Lounge. Both were located on East 63rd Street, and were owned by the same people. Lester was a humorist, a quiet, soft, gentle man. He always called me Lady Griffin and when Sonny Stitt was around, he called him Lady Stitt. Lester had a peculiar habit of speaking of himself in the third person. For example, if he was telling you that he fell down the stairs he would say, "The Pres fell down the stairs and hurt himself." Pres was always another person. Lester called everybody Lady. If he knew you, he made you a lady. Pres was always acting effeminate anyway, but he always had a woman on his arm, and the only sky piece I ever saw on his head was a pork-pie hat. Working with Lester Young was a gas when he was in good health and good spirits.

I had the unpleasant experience of working with Lester during his last days while he was here in Chicago. He was staying at the Pershing Hotel at 64th and Cottage Grove, and we couldn't get him to leave his room, except when we picked him up to take him on a gig in the evening. He would just lie in bed all day and listen to his old Count Basie records. Pres was so weak when we got on the job, we had to help him up to the microphone. He had been into drugs earlier, but he also liked to drink gin. In his final days, he switched to a weird concoction of bourbon and wine. He seemed to want to drink himself to death. He had a death look in his eyes, like Coleman Hawkins. I saw the same look in Billie Holiday's eyes, and she died just a couple of months after Pres. It's a sad commentary on our lifestyle that people prefer to die rather than go on with it.

I was saved from the kinds of pressures that killed both Pres and Billie Holiday by my first trip to Europe in December of 1962. It was a three month promotional trip, sponsored by Riverside Records. I stayed a month in Paris, a month in Stockholm, a month in London and a week in Holland. I came back to New York on my baby's birthday, which was on March 1, 1963, stayed two months and then Babs Gonzalez and I caught a boat back to Europe on May 19, 1963. I stayed there until September 11, 1978. I found that the average European has a great deal more respect for black jazz musicians than Americans do. I played the same halls

Gene "Jughead" Ammons, who became a legend in his own time as a tenor sax star.

as Arthur Rubenstein. I played the Berlin Philharmonic. It was not so much the halls that we worked in, but the people who operated those halls—they had respect for us as musicians. You take Carnegie Hall in New York. The employees there appear to hate jazz musicians. The stage hands seem to do everything they can to make life unpleasant for you, and that's true. In Europe, you're treated as an artist by the general public as well as by the establishment. You are on par with the classical musicians. But America has taken jazz musicians for granted.

Jazz is actually a dirty word in this country,—take expressions like "and all that jazz"—that's derogatory. Europeans would never graffiti-ize the jazz art form the way Americans have done. Europeans know more about American jazz musicians than the jazz musicians know about themselves. They study jazz composers just as they study Bach, Beethoven or Brahms. They view jazz music as an original art form.

This is July, 1983. I will bet you right now that there are more American jazz musicians working in Europe at this moment than there are working in America. This is the weekend of the Northsea Jazz Festival in Holland. In one huge building they will have seven concerts going on at the same time, from early afternoon until four the following morning. There are at least 550 American jazz musicians in just one building. At the same time, there is another large jazz festival being held in Sweden. The festival in Nice, France, has just started and will last for at least ten days. On top of this, there are festivals going on all over Italy and France. There will be festivals in Germany in the fall. Government subsidizes many of the

Left to right: Duke Ellington, Cat Anderson, and Johnny Griffin (extreme right) at Birdland in New York City.

festivals, particularly in Holland. Europe is saving jazz, and they have certainly saved my life.

As an art form, jazz has been lifted out of the black community. Black kids are not aware of our jazz heritage, because it has been transported out of the neighborhood and down to Carnegie Hall in New York or the Arie Crown Theater in Chicago. The American jazz audience today is predominantly white. Let's hope that those faithful white connoisseurs of jazz will hang in there long enough for the people back in the hood to get the message.

Left to right: Danny Barker, guitar; Milt Hinton, bass; and J. C. Heard, drums.

"Hey, Sporty! Get off that fiddle, and get you a horn!"

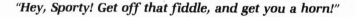

Milton Hinton

BIRTHDATE: June 23, 1910
BIRTHPLACE: Vicksburg, Mississippi
INSTRUMENT(S) PLAYED: Bass Fiddle, Violin
OCCUPATION: Instrumentalist, Instructor
FEATURED WITH: Earl Hines, Jabbo Smith, Eddie South,
Fate Marable, Cab Calloway, Count Basie, Louis Armstrong.

I was only three months old when my parents separated. We moved to Chicago from Mississippi in December, 1918, and although I left Vicksburg at the age of eight, my memories of my hometown are not very pleasant.

My mother's formal education was limited. She had, however, learned to play the piano and could read music and she was determined to make me a musician. She tried giving me piano lessons, but they would always end in a mother and son hassle.

Shortly after my thirteenth birthday on July 18, 1923, my mother purchased my first violin. She had been influenced by a fifteen-year-old kid across the street by the name of Quinn Wilson, who played beautiful violin. She sent for Quinn to come over to our house to show me how to tune the fiddle. She paid him twenty-five cents and he gave me my first lesson. Quinn later became the arranger and bass player for the famous Earl Hines Orchestra.

When I entered Wendell Phillips High School, Quinn, who was two years older than I, was already a lieutenant in the ROTC and playing bass horn in the band. He had become my idol and I was determined to follow in his footsteps. During my freshman year, I played violin in the school orchestra, but that did not satisfy me. I wanted to play the bass horn like Quinn. I applied to Major N. Clark Smith, musical director at Phillips and teacher of such artists as Ray Nance, Lionel Hampton, Eddie Cole (brother of Nat), Nelmatilda Woodard and Hayes Alvis, for a position playing bass horn. I was accepted in the marching band and given a brand new tuba that I mastered. However, I was more comfortable with the violin. Because I was a member of the marching band, I got a chance to travel with the Wendell Phillips football team. I remember my first trip with the team was to St. Louis where gas street lights were still in use.

Ed Burke, who lived next door to me, also attended Phillips and played first violin in the orchestra. His preference was a brass instrument. Major Smith permitted Burke to switch to the trombone in the school band. He became extremely proficient on that instrument. When the Walter Barnes Orchestra got the gig playing for Al Capone at the Cotton Club in Cicero, he hired Burke. Ed Burke was so good that he later became a star trombonist in both the Earl Hines and Cab Calloway bands. While Burke was making seventy dollars a week playing with Walter Barnes, I was still throwing 241 morning newspapers each day for nine dollars a week. In those days, people worked ten hours a day, six days a week, for twenty dollars. They managed somehow to rear families and send their kids to school on those wages.

Walter Barnes had the band that everyone wanted to join back in those days. It was not because Barnes was such a good musician or leader, but it was a known fact that he was Al Capone's pet, and the gangsters were paying him bigger dough than the Earl Hines Orchestra made at the Grand Terrace. The sidemen in Barnes' band were making seventy dollars a week and Hines' men were receiving only thirty-five dollars a week. Capone could afford to pay well because he had dollar bills rolling out of his toe nails. This was during Prohibition and Capone controlled the mayor and most of the liquor in Chicago.

Every morning I got up at four a.m. to deliver my 241 papers. I felt that delivering papers was a drag because I was as good a musician as most of the guys playing in Walter Barnes' band and could read music better than some of those guys. The violin was an instrument that very few of the jazz bands, outside of Erskine Tate and Dave Peyton, found any use for on the South Side.

Many mornings as I delivered my papers, Ed Burke would pass me in his

The Wendell Phillips High School Band. Extreme left: Major N. Clark Smith. Seated right, first row: Joe Collymore and Nathaniel Jones. Second row, extreme right: Henderson Smith, and at rear of room (violin section): Nelmatilda Woodard.

brand new car and stop to chat about old school days. He always called me "Sporty," and I felt a lot of envy, something that I'm not proud of. Deep within me I wanted to be a great musician and play in a nightclub orchestra like Burke and stop delivering those damn papers.

"Hey there, Sporty!" Burke would often call to me from his car. "Paperboy, you've got to get off that fiddle and get you a horn. Why don't you try the trombone, Sporty?"

Burke was kind to me. He bought a trombone and gave it to me. I asked him if it was a loan, and he said, "No, I want you to have it." Burke was like a big brother. He became my father confessor. He tried to encourage me, and even tried to teach me to play the trombone. I finally decided that since I was well acquainted with the strings of the violin, I would purchase a bass fiddle.

My newspaper route had some positive advantages in that I had an opportunity to meet a lot of people. Eddie South's mother was one of my customers. She lived at 42nd Place and South Parkway. Eddie South was called the "dark angel of the violin," and was probably the most accomplished jazz violinist that America has ever produced. One morning as I delivered the Sunday paper Mrs. South asked me if I were a musician. I told her that I was studying the bass violin and playing it under the direction of Major Smith at Phillips High School. She told me that her son Eddie was in Europe and when he returned she would introduce me to him. "Hopefully, some day you will get a chance to play in his orchestra," she said with a broad smile. That must have been in 1930.

During this period I started playing gigs at dance halls around Chicago. I remember specifically that one of my first gigs was at the Forum Hall, located at 43rd and Calumet. We used to play for a percentage of the gross receipts and I would carry my tuba and bass fiddle on the streetcar to that gig, which wasn't very far from my house at 4145 South Vincennes Avenue. However, it was a long distance for me to have to carry both instruments. When I returned home late one night from the Forum Hall, my mother asked how much I had made. I told her thirty-five cents, out of which I had already spent ten cents for transportation.

She said, "Son, you have got to do better than that." Of course that ended my career as a percentage gigger.

In 1932, Eddie South returned from Europe where he had been playing with a quartet and was contacted by Sam Scolding, a theatrical booking agent. The agent wanted South to put together a twelve-piece band to go into the Chin Chow Chinese Restaurant at 4709 South Parkway. We started rehearsing the band everyday at Chin Chow and Sam Scolding entered into a contract with Eddie South to pay each man seventy-five dollars a week for a forty-week period. Scolding finally got the bad news that the management of Chin Chow did not want to use string instruments or so-called "society bands" such as Eddie South had put together. They wanted a hot jazz band. Chin Chow had not consummated an agreement with Scolding. Scolding, who was a representative of MCA, was stuck with contracts for twelve men for forty weeks. In order to avoid difficulty with the musicians' union, he bought all of the contracts back by paying each of the guys $300 to cancel the agreement. Eddie South said to Scolding, "Don't give the bass player his $300 because I think that we can find work for him in a quintet that we're going to take up on the Near North Side to a place called the Rubaiyat." The club was operated by Eddie Pappan, an Al Capone henchman. The room was small and would only seat about sixty-five people, but it was considered a high class place and, of course, the tab for dinner and wine was higher than the class.

There was a guy playing piano with us by the name of Albert Spaulding, from Louisville, Kentucky, who played fantastically well. He had had an automobile accident and had a big scar across the right side of his face. He was an elderly man of about fifty, had gray hair and could play any kind of music you'd ever want to hear. He could play *Rhapsody in Blue* in classical fashion and *An American in Paris*. In fact, he was so good that Ben Bernie, Ben Pollack, Jack Teagarden and Benny Goodman would come by the club to hear this guy play and, of course, to hear Eddie South. South was the master of the jazz violinists. Stanley Wilson, the

Eddie South and his International Band. Second from right, standing: Eddie South, violin. Second from left: young Milt Hinton, bass violin. Right: Eddie South with a friend in Paris. South, called "the Dark Angel of the Violin", was a European favorite. His concerts were always sold out.

guitarist, was another fantastic musician with our group, and I can't forget Clifford King, a very cultured clarinet player, also known as the clarinet king. Working with Eddie South at that club was a great experience. Eddie taught me how to really bow a bass violin. Today, I am really proud I was able to study under a man who I still consider my musical father. Many young students in the colleges where I teach around the country marvel at my bowing technique. I always tell them I learned my bowing sitting at the knee of the master, and that master was Eddie South, the dark angel of the violin.

In the summer of 1932 I got a chance to double on gigs with Eddie South and play at the Congress Hotel for the Democratic National Convention. We played in the lobby by the fountain and I was told we were the second black group to have worked that hotel. It is my understanding that Fletcher Henderson's band played there in the mid-1920s, but it was a thrill for me as a young fellow to just observe that affair and see all those great congressmen come and go. I had an opportunity to see Franklin Delano Roosevelt, Al Smith, John Nance Garner, Speaker of the House, and many movie stars of that era who were in attendance. It was an experience I'll never forget. In fact, out of that gig at the Congress Hotel, Eddie received an offer to go to the West Coast and play in an exclusive nightclub in Los Angeles called the Ballyhoo Club. We played for an act that consisted of two Argentinian dancers—Carmen Miranda, who later became one of the popular musical screen stars of the late '30s and early '40s, and her partner, Caesar Romero, the tall, dark, Latin romantic screen idol of a later period. These wonderful experiences I attribute to Eddie South.

We stayed in California for twenty-six weeks before returning to Chicago. Joe Venuti was a great white violinist who loved Eddie South and who recommended him for many of our better gigs. I can remember one in particular. Joe Venuti was playing with Paul Whiteman at the College Inn in the Sherman Hotel here in Chicago and there was a woman in the show by the name of Bea Palmer, whom he always accompanied on the violin. When Joe Venuti left the Whiteman band, she literally had a fit. Bea informed Paul Whiteman that Joe had spoken well of a black violinist from the South Side by the name of Eddie South, and insisted that he be found. South was invited to the College Inn for an interview with both Bea Palmer and Whiteman and they agreed to hire him. Eddie would accompany this woman each night as a soloist. It was a solo gig, hence we did not join him. But he had to agree to play violin behind a screen enclosure. In other words, when Bea came out to do her number, Eddie had to be screened in so that he could not be seen by the white viewing audience, as opposed to standing five or six feet behind her as Joe Venuti had earlier. That said a great deal to me about Chicago and its attitude on race relations in 1933.

Somehow, that experience did not affect Eddie South's determination because he would stand behind that screen and play such beautiful violin obligatos that people would marvel at the sound. Of course, Bea Palmer received tremendous applause and was frequently called back for many encores. This meant that Eddie South got extra pay because every time he had to go behind the screen, it would cost an additional fee. I don't recall exactly what amount he said he received.

Joe Venuti, who died just recently, was a sensitive musician and also a very funny man. I remember he got Eddie South a job at a place called the Blossom Inn in Detroit, Michigan. He left a note on the piano saying, "Well, I hope you guys get out of here alive." Of course, we all got a big kick out of his humor. He was a fabulous man.

After about two years, jobs began to fade out for Eddie South. Luck was just not on his side. Therefore, I had to seek employment elsewhere. It so happened during that period that Louis Armstrong was leaving Chicago to go on his first big tour. He had been playing at a place called the Showboat down on Lake Street and they were looking for a fellow to follow him who played very good trumpet. The great Jabbo Smith, who was then living in Milwaukee, was selected and asked to organize a band. He chose Floyd Campbell for drums, as Louis Armstrong had suggested, Jerome Pasquall on sax, Cassino Simpson on piano, Ted Tinsley on guitar and yours truly on bass. Jabbo was fantastic; second only to Louie. I remember him as a handsome guy, a jet-black pretty boy and a ladies' man. The ladies would not let him make time. It was my job as the youngest member of the band to wake him up and make certain that he made some effort to get down to the gig by ten p.m. Even with my best efforts, Jabbo would never arrive before midnight, two hours after we started. Sam Beers, who was a partner in the Showboat and the last owner of the Three Deuces, which was at 222 North State Street, would almost pull his hair out because of Jabbo's unwillingness to make time. But then how can you stay mad at a guy that played so beautifully? Ultimately, of course, tardiness was Jabbo's downfall. I saw Jabbo when he came to New York a year or so ago in a show called *One Mo' Time.* He is an old man, but still playing beautiful horn.

You know, of all the trumpet players I have listened to, and I have indeed listened to many, I can't think of one that I've enjoyed as much as Jabbo on that Showboat job in Chicago. He had a mute that he used in his horn that looked exactly like a doorknob. It was roughly the same size. He could do more with that mute than anybody I had ever seen and, in addition to that, he was fast. He was as fast and as fluid as Roy Eldridge or Dizzy Gillespie. In fact, he was featuring those high notes at rapid speed back then, the same as Dizzy is doing today, and as Roy Eldridge did in earlier years. He is a top-flight guy.

It's a funny thing. People think musicians, drugs and alcohol are related. I can't remember ever seeing or hearing of Jabbo drinking or using any kind of narcotic. But it proves one thing, that it is not necessarily dope that can affect a man's behavior. Women can affect a man the same as dope. Women were Jabbo's narcotic: they rendered him ineffective and irresponsible. He never made it to a gig on time.

Jabbo was quite an egotist. I remember that on several occasions when Louis Armstrong was playing at the Savoy Ballroom, Jabbo would come in and say to Louie, "Hey, man, let me play your horn. I'm going to blow you out of this place." And of course that was always the joke around Chicago. Nobody blew Louie out of any place, but Jabbo was capable, and I would say that he came as close to doing it as any trumpet player at that time.

I remember one night Louie was talking to a group of us backstage at the Savoy when someone asked him, "How did you happen to start scat singing?"

He told us an interesting story. In 1926 he was recording a tune entitled "Heebie-Jeebies Blues" for Okeh Records in their studios located at 226 West Washington. They had gone over the song at least a dozen times, when Tommy Rockwell, who was supervising the session and subsequently became the head of the RKO Amusement Agency, said: "If you don't get it right this time, skip that number and go ahead with the others." They began the number again and in the middle of the song, Louie became so excited that he dropped the slip of paper containing the words.

"My memory," Louie said, "was always good so I acted as though I knew what was going on but I couldn't remember those words at that moment for the hell of me, so I blurted out something like 'umph-umph,' and then kept on and a guy in the studio named Richard Jones said, 'Do something!' and I said, 'Do-do-dah-dee-dee, et cetera.' The musicians became so amused and confused that they forgot and ended the song off-key. Of course, the producers of the record didn't release it. Later they decided to give it a try and 'Heebie-Jeebies' sold 150,000 copies in the first quarter."

That was really the beginning of the vogue for what is now called scat singing. The public thought that "Heebie-Jeebies" was intended to be that way and other bands borrowed the idea because of its popularity. Louie, in addition to being the father of the jazz trumpet, was also the father of scat singing.

After completing the gig with Jabbo Smith at the Showboat, I joined the Erskine Tate band for a very brief period. Then I went back with Eddie South and did vaudeville tours with Bea Palmer and Gene Austin, two very popular white singers during the '30s. Finally, South's band broke up and he returned to Europe. I took a job at the Three Deuces with Zutty Singleton on drums, Cozy Cole's brother on piano and Everett Barksdale on guitar. We played what they called "The Main Event," but, in my opinion, the intermission piano player was the main event. That was none other than Art Tatum. That cat played some piano. He, in my opinion, is the most exciting jazz pianist that the world has ever produced. It was during the gig at the Three Deuces with Zutty Singleton that I got an offer to join the Cab Calloway Orchestra in New York City. Cab was working at the famous Cotton Club. I still have in my possession a 1936 menu from the old Cotton Club that invited you to "fill up for $1.50." Now, keep in mind that the Cotton Club was a high-class, gangster-operated establishment. Yet for a dollar-fifty, one could have a good time. All of the Hollywood stars came and band musicians came. Although it was located in black Harlem, the Cotton Club catered exclusively to white crowds. The chorus girls were the prettiest I had ever seen; all very fine looking gals. In fact, a woman that Duke Ellington was once interested

Above: Milt and Cab Calloway. Right: The New Cotton Club at 48th Street off Broadway.

in, Lucille Armstrong, was the darkest girl in the chorus, and even she was light brown-skinned. All the rest were high yellow like Lena Horne and lighter. Now the girls in the chorus were divided into two components. Those called showgirls were the ones that would walk about in high-heeled shoes and just look pretty. And then there were the others who were called Ponies. They were smaller women who were the actual dancers.

The Cotton Club moved from Harlem to midtown at 48th Street and Broadway, right across from McGuinesses. Cab Calloway and Bill Robinson were the stars of the show. But one thing that is not well known is the fact that Bill Robinson was accused of being an Uncle Tom. Actually, he was a guy whom I learned to know well, as a man with an awful lot of dignity and a great deal of respect for black women. Bill used to sit at the door at the club as the chorus girls left, to make certain that they didn't have on heavy lipstick and were not overly made-up. He didn't want our colored girls walking around midtown on Broadway looking like prostitutes. He was a policeman without a badge and was always known as the "Honorary Mayor of Harlem." He was really a beautiful guy in the sense that he wanted to see our women always look their best.

White gangsters always messed around with the prettiest girls in the show, and even they respected Bill Robinson. The girls would never leave the club with gangsters. They would meet at McGuinesses, a bar directly across from the new Cotton Club.

Cab Calloway's band stands out, in my opinion, as the epitome of all bands. Cab was a disciplinarian. The discipline that prevailed during the sixteen years that I worked with Cab Calloway was tremendous; so much so, that he would make a U.S. Marine first sergeant look like a Boy Scout. I enjoyed the discipline and the musicianship. Cab was a great entertainer and his ability to perform actually overshadowed the band. Although he was not a musician, he respected us as musicians. Cab depended on the fellows in the band to rehearse themselves, and to find replacements, because he felt that we would use the best judgment.

Cab was a good enough businessman to not get in our way musically, but he ran a very tight ship. In fact, Cab paid us more money than any other black band on the road during that period, including the great Duke Ellington. The only complaint that some musicians might have had with Cab's band is that the arrangements were very tight, featuring Cab seventy-five percent of the time. It was actually his singing and entertaining that drew the crowds; therefore, there was not enough room for the fellows to solo. Ben Webster left Cab's band in 1937. I was with Cab and Ben when Ben said, "Man, I don't get but about eight bars at the most as a solo and I am not using my instrument the way I want to in order to get some real feeling out of it."

Ben later went to Cab and complained, "Hey, Twist," (which was the nickname Ben had given him) "I've got to quit."

Milt Hinton and Duke Ellington reminiscing about old times.

"What are you quitting for?" Cab asked.

"Man, I love you and everything is cool, but it just ain't enough music for me to play, and I've got to play, or move on to where I can play more," said Ben.

"Okay," Cab said. "If you want to go, I'm going to miss you, but you will have to find me another good tenor player."

"Yes, I can get you another good tenor player. I know a fellow named Chu Berry who is playing with Fletcher Henderson."

"How is he?" Cab asked, rubbing his chin.

"He's great."

"Well, call him and have him come to New York City."

Chu was making thirty-five dollars a week playing with Fletcher Henderson at the Grand Terrace in Chicago and Cab was paying $125 a week at that time. So when Ben called Chu Berry, he responded, "Yes, man, I'll come to New York as soon as I can give Fletcher a two-week notice."

Chu joined the band at the Trianon Ballroom in Cleveland, Ohio, and Ben stayed on for an additional week to teach Chu Berry the Calloway book. Chu was the best thing that ever happened to us in that band because he was a guy who talked with authority and Cab respected him. He actually permitted Chu Berry to reorganize the band. It was Chu Berry who was instrumental in getting Cab to organize a group called the Cab-Drivers, consisting of Chu Berry, Tyree Glenn, Dan Barker, Cozy Cole and myself. I will never forget when we were playing the State Theater in Hartford, Connecticut. We were out in the spotlight, playing up a storm, when all of a sudden a big wad of paper landed right in the spotlight by my foot. Cab was standing in the wings, saw the paper and shook his head.

After the show was over, Cab went to Dizzy Gillespie, yelling, "You son-of-a-bitch, you are fucking up all the time. We are out here trying to entertain the people and you're throwing spitballs like a kid." Everyone had left the theater except Dizzy, Cab, myself and a few others.

"Fess," Dizzy began. (We all called Cab "Fess.") "Fess, I didn't do that."

"You're a damn liar," Cab exploded. "I was looking right at you when you did it."

I could tell from his expression that Diz resented Cab's accusation, and could sense trouble.

Diz snapped back, "You're another damn liar!"

Two pretty girls that Cab had been talking to were listening intently to the argument. Of course, Cab wasn't about to stand by and let a little trumpet star call the great Cab Calloway a "damn liar." So Cab hauled off with an open hand and slapped Dizzy right across the head.

I'm a Chicago boy and I had delivered papers as you will recall. I had taught Dizzy how to open a knife. I had delivered papers with both hands, so I could open a knife faster than one could say "good morning." So when Cab slapped Dizzy, Dizzy came up with a knife. It appeared he was going right for Cab's stomach. Dizzy was larger than me, and I tried to slap the knife from his hand. Cab moved and the knife went right into his leg. By that time, Cab, who was a street fighter and tough, grabbed Dizzy's hand and they began scuffling. The guys in the band heard the commotion and rushed back onto the stage. Big cats like Benny Payne and Chu Berry were able to pull them apart.

The fellows pushed Cab into his dressing room and hurled Dizzy down toward the bandroom. We went down to visit Cab within minutes. The pantsleg of his white suit was blook-soaked. The knife was still plunged deeply into his thigh, but Cab was so goddamned mad, he hadn't noticed.

Moments later, Cab came and told the band members, "I guess you know that this cat cut me." He turned to Diz and said, "Get your things and get the hell out of here."

Diz picked up his trumpet and keys and left quietly.

We finished the last show that night without any further incident and caught the bus to return to New York. The bus would always deposit us at the Theresa Hotel at 125th Street and Seventh Avenue and from there we would go to our respective homes. This particular hotel was also our meeting place whenever we were leaving town for an engagement. When we arrived at the Theresa Hotel, the

Milt Hinton and his lovely wife Mona, who travels with Milt on all of his tours. Below: Milt reminisces with his old friend Eubie Blake on the White House Lawn.

bus came to a grinding halt. Cab, who always sat in the front seat of the bus, got off first only to find Dizzy standing at the bus door. He said to Cab, "Man, I didn't throw the spitball and I'm sorry we had this thing."

Cab walked from the bus, tapping him on the hand in a congratulatory way, or better known as giving him "five," and said, "Man, that's all over."

Jonah Jones, the star trumpet player and Cab's good friend, was never the same after the Calloway–Gillespie incident, the reason being that Jonah Jones had actually thrown the spitball, contrary to everything you might have read in many of the papers and magazines.

The war broke up Cab Calloway's band. There were just no places for us to play. My heart was broken when the war came because it broke up many great bands. We all had to leave to go into the service or defense work. It affected big bands, white and black. I would say 1942 and 1943 were the waning years of the big band era in this country.

In fact, while we were being installed in service, young kids sixteen and seventeen years old were asking $400 and $500 a week to play when they really weren't qualified.

Tommy Dorsey told me one day when the war was over, "I wouldn't hire a son-of-a-bitch unless he was forty years old."

Tommy just didn't want to pay money for unqualified people.

By the time the war was over and all the old guys were back, small bands were in vogue and nobody wanted to hire big bands anymore. I began working independently in a group called the New York Rhythm Section with Ocie Johnson, Hank Jones and Barry Gilmore. We were called the New York Rhythm Section because we played with everybody. We played on CBS television with Jackie Gleason, Patti Page and Percy Faith, the Woolworth Hour on radio, and went from one recording studio to another as a section. We had record dates by the hundreds, and were recorded with most of the great stars over the years.

I have known Frank Sinatra since the Tommy Dorsey days, and whenever he is in town, that is, in New York City, he always looks me up. I also knew Bing Crosby before he was a big movie star. When Bing decided to go back into show business, he contacted me, Joe Bushkin, Jake Hannah, and Johnny Smith and we went on tour. The money that he paid was incredible. You just couldn't believe the kind of money he paid us, in addition to permitting us to take our wives. He paid $1,500 per day per man, plus hotel expenses, limousine fees, and any other extras that you thought you might want, and he never looked back.

I played with Bing on his last gig at the Palladium in London. When I left him in London, he told me he was going to Spain to golf with friends, relax and have fun. I returned to New York and the following Monday I went to catch a train to Yale University for a meeting with one of my classes. I called my answering service to inquire about my messages. The girl said, "Have you heard what happened to Bing?"

"No," I replied, thinking to myself that Bing had won another award.

"Bing dropped dead," she replied.

The following day I received a note, dated three days before Bing's death, from his wife, Kathy, that read: "To Milt, Thanks."

AUTHOR'S NOTES

Milton Hinton, 73, is still busy teaching at various universities around the country. There is constant demand for him to appear at jazz concerts throughout the United States as well as in Europe. In between his many recordings and television sessions, he still finds time to appear in popular jazz clubs. He is a master musician who has never stopped learning. Milt is so highly respected in the field of music that he is now known as "The Judge."

Milt with Bing Crosby on Bing's last gig at the London Palladium, two days before Bing's death.

Art Hodes

"Chicago during the 1920s was swinging on a rusty gate."

Art Hodes

BIRTHDATE: November 14, 1904
BIRTHPLACE: Nikoliev, Russia
INSTRUMENT: Piano
OCCUPATION: Pianist and Bandleader
PERFORMED WITH: Louis Armstrong, Eddie Condon, Sidney Bechet, Bix Beiderbecke, Bud Freeman, Pops Foster, Pee Wee Russell, Wingy Manone, Gene Krupa, Chippie Hill and Bunk Johnson

My family moved to the United States when I was six months old. I was raised on Chicago's tough West Side in a neighborhood where hoodlums grew like vegetables in a garden. I took piano lessons at Hull House, on the near West Side, and my first gig was at a joint called the Rainbow Cafe on West Madison Street. The place was called a cafe, but it was really a buffet apartment. I remember counting the twenty-five steps I had to climb the first night I went there to work. At the top of the stairs was a room large enough to accommodate one hundred and fifty people. The year was 1925 and the only kind of booze you could get was bootleg. The establishment was owned by a Greek connected with the mob.

During the week I played piano there, and on Saturday the owner often brought in a small band to alternate entertainment. Every night there were two or more female entertainers who had to mix socially with the customers and encourage them to buy booze. Failure to accomplish that economic objective was cause for dismissal. The girls' income was heavily dependent upon their ability to hustle tips, which they had to split with the piano player: I was able to save my thirty-five dollar salary and live off the tips, which averaged about an additional forty dollars a week. The girls squawked about having to split their tips with me because at that time I could play in only about four keys, and one of them might not be the key they were singing in, so they would complain to the boss. For reasons unknown to me, the Greek liked me and kept me on, and in time I learned how to play in all keys and became somewhat accomplished. In spite of the beef from the entertainers I felt I really earned my money, because every night I had to sit down at the piano at nine o'clock, and I didn't get up until four in the morning. A couple of times a night I sneaked out to the little boy's room, but otherwise I was sitting at that piano and playing. The life of a buffet flat or cafe was dependent upon the piano player keeping the joint alive, because if it got too quiet the clientele would get restless and leave, and the boss would be unhappy. So I worked at it without killing myself.

It was a good gig for me. I was only nineteen, and I was able to buy a car, wear nice clothes and walk around with money in my pocket all the time. And I developed my craft at the Rainbow Cafe: I added hundreds of new tunes to my repertoire, and my ear became so sharp that the girls had to sing a new melody to me only once or twice at the most and I could take off in any key. My reputation as a piano player got around the streets. During my last days at the Rainbow I got offers right and left to work at other cafes.

During the roaring twenties nightclubs fell into two categories: a class operation, or a joint. A first class operation usually had a five piece band or larger, and a piano and singers for intermission. The orchestra usually furnished background music, and music for a minimum amount of dancing, which was not encourged, because when people were dancing they weren't spending any money and the bottom line when you operate a nightclub is that you sell booze in large quantities. The entertainers were very important to the bottom line: they sang little songs that brought tears to your eyes or aroused deep feelings about your long lost love, and that in turn generated a need for more booze. The piano player was important because he accompanied the singers. It was the band that had the lowest status in the nightclubs during that period.

The first high-class nightclub I worked at was on South Wabash Avenue. A buddy of mine named Henry Smith had the five piece band there. He played the drums, and he had the legendary Joe Sullivan on piano. My job was to play accompaniment for the singers. The fellows in the band were being paid sixty dollars a week; I was getting twenty-five. The boss told me when he hired me that if I ever made less than a hundred a week, with tips, I should quit. I stayed on that gig for several months and then one week I made less than a hundred dollars, and I quit. I used the shortfall in money as an excuse to leave because I wanted to move around and play at other clubs. My services were getting to be in great demand. Besides, I didn't like working with Joe Sullivan. We had arguments because I used his piano. He said, "You're an entertainer's piano player. Lay off my piano." At that time Joe was going out to the Apex Club on the South Side to listen to Earl Hines. It seems incredible but I had never yet heard a colored man play jazz.

It was during the summer of 1927 that I was introduced to jazz. I was working at a summer resort at Delavan Lake, Wisconsin, with a banjo-playing buddy named Earl Murphy, who had a collection of Louis Armstrong and Bix Beiderbecke records. He played them constantly and was always getting on me to listen, particularly to the rhythm section that played behind Louie. I soon bought a Victrola and some records of my own, and listened intently to Lil Armstrong, who pounded out solid chords as background for Louie's solos. I was definitely influenced by Louis Armstrong, but it was not until I heard Earl Hines on Jimmy Noone's recording of "Sweet Lorraine" that I felt like throwing my hands in the lake. I had never heard anyone execute so much piano as I heard Earl play in that "Sweet Lorraine" record.

That Delavan Lake gig marked a turning point in my life. When I got back to Chicago I hooked up with Wingy Manone, whom I had met at the Musicians Local No. 10 in Chicago. Subsequently we had become the best of friends. I became a member of Wingy's band, and his roommate as well. When Wingy got up in the morning he brushed his teeth listening to Louis Armstrong records. In fact the first thing he did when he woke up was listen to Louis Armstrong records. Through Wingy I met Armstrong, Hines, Carroll Dickerson and all the great cats on the South Side who were really making things happen. During the 1920s Chicago was swinging on a rusty gate. Outside of the South Side, it was a very bad scene, a cornball scene. The gangsters who owned speakeasies up on the North Side hired white musicians to play that "sock-it-to-you" sort of music which was right out of the cornfield when you compare it with the kind of jazz the black cats were playing out South. There was no comparison.

I remember the first time Wingy took me to see Louis Armstrong at the Savoy Ballroom at 47th and South Parkway. I can close my eyes now and still see the crowd of admirers carrying Louis Armstrong on their shoulders like a hero from the front door all the way to the bandstand. I would say there were at least two thousand people in the ballroom that night who loved Louie. I have never seen as much admiration for any musician as there was for Louie during that period. That was a scene I'll never forget.

After we listened to Louie play a couple of sets Wingy took me back to the bandroom behind the bandstand to meet him. Wingy looked up to Louie like a son looks up to a father. In fact Wingy followed Louie around like a little child follows his mother. King Oliver was in the bandroom with Louie that night, along with Carroll Dickerson. Louie was telling jokes that cracked everybody up. He was a great humorist and a fantastic human being. I was enthralled just being near him.

On another occasion Wingy and I went to the Savoy in the early afternoon to hear Louis practice with the Carroll Dickerson band. When we walked in we saw a porter sweeping the floor. Wingy said to the porter, "Man, what kind of nigger are you?" He was incensed because the porter was not sweeping in time with the music. Then we found out that the porter was from the Caribbean. He wasn't an American Negro, and that explained why he swept the floor out of step with the rhythm. Wingy just couldn't understand how anybody could be around Louis Armstrong's kind of music and not sweep on the beat. Wingy was a gas, to say the least. Incidentally, he was called Wingy because he had lost an arm.

We both used to take turns wearing Wingy's big bear coat. Often when we went to the Savoy Louie would greet us with, "Who's the bear tonight?" Louie was just always on your case. He was the center of the world for Wingy and me.

In the two years that I lived with Wingy I don't believe I read a single book, although I always loved to read. I didn't miss reading then; in fact, I almost forgot that books existed. Our days were loaded with listening to music and playing music, and going to see people from our world, which was the world of Louis Armstrong.

After the crash in 1929 it was difficult to make a living in Chicago playing music. There were small pickings, even for the best of us. Wingy used to answer the phone, and while I was standing there, he would say to anybody who asked for me, "No, this isn't Art. Yes, Art is working. Art's working with me." Of course neither of us was working and we needed the money but we had decided that we wanted to work together. That was the most important thing to us.

I admit freely that black piano players like Lil Armstrong and Earl Hines influenced my career greatly. But Benny Goodman would never admit anything like that. He acts like jazz music just dropped on him from heaven, and yet I know that he listened to Jimmy Noone and Johnny Dodds just as intently as I listened to Earl Hines and Lil Armstrong. Benny and I played together as teenagers and we both studied at Hull House. What he was playing back then did absolutely nothing for me. My most vivid memory of Benny Goodman and his clarinet is that he had a big head and a cocky attitude. He obviously began to hang out with black musicians in the late '20s because you can tell the difference in his style before 1931 and after 1931. You can really note the influence of Jimmy Noone and Baby Dodds on his clarinet work. Gene Krupa, whom I consider to be one of the great drummers, admitted openly that he was influenced by Tubby Hall, Zutty Singleton and Baby Dodds. Those were the black drummers who really turned him on. Krupa was smart enough to hang out with the right people, and young and vigorous enough to take the techniques that he learned from his black brother and use them. When he formed his band, the first cat he hired was Roy Eldridge, who was the hottest thing in the country on trumpet. During that same period Krupa used Charlie Ventura, who was as bad a tenor man as any white man who has ever put a reed to his lips. Ventura, Eldridge and Krupa were all into drive, drive, drive—the band had a force that would really hold your attention. You probably remember, Travis, the driving force that Gene Krupa put behind the old Goodman band back in the '30s. That fellow could drive. You could hear Zutty Singleton and Baby Dodds in his drumbeats. You could hear Tubby Hall too. In addition to being a great drummer, Gene was one of the great showmen.

We always talk about Fletcher Henderson as if he was a forgotten man, and I guess that he was forgotten economically, because he wrote all that beautiful material that made Benny Goodman famous, and Benny, if I know him, certainly wouldn't have paid much. Still that money was the only credit Fletcher Henderson got. Benny Goodman was what you might call the great white hope. The white public was looking for someone who could play black jazz in a style acceptable to them, and the crown fell onto Goodman's head. He dethroned the black musicians for the white public. He was to music what Jeff Willard was to boxing when he defeated Jack Johnson: the Great White Hope.

I remember the first time I saw Bessie Smith at the Grand Theater at 31st and State Streets. This big dark woman came on the stage wearing a shimmering white gown, and she never looked at the audience. For some reason she kept her eyes on the floor. The theater became mouse-quiet after she was greeted with thunderous applause. She stood on the stage silent for what seemed to be three or four minutes. Then she started to sing "Backwater Blues". The way she sang that song made your spine tingle. Her voice filled every crevice of that theater. There were no microphones then, but she didn't need one. She sang from the stomach, she sang from the heart and you felt the power of that message spewed from the depths of her soul. Except for gospel singers, I don't hear anyone sing today with that kind of voice and that kind of imagination and feeling.

Louis Armstrong played his trumpet with the force and spirit of a Bessie Smith. Louie didn't need a microphone either. In fact he usually had to stand back from the mike to avoid blowing the roof off the Savoy Ballroom, while Bix Beiderbecke, who was an excellent trumpet player, needed all the mike help he could get. One night Bix and I were in an all-night jam session and he didn't kill me at all. But when you heard his records he sounded like a giant, because in the recording studio they put him close to the mike and the spirit of his message would come through, because he had a tone like nobody else around. He was actually ahead of his time. If you listen to some of his earlier work you can see what that man has done.

It was not until 1940 that I got my first break in New York City, and it came from a black man. That man was Duke Ellington. He gave me a job playing opposite him on Monday nights at the Copacabana in New York. At that gig I implemented my rule, which is that I don't care what color you are, all I care about is how good you can play. Many times I found myself the only white cat with a six-piece band. I don't think I deserve any credit for that; I just feel you have to evaluate people for what they are able to contribute. Since I couldn't get Dave Tough or Gene Krupa on drums, I certainly wouldn't take a second-rate white drummer. I would take the best black drummer I could get. Kaiser Marshall was the drummer I used. He had worked with Fletcher Henderson, Cab Calloway and Coleman Hawkins, and in my opinion he was one of the best around. From 1940 on my band grew very black and I got a lot of flak from Local No. 10 in Chicago, but I didn't give a damn. They tried to tie me down but they couldn't. There was a difference like the difference between day and night between Local No. 802 in New York and Local No. 10 here. In New York I got no hassle about working with black musicians, but in Chicago I got plenty of flak.

The curse of the business for black artists is the way they are forced to live. Duke Ellington had to stay on the road constantly to keep his band together. Louis Armstrong traveled the world under Joe Glaser for the same reason. Count Basie is still working like a teenager when he should be resting on his laurels. Black bands have never had the luxury of playing the long hotel gigs that Woody Herman, Benny Goodman, and Tommy Dorsey played. Goodman would check into a hotel like the Congress in Chicago or the Waldorf in New York and play for sixteen, eighteen, twenty and thirty-eight weeks out of the year. Because they were white these men were able to live some sort of orderly lives. But black musicians were constantly doing ninety to one hundred and twenty straight one-nighters. I have had that experience working with black bands and I know it is not easy. You can do it when you're twenty, or perhaps until you're forty, but after that time takes its toll and you can feel the difference. I believe that if Louie could have lived differently he would have lived longer, because every day of his life—or at least during the last fifty years of his life—he took a laxative called Swiss Kriss to make his system function regularly. It appears to me that a man of his stature should have had time to get to a doctor who could straighten out whatever his problem was. As you grow older of course your body cannot take the punishment it once could take. Eubie Blake said, "If I had known I was going to live this long, I would have taken better care of myself." I don't know where the hell he got that line, but it's a good one.

The lives of many black musicians have been shortened by the oppressive racial conditions which they were forced to accept. I remember taking a band down to New Orleans in 1965 to celebrate that city's two hundred and fiftieth anniversary. Rail Wilson was playing bass for me and I recall he had to wait at the airport for a long time before a black cab driver showed up because no white driver would take him. On that same trip when he bought a bottle of beer in a liquor store he would be told that he had to take the beer away and drink it somewhere else. I'm not talking about 1865, but about 1965. I remember another time I was with Buddy Smith the drummer in Columbus, Ohio; we were walking down the street and we wanted to get something to eat. No place in that city would serve us, outside of the black community. Buddy said, "Look, let's not start anything. Let's go back to the train station." We knew that the railroad station always had a facility to accommodate black train riders, even if it was a Jim Crow facility.

I believe it is our mission to preserve jazz music by bringing it to the attention of people who have not had an opportunity to hear it. High school and college students get their music from the radio and from record shops. Ninety-nine percent of that music is mickey mouse popular music, with a small amount of classical. There is little or no jazz, and yet jazz is the only original American art form. So I spend a great deal of my time lecturing in colleges, universities and high schools. I want to tell young people about this great music that has made a difference in my life. I think if they learn to know it they too will love it, and it might make a difference in their lives too.

Franz R. Jackson

"We had to be exploited in order to make any headway in the music business."

Franz Jackson

BIRTHDATE: November 1, 1912
BIRTHPLACE: Rock Island, Illinois
INSTRUMENT(S) PLAYED: Tenor Saxophone, Clarinet
OCCUPATION(S): Arranger, Composer, Bandleader
FEATURED WITH: Roy Eldridge, Fats Waller, Cootie Williams, Fletcher Henderson, Earl Hines, Jimmie Noone.

My mother played the piano a little by ear. She could not read a note as big as the Sears Tower but she was sensitive to music and loved to listen to it. My mother had a friend by the name of Jerome Pasquall, a tenor sax man who had played with Fletcher Henderson and who, in 1926, was working at the White City Ballroom at 63rd Street and South Park Avenue with Charlie "Doc" Cooke's Orchestra. He gave me my first saxophone lesson when I was fourteen years old.

My father died when I was about three and my mother had to support three children with her earnings from dressmaking. In order to make a decent living she had to pass for white to get employment in the Chicago Loop dress shops. Most colored women at that time were employed as domestics—cleaning some white folks' homes, cooking in their kitchens, washing their clothes and taking care of their children.

The first gig I had I worked for tips. I played dance music on a boat that ran from Jackson Park to Navy Pier and back. The boat repeated that cycle at least a half dozen times a day. At the end of each excursion a member of our musical group would pass the hat. The daily tips averaged about two dollars per man per day. The boat owners did not give us a meal or even a small stipend.

The first real job I had with fixed pay was with Albert Ammons, the boogie-woogie piano player. In addition to me on tenor sax, he had Punch Miller on trumpet, Al Wynn on trombone and Francois Mosley played the drums. We would ride around the colored community tailgating on the back of a truck, with a big sign advertising Illinois Central round-trip weekend excursions to New Orleans and Memphis. A barker would sell the train tickets directly to people who gathered around the corners to hear us play when the truck stopped at 31st Street and Cottage Grove Avenue, 35th and State streets, 47th Street and South Parkway, and the many stops in between.

The excursion train would leave Chicago on Friday night from the 12th Street Station, which was located a half block east of Michigan Boulevard at 12th Street, and return to the Windy City on Monday morning. The baggage car at the front of the train next to the "For Colored Only" car would be converted into a dance hall on wheels with piano, drums and a makeshift bar. The people would Charleston,

The Cassino Simpson Orchestra at the Roof Garden in Milwaukee, Wisconsin in 1930. Cass at piano, Franz Jackson (seated third from right), and Milt Hinton on bass.

Black Bottom, and Shimmy throughout the night as the train rolled south to Memphis. Upon our arrival in Memphis we would check into a Beale Street hotel and sleep until late afternoon. The excursion's promoters would put on another dance for the weekenders at a local dance hall that Saturday night. On Sunday we would rest before returning to the train Sunday night. Those dancing souls who still had enough energy left would dance across the states to the beat of the drum and the clickety-clack of the train wheels as they rattled north to Chicago. We would not play our last blues note until daybreak Monday morning when the train had pulled to a dead stop at the 12th Street Station. I never had more than three or four dollars in my pocket when I returned from one of those train trips.

I cannot thank Albert Ammons enough for giving me the opportunity to get that experience. Whenever I think of Ammons, I think of one of those Clydesdale horses, you know, the regal ones that have feathers on their legs and prance. That's the way Ammons played the piano. His fingers pranced on the keyboard. He sat up straight, proud and poised. Ammons sat on the piano stool so erect that from the rear he looked as if he were riding a bicycle.

The members of the Ammons band did not have to read music. Neither did the guys who worked with me in the Francois Mosley Orchestra. All the numbers we played were head arrangements. When we had to replace a musician, the band would be in total disarray until the new guy could learn our material by ear. It was at this point that I decided to become an arranger. I felt like the band was going out of the world backwards in the absence of a written musical score. Without that music sheet in front of you, there was no instrumental organization.

I attended Chicago Musical College for almost two years and learned how to write without piano, solfeggio. I did not get an opportunity to fully put my musical training to work until I joined Cass Simpson's band at Sam Beer's Showboat in Chicago's Loop. The Showboat was a mob-controlled speakeasy where we got our money every night. We were paid on a nightly basis because the next day the place might be burned down by a competing group of gangsters or padlocked by revenue agents. The sidemen in the band were paid four dollars per night, plus a meal. In addition, we picked up sixteen to twenty dollars per man in tips from the big Prohibition spenders. Our nightly tips were equal to the average colored person's weekly salary during that period. That was good money when you consider my weekly room rent was only two dollars and the average meal would cost me about thirty-five cents.

In 1934 I joined Jimmie Noone's Orchestra at the Platinum Lounge, which was located in the basement of the Vincennes Hotel at 36th Street and Vincennes Avenue. Benny Goodman would come down to the joint every night he was in town. He loved Jimmie's style of playing. Benny and Jimmie had the same music teacher. I believe his name was Shepp. Whenever Jimmie would go downtown for his lessons, Shepp would invite Benny Goodman down to listen to them play

Chu Berry.

Jimmie Noone.

James P. Johnson. Inset: Fats Waller.

Ben Webster.

duets. The teacher was trying to help Benny learn Jimmie's technique and tonation. Noone had a light, airy and melodic wail, whereas Goodman had a gutty style. Although Goodman was the white media's "King of Swing," he was never able to perfect that wailing soul tone that was very lyrical and characteristically black. As a matter of fact, most black musicians never reach Noone's clarinet-playing plateau. The only exceptions that come to mind are Barney Bigard from New Orleans and Buster Bailey of Memphis. I could not touch Jimmie Noone with my clarinet and a ten-foot pole. His sound was so beautiful that he made my efforts sound like I was playing a set of plumbing pipes. I kept my clarinet in its case the entire period that I played with the Noone orchestra and I was considered a good clarinet player by my peers. His tone on such songs as his theme song, "Sweet Lorraine," was pure, open and big. My tone was a "legit" clarinet sound but it was tight and closed.

Now I could really bark on a tenor saxophone. I remember being with Jimmie Noone at the Platinum the same time Fletcher Henderson's Orchestra was at the Grand Terrace. One night during our radio broadcast, Chu Berry, the star tenor man with Fletcher's band, came down to the Platinum Lounge seeking me out like a cowboy at high noon looking for a gun duel. He jerked his sax from its case and walked upon the bandstand and started blowing. Although we were on the air, Jimmie did not stop him. Noone said: "Oh, what the hell!"

Chu and I had a non-stop tenor sax duel that lasted till the end of the half hour radio broadcast. Chu was a "bad" tenor man. He was killed in 1941 in an automobile accident near Conneaut, Ohio, when the car in which he was riding skidded on the road into a concrete bridge. He was only thirty-one years old.

In 1937, I joined Roy Eldridge at the Three Deuces, which was located at 222 North State Street. Chu Berry had left Fletcher Henderson to join Cab Calloway. Ben "Brut" Webster, the other tenor with Fletcher, left cold without notice. I had always wanted to play the Henderson book and I just went over to the Grand Terrace and sat down in Ben Webster's seat and started playing. Nobody ever asked me why I was sitting in Ben's chair, and I didn't volunteer any information. I just simply took the job. I was never officially hired or fired. I got paid every week during the fifteen months I remained with the band.

I thought that I had learned all of Fletcher's arrangements, but I didn't really find out until one night in Bunkersville, West Virginia. I got drunk that day and the fellows had to set the book up on my music stand that night because I was too far out to manage it myself. I played all the arrangements that evening without being physically able to focus my eyes on the music. Subconsciously, I had memorized the entire Fletcher Henderson book.

Fletcher was a poor disciplinarian and a weak band leader. However, you had to respect him for his superior arranging ability. He was among the best. I quit the band after completing a St. Louis gig in December, 1938. I had grown tired of traveling and I wanted to spend some time with my spanking brand new wife. I rejoined Roy Eldridge at the Arcadia Ballroom in New York City in 1939. Prince Robinson was with the band on clarinet. He had an excellent style that was reminiscent of Jimmie Noone. I liked hearing him better than I did hearing myself. He had a jump style that really kicked off. I stayed with Roy until I joined Earl Hines in 1940.

The Hines' band was at its musical best in 1940. All the guys were young and musically sharp. The band was playing some hot arrangements, such as "Boogie Woogie on the St. Louis Blues," "G. T. Stomp" and "Jelly, Jelly." I remember when we recorded "Jelly, Jelly" in December, 1940. No one thought much of it because it was nothing but the basic twelve-bar blues. We did not realize it was a big hit until we reached the Apollo Theater in New York City. There were cops on horses outside the theater trying to keep the huge crowd under control while they were waiting impatiently for the doors to open. When Billy Eckstine began to sing "Hello, baby, I had to call you on the phone," the house went berserk. The women started yelling and screaming and some dude got so excited that he fell from the balcony to the main floor.

Earl asked me to rejoin the band after I left in 1941. I went back and played a one-night stand and left again. World War II had started and we were forced to travel by train instead of bus because of the gas shortage. I didn't like the idea of running to catch trains, carrying my instrument and suitcases. That was heavy, man! It was comparatively easy when we could walk right out of the hotel with our bags and get on the bus. In addition, the draft was going on and the draft board treated you like a criminal if they could not find you on short notice. That kind of pressure got on my nerves because the only people who knew my whereabouts were my mother and my wife, when I took time to write.

After leaving Earl, I gigged around New York City with James P. Johnson. He was the king of the stride piano players. I loved his style so much that I tried it myself. I will never forget the night we played Carnegie Hall and he brought the house down. He knocked them out. Fats Waller was a Johnson student and a master of his style.

Fats Waller was a big robust man with a robust piano style. James P.'s style was lighter, more tonated and intricate. An untrained ear could hear the replica of style, and also recognize the difference in presentation. Musically, Fats Waller was an extrovert because he talked extensively while he played as did "Willie the Lion" Smith who ran his mouth continually as he stroked the "eighty-eights." The thing I resented most about Smith was the fact that he covered up his excellent stride piano style with his big mouth. Smith, like Waller, was continuously selling as he played. "Pine Top" Smith was another piano player who described what he was playing as he played it. The two Smiths and Fats Waller were loud talking, extroverted piano players, whereas James P. Johnson was the exact opposite,

Fats Waller's band in 1941. Third from right is Franz Jackson, and seventh from right is Fats Waller.

and this was reflected musically on the individual keyboards. Fats Waller, the student, got all the credit for the Johnson style of piano playing. If you compare the recordings of Fats Waller and James P. Johnson, Fats sounds like a little boy playing in a contest against Johnson, his musical father. Johnson was subtle and played the finest kind of piano you ever wanted to hear.

I worked with Fats Waller in a little pick-up band around New York City, and was also in the last big band that he took on a Southern road trip. We played in huge tobacco warehouses to accommodate the large crowds that wanted to hear Fats play his latest recordings. His records were extremely popular during the period of 1941 and 1942. There was another tenor man in Fats Waller's band named Eugene "Baby Bear" Cedric. Fats would constantly push us into jam sessions. Fats liked the excitement. Although Fats would always do his numbers on the piano, he would leave a lot of room for his soloists. He would say, "What are you guys going to do?" He would back you up with some solid accompaniment. He would never try to outplay you. Whatever he was doing it was helping the band.

Fats was a very emotional person. He could turn his personality on and off like a light. When he was at the piano, he was a different fellow than when he was seated on the bus, where he generally remained very quiet. He was very pensive. He had to have someone with him all the time. He had a fellow who traveled with him as a companion. This fellow would go out and get whiskey, food or girls for Fats when he did not feel like leaving his room. When Fats couldn't sleep, he would send for me to come up to his room. My presence was all that he needed to start playing the organ. This private musical concert would sometimes last until daybreak. He had to have somebody to sit down and listen to what he was doing. He needed a person to play to.

Waller usually had a portable organ in his room. He often told me the story about the Christmas Eve he spent in Chicago at the Ritz Hotel located on South Parkway (King Drive) and Oakwood Boulevard. That night after he finished work he went to his room with a friend and started working out on the organ. The room was literally rocking when it slowly began filling up with piano players. Duke Ellington, who was staying in the hotel, was the first to drift-into Waller's room, followed by Earl Hines, who was working next door at the Terrace. Billy Kyle, the pianist with John Kirby's orchestra, was also staying at the hotel, and he came downstairs to Waller's room feeling good and just flopped down on the bed. Not too much time had passed before Duke pulled out his handkerchief, pretending to wipe his nose. Earl Hines started rubbing his eyes as though they itched. There was not a dry eye in that room because all the "cats" had become homesick and were moved by Waller's sensitive renditions of "Silent Night" and other holiday songs.

Fats Waller was a lonely man and frequently needed a pacifier. His companion and road manager attempted to fill that need when Fats would get homesick and lonesome in the middle of a successful tour and threaten to go home. His companion usually managed to talk him out of that notion. However, there were times when Fats would ignore the tour schedules. He would stop the bus and throw his suitcases into his chauffeur-driven Lincoln and scream "Holland Tunnel" to his chauffeur, Buster Shepherd. Off they would go to Harlem, leaving his manager Ed Kirkeby behind to deal with the irate promoters and theater owners. Offstage, Fats was shy and alone in the midst of a crowd.

New melodies bubbled out of Fats Waller's creative brain like water spouting out of the head of a whale. He wrote songs with such ease that he never fully realized the value of his musical contributions. He wrote "I Can't Give You Anything But Love, Baby" and "On the Sunny Side of the Street" without ever getting any royalties or credits. In the summer of 1929 he sold the rights to 21 of his songs, including the ones from the musical hit, *Hot Chocolates,* to Irving Mills for $500. Fats Waller was so creative that he could have set the phone book to music. Unfortunately, he did not have a head for the bulk of business that he created.

The Fats Waller experience pushed me into trying my hand at composing music. I soon found that the key to the door for getting into that business was called "connections." I met a fellow named Edgar Battle in New York City who was a song hustler and my key to getting heard. I would give him a tune to record, and he would put his name on the credits. That was the way I got into the song-writing business. I had to cut somebody in. Half the battle of song writing is to get someone to play your tune. Edgar Battle had those type of contacts. I remember I spoke to Jack Teagarden about a couple of tunes I had written and that he had recorded. When I told him those were my songs, he said: "Well, I thought Edgar Battle wrote them." It floored me that Teagarden thought somebody else had written those tunes. Battle was a member of ASCAP (American Society of Composers, Authors and Publishers), and anything with his name on it was protected for royalties. I was not a member and therefore I had no protection or credibility.

You know, there is an old saying: "You are not worth the price of a song." There is a lot of truth to that statement because a song standing by itself is nothing. It's the arrangement of the song that puts it over. "Tuxedo Junction" is really nothing musically. Its success came from the way it was presented, the way

Franz Jackson's Original Jass [sic] Band: (Left to right): Preston Jackson, Little Brother Montgomery (piano), Dolton Nicklison, Jim Herndon (drums), Jeanie Carroll, and Franz Jackson.

it was arranged and played by the Erskine Hawkins band and later by the Glenn Miller Orchestra.

Although I have never received over $500 in any one year from the gobs of records that I have made, I met some interesting people. Jelly Roll Morton was one of the most interesting characters. He was in a class by himself in that he was an uncrowned musical genius with an elephant-sized ego. Jelly Roll was a nonstop braggart. I will never forget the summer of 1939 when I was standing in front of the Brill Building at 1547 Broadway in New York City and Jelly Roll Morton was complaining to a group of musicians about the fact that W. C. Handy had not invited him into ASCAP.

I said: "Man, they don't ask you, you ask them. You've got enough tunes behind you to fox trot in. All you have to do is go to a publisher and get them to recommend you."

A couple of weeks later I heard he had been accepted. He subsequently collected back credits on the thousand-plus songs he had written.

Left to right: Hilliard Brown, drummer; Unknown; Art Hodes, and Franz Jackson.

Jelly Roll Morton and W. C. Handy were contemporaries who did not respect each other. Jelly Roll "bad-mouthed" Handy because Handy, by his own admission, copied what he heard in blues' expressions and work songs from the guy on the street, whereas Jelly Roll created his material in his head. Hence, the conflict and envy.

I found a conflict in my desire to play jazz when I returned to Chicago in the mid-1950s and discovered that the only regular gigs I could get was playing New Orleans "gut bucket" music for white folks. I made the adjustment by organizing the Original Jass All-Stars in 1957. I had Bud Shoffner on trumpet, Al Wynn on trombone, Joe Johnson on piano, Lawrence Dixon on banjo, Richard Curry on drums and Bill Oldham on tuba. Those swing era cats played that two-beat "jive" so naturally that we became an instant success. A two-week gig at the Red Arrow Club turned out to be a 10-year engagement.

You know, jazz originally had bad connotations in that it was associated with sporting houses. The origin of jazz came from the word "jass" which was derived from the French verb, jaser, meaning to speed up. Man! I am seventy years old and can't slow down.

Viola Jefferson

"No one wanted to hire you if you were too dark."

Viola Jefferson

BIRTHDATE: July 11, 1916
BIRTHPLACE: Helena, Alabama
OCCUPATON: Vocalist
PERFORMED WITH: Ray Nance, Horace Henderson, Jimmy Johnson
and Larry Steele's "Smart Affairs".

My family moved from Helena, Arkansas, to the small, coal-mining town of Dewmaine, Illinois, in 1921. The closest city to Dewmaine was Carbondale. I was the youngest of nine children. My father and three older brothers worked in the coal mines. My mother was my father's slave, and I was the original coal miner's daughter. As the youngest child, I was able to see and hear an awful lot, and it really turned me against the idea of being a mother or a housewife.

I made up my mind at an early age that I wanted to live a different type of life from my mother's. It was in a Dewmaine Baptist church that I discovered I had a talent as a gospel singer. I won the first prize in a gospel-singing contest and decided that maybe I could really be somebody.

In 1930, at the age of fourteen, I moved to Chicago to live with my sister Ethel, and help babysit her children. Ethel was my biggest inspiration, because she was always encouraging me to do something with my voice. Shortly after I arrived in Chicago, I heard Jack L. Cooper's radio show "The All-Negro Hour", which was broadcast every Sunday at five p.m. over station WSBC from the Brookmont Hotel at 39th and Michigan. After listening to Cooper's show for about three months, I got up enough courage to go down to the Brookmont Hotel and introduce myself to him. To my surprise, Mr Cooper was a very friendly man, and a person who seemed to want to help those who were willing to help themselves. It was through Jack L. Cooper that I received my initial training in radio technique. He showed me how to use a microphone, and he let me come down every Sunday and just watch, and after I had watched for three or four weeks he let me sing a spiritual on his show that was a big boost to my self image. I felt that I was really on my way, and then I met the city slicker: my first husband. He thought that my career as a singer was secondary to my career as his wife, and of course being the original country girl and coal-miner's daughter, I agreed with him and left my potential singing career.

I had been married a little less than a year when I finally made up my mind that I wanted to be a show business personality, and I realized that I could not make any money singing spirituals. My husband was hell-bent against my becoming a jazz singer. He told me that all show people were either freaks or dope addicts, and that I would probably turn out to be a whore. I considered his statement a personal challenge, and I was determined to prove that he was wrong. My husband worked nights downtown as a valet so I could test my wings in show business without his finding out. I had been gigging for over a year when he finally found out, and he told me that if I was going to stay in show business, I couldn't use the name of Maisley. I told him I didn't need to use his name. I had a name before I met him, and that's how I reverted back to using my maiden name, Jefferson.

My real show business break came when I won first prize in an amateur contest at the State Theater at 3507 South State Street. A week's engagement at Dave's Cafe, at 343 East Garfield Boulevard, was part of the prize. While I was working that one-week engagement at Dave's Cafe, I realized that being dark was a handicap in show business. My first week's engagement was so successful that Dave Heighly, the owner of the cafe, wanted me to stay over another week and it was then that I learned through the grapevine that the other colored people in the show said that they didn't want me to stay because I was too dark.

I remember Clarence Weems was the M.C. of the show. Joe "Ziggy"Johnson and a girl named Margie Tubbs had a dancing act. There was also a chorus line of high yellow women. They were all dead-set against my staying. The owner had

Left: Viola the bombshell, in action. Right: Viola is greeted by Willie Bryant on stage at the Apollo Theater in New York City.

just the opposite opinion. He was insistent that I stay because he thought that I was a good entertainer and the patrons liked my act. Since the man liked me, I made up my mind that I was going to go out there and sing my buns off. This was the only way I could fight against the color situation. I said to myself, I can't help it because I'm black, but I will never let anybody say that I can't sing. I was deeply pained to find that colored people in show business were as racist as those crackers that I left in my homestate of Alabama, and the other rednecks I had encountered in Dewmaine, Illinois. As they used to say back in those days: "If you're white, you're right; if you're yellow, you're mellow; if you're brown, stick around; if you're black, get back." Getting back was something that never registered in my psyche. In contrast to the other people in the show, the band boys always treated me fine. Ray Nance, who later went on to become a star trumpet player with the Duke Ellington band, was the leader of the six-piece combo. He treated me with a great deal of respect. I never had any problem with the musicians.

Following the one-week engagement that was extended to six weeks at Dave's Cafe, I found myself among the unemployed until I got an offer to work with the Jimmy Johnson Band at a Blue Monday Party at a little place called Brownie's

Deauville Palace Number One, just two doors east of Prairie on the south side of 61st Street. At Brownie's, I had my first real feeling of success. I was making only three dollars but we packed that place every Monday night, and the people just loved me. In fact, it was there that Jimmy Townsend gave me the name of "Kiki'. Although the Jimmy Johnson Band had only six pieces, on Monday nights there would be as many as twenty musicians sitting up, blowing their hearts out all night long for kicks, and there was always a bunch of cats around the wall waiting their turn. When a trumpet player dropped out, another would come right in and take his place. The same with the saxophone and piano players. It was just an absolute ball. I would say that those were real jam sessions. We don't have sessions like that anymore. The guys really enjoyed listening to each other, playing for each other, and the unions didn't interfere.

I really think I began to create a name for myself on that gig because Jimmy Johnson was able to get a couple of extra gigs a week because I was his singer. We started to get gigs downstate, which kept us busy at least four nights a week. That was a lot of work when you consider that we were in the midst of the Great Depression. It was during my engagement with the Johnson band that I came in contact with the Pintozzi brothers, who owned the Cotton Club, three doors south of Roosevelt Road on Blue Island Avenue. They offered me a job working in their club seven nights a week, and of course I jumped at the opportunity because a steady gig was something every singer and musician was thirsting for during that period. I guess I must have worked at the Cotton Club, along with Billy Mitchell and Sporty Odie, for better than a year. They had a full show. We must have had twenty to twenty-five people in that show: a full chorus line, comedians, dancers and a large band. Billy Mitchell, the comedian in the show, was the funniest man I have ever had the privilege of working with. He was the Richard Pryor of his time. He had a bushel basket of risque songs he used to do. I remember one called "I Can't Get Her Started", which went as follows:

> I can't get her started,
> I can't get her started,
> She won't turn over for me.
> Last night, while we were out in the woods,
> I looked under her hood,
> But I couldn't get her started.
> And I just couldn't get her started.
> I couldn't get her started,
> She wouldn't turn over for me.

There were more words to the song than that but I just don't recall them. All of his songs had a double meaning. There was another funny one that comes to mind, called "The Bed-Bug Song":

Vi Jefferson with Horace Henderson and the brass section at a battle of swing against Harlem's Chick Webb, (below).

The bed bugs were marching,
Oh, the bed bugs were marching.
I turned on the light,
And one took a bite,
And they kept marching on.

At that point, Billy Mitchell would do a little step like a crippled bed bug, and he would hop around the stage and everybody would just absolutely crack up. He was indeed a funny man. He had another one he used to do that I thought was pretty funny. I can only remember a couple of lines:

Two old maids in a folding bed.
One turned over,
And the other one said,
I'm coming, I'm coming!

The people would just crack up. He was a gas!

The Pintozzis loved my act so much that they told me that I could work there as long as they had the club. In fact, I was at the Cotton Club when Horace

Henderson discovered me. Horace Henderson, who is the younger brother of the late Fletcher Henderson, was organizing a band to go into the 5100 Club at 5100 North Broadway. One of the members of the band told him they thought that since he was looking for a singer, he would do well if he came over and listened to that little black girl working at the Cotton Club on 12th Street.

One night, the great Horace Henderson showed up and sent the waitress backstage to ask me to come out and join him at his table. When I came out, he told me that he had enjoyed my act and would like me to become the singer in his band. I've always been a skeptic, so I asked him, "What else do I have to do besides sing?" He said, "Nothing."

You see, Travis, as I look back, I think that my drawing the line around myself is really the reason that I didn't get any further in show business. I always wanted to move ahead on the merits of my talent and nothing else. That may have been a mistake, but I don't think so. During my initial conversation with Horace Henderson, he told me that I would have to travel a lot because they planned to do a lot of one-nighters throughout the country. I had some reluctance about accepting his offer, because I had a small daughter at that time and I didn't want to leave her here when I traveled on the road. Again, my sister Ethel who was my initial inspiration, told me, "Whatever you do, Vi, take it. We'll find a way to take care of your child while you're gone."

Incidentally, Danny Thomas, the star of movie and television, was the M.C. at the 5100 Club when I worked there. Horace left the 5100 Club after about a year and went into the newly refurbished Savoy Ballroom. The Savoy had initiated a five night dance program with live radio broadcasts nightly.

The night of nights at the Savoy was July 31, 1938. It was billed as the "Swing Battle of the Century": "Harlem's Chick Webb, America's Outstanding Swing Band, versus Bronzeville's Horace Henderson, Creator of the Jump Band." Ella Fitzgerald was featured with Chick Webb and I was featured with Horace. Horace had made an arrangement of "Ticket-A-Tasket" for me that was almost identical to the one Chick Webb had made for Ella. The Savoy people had been hearing me sing that song, so when they set up this Battle of Swing between Horace Henderson and Chick Webb, the Chicago bunch wanted to hear me do it again. I really didn't want to sing that song because I felt that "Tisket-A-Tasket" was Ella Fitzgerald's song and there was no reason for me to invade her territory on my home ground. The Savoy audience wouldn't stand still until I sang "Tasket"; they kept screaming and yelling: "Vi, sing "Tisket-A-Tasket!" Ella had just finished singing the song in the Chick Webb set, and Horace said to me, "Come on, Vi. The people want you to sing it." But I kept saying I didn't want to.

He struck up the band with "Tisket-a-Tasket", and of course I had no alternative except to go out there and do my number. When I finished singing, the crowd just roared and screamed and practically walked the walls. Horace was

Viola Jefferson getting down and selling her song.

standing there smiling and his smile got wider and wider and wider and of course, that gave me a great feeling. I'll never forget that night. It was as hot as the devil's oven. In fact, it was so hot that they actually had to move the bandstands to the outdoor pavilion. That was probably the largest crowd in the Savoy history.

To this day, Ella Fitzgerald and I are very close friends. Whenever I'm in New York, I visit her and she does the same when she's in Chicago. However, I've always resented the way Horace Henderson billed me as "The Second Ella Fitzgerald" because I think that nobody in second place can be very good, and all I wanted to be was the first Viola Jefferson. The fellows knew how I resented this second-place badge Horace had hung on me. They kidded me by calling me "Viola Fitzjefferson", and I just steamed whenever Dave Young, the tenor man, did it. To this day, Dave Young still gets a big chuckle out of calling me "Viola Fitzjefferson".

Betty Hutton, the singer and movie star, came to the Savoy one night to listen to me, and she watched my every move like a hawk. That particular night I did a song called "I Got Rhythm". As you probably remember, whenever I did that

Above: Viola Jefferson performing in Berlin, Germany.

tune, I would carry the mike across the stage singing and walking. I would walk and do little rhythmic dance steps to sell the song. Would you believe that the next time I saw Betty in a movie, she was doing my act? The same gestures, walk and everything. Of course the only difference was that she got the big mega-bucks for doing it, whereas I was making sixty dollars a week.

After we completed our engagement at the Savoy Ballroom, we went on the road for sixty days of one-nighters across the country, and came back to Chicago and opened up at Benny Skollar's Swingland, which is actually the same place as Dave's Cafe. They simply changed the name. I stayed there with Horace for six or seven months, and when the band decided to go back on the road, I quit because I was tired of the road and I wasn't making any money or getting the proper recognition. Horace never stopped billing me as "the Second Ella Fitzgerald", and I felt it was impossible for me ever to feel good about being the second anything.

Sammy Dyer, producer and choreographer at the Club DeLisa, invited me to join the new show that was opening at the New DeLisa in April of 1941. I worked there with the DeLisa aggregation for better than a year. They started me with a big-time salary of sixty-five dollars a week. That was considered big money because I was famous. At that time, the chorus girls were making only fifteen dollars a week. People have often asked me how chorus girls could make it on so little. Some of them couldn't, but they were generally glad to be able to work with the public because they never had to buy any drinks and they were generally having a good time. They loved that kind of work, and I guess some work transcends the need for money. I've never understood it, but it happens.

After Club DeLisa, I joined the Larry Steele show at Club Harlem on the Boardwalk in Atlantic City. Larry used me, more or less, as his house singer on all of his engagements along the East Coast. I'll never forget, he took me into Club Baron in New York City where Ivy Anderson was the star and I was the opening act, and I did another number in the middle of the show. I used to sit in my dressing room and say, "Oh, listen, honey, my nerves are bad!" I would say that all the time, and evidently Ivy, who had never seen me work, thought that I was really a nervous person. I think she decided early on that I was somebody she didn't have to worry about because of my nerves. When I went out the first night to do my act, the audience wouldn't let me off the stage.

Now Ivy the star was down in the dressing room knowing that she had to come up as the star attraction, and here this little black girl who was so nervous had just stopped the show cold. She never said anything to me about how I was stopping the show every night. I didn't know how Ivy felt about me until a month later. They were bringing in a new show at Club Baron and the new star attraction was going to be Ethel Waters. Ethel Waters came in to see the show, and of course she saw me. She immediately told the boss: "I will not open in this show unless you get rid of that singer." So I was fired.

Several nights before our show closed, Ivy Anderson and I were sitting at the bar having some drinks and talking about going out and having a ball. One of the chorus girls came up and said, "Don't you think it's horrible what they're doing to Vi? They're going to fire Vi because that old Ethel Waters is coming and saying she will not open if Vi is still in the show!" Ivy Anderson looked at me and said, "Now listen, honey chile, I've got news for you! If I had known that you were going to raise as much hell on that stage as you did during the past month, I wouldn't have had you in my show either!" I admired her for admitting that she didn't want to deal with that much competition.

I went to Europe in 1949 with the help of June Richmond, former singer with the Andy Kirk band, and a great all-around entertainer. I had no idea that June considered me one of her friends. Usually, you don't find one singer helping another as she did me. When June got to Europe and found that the field was wide open for black American singers, she called me long distance, and said, "Look, if you want to come over here, the field is wide open, and I will talk to my agent and see what he thinks about helping you make the trip."

She knew I didn't have the money to go to Europe, so her agent advanced the money to me for a one-way ticket from Chicago to Sweden. After I got to Europe, I told June's agent that I would reimburse him as soon as I got my first engagement. I got my first engagement in Oslo, Sweden, and I never stopped working from that point in 1949 until I returned to the States in 1954.

My success in Europe would certainly have to be credited to June, because she taught me how to handle a European audience. She told me to choose American songs that Europeans would recognize; she said they would appreciate them even though they didn't understand the language. She also explained to me the importance of speaking slowly and very distinctly because there were many people in Europe whose English was not perfect. I found that the Europeans loved spirituals. In fact, I ended up putting two spirituals in my act.

The difference between a European audience and an American audience is that the Europeans continue to love you, no matter how old you are. As long as you can deliver the song, they always seem to appreciate you and they show it in many ways—through gifts, flowers, extended visits in their homes; a kind of a loving relationship you just don't find in America. In fact, Travis, those two wooden horses over there on my mantelpiece were given to me in Sweden. A couple came into a club one night and told me that they had enjoyed hearing me on an earlier occasion, and they thought that one way to thank me for the evening was to present me with that gift.

While I was in Europe, I got a contract with the Army Special Services and I joined a unit that was entertaining the troops; the other members were Frank Sinatra, Janet Leigh and Tony Curtis. This was about 1952, shortly after Tony and Janet were married. It was the first time that I had worked with an integrated show in Europe, and I told the commander that if I was going to travel with the show, I wanted to be treated just like everyone else, and he promised me that I would, so I stayed in the best hotels, ate the best food and had a chauffered car at my disposal.

The racism that I knew at home was either very subtle or non-existent in most of the European countries. I can recall some of my earlier days traveling with Horace Henderson to Illinois and Indiana. We always had a white bus driver and he would be the one to go in and get sandwiches because they wouldn't sell them to blacks, and we would wait on the bus until he returned. On one occasion, I had to go to the rest room, so I got off the bus and went around to the rear of the place where the toilets were usually located and there was a notice on the door which read: "No Niggers or Dogs Allowed". That was one of the most shocking experiences I had had since I left the southern part of Illinois. As I recall, the incident occurred just outside of Fort Wayne, Indiana. That brings to mind another experience. I was working with Joe "Ziggy" Johnson in St Louis at the Plantation, and that's exactly what it was, a plantation. It was a white club, white owners, white audiences and black entertainers. We were not allowed to go out into the front part of the plantation for anything. We had to go to the stage through the kitchen and when we finished our show, we had to go back through the kitchen to our dressing rooms. We were not permitted to move around at all. That was a most unusual kind of situation. We were almost afraid to ask them to deliver sandwiches from the kitchen. Their attitude toward blacks was hostile, yet we were there entertaining them and making them laugh every night.

Of course, we had a similar experience in Chicago. The Horace Henderson Band was engaged to play at the Hotel Metropole, at 23rd and Michigan Avenue. I remember when we arrived the doorman directed us through the lobby and straight to the freight elevator. We took the freight elevator to our suites, and that's where we stayed. We stayed in those rooms until it was time to go down to the ballroom to play and when we finished, we had to go directly back to the rooms and anything that we wanted to eat or drink was sent up to us. We were not allowed to use any of the hotel facilities. Remember, this was on the South Side of Chicago within five blocks of a predominantly black population. I'm not talking about the Reconstruction period. This was in the late 1930s.

The 5100 Club on North Broadway was not much different. The owner there, Harry Eager, didn't permit the band or the entertainers to mingle with the patrons under any circumstances. The thing that still amazes me is how we could be so effective as entertainers under such depressing conditions.

AUTHOR'S NOTE

I had the pleasure of seeing Viola work at the Cotton Club, the Savoy, and the Swingland. She was undoubtedly one of the best vocalists on the scene during the 1930s and '40s. When she returned from Europe in the '50s she was ill and she finally left show business to pursue a career in business administration. Inter- and intra-race prejudice capped her career just as it put a lid on thousands of careers because the individuals were born with America's most unpopular pigmentation. Black.

Eddie Johnson

"Louis Jordan was rocking and rolling before the Beatles and the Rolling Stones were introduced to their first rocking chair."

Eddie Johnson

BIRTHDATE: December 11, 1920
BIRTHPLACE: Napoleonville, Louisiana
INSTRUMENT PLAYED: Tenor Saxophone
OCCUPATION: Instrumentalist and Bandleader
FEATURED WITH: Johnny Long, Horace Henderson, Moral Young, Cootie Williams, Louis Jordan and Coleman Hawkins

My mother and I moved to Chicago when I was two years old. I can't remember my father because he died before I reached my second birthday, but I have a picture of him with a trombone. He worked as a dock laborer in New Orleans during the week and played gigs with his horn on weekends. As a child, I used to listen to the Mills Brothers on the radio and I also listened to some Phillips High School students who called themselves Austin Powell and his Harlem Harmony Hounds. Two neighborhood friends, Jimmy Jones and Leroy Wimbush, often listened to

The Melody Mixers. Left to right: Jimmy Jones, fifteen years old; Leroy Wimbush, seventeen; and Eddie Johnson, thirteen.

the radio with me. Remember, most people didn't have a radio back in the Depression. One day Leroy decided to organize us into a vocal group, to be known as the Melody Mixers, that would sound something like the Mills Brothers. Jimmy Jones played the ukelele and was our musical prime mover. He had never studied music formally, but he had an amazing grasp of chord structure and harmony. He would give us our harmonic parts and then glare at Leroy and me if we got out of tune. I remember once Roy brazenly took us backstage at the Regal where the Mills Brothers were appearing and, right in their presence, we just started singing. The Mills Brothers were surprised at the harmonic togetherness of the group and they gave us a great deal of encouragement. As you know, the Mills Brothers were at their peak back in the early '30s.

We became quite popular around school and at house parties and that led to bigger things. Before I reached my thirteenth birthday, the Melody Mixers were working regularly on WCFL radio under the sponsorship of the Hoover Vacuum Cleaner Company. Can you imagine three punks like us working a fifteen minute daily program over the radio back in 1933? The funny thing is that neither Jimmy

Jones nor I was impressed with what we were doing at that time. I remember Leroy Wimbush used to have to come and look for Jimmy and me to rehearse, and he would usually find us shooting marbles. We resisted going to rehearsals because we really preferred shooting marbles to singing. Leroy, who was then seventeen years old, insisted that we rehearse and be prepared for our daily radio show. He was always right on target.

Our reputation as singers spread fast as a result of the radio show and we got another gig playing at the World's Fair in 1934—the second year of the Fair. We were employed by the Swift Packing Company to play at the Swift Bridge of Service on the Fair grounds. We did two shows a day there, seven days a week. I was making more money than my mother Agnes, and she was a professional seamstress. The Harmony Hounds continued going strong throughout 1934, and then our voices started to change and that broke up the group. You can't successfully sing for your supper with a cracking voice.

I didn't think about playing any kind of musical instrument until I was in my sophomore year in high school. My brother Fred, who is now a retired policeman, had an old Selmer tenor sax in the closet. Mother had bought it for him because she believed he had musical talent. Fred couldn't carry a tune in a barrel and I decided that I would borrow the horn and have my uncle, Joe Poston, teach me how to play it. He had played with Erskine Tate, Jimmy Noone, and Doc Cook in Chicago, and earlier in his life, he had played gigs around New Orleans. Uncle Joe was my first teacher and instrumental influence. After Uncle Joe started me off I just kind of drifted with the instrument. I didn't really get a great deal of formal training. I played around high schools a bit. My instructional push came through the music programs that were started under the Work Projects Administration by President Franklin D. Roosevelt during the Depression. WPA offered classes in churches throughout the black communities and music lessons were free. I used to spend hours in the church at 60th and Prairie where they were giving these free music and harmony lessons. The WPA programs gave me a basic music education. In fact, I became proficient enough on my horn to get a professional job with the Danny Williams Orchestra.

Danny Williams was a fellow student at Englewood High School, and he had one of the popular younger bands around town. The high school kids and young social set hired either Danny Williams or the Tony Fambro Orchestra for their parties. Club dances were given by high school kids in each of their four years. I played with Danny Williams for about three years.

During that period, Alabama State College used the Bama State Collegiates Orchestra as kind of a flagship to promote the College. Kentucky State got the idea that they should get a band and do the same thing in order to promote their college. They sent the registrar to Chicago to sign up the entire Danny Williams band for a scholarship that included free tuition and board. They even gave us free books. All we had to do was to attend class and play for the school functions. On weekends, the band would gig in the small towns around Franklin, Kentucky. As a group, we didn't stay in Kentucky more than a year. In fact, some of us started coming back to Chicago after the first six months. I remember Nick Cooper the trumpet player stayed down there with Jimmy Jones. Jimmy had elevated himself from the ukelele to the piano. I came back after nine months and enrolled in Wilson Junior College. The only two musicians that stayed and graduated from Kentucky State were "Bally" Beach, and Joe Burton. After they returned to Chicago, the fellows went their respective ways. Although most of the guys are dead now, Danny Williams is still around repairing instruments and looking well.

When I returned to Chicago, I became affiliated with the Johnny Long Orchestra through our mutual friend Dave Young, the tenor sax man. Johnny Long was the real musical force in Chicago during that period. He had all of the jobs locked up and his band worked regularly playing social club dates on the South Side of Chicago. As I remember, Johnny Long was a businessman and between me and you, he had the B.S. that it took to front a band. He wasn't a good player by any stretch of the imagination, although he had a way of projecting himself in the image of Louis Armstrong, even to the mannerisms. If you analyze what he was doing, it was just pure B.S., but people bought his stuff. Johnny had real business acumen. He was also smart in his selections of musicians. He always picked the best musicians available: fellows like Gordon Jones, Nat Jones, Dave Young, Henderson Smith, and Gail and Charlie Brockman.

The band never went on the road because they stayed busy just playing gigs around Chicago. I can remember only one regular job that Johnny Long ever played, and that was at Squares Lounge, which was located just east of Michigan on Fifty-First Street. It was a very popular place back in the '30s. Johnny played there for about a year. He followed Lonnie Johnson, the famous guitar-playing blues singer on that job.

After leaving Johnny Long, I went into Swingland with the Horace Henderson band in 1937, and I worked there for almost a year. I left Henderson and joined Moral Young who was rehearsing a band that was to open at the same club. I will never forget Moral Young who was a top notch musician and probably one of the best Chicago ever produced. He was a heck of a piano player, arranger, composer and a leader of men. (In the 1950s he became musical director of the *I Love Lucy Show*.) I remember one time Charlie Parker came to Chicago looking for a job and Moral hired him to play in our band. Parker lasted only three weeks. He just didn't seem to be interested in playing the musical score for the show or even playing the dance arrangmenets. Keep in mind that the "Bird" could read. But all he wanted to do was solo. He would lay out and just wait until a spot opened up on the score for a solo and it could be marked trombone, piano, clarinet, etc. and

Jimmy Jones, pianist.

Charlie Parker would jump in and just start blowing. He and Moral Young had many conversations about his unconventional habit, which ultimately led to Charlie being fired. Moral said that when he writes his book, he is going to call it, "I Am the Only Man Who Ever Fired Charlie Parker".

Young was a product of Englewood High School, along with Joe Williams, the international renowned singer. Joe Williams and I played baseball at Carter playground at Fifty-eighth and Michigan and later at a big vacant lot at Sixty-first and Prairie Avenue. Even then, Joe showed unusual ability. He was a great athlete and could very well have had a professional athletic career if he had pursued it. I recall how Joe Williams used to sing while he was standing at second base, third base, or in the outfield. He would tell us that someday we would have to pay to hear him sing. We laughed, but inwardly I felt that he had something going for him. He had more self-confidence than any man I've ever met. I have always marveled at his diction. It's almost perfect. He certainly didn't learn it at school, because we were there together. He either taught it to himself or learned it at home, but it was something that he and Nat Cole managed to master.

Coleman Hawkins was another highlight in my career. I opened with the Hawk at White's Emporium on East Garfield Boulevard in February, 1941, when he returned to Chicago after a lengthy stay in Europe and in New York City. It was an experience just playing with that man. I remember he detested playing "Body and Soul", but he had to play it because it was the tune that really made his name a household word with the public and the musicians. When Hawk picked up his horn, it was mandatory that he play "Body and Soul". So in order to avoid boredom from playing the same tune, he would actually change keys every eight bars. He might start off in "F", go to "D" and then to "A" or go into a minor key. I have never seen anything like it, and the piano player obviously had to follow him. You could hear the piano player modulating from one key to another, and Hawkins was gone. I had never worked with a living legend. Neither have I ever worked with anyone with that kind of harmonic skill and versatility on an instrument. The man was a genius.

I remember some nights Hawk would get so bored, he would drink a little more of his Seagrams Seven than he could comfortably handle, and when he got up to solo, he wouldn't stand out in front of the band. He would get in the arch of the grand piano in order to brace himself so that he wouldn't fall on his face. He would open up on his horn some nights and blow for an hour and a half nonstop. The rest of the band just sat gap-mouthed and listened. That's an experience that very few people have had. It's unfortunate that those sessions were not recorded. That was some great music. It was something for the archives. It will always be stored in my archives.

There was something else I noticed about Hawk. He seldom, if ever, had to tune his horn. Hawk always managed to be in tune. Regardless of where the piano was, he was in tune. I don't understand it to this day, but it happened. I remember that we always tried to get next to the Hawk, but he was a very shy and private person and stayed to himself. He didn't talk to many people. To get him to talk was an effort. There was one exception. I remember one morning after work, he had had an extra fifth of Seagrams Seven and he invited "Goon" Gardner, the alto player, and me down to his room at the Ritz Hotel on Oakwood Boulevard and South Parkway. We were with him for about three hours that morning, and he played his horn and explained to us what he was doing and how he did it. He gave us a private lesson—one like I've never had before and I've never had one like it since. Those were the only private hours I spent with the great man during the entire year I worked for him.

We left White's Emporium after several months and went on the road. We arrived in Kansas City, Missouri, on December 7, 1941, just in time to hear President Roosevelt announce that Pearl Harbor had been bombed. Hawk contacted his management people, and they directed him back east to a place called Mason's Farm, just outside of Cleveland. We played at Mason's Farm for three months and returned to Chicago for another three months at White's Emporium. That period with Hawk will always be deeply etched in my memory.

Following my experience with Hawk, I joined the Cootie Williams Band.

Cootie, as you know, was the former ace trumpet player with Duke Ellington for many years and when he decided to go out on his own, he showed an uncanny ability to organize and rehearse a band in a relatively short period of time and make them sound like something. He would do it overnight. I remember many things that I found unique about Cootie. Sometimes he would stand in front of a band and would be counting off for a tempo, and to the audience, it must have seemed as though he was taking forever, but we understood what he was doing. You could actually hear him humming and when he finally got the tempo that he thought he wanted that song to rock on, he would give the downbeat, and you can bet your bottom dollar, when he gave the downbeat, the tempo was right. He had a sense for setting tempo unlike any musician I ever worked with. I remember for a period there, Ella Fitzgerald was working with the band as a vocalist and of course my old friend Danny Williams was with the band briefly on baritone sax. Cootie had a peculiar kind of personality, somewhat like Hawk. Maybe that's the badge of genius. He did not communicate after rehearsals. There was nothing other than music that Cootie would talk about. We would get on the bus and ride for 300 miles, and he wouldn't open his mouth, even if he was spoken to, unless he thought it was something important. We initially thought it was because he had worked with the great Duke for so many years but it is my understanding that that was his attitude with the members of the Ellington band all the years he was there. He did his job, but never had anything to say. He is one of our great trumpet players, a great contributor and a man that I credit for enlarging my understanding of music.

In 1945, I joined Louie Jordan, the uncrowned King of Rock-'n'-Roll. He was rocking and rolling when the Rolling Stones, the Beatles, and Elvis Presley thought the only rock was in a baby's rocking chair. His "Choo-Choo-Choo-Boogie", which is pure rock and roll, sold over two million copies in the early '40s.

Jordan was a real groove to work with. His apparent laid back, spontaneous rocking style was well rehearsed. He was a perfectionist. He wanted everything around him sounding good and looking right: even the musicians' shoes. I will never forget the first job that I had with the Jordan band. It was at the Paramount Theater in New York City. The Jimmy Dorsey Orchestra was the back-up band, and Jordan's Tympany Five was one of the acts in the show. In other words, we would do fifteen or twenty minutes and be followed by another act. Jordan's segment of the show was always a show-stopper. He could sell a song like few, if any, on the stage today. In addition to being a good musician, he was an actor. He actually mugged and pantomimed the lyrics to all of his tunes. Many of the tunes that Jordan played were written by him, and they all were songs that people could relate to in life. For example, "Don't Burn the Candle at Both Ends" was a very successful number, along with some of the earlier ones, like "I'm Going to Move to the Outskirts of Town", "Knock Me a Kiss", "Run Joe", which was a calypso song, "Beware", and "Cold Stone Dead in the Market".

I'll never forget the first time I went on the road with Jordan. I found that he was a stickler both for time and for neatness. In fact, he actually furnished us with six or seven uniform changes so we didn't have to buy anything except shoes. We had a gig in South Carolina and I had to walk through some mud in order to get to the tobacco warehouse where the dance was being held. When I got up on the bandstand, Jordan looked down at my shoes and saw that they were muddy. He said, "Those shoes are going to cost you a ten dollar fine. I'm furnishing your uniforms and I'm paying you the same kind of money to play in South Carolina that I pay you to play in Chicago or New York, and I expect for you to look the part." From that point on, I carried an extra pair of shoes just in case they got dusty or muddy when I reached the bandstand.

Jordan was paying good money at that time. He was paying something like forty dollars a night as compared to Duke, who made me an offer at the same time that I received the offer to go with Jordan's band. I selected Jordan over Duke, because Duke's salary at that time came to just a little better than $100 whereas Jordan's, based on a seven night week, was almost $300, and sometimes it exceeded that because he would give us small bonuses. As I look back, I sometimes regret that I didn't go with Duke for the experience of working with

Left: Eddie Johnson and Louie Jordan in the rear of the Royal Theater in Baltimore. Right: Louie Jordan sings a chorus of "Caledonia".

First row: Johnny Long; Everett Barksdale; Unknown; Unknown; Gordon Jones; Nat Jones; Henderson Smith; Lurlene Hunter. Back row: Unknown; Moses Gant; Rudy Martin.

the great man. On the other hand, I had just gotten married to Clara, and it was important to make enough money to support a new family.

Jordan was making so much money himself that he only worked about eight months out of the year. We were told that he didn't work more because he didn't want to pay additional taxes. Chris Columbus, who was the drummer for the band, and I got together and went to Jordan and told him that he should pay us more money and let us pay the taxes on it. I am of the opinion that that approach didn't sit well with Jordan. Possibly he thought that we were interfering with his business and trying to be too slick. Shortly after that, we played an engagement at Billy Berg's in Hollywood. It was a nightclub hang-out for movie stars and celebrities. When we closed there, Billy Berg and Louie decided to give a farewell party for all of us. Little did I know that that farewell party was actually a notice that the band was going to be disbanded, because within a couple of days we were called and told that Louie was not going to play for awhile, and we could go back home. To this day, I'm not exactly sure why Jordan disbanded at that time. I suspect that it was the conversation that Columbus and I had with him that might have set the whole thing in motion. I missed that guy because, in spite of his strict rules, he was a real joy to work with.

I returned to Chicago after leaving Jordan in 1947 and took a gig with Roy Eldridge and Lockjaw Davis at the El Grotto Supper Club in the Pershing Hotel at 64th and Cottage Grove. Working with Roy and "Jaws" was a gas. I have never

Above: A party given by Billy Berg on December 8, 1947, at his club in Hollywood. Louie Jordan (third from left); Eddie Johnson (directly behind); Billy Berg (at mike); Dallas Bartley with bass (extreme right). The group appeared together at this party for the last time. Left: the Pershing Hotel. Right: the Pershing Lounge, where Ahmad Jamal, the jazz pianist, and others appeared.

worked with two more competitive people in my life. "Jaws" did not want Roy to outsolo him. Although Roy was the leader, Jaws wanted to solo as frequently and as long as Roy. I'll never forget that in Roy's efforts to outdo Jaws, he literally lay down on the dance floor at the El Grotto Supper Club and blew four consecutive choruses on "After You've Gone". That broke up the house and broke Jaws up too. Those guys would sometimes demonstrate this competitiveness on the air, during our radio broadcast. They would actually get on the air and attempt to outblow each other. I really had opportunities to play with some of the great giants of the '30s, '40s, '50s and '60s. Having been in that kind of fast company for such a long period of time, I could only improve as a musician.

AUTHOR'S NOTE

Eddie Johnson, at sixty-two, is still going strong on the Chicago jazz scene. He is in constant demand for record dates and he's a regular at several of the better known clubs on the Near North Side. It is always a pleasure to listen to him play, and I feel fortunate to be able to count him among the people I've known for most of my life.

George Kirby

"Cold turkey caused me to hemorrhage blood through every crevice in my body, including my eyes."

George Kirby

BIRTHDATE: June 8, 1924
BIRTHPLACE: Chicago, Illinois
OCCUPATION: Mimic Extraordinaire, Singer, Dancer, and Comedian
PERFORMANCES: All major television shows, including Johnny Carson and Ed Sullivan. Has also starred in the majority of night-clubs and theaters in the continental United States.

I was born in Chicago's Cook County Hospital in 1924. My parents were living at 3130 South Indiana at the time. I went to Douglas Elementary School at 33rd and Calumet except for a two-month period when I was enrolled at the Doolittle School at 35th near Cottage Grove Avenue. My folks moved whenever the rent was due.

When I was nine years old Louis "Pops" Armstrong was our first floor neighbor at 35th and South Parkway. He used to come up on our back porch on the second floor and talk to us youngsters. Frequently he would say, "I want you kids to listen to some nice pretty tunes." Then, clad in undershirt, pants, white socks and black slippers, he would sit in our old porch swing, take his trumpet out of the case, place a mute on it and play, swinging back and forth, for two or three hours. I was too young to appreciate what Pops was trying to teach us.

I always liked to mimic people. I used to listen to a fellow named Dean Murphy on the radio; he was the top impressionist in the country at that time. He did Franklin D. and Eleanor Roosevelt and a lot of the movie stars. I thought to myself that I knew how to imitate people and I should be making some money doing it. But at ten years old I did not have much opportunity to display my talents except at school. I remember I used to mimic my fifth grade teacher, Mrs Simpson. She caught me one day and took me down to the principal of Douglas Elementary, Mrs Maude L. Bousefield. Mrs Simpson told the principal that I was incorrigible, that I had been acting up in class. Mrs Bousefield asked Mrs Simpson to leave the office for a moment while she talked with me. As soon as the door closed behind Mrs Simpson, Mrs Bousefield said, "Let me see what you have been doing."

I mimicked Mrs Simpson for her, and Mrs Bousefield said, "Can you do me too?"

I did my impression of Mrs Bousefield, and she smiled, patted me on the head, and sent me back to the classroom with instructions not to mimic the teacher in the classroom any more.

The kids in the neighborhood were always eager for me to go to the movies on Saturday because they wanted me to come back and do impressions for them of what I had seen. We would sit on the back steps and I would run through the main feature and they would say, "You sound just like Wallace Beery, James Cagney, Marie Dressler. . ." I know my mimicry was amateurish but still it was pretty good for a ten-year-old kid.

I dropped out of high school in my second year because I had to go to work to help the family. My first job was hustling on the street. That's where I ran into Redd Foxx, who had a tramp band working the street corners. I never worked with his group, but I took advantage of their audience: I did a little step and sang a little song on the edge of the crowd so I could collect as much money as possible before Redd threatened me with violence if I didn't move on.

Foxx was a very talented fellow: he won an amateur contest at the Avenue Theater at 31st and Indiana. Then he won first prize in a talent contest at the Indiana Theater on 43rd Street. When he went to New York, Redd won the top prize on Major Bowes Amateur Hour on national radio. He was in orbit.

Since I had no job skills, I could get only menial jobs: I worked as a porter at Pops Drug Store at 33rd and Indiana and then as a laborer at the Excelsior Laun-

George Kirby backstage at Regal Theater in Chicago.

dry and at the Chicago Towel Laundry. When the rent was due the family had to move again, this time to 33 East 55th Street.

The Rhumboogie Club was right down the street from us on 55th. I got a job there as a dishwasher, and met Joe Louis, Charlie Glenn, Joe "Ziggy" Johnson and stars like Pot, Pan and Skillet, T-Bone Walker and Mabel Sanford. I used to stand in the wings and watch those stars perform and I'd think, Wow, I can do that, and I would go back in the kitchen and rehearse their routines. Finally I got up the nerve to ask Joe "Ziggy" Johnson to give me a chance in the show. Ziggy said, "Don't see me, see Charlie Glenn. He runs everything."

I went to Charlie Glenn, and Charlie said, "Hey, Joe "Ziggy" Johnson is the producer. Don't ask me, ask him. If he says it's okay, I'll put you in."

I went back to Joe and he said, "Oh, you know better than that. Charlie is just trying to pass the buck."

They did this for about a week and I got tired and disgusted. I waited until Saturday when the dishes had piled up to the ceiling and then I went to Charlie

Glenn and I said, "I want my money right now." The cooks and bartenders obviously did not want me to leave, because I was handicapping their operation with all those dirty dishes and glasses in the sink. But I was tired of being pushed around and I just walked out.

I went to Washington Park, a half block east of the Rhumboogie, and sat down on a bench and cried, because I was hurt. After I ran out of tears I walked slowly home. Just as I was going in my front door I heard loud music coming from the Club DeLisa around the corner. It was Saturday night and the brothers were spending their stockyard paychecks. I stood outside and listened to the music and whenever the door opened, I peeped in. I stood there for a while, thinking that maybe I could get a job there. And lo and behold, staring me in the face was a sign in the window saying, "Porter wanted". I walked in and took the sign out of the window and said, "I'm your porter."

Mike DeLisa said, "You're agonna do the job?"

I said, "I'm agonna do the job."

"Okay," he said, "I am gonna show you what to do right now."

He took me downstairs and showed me everything I had to do. He said, "Now you start at four tomorrow afternoon, and your first duty is to get a hundred pound cake of ice out of the walk-in cooler and chip it up with the tongs and make ice cubes. And you continue to make ice cubes until you've filled those three wooden barrels out there." He pointed to the barrels upstairs.

The DeLisa job paid seventeen dollars a week. I noticed that the bartenders were making that much a night in tips while I was fixing ice and washing glasses for them. So I asked one of the bartenders to teach me how to do his job.

"Okay," he said. "I'll teach you if you wash my glasses."

So I washed his glasses and he taught me some of the rudiments of bartending.

I went to Mike DeLisa and I said, "Look, I know how to tend bar. Why don't you give me a job as a bartender?"

He said, "Okay, I'll give you a job, but you have to continue to do the job I already gave you, in addition to bartending."

He gave me a bartending post that was directly behind the door as you walked into the DeLisa. My bar station was invisible, so I figured out a gimmick. I started talking out loud to myself in various dialects like the movie stars. Of course this attracted attention and people began to sit at my station. Word got around the Stroll that there was a bartender at the DeLisa who could do a lot of funny stuff while he served drinks. My tips started to pile up. I began to feel like moving ahead.

One morning I saw Sammy Dyer, the producer of the DeLisa floor show, come in. I jumped over the bar and said, "Sammy, give me a chance in the show."

He said, "Well, what do you do, George?"

"Well," I said, "I talk like other people."

He wanted to know what I meant, and I told him I would show him. I did Amos and Andy, Edna Mae Holland, Marie Dressler, Wallace Beery, Jimmy Durante and James Cagney. He looked at me and said, "My, my! You're a mimic!"

When I got home I looked up "mimic" in the dictionary because he was gay and I didn't know what he was calling me. Sammy recommended that Mike put me in the show. So when the new show started, I was in. After I came off my first act, Mike DeLisa said to me, "You're good, you're a funny son-of-a-bitch. You're in the show and we're going to keep you in the show!"

I thanked him.

"But right now," he said, "get back to the bar."

I was still portering and tending bar while I was working the show. I did that for about nine months and then finally Mike said, "You can do just the show." He agreed at that point to pay me big money: forty-five dollars a week. It wasn't too bad, considering we were just coming out of the Great Depression.

I got the big head because of my new status in the show. My friend little Freddie Cole, the chorus captain, called me into her dressing room. She got on my case, cracked the whip on me and brought me down to size. I've always had a great deal of respect for her and I've never really let my feet leave the ground again.

There was no one on the DeLisa show who I couldn't imitate. There was a team called "Phil and Audrey". One night Phil got drunk and couldn't make the show. Sammy Dyer asked me if I would fill in and do the jungle number. In that number Phil would come out of a casket all oiled down, wearing only a brief and carrying a small flashlight. The drums would roll and Audrey would come out with a whip. They would square off. She would whip him and they would fight. Sammy told Mike DeLisa not to worry. "George Kirby will do it," he said.

I was slim then, and I put on the oil and got in the casket and then I got out and did Phil's dance and I suddenly remembered that Audrey was supposed to whip me. I danced over to her and said, "Now don't you hit me with that whip!"

She was already working herself up for the rest of the act. She yelled, "BAA TE-LA-ZA! BAA TE-LA-ZA!" and started cracking the whip.

I said, "Don't hit me with that whip!"

She came out there and hit me across the behind with that whip and we got into a real fight right there on the stage. Mike DeLisa came backstage after we finished and said, "That's the best act I've ever seen! Phil isa out! No more Phil! You do the show! You do it!"

Hell, I never performed Phil's act again. I will never forget that incident.

I was enjoying my long engagement at the DeLisa when one morning two white men in blue suits showed up and one of them said, "Are you George Kirby?"

I said, "Yes, what can I do for you?"

The man said, "You can't do anything for us. But you'd better do something for Uncle Sam. You're supposed to be in the Army."

I said, "Oh, I went down, but they sent me back home."

"They sent you back home for just twenty-one days," he snarled. "So be on the next streetcar heading for the induction station."

That was the end of my entertainment career for a couple of years.

When I got out of the Army I changed my act. I realized that mimicking alone was not enough so I added one-liners and story lines, jokes, and later singing and dancing. Then I began to play the piano. I felt that I should keep building and of course it paid off. I was booked into most of the major houses and I appeared all the time on major television shows.

My friend Nipsey Russell in my opinion is a genius. Here's a man who was promoted on the field during World War II from private to captain. Today he is one of the most articulate entertainers in the business and he's the only fellow performer who took his entire book of material and handed it to me. He said, "Man, get what you want out of it. You can use whatever I have." No one else ever did that for me, man, and I have some people around who are supposed to be good friends. But they never offered a hand like that. Nipsey is a marvellous man and a wonderful entertainer. A lot of people thought he could only do disco stuff but when he played *The Wiz* he put down a lot of iron and of course then they recognized that this man had multiple talents.

I went into Las Vegas for the first time around 1950 to appear at the Flamingo Hotel which had just been built. We came from California with a big show headed by Count Basie, Thelma Carpenter, Bill Bailey and several other acts. Ben Siegel, the man in charge of the hotel, sent a bus to pick us up. When we arrived at the Flamingo the bus didn't stop in front; it continued around to the back of the hotel.

Siegel said to us, "Now I've got half the pool blocked off out there for you. You people can relax there. Your dressing rooms are also in the back. You'll eat in the employees' dining room. You can't use the casino at all, and you must leave the hotel by the back door as soon as you've completed your last set."

I said to myself, These guys have got to be the most original racists in the world. I've never heard of anyone blocking off water in a pool, but that's exactly what they did. I never used the pool. We all just stayed in our dressing rooms and never went out at all. That was a horrible trip.

Speaking of pools, on another occasion Eartha Kitt sent her little girl out to the pool and the hotel people actually drained all the water out of it. Simply because the child was Negro.

The first black person to stay on the strip was Nat "King" Cole. He stayed at the Colonial House. Many people think Joe Louis was the first, but he wasn't. Joe

stayed at the Moulin Rouge Hotel, where he was one of the investors, and the Moulin Rouge was on the west side of Las Vegas in the Negro community, and not on the strip.

If we wanted to eat outside of the hotel employees' diningroom we had to go all the way over to the west side. If you went down on Fremont Street to buy anything you had to be sure it was your size, because once you removed it from the rack and tried it on, it was yours. If you went downtown to the theater, you had to sit on the left or right side; you couldn't sit in the orchestra seats in the center. Las Vegas was a trip. Mr Charlie is also a trip, and don't you forget it.

Speaking of trips, I've been on a few. Early in my career I thought that smoking a reefer made my jokes funnier and my singing better. I discovered after a short while that in order to maintain that same lift I had to smoke two reefers. Then three. Finally I was smoking grass by the cigar box, but I wasn't getting that initial high that I needed to deliver fresh material with a punch for my public. At this point I found some dynamite stuff that was guaranteed to do the job. They call it speed. That's mixing cocaine with a little horse. It really gives you a different feeling. Then suddenly you find that you are leaving out the cocaine and just doing the horse.

One morning I said to my buddy, "Man, I've got a terrible cold. My nose keeps running and my stomach feels nauseated. If I don't take something, my cold is going to cause my ulcers to start bothering me."

My good buddy replied, "Man, that ain't no ulcer and you ain't got no cold. You've got the habit."

"What are you talking about, man? I ain't got no habit."

"All right. Take this cap and see if that cold won't go away."

I took the cap and sure enough, the symptoms went away. I said to myself,

Well, I'll be damned. I've got to wean off of that stuff. It's almost the way Richard Pryor said it: "The first time you do it you can walk away and leave it. The second time you do it, you go halfway away and then all of a sudden you can't get away from it at all."

I went from snorting to using the needle because they say it's more economical that way. That's true, because when you snort you take the whole cap and it's gone. Now with the needle you only shoot half a cap into your vein, the high is sustained and you don't have to use the other half cap until the next morning. But constant use of heroin will ultimately require that you use the whole cap for shooting and then it builds up and you need two caps, and so on to the point that when I was down in Florida I looked in the mirror and saw a skeleton with meat hanging on it, and I said to myself, I've got to do something about this.

The problem came to a head while I was playing a gig at the Hollywood Hotel in Miami Beach. After I finished the gig I looked at the money I had made and realized that if I spent any for bus fare back to Miami, I wouldn't have enough to buy a cap. So I walked. After I got back to Miami I bought some horse and went over to the Hotel Carver where I was staying and sat down on the side of the bed, cooked the stuff, and shot it. Then I looked in the mirror and like I said, I saw skin hanging on a skeleton. I dropped the syringe on the floor and stepped on it.

I left the room, leaving all my personal belongings behind, and went directly to the United States Post Office to turn myself in. A U.S. Marshall put me in the county jail where I was supposed to see a doctor who would administer morphine or something to hold me down until I reached the rehab center at Lexington, Kentucky. No doctor appeared during the night and the next morning I was really having problems. I was sick as a dog. I was lying on the concrete floor because they had removed the bed. I started hemorrhaging from my nose, mouth, penis, rectum and eyes. I don't know how it started; it just started.

The rats smelled blood and started coming at me. There was a Black Muslim in the cell with me. He was wearing big C.C. work shoes with heavy steel toes, and he started beating the rats off and shouting, "Man down! Man down!"

A guard came into the cell. "Let me see the son-of-a-bitch," he said. He looked at me. "Oh, that's the dope addict fiend of a mother," he said. "Let him die." He walked out and locked the gate. I don't know how long I hemorrhaged but it stopped as quickly as it had started. The Muslim got some rags and wiped up the blood around me and helped me over to the basin to wash up. He said, "You're starting to come around."

I said, "I hope so."

He said, "Get up off that concrete floor and use my cot for a while."

The guys on the other side of the tier said, "Hey man, the buzzards are still out there. When you started bleeding at least a dozen buzzards started flying around outside your cell window."

Finally they brought in some beans in a pie pan. Waterbugs were crawling all over the beans. I simply knocked them off and ate like it was my last meal. Shortly after I finished eating, a Federal Marshall named Peoples came in and said, "My God, George, you still here?"

He went downstairs and got extradition papers from Judge Schultz. He came back and said, "I've got your papers. We're going to take you to Lexington. I know that's where you want to go to get straight."

I said, "I sure do."

He said, "I'm gonna have to put you in chains, George, because I've got a moonshiner who I've got to take halfway to Lexington and it wouldn't look right for me to be riding around with a black boy without chains and a white boy in chains. It shouldn't be necessary, but I just can't afford to have it look any way but democratic."

I stayed in Lexington for two years—from September 7, 1958 to October, 1960. I was lucky. I went right from Lexington to the Ed Sullivan TV show with brand new material. My career was off again at jet speed, and that caused me to break a promise. When I got out of Lexington, I had fallen onto my knees and said, Lord, I'm going to help other people and I'm not ever going to go wrong again. But success caused me to think less and less about my career and more and more about other kinds of grinds. And as a result, I fell a second time. I pray every night that there will not be a third fall.

AUTHOR'S NOTE

I've known George for forty years. He's bent on making sure that youngsters don't make the same mistake he made. He gives his time to talk about it in schools, universities and prisons—wherever he gets an opportunity. I interviewed him on June 11, 1983, and he told me that June 11th was the anniversary of his release from prison for the second time. He did not want to discuss his second fall because he plans to write a book about his experience with the drug scene in order to prevent as many people as possible from following in his early wayward footsteps. He is a remarkable man, and a remarkable entertainer.

Sy Oliver

"I think records influence music writers just as books influence literary writers."

Sy Oliver

BIRTHDATE: December 17, 1910
BIRTHPLACE: Battle Creek, Michigan
INSTRUMENT(S) PLAYED: Trumpet
OCCUPATION: Instrumentalist, Arranger, Vocalist, Composer and Bandleader
FEATURED WITH: Zack Whyte, Alphonso Trent, Jimmie Lunceford, and Tommy Dorsey.

Both of my parents were musicians. My father was a professional singer and choir director. He also played all the string and brass instruments. Mother was the church organist. My folks started teaching me piano before I was six years old. I didn't like it and I didn't want to practice. But I can't remember when I couldn't read music. It seems to me as if I have been reading music all my life.

My family moved to Zanesville, Ohio, from Battle Creek, Michigan, when I was ten years old. In Zanesville, I met a boy my age named Al Sears, who was really a child prodigy. He was a good tenor player, even at that time. As a matter of fact, Al used to play and rehearse with a local band under the direction of Cliff Barnett, and I used to hang out and listen to them rehearse in the evening. My big problem was that I couldn't stay out after dark, and they would sometimes rehearse until ten or eleven at night. When something happened to the trumpet player and they needed a replacement, I told my father that I wanted to learn how to play the trumpet. He was tickled pink. He got me an instrument right away, and showed me how to run the scales on the trumpet and how it related to the piano keyboard. I learned to play that instrument very quickly. I guess I must have had some innate talents because in a matter of months I was ready to join the band so I could stay out nights.

Both Cliff Barnett and Al Sears thought that I had become accomplished enough on the trumpet to play in their orchestra. I went to Dad and told him that I had been offered a job and of course the first thing that he wanted to know was what I would be doing. I told him playing with Cliff Barnett. He said, "Not under any circumstances. I want you to get an education."

Keep in mind that when I was born in 1910, the only salvation for a Negro was education and of course there were two societies in the black community: the educated on one side and the uneducated on the other. They led totally different lives. My father was gung-ho on seeing that I got a good high school education and then went on to college. Unfortunately, my father had a stroke when I was in my sophomore year in high school, and since I was the oldest of six kids, I began to play trumpet professionally to earn enough money to stay in school.

I worked with the Barnett band for a little over two years until I had finished high school and at seventeen, I joined Zack Whyte's Cincinnati-based band, which was the most popular and successful band in the region. My friend Al Sears was also a member of the band. We got a chance to tour extensively throughout the midwest. My first trip to New York was with the Whyte Orchestra.

As a young member of that group, I guess I was a bit intolerant of the ignorance that prevailed among the musicians. In fact, I used to get into some serious physical fights with members of the band because they didn't understand me and I certainly didn't understand them. In order to avoid arguments and fights, I decided that I would write out the arrangements, introductions, endings, and bridges so the band could have some consistency. The musical things that they were doing, in my opinion, were harmonically ass-backwards, and I felt that it was much simpler to run the voices along a consecutive line. Sometimes I would make an effort to try to explain an arrangement to the group and they would tell me to shut up because I was a youngster and that would provoke more physical violence. As a young hot-head, I didn't run from fights. In fact, I was pretty good at them. I used to go down to the gym and work out, and to this day, I have large knuckles as a result of working out on the sides of people's heads. My peaceful side dictated that after three years I quit that band and move on to some new musical adventures. Incidentally, it was in that band that I got my nickname "Sy". They used to call me "Professor", but that didn't work because of my age; a kid with glasses looked too young to be a professor. Then the drummer in the band started calling me "Psychology", for no reason except that it was a big word and they always associated me with big words. Somehow that name stuck, and they subsequently abbreviated it to "Sy".

I left Whyte and moved to Columbus, Ohio, where I was in the kind of atmosphere that my father loved; that was the University atmosphere. Although I wasn't a student at the school, I was able to get gigs at small nightclubs around Columbus. In addition to that I made arrangements to teach many of the college students at Ohio State. It was in Columbus that I met the famous Alphonso Trent, the bandleader. I joined the Trent organization in order to write them a new book because all of their music was lost in a nightclub fire in Cleveland where they were working. Stuff Smith, the renowned jazz violinist, had been fronting the band in Cleveland and I was his replacement. The Trent band was one of the smoothest black bands that I had ever heard in my life. They had class, and were a beautiful bunch of guys. They all dressed immaculately and they played well. They knew their instruments. Snub Mosley was one of the real backbones of the

The Lunceford Band on the stage of the Lafayette Theater in New York City, 1933.

Trent band. He was a most proficient trombone player, slide saxophone player, and, too, he was no slouch when it came to singing. I traveled with the Trent band during the latter part of 1930 and a couple of months in 1931, before returning to Columbus where I joined the Jimmie Lunceford Orchestra.

I carried my bad temper and reputation with me into the Lunceford aggregation. I felt that I would be able to modify my behavior because the Lunceford band had everything I had ever looked for in a group of musicians. They wanted to play things right; they rehearsed in sections in great detail. However, anytime there was a conflict between the band personnel and myself, Lunceford always sided with the other fellows. He never sided with me, so finally one day I told Mr Lunceford I was getting tired of what was going on. I told him I was trying to build the damn band and every time there was a problem, he would side with the members of the band. I asked him why he had hired me in the first place.

He replied: "I'll tell you why I hired you, Sy. The reason I side with the fellows is because I understand what they are up against. They don't understand what you're doing all the time. The things that you're doing are new to them and they just can't follow them. And you are extremely impatient. You don't give them a chance to learn. If they all thought like Sy Oliver, they all would be Sy Oliver, and I wouldn't have had to hire you. You know, I always investigate everybody carefully before I hire them, and you are the only person I have ever inquired about that nobody ever had a good word for, and I thought that anybody who could alienate the world must have something special, and I thought I could control you."

I accepted those words from Lunceford without any feeling of hostility. I learned a lot from him, both positive and negative.

I learned that it's stupid to write things that no one could play. Many of the songs that I wrote, such as "For Dancers Only", were things that the fellows played themselves in solos. Joe Thomas, the tenor man, played that particular piece. I began to recognize that I was simply part of a unit. Whether I had been there or not, the Lunceford band would have been Lunceford's band. The unique thing about the Lunceford band was that it was the first black band that played for everybody. At the time that band came along, there were actually two worlds of music in New York City. There was music that was above 110th Street, which was Harlem, and there was music that was below 110th Street, near the east side, and mid-town Manhattan. The black bands played the Harlem style, and the white bands played the mid-town Manhattan style. The white bands tried to copy the Harlem bands, but they didn't do it very well. Lunceford came along and played for both groups. He was as successful at the Waldorf Astoria as he was at the Apollo Theater. Nobody thinks of it, but his band was actually the first band to bridge the gap. There were no other black bands playing tunes like "Dancing on Park Avenue", "My Blue Heaven", "Since My Gal Turned Me Down",

"Sleepy Time Gal", "Sweet Sue, Just You", "Ain't She Sweet", "Swanee River", "Annie Laurie", and "Put On Your Old Grey Bonnet". Those were tunes that the white audience understood, and the two-beat rhythm that we added to those songs gave such a rhythmic impact that black folks couldn't refrain from tapping their feet. So we bridged the gap between the two musical worlds. In addition to that, we were able to bring in a fellow named Dan Grissom from Chicago who sang in a falsetto and was very successful with both white and black audiences. He sang songs like "Jealous", "Charmaine", "Linger A While", and "My Melancholy Baby", and, believe it or not, the audience enjoyed both my arrangement and singing of my composition, "Dream of You", which was a melancholy tune with a Lunceford bounce.

The impressive and distinguished Jimmie Lunceford.

There were many creative and innovative people in the Lunceford band. There was a trumpet player named Tommy Stevens who taught the band a lot of high note trumpet playing before he left in 1935, and in addition he gave us instructions on instrument choreography. He helped make the band as much fun to watch as to hear. When the band went through its instrumental choreographic paces, you would see the trumpets and trombones moving together or in contrast with trumpets to the left and trombones to the right. Stevens would have the saxophones pointing down toward the floor while the trombones would slip their slides toward the roof. There was nothing more interesting in a jazz scene than the sight of the three trumpet players throwing their horns exactly the same distance straight up in the air on the beat and catching them at precisely the same moment, and bringing them back to our lips on the right beat and on the right note. The only band that has come anywhere near paralleling that kind of instrumental choreography was the Lionel Hampton Orchestra of the mid 1940s. The Lunceford band had an excellent mixture of showmanship and creative musical talent.

I will never forget that night in the fall of 1933 when we opened at the Lafayette Theater in Harlem. The band did a glee club number which absolutely left the audience spellbound. We were an overnight success. The people weren't impressed with the band's ability to hit high notes or solo or anything like that. They were impressed that everybody in the band could sing. The only exception was Jimmy Crawford, the drummer, who could not carry a tune if you bottled it. Those male voices were absolutely beautiful. We were as together vocally as we were instrumentally. The pleasant feeling of that evening is etched in my memory, and I hope that it will never be erased. It was beautiful. Absolutely beautiful.

After the Lafayette Theater, we did a tour in New England and opened at the famous Cotton Club in New York City on March 11, 1934. The Cotton Club was noted for great bands like Cab Calloway and Duke Ellington. They were certainly great bands. But the management told us that there had never been a band playing the Cotton Club show with our precision, and nothing ever came close to it. I guess you would have to attribute that to Lunceford's leadership and the total musical code he instilled in the aggregation. We were so good that we could even take some of Irving Mills' idiotic songs and make them sound sane. I remember Mills had us play some of Will Hudson's tunes during our initial Cotton Club engagement. Mills, in addition to being Duke Ellington and Cab Calloway's manager, owned a publishing company. Will Hudson had some tunes that were really poor imitations of some earlier Henderson works Mills had published. "White Heat" and "Jazznocracy" were two of them. Mills had the band play those numbers at the Cotton Club and recorded them in January of 1934. We took a nothing number like "Jazznocracy", arranged it to fit the Lunceford style, and turned it into a jazz classic of that period. In fact, we used "Jazznocracy" as our theme song for a number of years.

There was a trio in the Lunceford aggregation. We would take simple child-like tunes and put them together in a suggestive and risque fashion. I did a thing on an innocent tune called "Four or Five Times", which caused a number of men to have heart attacks because they tried to follow the song's risque suggestion. There were other songs like "It Tain't What You Do, It's The Way That You Do It",

The Lunceford reed section. Left to right: Earl Carruthers, Joe Thomas, Willie Smith, and Jimmie Lunceford, standing.

Trummie Young's "Cheating On Me", "Baby, Won't You Please Come Home", and of course Trummie's rendition of "Margie", which was our standard. We couldn't play anywhere without the audience demanding that Trummie sing "Margie". I remember one night Trummie was in the hospital with a borderline case of pneumonia, and Jimmy had to send an ambulance to pick him up, bring him to the ballroom to sing "Margie", put him back in the ambulance and send him back to bed. That was the kind of thing that the public of that period demanded of the band and its musicians. Of course, I always warned the boys in the band that the crowds that followed the band knew our records better than we did, and if we didn't play them exactly the way we recorded them, we'd get a lot of complaints right on the spot. The people would scream at us to play it just like the record. I think the Lunceford band offered a unique consistency.

I'm often asked by writers and fans what made my arrangements so unique for the Lunceford band and later for the Tommy Dorsey band and I must say I have never analyzed why I write the way I do. I just don't believe in analyzing a writer. I believe it's instinctive. For example, a simple tune like "Organ Grinder's Swing" was a great success for the Lunceford band back in 1936. It was my arrangement and I can't tell you how or why I wrote it. I took the nursery rhyme and wrote an organ grinding voicing for the brass and reed section, and then

Trummie Young (left), and Jimmie Lunceford.

The Lunceford Band at Midway Airport in Chicago.

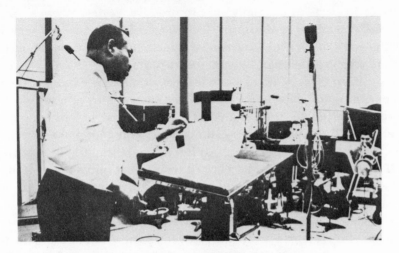

Sy Oliver, songwriter and arranger, directing a recording session.

added a two-beat rhythm and a Lunceford tempo, and the public responded.

My earliest writing came from records. I think records influence most music writers just as books influence literary writers. Duke Ellington's arrangements were the first to come to my attention; specifically, Duke Ellington's "Birmingham Breakdown", and his "East St Louis Toodle-Oo". Both stand out in my mind as the earliest tunes that influenced me. At the same time I was listening to Fletcher Henderson, who was certainly the master of that period. I'm thinking of Fletcher Henderson's recording of "Stampede", with "Clarinet Marmalade" on the reverse side. Both arrangements in my opinion are musical classics. When you write, you write for the people that you are working with, as I have said so many times.

The Duke Ellington sound is unique because Duke wrote for the men in his band. There was nobody else in the world that sounded like Johnny Hodges and Lawrence Brown. I don't care what band you put them with, the sound would still be unique, and in Duke's band, it was a combination of his writing and the men in the band. The same was true of the Lunceford band. Lunceford's group were unique players. We played a different sort of thing from the Ellington band. Duke's men were all master soloists, while the Lunceford fellows were more or less a cohesive group of unit-type players. The authority of the Lunceford band rested in its ensembles. The saxophones were doing their own thing, all in unison; the trumpets blew alone or in tandem with the trombones. The rhythm section drove the reeds and the brass with a two-beat swing. The Lunceford band had a distinctive sound, which could best be described as light, loping, and swinging. The collective personality of the Lunceford band was as satisfying to listen to as the work of an individual soloist in the Ellington band. The Lunceford band as a unit or in parts was usually very impressive. Someone once said that the intensity and infectious enthusiasm of the Lunceford band was enough to knock down the walls of Jericho. I have always maintained that the whole of the Lunceford band was greater than the sum of its parts.

Jimmie Lunceford himself was a born leader, who led by example. He was a very private person who never had much to say. He was sort of a father figure. Everybody wanted to please Pops. Lunceford was impressive looking: tall, and with an athletic build. He looked very distinguished and gentle, waving that extended baton in front of the band. On the other hand, he ran the orchestra with an iron fist. If a musician was a minute late, it would cost him a dollar. If he was very late, it was suggested that maybe he'd better not show up again at all. Lunceford was not only quiet, he didn't smoke, drink or allow women on the bandstand or the bus. He didn't even allow our wives or girlfriends to travel with us. He was a man of high moral principles. I loved Jimmie, but at the same time I resented him. I had a love/hate relationship with him that until this day I have never fully understood, and yet he's one of the few guys that I can recall that I

Jimmie Lunceford and Tommy Dorsey (inset). Both men benefited greatly from the musical creativity of Sy Oliver.

always respected. Of course I recognized that he was the world's greatest square.

When Lunceford walked into a room or onto a bandstand, he had an awesome presence. Maybe I resented that powerful presence and the fact that Lunceford made the organization what it was, without contributing one darn thing musically. He was a leader. Everything went on around him, though not ever in a musical sense.

After working with Lunceford for six years, I went with the Tommy Dorsey band. The Dorsey music required quite an adjustment on my part. At the time I joined him, Dorsey had a Dixieland band. Tommy saw that swing was the coming thing and wanted to change his band to fit the coming style and of course he needed somebody who could write swing. At the time he had the best musicians available to do what he was doing. But the band was not readily adaptable to what we wanted to do. Gradually, he had to change his personnel and within a year, he had a completely new band. There was only one man left in the band who had been there when I joined a year earlier. Dixieland and Swing are two different types of music which require different approaches. As I said, Tommy had the best Dixieland band available and he decided to get the best swingmen available: fellows like Buddy Rich on drums and Ziggy Elman, the trumpet man. I'll never forget, sometimes I would turn a piece of music over to the band at rehearsal and one of the guys would yell "Jesus Christ, Sy! I'm not Trummie Young! I can't play this!" And he couldn't play like Trummie Young. Trummie Young was a genius. Dorsey was also a genius in his way. Tommy and Trummie may as well have been playing different instruments as far as their approach to music was concerned. The most difficult thing was writing for drummers in the Dorsey band. After working with Jimmy Crawford in the Lunceford band for six years, it took me years to adjust to other drummers. In fact, I'm not sure that I ever really adjusted. When I stopped writing for bands and began doing commercial arrangements for record companies, I always used Crawford on record dates. I have changed many a record date just to make sure that I was able to fit it into Crawford's schedule.

Crawford and I found out years later that we were not working for Jimmy Lunceford. We discovered that Jimmy was working for Harold Oxley and that Oxley owned the band and we were working for him, and that Jimmy was getting a salary just like the rest of us. That kind of working arrangement was not unusual among name black bandleaders of that period. In some quarters, that same type of arrangement still prevails today.

I think that what caused the decline of the Lunceford band was Jimmie's perfectionism and his continual search for highly trained musicians with good character and intelligence. He found them. He found guys who were intelligent enough to mature, and realize that there were other things in life besides travel-

Top: Frank Sinatra, Finnis Henderson and a Carnegie Hall official watch Sy Oliver (below) rehearse the band in preparation for Sinatra's concert, to be held at Carnegie Hall that evening.

A 1930 Sy.

A 1983 Sy.

ing all year long and living in Jim Crow rooming houses and hotels and eating inferior food.

Till the very end, the Lunceford band kept plugging away and Jimmie remained the first class leader that he always was until the day he died on July 12, 1947 in Seaside, Oregon, at the age of forty-five. Lunceford suffered a fatal heart attack while he was signing autographs in a music store.

AUTHOR'S NOTE

The Lunceford band gave me some of the most exciting jazz experiences of my life. I feel that I was extremely fortunate to have lived through that period and heard that great band on many occasions. I'm lucky to have stayed around long enough and retained enough energy and interest to want to share what I saw and heard with those who will never have that pleasure, except through recordings.

Sy's talents as an arranger and musical director are still in great demand by major recording studios. For over ten years, Sy has been directing his own very fine band in the plush Rainbow Room on top of Radio City in New York. A night never passes when the patrons do not request that Sy play some of his old Lunceford arrangments.

Maxine Sullivan

I received twenty-five dollars, and signed a no royalty contract for recording 'Loch Lomond'."

Maxine Sullivan

BIRTHDATE: May 13, 1911
BIRTHPLACE: Homestead, Pennsylvania
INSTRUMENT: Valve Trombone
OCCUPATION: Vocalist
FEATURED WITH: John Kirby, Louis Armstrong, Benny Goodman, Glenn Gray, Henry Busse, Bobby Hackett, and Fats Waller

Neither of my parents were musicians but my father's youngest brother, Harry Williams, was a drummer with Louis Deppe's band in Pittsburgh—Earl Hines played with the Deppe band before moving to Chicago in 1923. My Uncle Harry didn't like playing drums so he switched to the saxophone and moved back to Homestead in the late '20s and formed his own group called the Red Hot Peppers. I used to go on gigs with my uncle and his band and occasionally Uncle Harry would let me sing a few songs. I never made a conscious effort to become a singer. I guess the fact that I was good enough to sing on gigs should have told me something, but it didn't.

My hometown, Homestead, was very small, and offered few opportunities for young people. When I wasn't hanging out with my uncle and his band, I waited on tables in small cafes around town. In Pittsburgh, which was near Homestead, there were lots of things going on. They had clubs and female singers, but I always felt that I couldn't compete with those singers because their voices were so loud they could actually stand in the middle of Yankee Stadium and be heard in its furthest corner. I'm talking about a time when there were no microphones; my voice was soft and it handicapped me. I couldn't belt it out like Mamie Smith, Bessie Smith or Ethel Waters. I'm not even sure I wanted to do it. I wasn't exactly into the blues. They didn't appeal to me.

My first break came when my uncle introduced me to a female pianist named Jeannie Dillard who worked in Pittsburgh in a place called Benjamin Harris' Literary Club, which was actually a speakeasy before Prohibition and after Repeal. It was a private club, and one of its advantages was that it did not have to observe the two a.m. closing mandatory in Pittsburgh. People came there after two a.m. to drink and most of the musicians and a lot of the entertainers hung out there. It was a good room for me, because it was small. It had only eight tables. I could be seen and heard by a lot of the professionals who came through. Duke Ellington, Fats Waller, Earl Hines, Cab Calloway and all the famous musicians who came to Pittsburgh stopped in at some point at the Literary Club. It was a steady job but it only paid fourteen dollars a week plus tips.

When the Ina Ray Hutton Band came to Pittsburgh, the piano player, Gladys Moser, stopped by the Club one morning after work. She was impressed with my singing and she encouraged me to come to New York. She made me promise that if I came I would look her up. She was going to be my contact. I worked at the Club for another six or eight months and saved my money, and finally I decided to take a Sunday excursion to New York. Jeannie Dillard, the Club pianist, decided to go with me. We didn't tell anyone that we were going, because we figured that if I didn't succeed we would just return to our old Monday night job. I was naive enough to believe that I could make something happen in one day in the Big Apple.

Jeannie Dillard's brother lived in New York and through him we contacted Gladys Moser. It was lucky for me that the Hutton Band happened to be playing at the Paramount Theater in New York at that time. I'm not sure that Gladys remembered me but we talked, and she wanted to know when I was leaving. I told her I had to leave the next day because the excursion was only overnight. She said, "You can't do anything overnight, so you'd better make up your mind whether you want to stay or not."

Stuff Smith, an Onyx regular.

Buster Bailey

It was a tremendous decision for me because I had left my job in Pittsburgh, but I decided to stay and sure enough she contacted me the next day. She had gotten in touch with Claude Thornhill the musician-arranger who arranged for Andre Kostelanetz, and the two of them came up to Jeannie's brother's house on Wednesday and we auditioned in every gin mill from 155th Street all the way down to 52nd Street in one day. When we reached the Onyx Club, at 62 West 52nd Street, the manager was not there. He was out on the West Coast trying to get Stuff Smith to come back East to play at his club. However Carl Crest, the famous guitarist, was a silent partner at the Onyx Club and he arranged for us to audition that evening. Two days later we had a regular job as intermission entertainers at the famous Onyx Club. Right out of the smokey hills of Pittsburgh to 52nd Street—big time on a fast track. I even met my husband at the Onyx Club: he was John Kirby the Onyx bandleader.

The first song I sang at the Onyx Club was "I Can't Get Started With You". I will never forget that because I felt that I had really arrived. A pick-up group was playing at the Club with John Kirby on bass, Frank Newton on trumpet, Buster Bailey on clarinet, Pete Brown on alto sax and Leon Watson on drums. About six months later some of them were replaced by Billy Kyle on piano, Charlie Shavers on trumpet, Russell Procope on clarinet and O'Neal Spencer on drums. That was the beginning of the John Kirby Quintet.

Claude and Gladys had become my managers and they were out trying to make contacts for me. They knew that if I was going to become an important singer they would have to come up with a new way to present me. Claude took a page from Tommy Dorsey's book. Tommy had just recorded a hit tune called "A Song of India". Claude, among others, was looking for classics and folk songs which could be adapted to a swing beat. Claude came up with the idea of making arrangements on "I'm Coming Virginia", "Blue Skies", "Laurie" and of course "Loch Lomond". The adaptors of classics had a good idea because those classics were in the public domain, but the adaptor collected composer's royalties. Being from the hills of Pennsylvania I wasn't hip to all that stuff back then.

Claude Thornhill got dates for John Kirby and me to record "Loch Lomond". I received twenty-four dollars and signed a no-royalty contract for doing the number. It was unfair, but in those days I guess I was lucky even to get a recording date. A short time later I discovered that "Loch Lomond" was causing a stir. The CBS Saturday Night Swing Club played it on a Detroit station and the manager, Leo Fitzpatrick, cut it off the air because he considered it sacriligious to play a swing rendition of a Scottish song. Fitzpatrick's protests fell on deaf ears because CBS brought the Saturday Night Swing Club's production to the stage of Loew's Theater on Broadway and made me the featured singer. "Loch Lomond" went into orbit. My salary went from forty dollars a week at the Onyx to eighty and then to one hundred fifty which in the late 1930s was considered a great deal of money for anyone, and for a colored girl it was a fortune. Yet I was making less than singers with some of the large bands who had a lot less talent than I.

After the recording of "Loch Lomond" in early 1939, Hollywood beckoned to me. I went out there and had a cameo spot in a movie called *St Louis Blues* with Dorothy Lamour and Lloyd Nolan. The movie had nothing to do with W. C. Handy and I played a waif washing clothes in the backyard with the usual bandanna on my head. But I sang several songs in that movie. While I was in Hollywood I made *Going Places* with Louis Armstrong, Dick Powell and Eddie "Rochester" Anderson. "Jeepers Creepers" was the hit song that came out of that movie. Louis played a groom for a horse named Jeepers Creepers. I played a maid in *Going Places* and the big number was a scene on a lawn where I sang "Mutiny in the Nurseries". The Andrews Sisters were in that scene with me, along with Nicodemus.

After we finished that picture, I came back to New York with Louie and we opened at the Cotton Club which had moved downtown to 48th Street. A scene from *Going Places* was used as an opening number for the Cotton Club revue. A clip from the film was projected on a paper screen every night and Louie and I would walk through that screen, creating an unusual effect. Louie was dressed as a groom and I wore my maid's uniform. We did our respective parts from the movie and then we did a couple of numbers together. Louis Armstrong and I

Louie Armstrong with Bob Crosby. Louie and Maxine appeared together in a movie entitled Going Places, *in the stage production of* Swinging the Dream, *and in the last floor show at the Cotton Club before it closed.*

were the last act to play the Cotton Club before it closed on June 10, 1940.

Louie and I later played in a theatrical extravaganza called *Swinging the Dream,* a swing version of *A Midsummer Night's Dream.* I played the part of Titania, Queen of the Forest. "Darn that Dream", one of the tunes especially written for me to sing in that show, has become a jazz standard.

During 1941 John Kirby's band became the biggest road band in America. His popularity caused a rift between us and I divorced him in 1941. It was impossible to have a marriage with two partners going in separate directions. The only time after our divorce that we worked as a team was when I had my radio show, *Flow Gently, Sweet Rhythm.* It was a big thing, a CBS network show that stayed on the air two years. John Kirby died on June 14, 1952.

In 1943 I began travelling as a single and was featured on bills with major bands in the country. I did several jazz radio programs and theater engagements with Benny Goodman. I gigged also with Henry Busse, Johnny Long, and Glenn Miller and his Casa Loma Band. I finally settled down in New York on the east side at a club called Le Reuban Bleu. I was there for six years. I also worked at the Village Vanguard for four years. For over twenty years I was a very busy lady in show business.

I retired in 1956 and devoted my energies to being a wife, mother and PTA leader. It wasn't until 1968 that I was lured back into show business by the owners of Blues Alley in the Georgetown section of Washington, D.C. Since then I have slipped back into the mainstream: I toured with Jack Lawson and Bob Taggert's World's Greatest Jazz band, did a stint at the Riverboat in New York with Bobby Hackett and did gigs around the country, including my current one at Rick's Cafe Americain in Chicago.

AUTHOR'S NOTE

Maxine Sullivan, who carried all our hearts to Scotland with her rendition of "Loch Lomond" in 1938, set foot in Scotland for the first time in 1948.

Clark Terry in 1940.

"Some people might say I'm picky. That's true, I won't play if I have to sacrifice my integrity."

Clark Terry

BIRTHDATE: December 14, 1920
BIRTHPLACE: St Louis, Missouri
INSTRUMENT(S): Trumpet and Flugle Horn
OCCUPATION: Instrumentalist, Composer, Vocalist, Band Leader
Teacher
FEATURED WITH: Fate Marable, George Hudson, Charlie Ventura,
Eddie "Mr. Clean Head" Vinson, Count Basie, Duke Ellington, and
the NBC Staff Band for Johnny Carson's Tonight Show.

My parents had ten children: seven girls and three boys. I was the seventh child, born in the twelfth month of the twentieth day of this century. My family was poorer than church mice in Russia. In order to relieve the economic strain on my mother and father, I moved in with my oldest sister and her husband when I was about nine years old, and earned my room and board by hauling ashes for people. I was what you would call real cheap labor. I only charged pennies for my services. I used to promote my hauling business by passing out paper mills (currency value of one tenth of a cent) inscribed: "Let the Terry Brothers do your Hauling."

Sy, my sister's husband, was a tuba player with the Dewey Jackson band, which was one of the top bands in the territory at that time; they were known as the Musical Ambassadors. Sy was a great tuba player: in fact, he was one of the best that ever came out of St Louis. The Jackson band used to rehearse at our house and of course I hung around and listened to what was happening. I found myself digging jazz very early. I became very closely attached to a trumpet player in the band named Louis Caldwell because he was extra nice to me. He used to bring me candy. I remember vividly the Mary Janes and the yellow caramels, which were favorite candies for kids back in the late '20s. In addition, Mr Caldwell gave me pennies when the band took a break, to watch his horn. I remember once he came back from his break sooner than I expected, and he caught me trying desperately to get a sound out of his trumpet. He caught me huffing and puffing and said, "Say, son, you're going to be a trumpet player!" I was stupid enough to believe him, so I hung in there from that point on.

The radio helped my musical education. We used to put our little radios in a bowl to give them a bigger sound. We kids used to try to imitate the sounds of the bands that we heard on the radio by creating make-shift instruments. My brother wanted to play drums and since we could not afford to buy a set, he devised a drum out of a worn-out ice pan—the kind that was used to catch the drippings from the seventy-five to one hundred pounds of ice in the ice box. Remember, the ice box is what everybody used before the refrigerator. The ice pan atop a tall, upside-down bushel basket made an excellent snare drum. Old chair rungs were great substitutes for drumsticks. To get a tuba sound, we took a big, round tin beer mug, wrapped a vacuum hose around it, blew through it, and got a fantastic bass noise. I made a trumpet by coiling an old hose and putting a kerosene funnel on one end to look like the barrel of a horn and a pipe on the other end for a mouthpiece. Admittedly the contraption didn't look very musical, but it actually produced a sound like a trumpet.

I didn't get my first instrument until I reached Vashon High School, on Garrison and McLeed in St Louis, Missouri. I registered for the band on my first day in high school because I wanted to learn to play the trumpet. Clarence Hydon Wilson, the bandmaster, said to me: "I understand you want to play the trumpet. I'm sorry, we don't have a single trumpet left. But I've got an old valve trombone hanging over there in the corner that you can use. The fingering on that instrument is exactly like a B-flat trumpet, and you can make a lot more noise with it. Take it and get the heck out of my face."

I took the trombone home and went to work on it. I got my fingering together and learned the skills because as Mr Wilson said, the fingering was exactly like a trumpet. I never became proficient on that instrument but I learned to appreciate it a great deal. Mr Wilson was an excellent music teacher and I stayed right with him until my senior year when the economics of the times dictated that the Terry Brothers drop out of school in order to chip in and help my old man and unmarried sisters.

I was lucky because I got involved immediately in playing jazz music as a profession through my brother-in-law, who took me on my first gig. He later introduced me to a bandleader named Dollar Bill. I got a chance to gig around St Louis with Dollar Bill and his Small Change. I was initially one of the pennies. I eventually worked up to be a nickel. Later I played with Fate Marable who was the giant among musicians in the St Louis area.

My first road gig was with Willie Austin, a trombone player and bandleader from St Louis. We traveled with the Reuben & Cherry Carnival Show. The carnival and medicine shows during that period were a means of survival for many a musician. Both Roy Eldridge and Harry James got some of their earlier experience working with the carnival shows. The Reuben & Cherry Carnival Show was a biggie for me until it went bankrupt in Hattiesburg, Mississippi. There we were, stranded without any money in the middle of cottonland. Luckily a fellow with the carnival who had a monkey show also owned a truck, and Willie Austin was able to con the man into letting him and his lady ride in the truck and I and a couple of other fellows had to ride in the rear of the truck with fifteen active monkeys for 750 miles. That was some experience. However during the course of the trip, we learned to know the monkeys by their names and I'm sure they knew us by ours.

The next time I hit the road was with a blues singer by the name of Ida Cox, and her Dark Town Scandal Show—a great experience. We used to travel in an old, broken down bus and every time we came to a hill, everybody had to get out of the bus and push. There was a midget named "Prince" on the show and he just sat in the bus while the rest of us pushed. Ida Cox asked him one day, "What are you doing sitting in the bus while we are all out here pushing?"

He said: "I'm too small to push."

"We've got a tiny little place for you to push here at the back of the bus," Ida said.

I'll never forget that. Her sense of humor always cracked me up.

After I arrived back in St Louis after the Cox tour, I started to work with Fate Marable who had one of the celebrated riverboat bands of the day, and had worked with such stars as Louis Armstrong and Jimmy Blanton, the great bass player. Fate was quite a character. He had changed his name from Marble to Marable. Whenever Fate was going to fire a person, he'd take one of the fire axes from the wall of the boat and put it in the cat's seat. When the guy came on board, we would start playing. Naturally the cat would figure he was late, and as he ran up to the band, we would start playing "There'll be Some Changes Made." I believe to this day that "getting the axe" when one was going to get fired was an expression that was actually originated by Fate Marable of St Louis.

In 1942, I signed up with a Navy recruiter in St Louis and was immediately shipped directly to Great Lakes Naval Base, just north of Chicago. During the next three years, I played with the Navy All-Star Band under the direction of altoist Willie Smith of the Jimmie Lunceford Orchestra. Some of the cats who passed through Great Lakes were Dave Young, the tenor player, formerly with Fletcher Henderson and Roy Eldridge, and Pee Wee Jackson, the trumpeter with Earl Hines and Jimmie Lunceford. I could name others. I had a terrific jazz experience in the Navy.

After I was discharged in 1945, I joined Lionel Hampton's band for a short time, and then I went back to St Louis and spent the next eighteen months as the straw boss and lead trumpet player with the George Hudson band. Hudson built a solid reputation for himself in St Louis with his house band at the Club Plantation which was to St Louis what the Cotton Club was to Harlem and the Grand Terrace was to the South Side of Chicago. George Hudson selected a number of musicians who were serious about their craft: Singleton Palmer on string bass, Weasel Parker the tenor sax man, and myself. When new acts came into the club, we'd rehearse their music as if it were our own. The performers loved the band because we played their music right. Many of them told us that they had never heard their music played so beautifully. Our conscientiousness paid off because the entertainers spread the word about how well the George Hudson orchestra performed and of course our reputation had preceded us when we reached New York's Apollo Theater in 1946. Our little tenor man, Willie "Weasel" Parker, played such a bad solo on "Body and Soul" during the first show at the Apollo that Illinois Jacquet, who was a big star at that time, ran backstage and told Jack Schiffman, the owner of the Apollo, that he had to "Take it out! Take that number off!" The George Hudson band was just that bad.

In 1947 while I was still working with George Hudson at the Club Plantation in St Louis, I received a call from Charlie Barnett, the millionaire orchestra leader who played music for kicks in Los Angeles. Barnett told me that my good friend Gerald Wilson had recommended me highly and he wanted to know if I would be interested in joining the orchestra which was playing Hermosa Beach. I told him I would love to. He asked me if I wanted to drive, fly or take the train. I told him I wanted to take the train in order to think about it while traveling so I wouldn't seem like I was rushing into things too fast. Barnett sent me the ticket by airmail special delivery. I had a three-day train ride in which I contemplated my future. Gerald Wilson met me at the station and took me right out to Hermosa Beach where Charlie's band was performing. They were on the air when we walked up

Above: The chorus girls of Club Plantation in St. Louis, Missouri. Below:
Chorines, left to right: Edith McKinney, Ernestine Moore, Faye Barnes, Stella
Halloway, Hortense Allen, Sadie Hogan, Emma Lee McDonald, Martha Weaver,
and Wilma Harris.

Charlie Barnett, bandleader.

to the bandstand and in the middle of a coast-to-coast radio broadcast; Charlie Barnett signaled that I should take my horn out of the case. He then announced, "And now, our new trumpet player," and I had to go right into a number. I don't remember the name of the tune, but I know it was a number that had a standard set of changes like maybe "Lady Be Good", so once I heard the first chorus, there was no pain. That was Charlie Barnett's style of doing things. Charlie Barnett is a beautiful man. In fact, we are still the best of friends. His mother Charlotte owned controlling stock of the New York Central Railroad, and when she passed, of course all of the money went to Charlie. He used to give the guys in the band presents of Buicks, Cadillacs, Packards and what have you for Christmas. Of course when I joined the band he was only giving out fifths of whiskey. That's the story of my life. Some of the guys who had been with him earlier said that Charlie ran through a million dollars in a very short time with his first orchestra. In addition to giving big gifts, he paid astronomical salaries.

In 1948, Count Basie asked me to join his band, and I had not worked with him for long when he began to encounter financial problems. His managing agent in New York told him that he had to reduce the size of the band immediately. I returned to St Louis but I had only been there a little while when I received a call from the Count asking me to rejoin him at the Brass Rail in Chicago, and to bring along a good tenor man. I brought a young white boy named Bob Graff with me. The other guys in the group were Freddie Green on guitar, Gus Johnson on drums, Jimmy Lewis on bass, and Buddy DeFranco. When Bob Graff was recruited by Woody Herman, we replaced him with Waddell Gray. Basie had apparently been able to resolve his financial problems because in less than six months he started reorganizing the big band. While we were playing at the Strand Theater in New York City Basie said he needed another alto sax player. I told him I had a friend in St Louis who could fill the bill. Count said, "Call him up."

I went directly to the phone and called Ernie Wilkins, who had never played an alto in his life, and very quietly I said, "Can you get an alto? Do you want to come and join Basie?" So Ernie borrowed one of those silver-colored high school students' saxophones (we used to call them the "grey ghosts") and came to New York the next day. The Basie band was still playing the old Kansas City book and I suggested to Basie that he let Ernie Wilkins write some new material. That might have been the best suggestion I ever made, because from that point on the band's reputation simply skyrocketed. Ernie wrote all of that great material for Joe Williams. And just think—all of those good things came as a result of a whispered telephone call!

In 1951 Duke Ellington dropped in on one of Count Basie's dates to scout. Duke subsequently had his managing agent work out a deal where I would leave Count Basie because I was tired and needed a rest—he agreed to pay me $200 per week while I rested in St Louis. This ploy was used because Duke wouldn't dare lift a guy out of his good buddy's band. Incidentally, Count had just given me a ten dollar raise for a grand total of $125 per week, and he immediately took back that raise when I handed in my notice. Duke made a big boy out of me because he literally threw me into one of the most awesome trumpet sections in the nation: William "Cat" Anderson, Harold "Shorty" Baker, and Ray "Little Dipper" Nance. All of those cats had their act together. Duke never wrote parts like first, second, third and fourth trumpet. He simply wrote Anderson, Nance, Baker, and Clark. Those were the parts. You didn't know whether or not it was first, second, third or fourth until you actually played it. He started this system way back in the early days of his orchestra, because he found that Rex Stewart had an uncanny way of playing an E-natural on the horn. Stewart used to play it with a semi or suppressed valve, which is called a cock-valve. Therefore whenever this note appeared in a chord, Duke automatically gave it to Rex Stewart. It didn't matter if it was first, second, third or fourth, so your part could jump all over the place. I'm sure you've heard many times that Duke's band was his instrument. It's true. Duke surrounded himself with talented musicians that he dug, and he used them to extend his feelings musically.

Clark Terry and Sarah Vaughan in 1971.

Let me tell you about Duke. He had a way of getting things out of you that you didn't realize you had in you. Let me give you an example. We were doing an album called "The Drum is a Woman", and Duke came to me and said: "Clark, I want you to play Buddy Bolden for me on this album."

I said, "Maestro, I don't know who the hell Buddy Bolden is!"

Duke said, "Oh, sure, you know Buddy Bolden. Buddy Bolden was suave, handsome, and a debonair cat who the ladies loved. Aw, he was so fantastic! He was fabulous! He was always sought after. He had the biggest, fattest trumpet sound in town. He bent notes to the tenth degree. He used to tune up in New Orleans and break glasses in Algiers! He was great with diminishes. When he played a diminished, he bent those notes, man, like you've never heard them before!"

By this time, Duke had me psyched out! He finished by saying: "As a matter of fact, you are Buddy Bolden!" So I thought I was Buddy Bolden.

Duke said, "Play Buddy Bolden for me on this record date."

I played and at the conclusion of the session, Duke came up to me and put his arms around my shoulders, and said, "That was Buddy Bolden."

Duke Ellington was a genius. His black skin prevented him from earning top dollar during his lifetime. There was a limit on where and how he could work. You wouldn't believe it, man, but there was a time, when we played the Hotel Flamingo in Las Vegas, that Duke had to come through the kitchen in order to get to the bandstand, although his name was the top billing on the marquee. It was bigotry. It had a lot to do with the whole economic scene. They would not give this man an opportunity to put his music in a proper perspective. They wouldn't let it reach the height it should have reached until after he was gone. He had to hustle and go out on the road and do one nighters right up until the end. He never had an opportunity to do a radio or television show like Benny Goodman or Tommy Dorsey. They kept him scuffling and batting his head against the wall and he was a courageous man because he did it. He believed in his music and himself and he kept his band together until he couldn't stand up anymore. Count Basie is caught in that same exploitation trap.

In 1959, I left Duke to join Quincy Jones in Europe in the Harold Arlen's Blues Opera—free and easy. I returned to New York in 1960 and became the first black staff musician for NBC. That job was a by-product of an Urban League Affirmative Action campaign against NBC for not employing more minorities. The staff band subsequently became the Johnny Carson *Tonight Show* regular band. It would be difficult for me to categorize that band because we had to swing, we played classical music, and in fact, we had to play any kind of music that came along. It was a unique band to say the least.

After Skitch Henderson left the show by special request, NBC received many letters asking that I be made the bandleader. The management people at NBC thought that a black leader would affect their southern market, so they wouldn't give me the job. I also had the first shot at becoming the bandleader on the *David Frost Show*. But I turned that down because they wanted the band to play behind a screen out of sight of the television audience.

Some people might say that I'm picky. That's true—I won't play music if I have to sacrifice my integrity. My television exposure has led to my ongoing involvement in education. Listeners would write in requests for different members of the *Tonight Show* band to appear at various high schools and colleges. The instrument companies would sometimes sponsor these appearances and I soon found myself involved in the music clinic circuits full blast. It has really given me an opportunity to stay involved with jazz education and I love working with kids, so I get around to the universities and colleges, high schools and grammar schools all over this country and in other parts of the world, just to stay involved with the perpetuation of my craft. It's refreshing to me and it keeps me on the ball. I know that my craft is in good hands because the kids are getting into it.

The only thing that I find disturbing is that the black kids are letting it slip through their fingers like sand. And it disturbs the hell out of me that black people are not interested in perpetuating their own culture—America's original art form—jazz.

Joe Williams

*"My light skinned black brothers really whipped a racist color game
on me."*

Joe Williams

BIRTHDATE: December 12, 1918
BIRTHPLACE: Cordele, Georgia
OCCUPATION: Vocalist

I was born Joseph Goreed. My family moved to Chicago when I was four years
old. Although my mother had received some college education in Georgia, her
first job in the North was as a domestic. Mother would bring me discarded *National Geographic, Life,* and *Liberty* magazines from white folks' houses. As a child
I used to enjoy lying on the floor, looking at the pictures and reading the captions. There were many things that I did not understand, but mother would
always take the time to try and make them clear to me. I was able to read and
understand magazine and newspaper editorials long before I reached high
school. Although Sexton Elementary School at 6020 South Langley Avenue was
eighty percent white when I graduated in 1932, I was in the top ten percent of my
graduating class.

My mother was musically inclined and very religious, so I was used to hearing her sing church hymns around the house. Although I always participated in the family musical hours, my real interest was in sports. I was considered a good athlete until tuberculosis struck me down at the age of fifteen. My left lung collapsed and I had to give up strenuous activities. I dropped out of high school in my junior year and drifted from one menial job to another, working as a short order cook, store porter, and as a men's washroom attendant.

In 1935 I formed The Jubilee Boys and we sang at local churches, weddings and funerals. Local bandleaders like Erskine Tate would encourage me to sing but they never paid me any money. My first professional break came from Johnny Long, a bandleader who called me one evening about 8:30 p.m. and said: "Man, I've got a gig at Bacon's Casino that starts at ten p.m. and I will be by and pick you up within forty-five mintues." In the 1930s and early '40s, Johnny Long had one of the most popular club dance bands on the South Side of Chicago. I would sing beautiful ballads and waltzes with Johnny Long's orchestra but, internally, I was in conflict with my role as a crooner. My image of ballad singers was "pretty boys" like Herb Jeffries, Billy Eckstine and other light-skinned fellows. I was reddish black and unattractive. I didn't fit the matinee idol mold of the 1930s. As a matter of fact, when I decided to give singing the old college try, I went to Charlie Glenn at the Rhumboogie, which was located at 343 East Garfield Boulevard. Charlie would not hire me because I was too dark. I also begged Joe Hughes, the owner of Joe's Deluxe at 6323 South Park Avenue, for an opportunity to work. About two or three weeks before Christmas I would go to Joe Hughes and say: "Hey man, I need some money to get some presents for my mother and grandmother. Give me a job. I will work for twenty-five dollars a week."

Joe Hughes replied: "Aw, come on, man! I can't hire you for that little bit of money. You sing too good. You're just too good. You're overqualified."

The truth is that my skin was too shady for both club owners. They were both light-skinned pretty boys. The darkest male singer ever to work for Charlie Glenn was "Gatemouth" Moore, and he was a teasing brown. My light-skinned black brothers really whipped a racist color game on me. I was about twenty-five or twenty-six years old before I felt comfortable enough with my blackness to remove that cross of inferiority from my shoulders.

Nat "King" Cole, who was blacker than I, struck it big nationally through his recordings before most people outside the black community knew he was black. There were no televisions in those days, so you couldn't see him. As you remember, he had perfect diction, the kind my mother taught me to speak around the house. Since Nat Cole was darker than I was and making it big singing ballads, I felt that I should try my luck as a professional singer. Nat Cole opened the doors for darker-hued male entertainers two decades before the "black is beautiful" crusade of the 1960s.

Nat "King" Cole.

Chicago offered me a fertile musical training ground. The Windy City gave me an excellent opportunity to hear the best jazz in the country being played at the Regal Theater and the Savoy Ballroom. Since the Regal was my second home, I constantly digested the sounds of Ethel Waters, Louis Armstrong, Big Joe Turner, Eddie "Cleanhead" Vinson, and Jimmy Rushing. Their shouts and cries reminded me of the alley hucksters' lament that fascinated me a a young boy. Their sounds were pure and spine-tingling, like a house-rent party blues.

I also had an opportunity to do nightclub and radio work with the Jimmie Noone band at both the Cabin Inn and the Platinum Lounge where we did live broadcasts nightly. I toured with the Les Hite band throughout the Midwest during 1939 and '40. I was working hard at my craft, but I was not earning very much money.

Ken Blewett, the manager of the Regal Theater, got to know me well because I had been hanging around the theater for years. One day in 1942 Ken said: "Joe, I need somebody backstage who knows what's happening. I don't have a stage doorman back there. Balaban & Katz have a multi-million dollar showplace here on the South Side and I need somebody that I can trust to cover my rear."

I hastily replied: "Man, I would be glad to take the job."

Ken rubbed his chin and said: "The job doesn't pay much. I can only pay you forty-two dollars per week."

"That's all right. I'll do it, man. Don't worry about a thing. Oh! I forgot. I have one request. On Tuesday nights, you'll have to get somebody else to relieve me because I have a regular gig singing next door at the Savoy Roller Skating Rink with Tiny Parham, the organist, during the intermissions."

So every Tuesday, Ken Blewett would let me off to sing at the Savoy and I continued working for him six days a week at the Regal for better than a year. I enjoyed the job as a doorman because it gave me an opportunity to meet all the musical greats. Some of the cats would tip me when they finished their one-week engagement. There were others who wouldn't drop anything in my hand but hot air because in spite of their stardom they had less than I did. Many of them either gambled their money away or gave it to the girls.

Ken Blewett was a good friend of both Lionel and Gladys Hampton. Early one afternoon Hamp and Ken brought Dinah Washington backstage for an interview. I was still the stage doorman at that time and Dinah had a regular gig singing downtown at the Garrick Lounge at Dearborn and Randolph. After the interview she handed in her notice at the Lounge and joined Hamp's band. Later in 1943, Ken Blewett called me into his office and said: "Hamp wants you to come and join him in Boston. He has agreed to pay you eleven dollars a night."

"That's okay with me," I replied with a grin that must have been a mile wide.

I will be forever grateful to Ken Blewett because he was directly responsible for my getting that break with the Hampton aggregation.

Dinah and I were the male and female vocalists featured in Lionel Hampton's very popular band. When I arrived in Boston the next morning I went right into rehearsal. That night I was singing "Brazil," arranged by Milt Buckner, on a national radio broadcast live from the Tic Toc Club in Boston on Freemont Street. Man! I went from the stage door to the microphone, broadcasting from coast to coast, in twenty-four hours. Lucky for me that in 1938 I had had radio experience in Chicago with Jimmie Noone.

I was the replacement for Rubel Blakely, Hamp's former male singer. That was some band. In the brass section Hamp had Joe Morris, Joe Newman, Lamar Wright and Joe Wilder on first trumpet. Arnett Cobbs was blowing lots of tenor sax, Eric Miller was on guitar, George Jenkins played drums, and Milt Buckner rounded out the rhythm section on piano. The musician union's recording ban of 1943 prevented me from recording with that fine group of musicians. That was a crucial time in jazz history. I believe the inability to record delayed my career at least ten years.

I left the Hampton band in early 1944 after three months and joined the touring orchestra of Andy Kirk. In the same year, I worked briefly with the two masters of the boogie-woogie piano, Albert Ammons and Pete Johnson. I started working intermittently at Club DeLisa in Chicago with Red Saunders' band from 1945 to 1954. I didn't make my first record with Red until 1950 (as "Jumping Joe

Above: Left to right: Jimmy Rushing; Erskine Hawkins; Dinah Washington; Count Basie; and Ida James. Below: Joe Williams (left), Dr Jo Jo Adams at the mike, and Finnis Henderson.

Williams") on the Columbia label. But it was not until 1951 that I started singing "Every Day" as part of my act. That was my big number and it is still holding up after thirty-two years.

Club DeLisa wasn't like any other club in the world. I can't describe it or put it in a category with any room I ever worked. Believe me when I say I have never found anything comparable in the clubs I have sung in throughout America and Europe. You could buy anything you wanted within the DeLisa compound in the 5500 block on South State Street. The DeLisa brothers owned the hotel, the gambling operation, the liquor store, and the dainty-looking girls who worked the bar stools inside the club. You could even buy whiskey on election day.

Mike DeLisa and I got along okay. I never sought him out. I never borrowed any money from him. I was never a part of the plantation system. Our conversations were always strictly business. He'd walk by me and say, "Hey, Joe!"

I'd say, "Hi, Mike," and that's all.

Count Basie, the man who affectionately refers to Joe Williams as his "Number One Son".

Years after Mike died, a white fellow came up to me and placed his hand on my shoulder backstage at the Apollo Theater in New York City and said, "Mike DeLisa told me that you had more character than anybody who ever worked for him."

Memphis Slim's "Every Day I have the Blues," did not really catch fire nationally until I joined Count Basie's band for the second time in 1954. I had worked briefly with the Count Basie Septet in 1950 in downtown Chicago at the Brass Rail. They had the swingingest seven-piece outfit you ever wanted to hear. In the band were Clark Terry, Wardell Gray, Buddy DeFranco, and in the rhythm section we had the Count, Freddie Green, Jimmy Lewis and Gus Johnson. Those cats could play you into bad health. Wow!

Basie agreed to pay me seventy-five dollars per week on the second go-round when I rejoined him in 1954, but when "Every Day" broke big in the spring of 1955, my salary was immediately increased to $300 per week. I was instantly

The end of a hot jazz set in 1970. Left to right: Duke Ellington; Joe Williams; Woody Herman; Paul Gonzales; Joe Benjamin, and Harold Ashby.

catapulted into national fame after twenty years of paying dues. My career pattern reminds me of something the great Duke Ellington once said: "They don't want you to get famous too young. You might get a chance to enjoy it."

I enjoy singing the blues; however, fifty percent of the numbers in my repertoire are ballads. It's funny that when white writers write about black singers, they invariably label them as blues singers. The only two people who come to mind who have managed to escape that connotation are Nat "King" Cole and Billy Eckstine. They were "romantic balladeers." When Sinatra does a blues tune like "One for the Road," it's called a saloon song. When Helen Morgan does it, it's called a "torch" song. When I do the same numbers they are called the blues. Don't get me wrong, I love blues because it's so natural. It's life, man.

In 1961 I left the Basie band with the Count's blessings. As a matter of fact, I opened at Storyville in Boston three days after I left Basie. Count always called me his No. One son and he treated me that way. He actually took time off to ride up to Boston with me in the club car. When we arrived in front of the Bradford Hotel, there was a sign: "Count Basie Presents" in very small letters and "Joe Williams" in very large letters. Basie stayed in Boston that night and introduced me at both

A taping session at Public Radio station WBEZ in Chicago. Left to right: Joe Williams, moderator Sondra Gair, and the author.

shows. He went back to New York the following day. What a beautiful man: Count Basie, Count Basie.

Author's Note

Joe Williams is now an international star, which is certainly evidenced by a list of just a few of his awards and honors:

Downbeat Magazine's readers' poll for Best Male Band Singer—1955, 1956.

Downbeat Magazine's International Critics Poll for Best New Star Male Singer—1955.

Rhythm & Blues Magazine's plaque for Top Song of 1956 ("Every Day I have the Blues").

Billboard Magazine's DJ Poll for Favorite Male Vocalist—1959.

Downbeat Magazine's International Critics Poll for Best Male Singer—1974, 1975, 1976, 1977, 1978.

Nancy Wilson

"The story line in the lyrics determines what's going to happen for me musically."

Nancy Wilson

BIRTHDATE: **February 20, 1937**
BIRTHPLACE: **Chillicothe, Ohio**
OCCUPATION: **Vocalist and Actress**

When I was four years old my father, Olden Wilson, and my mother, Lillian Ryan, were divorced. My younger brother Michael and I went to live with my grandmother on Whiskey Run Road, about two miles outside the Columbus suburb of Richmondale. I can still remember in detail Grandmother's big, rambling Victorian house. I enjoyed living there: it was comfortable and it was in a rural area so we could plant and harvest tomatoes and potatoes. When I recorded "Raindrops" I thought back to the days when I used to lie in my bedroom and listen to the rain pattering on the roof. It was there in that house that my musical education began. Grandmother had a small organ and a piano; my aunts used to play them. I can't really remember any time after the age of four that I was not surrounded by music, but no one in the family except me became a professional musician. My grandmother and my aunts sang in the church choir, but the first song that I remember singing was an old pop tune called "Margie". I was five years old, and I sang "Margie" and went into a little act.

Our church was Pentecostal and I was not allowed to sing in the choir because I liked to sing popular songs like "Margie" and "Street of Dreams" and others. I was considered to be a sinner at a tender age.

Although I never did sing gospel as such, I believe in the words and the message of the songs. The lyrics are strong and the quality of God is there. I feel it and I believe it. Gospel songs tells stories about a people, their hopes and desires. A song can be a short story or a novel. It depends on how much you want to say. My whole approach to singing has been dual, because I am both an actress and a musical storyteller.

The first singer who influenced me professionally was Little Jimmy Scott. I heard him singing with Lionel Hampton's band in 1947 when I was ten years old. His phrasing and mine are almost identical. I once heard him do a song that I had recorded without ever having heard him do it first: a comparison of the two renditions was scary: they were almost identical. If I had not been looking at Jimmy when I first heard his voice, I would have thought he was a woman. His voice was high and his phrasing was beautiful.

I was fifteen years old and a sophomore at West High School in Columbus when I entered a student talent contest sponsored by the local TV station WTVN-TV. The station managers heard me sing only a couple of bars of one song before they pulled me out of the competition and gave me my own fifteen-minute TV show. It was called "Skyline Melody" and it aired twice a week for thirteen straight weeks. I sang birthday songs and anniversary requests. Despite the responsibility of carrying that show, I still managed to maintain my B + /A— grade average in high school. I also played on the softball team, and I was president of the French Club.

In 1954 when I graduated from high school I was seventeen years old and an experienced entertainer; I had been working weekends in nightclubs and earning fifteen to twenty dollars a gig. I traveled with a band called the Sultans of Swing, headed by a fellow named Rolly Randolph. We went as far south as Cincinnati and as far west as Fort Wayne, Indiana. I took my younger brother Michael along as my chaperone.

I worked in Chicago for the first time in 1956 with Rusty Bryant's band. Rusty was an Ohio boy who became popular back home playing tunes like "Castle Rock" and "Night Train". We were booked into the Crown Propeller Lounge on East 63rd Street. Paula Grier also worked there, along with a shake-dancer and a couple of other entertainers. The owner of the lounge insisted that when the girls finished their numbers on the raised stage behind the bar, they go out front to

Little Jimmy Scott, the young man who influenced Nancy's style.

the bar and sit and drink with the customers. Paula told me the girls always did that. I didn't. After I had been working there a couple of nights the owner came up to me and told me to go and sit on a bar stool. I said I didn't care what the girls had always done. I told the owner I wouldn't do it; I had been hired by the band and the band paid me to sing and that was all I was going to do in the Propeller Lounge. That was the only really bad experience I had in Chicago.

My next memorable trip was to New York in 1959. I went there in search of fame and fortune with money I had saved from gigging. I didn't think I was going to set the world on fire but I was confident that I could get some kind of job. The first job I got was receptionist for a handbag manufacturer in the garment district in midtown Manhattan. Then I got a job as a Girl Friday at the New York Institute of Technology, where I didn't have to punch in until noon, so I could look for a singing gig in the evening. I was lucky enough to get a job singing weekends at the Club Morocco in the Bronx. It was there that my friend Cannonball Adderley brought in John Levy to hear me sing one night. Levy managed Dakota Staton, Joe Williams, George Shearing, Ramsay Lewis and of course Adderley himself. Levy liked what he heard, and told me he would call me the next day, which he did. Subsequently he had me make demo records which he airmailed to Capitol Records in Los Angeles. Within five weeks I was signed as a recording artist for Capitol, and there I met the late great Nat "King" Cole. We became fast friends.

I recorded my first album for Capitol in December, 1959. It was "Like in Love", released April, 1960. Later that year I played the Sutherland Show Lounge in Chicago at 47th and Drexel Boulevard with Cannonball Adderley and Flip Wilson. Disc jockeys Sid McCoy and Daddy-O Daylie picked up my album and gave it a big play. Sid McCoy began to call me "Sweet Nancy". These two disc jockeys really made it happen for me. Later a fellow in Los Angeles named Johnny Mangus, who was considered one of the most knowledgeable record spinners in the country, picked up the Nancy beat on the West Coast. I had national recognition. Mangus was almost embarrassing. He said, "Nancy is singularly the most important singer of the decade. She can lift a song off the printed page and groove it to her own identity. She has broken a sound barrier and made a success of pure talent."

My love affair with Chicago started at the Sutherland Show Lounge—I consider that the foundation for what's happening for me today, nationally and internationally. It's a love affair that's been going on for over twenty years. After the Sutherland Lounge there were Mr Kelly's, the Palmer House and later the Blue Max. Currently it's Rick's Cafe. I've also done concerts at the Civic Opera House, the Arie Crown Theater and the Auditorium Theater. Of the large houses, I think that the acoustics and the sound system at the Auditorium are as close to perfection as anything you will find. I regret I cannot say the same thing for the Arie Crown.

Chicago is my number one city. Sales records were broken here for my first album and this town still leads the country, as it has for twenty years, in sales of my records. I don't want to sound like the Chicago Chamber of Commerce, but I had to tell it like it is. Chicago has been wonderful. It's just great.

I don't try to impress people with how high or how low my voice is, or what I can do with it melodically. I look first at the story line in the lyrics; that tells me what is going to happen for me musically. I never thought Billie Holiday had a voice, but she phrased the story so well you wanted to hear what she had to say. Her "Strange Fruit" and "Fine and Mellow" are good examples of this. Lena Horne has never been accused of having a great voice but she can work miracles with strong story lines. I loved Dinah Washington's work for the same reason. She was a great phraser. I didn't care too much for her songs but I liked her laid-back

Cannonball Adderley, the sax genius who discovered Nancy in Brooklyn.

style, and she always told the story like it was. I loved her.

In my book the real singers are Sarah Vaughan, Ella Fitzgerald and Carmen McRae. I think there will never be another voice like Sarah Vaughan's. There is no other singer in her category, and she's getting better all the time. She's just absolutely magnificent.

Many of my Chicago fans have asked me what goes on inside of me when I sing "Guess Who I Saw Today". My answer is—"Nothing." I'm an actress, so it's not personal. If it were, there would be no way in the world that I could perform that song every night for twenty-three years and not be devastated. I have to divorce the personal trauma of that song from myself when I sing it. I have to be realistic and recognize that singing is my job. I couldn't handle it any other way and survive.

I have had problems in the past because I am too believable on the stage. When I toured the East some years ago, some listeners thought they detected a

Nancy Wilson, the girl with a thousand beautiful faces.

personal sorrow in "Guess Who I Saw Today". In a little while there were newspaper items: "Friends find it hard to believe that Nancy and her husband have reached a parting of the ways. . ."

Something else like that happened when I was filming a scene for *Hawaii Five-O*, the television show. I was playing a junkie, and it was my death scene. My mother and son were sitting on the set having coffee when I was called by the director to play the scene. One minute I was talking to my mother and the next minute the director said "Action!" and I became a totally different person. I stumbled across the stage and died, and my mother could not believe it. We were talking family matters one second and I was a street person the next. It was more

Nancy Wilson and the author.

than she could handle, and she has never come to watch me act anything similar since. She was very upset. You can draw a parallel between that kind of acting and singing. They are the same: you know your lines and you deliver them, showing whatever emotion is called for by the part you are acting or singing, and that is it. I sing "Guess Who I Saw Today" twice a night, seven nights a week, and sometimes for thirty consecutive nights—that's sixty times in a period of thirty days. I couldn't let myself get involved with that kind of emotion every night. It has to be *your* husband I'm talking about, not *mine,* in order for me to perform. I'm not singing my feeling but your feeling, the feeling of the audience.

I have a gift. I sing and act. I don't think about how I do it. I have never studied it, I don't want to dissect it. I don't want to know how it works. I just want it to work. For example, I can't explain why, when I have laryngitis, I can't even say hello but I can sing a complete show without faltering.

I don't object to singing "Guess Who I Saw Today". I have to do it every show. Another number that I always used to do was "You Can Have Him"; I can take that one out from time to time but I always have to put it back. It's just something that my public wants to hear.

AUTHOR'S NOTE

Nancy Wilson wears thirty-two years in showbiz like the latest Paris fashion. It fits her perfectly. She is more attractive today than the first time I saw her at the Tivoli Theater on a cold January night in 1961 in Larry Steele's production of *Smart Affairs.*

She is the most exciting singer on the world circuit today. Her stylistic vocals please the crowds and stop the shows. She has the same kind of vocal freedom as Billie Holiday and Dinah Washington. And she delivers her lyrics with intense personal conviction.

Guess who I saw today?

David A. Young

"You can't blow your god-damned nose."

David A. Young

BIRTHDATE: January 14, 1912
BIRTHPLACE: Nashville, Tennessee
INSTRUMENT PLAYED: Tenor Saxophone and Clarinet
OCCUPATION: Instrumentalist
FEATURED WITH: Roy Eldridge, Carroll Dickerson, Fletcher
Henderson, Horace Henderson, Lucky Millinder, Walter Fuller,
and King Kolax.

My family moved to Chicago from Nashville in 1914. The first address that I can
remember was a rented house at 5244 South LaSalle Street which was adjacent to
the Rock Island Railroad yard. My father was a chef cook on the California-bound
Golden State Limited. All my dad had to do was go across the street and hop on
the train to get to work.

I was ten years old when a friend of my mother asked me what I wanted to be
when I grew up. I said, "Nothing."

In dismay, he responded, "Damn it! You are going to be something. I've got a clarinet at home and you're going to learn to play it."

The following Sunday he brought the clarinet over and gave it to me. I had never seen one before. I put it in my mouth and blew. I did not get even a squeak out of it. I fingered around with it all summer. When school started, I put it under the bed and I did not take it out again until the following summer. I dusted it off and poured water through it and went out on the back porch where I inexplicably blew my first sound. I had created something. That spurred me to want to learn to play.

In 1923, every neighborhood had a music teacher that taught the local kids. Our teacher was John A. Willis who lived up the street from me at 5308 South LaSalle Street. He charged fifty cents per lesson. My mother had to struggle each week to get the money together. My father would not support the idea of my learning to play clarinet because he considered studying music to be foolishness. One week we did not have the money and I didn't go for my music lesson. The next day Mr Willis came to my house and asked my mother why I had not shown up for my lesson.

She replied, "I did not have the money so I felt there was no need to send him."

Mr Willis smiled. "Your boy has very good potential," he said. "You can send him to me forever with or without the money."

I started back with Mr Willis on a regular basis. After about two years, he had me teaching his beginning students. Mr Willis taught a lot of future jazz giants such as Gail Brockman, the Earl Hines' trumpet star; Moses Gant, tenor man with Horace Henderson's Orchestra; Gordon Jones, Johnny Long's alto sax soloist; and a host of others.

All the neighborhood theaters had small bands. The theater that we frequented was the Owl at 47th and State Streets. There was a famous piano player there named Clarence Williams. When he started playing the crowd would start tapping their feet or clapping their hands in a rhythmic fashion. His music made me feel very good and it was at that point that I decided I wanted to play music and help others get that good feeling rather than work in a factory as a laborer. Mr Willis was a Prince Hall Mason and he played in the Masonic bands. As we neighborhood kids became proficient with our instruments he pushed us into joining the junior Masonic marching band. Every Sunday, we would go to some small town to play in a parade. We all had bright colorful uniforms. This put us several cuts above the other guys in the neighborhood.

My next step up the musical ladder was with the *Chicago Defender* Newsboy Band under the direction of Major N. Clark Smith. Lionel Hampton had been a member of that band shortly before I joined, and over the years Major Smith turned out a number of topnotch musicians, such as Bill Oldham, the tuba player who doubled on string bass with Louis Armstrong; Scoops Carry, the great alto sax man in Earl Hines' Orchestra; Ray Nance, violinist and trumpet star with the Duke Ellington band; Milt Hinton, Cab Calloway's top bass man; and hundreds of other kids who later did very well in the music profession. We got a real solid musical foundation in the *Chicago Defender* band with Major N. Clark Smith.

In 1923, Samuel Insull, the Chicago billionaire who controlled utilities and holding companies, providing electricity, gas and transportation to thirty-two states, purchased an old mansion at 3947 South Michigan Boulevard (present site of the Donnelly Youth Center) and had it completely refurbished. Insull and his lawyer, Daniel J. Schuyler, organized the South Side Boys Club for Negroes. The big mansion became our youth center. It was a large-scale, well-financed facility that included vocational training, recreation and a music department. Mr Insull

Clarence Williams & Sarah Martin at the Owl Theater in Chicago.

hired Major N. Clark Smith, who was a music instructor at Wendell Phillips High School, to direct the band. Mr Insull took Major Smith downtown to the Lyon & Healy music store on the northeast corner of Jackson and Wabash to buy instruments for the band. Mr Insull told the sales clerk he wanted to buy enough instruments for a seventy-five-piece symphony orchestra.

Apparently Major N. Clark Smith was either invisible or a non-person to the white clerk because in Smith's presence, the clerk said to Samuel Insull, "Mr Insull, these aren't the kind of instruments you should buy for Negroes."

Mr Insull thanked the clerk for his advice and acidly asked, "What time can I expect delivery?"

The instrument truck arrived at the South Side Boys Club loaded with oboes, flutes, English horns, bassoons, and the traditional trumpets, trombones, saxophones, clarinets and drums. Man! We kids had never seen that many brand new instruments in our lives. Once the excitement of seeing the instruments was over, we became cry babies because there were not enough saxophones and trumpets to go around. Nobody wanted to learn to play the oboe, flute or bassoon. I wanted to play the sax and Major Smith told me he did not need a saxophonist. He wanted a clarinet man. However, he compromised and told me that if I played the clarinet in the band he would let me take the saxophone home provided I would take care of it and bring the clarinet to band practice. That was how I got my first saxophone. Major Smith left for St. Louis in the early 1930s and was replaced by Captain Walter Dyett, his assistant at Wendell Phillips High School.

When I was sixteen years old, Charles Letchell, a trumpet player, sent me out to play my first night club gig in his place. When I started to play my solo, one of the band members said: "Kid! Don't play. Just lay out. We are going to pay you."

I must have sounded pretty bad for those guys to pay me for not playing. That experience sent me back to the musical woodshed because I was determined to play and play well.

The next real job I had was with the Melvin Draper band in a road show traveling to Cincinnati, Ohio, on the T.O.B.A. (Theater Owners Booking Association) circuit known in the trade as "Tough on Black Acts." The show became stranded in Cincinnati. We were staying at the Sterling Hotel, the largest and most ragged hotel in America, located at Sixth and John in the heart of Cincinnati's black community. My rent was two dollars a week and I was eight weeks behind. The hotel owner knew that we would be there awhile and suggested we work for him in the hotel nightclub for a dollar-fifty per night, plus a meal. He then took a hard look at each member of the band and show and pointed his finger, saying, "I will take you, and you and you."

"Me?" I inquired anxiously.

He replied: "Hell naw! You can't blow your god-damned nose. What would I want with you?"

    I had never had anything hurt me so bad in my life. I wrote my mother a penny post card and asked her to send me two dollars and eighty cents for bus fare. On that bus trip home, I made up my mind that nobody was ever going to talk to me like that again. I was going to be number one and never less than number two in any future musical aggregations that I joined. When I got home, I ran my family crazy for almost three months. I practiced all day every day, and at night I would go out and play in the jam sessions. The next day I would practice the best licks I had heard played by the older, experienced musicians the night before.

    My professional music turning point came when I met Everett Barksdale, a guitarist who later became Art Tatum's and Eddie South's favorite sideman. Barksdale taught me basic harmony and chord structure and I have not looked back since.

Art Tatum.

My next step up was with Bob Short's band. The Short Orchestra was fronted by Frankie "Half Pint" Jackson to play dances throughout the Midwest. The unique thing about Half Pint was that he was a black man directing an all-white, fifteen-man studio band on a national radio show sponsored by "Muscle Tone." Man! That cat was making big dough in 1933 right in the heart of our worst Depression. Those were the days when white folks would not even permit black smoke to come out of their chimney. Dave Kapp, brother to Jack Kapp, Bing Crosby's partner in the Decca Record Company, was the booking agent for the Jackson white radio band and also for his black dance orchestra. We were making twenty-five dollars per man per night when almost twenty percent of the country was unemployed and the average weekly salary was less than our nightly pay scale.

Half Pint Jackson's theme song, "Fanning," was popular in those days. Everybody was singing:

> When the sun gets hot,
> Cool it if you can,
> Cool it by buying yourself
> a ten cent fan,
> And fan it.

Frankie "Half Pint" Jackson (on top of piano), a leading vaudeville performer with considerable jazz feeling, worked in the mid-20s with this group which includes trumpeter Bob Schoffner and drummer Tubby Hall.

Jackson could sing that song with spark and soul. He was a hell of an entertainer. They called him Half Pint because he was smaller than our Sammy Davis
Jr. Bing Crosby and the Kapp brothers loved him. They had enough clout, collec-
tively, to get King Kong a gig playing at a Presidential Inaugural Ball.

I left Bob Short's band in early 1934 to freelance with the Kenneth Anderson,
Jimmy Bell, and Carroll Dickerson orchestras between 1934 and 1936. I joined
the Roy Eldridge band at Sam Beer's Three Deuces at 222 North State Street in
September, 1936. That was a real growing experience. Art Tatum was playing
piano during intermission. He played so much piano he made my hair ache. Chu
Berry, who was working at the Grand Terrace with Fletcher Henderson, would
come down to the Deuces after work to blow with Eldridge. I would just sit back
and listen to the three giants of jazz: Art Tatum, Chu Berry and Roy Eldridge.
Man, if you can't learn and grow in that environment, there must be something
wrong with your skull.

I will never forget the night Roy was in the midst of hitting all those beautiful
high notes in rapid succession when he suddenly rushed from the bandstand.
We didn't see him again for over two hours. We later found out that he had taken
a cab to his South Side apartment at 343 East Garfield to take a bath and change
all of his clothes. The moral of that story is to close all your apertures when you
blow high notes.

*The Roy Eldridge Band at the Three Deuces in 1936. Left to right: Scoops Carey, alto sax; Zut-
ty Singleton, drums; Dave Young, tenor sax; Teddy Cole, piano; Roy Eldridge; John Collins on
guitar; and Truck Parham on bass.*

The most exciting experience I had with the Roy Eldridge band took place on June 22, 1937, the night that Joe Louis defeated James Braddock for the heavyweight championship of the world. We were playing at the Eighth Regiment Armory at 35th and Giles in a battle of the bands against Benny Goodman. Although we only had eight men in our band, we gave Benny Goodman's fifteen-piece orchestra hell. We had John Collins on guitar, Scoops Carry on alto sax, Joe Eldridge on alto sax, "Truck" Parham on string bass, Harold West on drums, Cozy Cole's brother on piano (for the life of me, I can't remember the piano player's first name) and I was on tenor sax. Roy was in great form that night. We blew the ceiling off that place and the dance crowds went wild. The Goodman band followed us with their best shot. They opened their set with "King Porter Stomp" by Jelly Roll Morton and followed it with a Fletcher Henderson arrangement of "Big John Special." They went right through the ceiling and the crowd went with them. Those white boys were playing those black arrangements with a togetherness you wouldn't believe. That was some night.

In 1939, I left Roy's band in New York City and returned to Chicago where I joined Fletcher Henderson at the Grand Terrace. On my first night with the band the other musicians sat back wondering how I was going to handle the Chu Berry solo in a number called "Stealing Apples." For me, it was like throwing a rabbit in a briar patch becuse I had learned most of Fletcher's book from Roy. When it came time for me to solo, I played the first three choruses exactly like Chu Berry and then laced it with two choruses of my own. From that point until I left the band in 1940 I was king in that orchestra.

In 1942, I joined Lucky Millinder's Orchestra. It was loaded with talented musicians. "Dizzy" Gillespie and "Cat" Anderson were in the trumpet section; "Panama" Francis was on the drums; Thelonious Monk was holding down the piano; and Bill Doggett was the organist. There were a total of sixteen swinging cats in the band.

The Millinder band was actually a back-up touring orchestra for the Four Ink Spots who were at the height of their popularity during that period. Their "If I Didn't Care" number was still breaking up the house. But for some reason, tall, slim and handsome Bill Kenny, the lead singer and star of the "Spots," was jealous of the short, chocolate brown Deak Watson. On many occasions after they had taken their bows and were waiting offstage for the applause, Bill Kenny would haul off and hit Deak Watson in the mouth and then both of them would run back on stage as if nothing had happened. Hoppy Jones, the baritone who owned and organized the group for radio station WLW in Cincinnati, would frequently remind Bill Kenny, who was born in the West Indies, that when they picked him up he was on his behind and they could leave him the same way. That would have been easy because Bill Kenny gambled away his money almost as fast as he made it. He would sometimes lose as much as $4,000 a night with Jimmy Cooper

Left: Lucky Millinder, renowned bandleader, a product of Wendell Phillips High School in Chicago. Below: The internationally famous Four Ink Spots.

who ran a twenty-four-hour crap game at the DuSable Hotel at 764 East Oakwood Boulevard. Charlie Cole, one of the owners of the DuSable Lounge, used to say that Bill Kenny worked to gamble. Jimmy Cooper made enough money out of those games to buy the Ritz Lounge, which was located in the basement of the Ritz Hotel at 409 East Oakwood Boulevard, just twenty-five feet east of South Parkway [now King Drive].

After two years in the Navy playing with Lonnie Simmon's Navy band, I organized a group called the Four Vets. The men in that group were Pee Wee Jackson on trumpet; Curtis Walker on drums; Rozelle Claxton, Pearl Bailey's current piano player; and I held down the tenor sax chair. Our first gig was at the Cabin in the Sky Club located near 63rd and South Cottage Grove. It was owned by Ethel Waters, the popular singer and movie star who had starred in the moving picture entitled *Cabin in the Sky* in 1943. The East Woodlawn community was in a state of racial transition during that period; however, Ethel Waters thought her popularity would draw the whites who lived east of Cottage Grove into her Cabin. She did not understand Chicago racism. Whites did not want blacks invading their neighborhood. Ofays looking for kicks may have been happy to come to the Cabin in the Sky if it were located in the heart of the black ghetto. Because the Cabin was outside of "nigger heaven," it was a financial disaster.

William "Lefty" Bates approached me in early 1947 and begged me to replace him on a gig at Jimmy Cooper's Ritz Lounge. Lefty had a better gig downtown and he did not want to leave Jimmy Cooper high and dry.

I went into the Ritz Lounge in February 1947 with a six-piece combo which included Pee Wee Jackson on trumpet, Goon Gardner on alto sax, Curtis Walker on drums, Rudy Martin on piano and Bill Settles on bass. The Ritz had a blues loving crowd. Jo Jo Adams, a blues singer, was one of the main attractions at the lounge when we started. He obtained a better gig at Club DeLisa and gave Jimmy Cooper his notice.

Billie Holiday was in town working at the Colosimo Cafe at 2126 South Wabash Avenue. Lady Day and Jimmy Cooper were very good friends. Cooper and I went down on South Wabash to persuade her to come out and work at the Ritz Lounge after she closed at Colosimo's.

Billie said: "Jimmy, I can't do it, but I know a black bitch who has never made more than a hundred dollars a week in her life who could do you a lot of good. You take this bitch and put her in your place and when she opens her mouth and starts singing, the plaster on the wall will start shivering. Here is her telephone number. Her name is Ruth Jones, but she works under the name of Dinah Washington."

Jimmy laughed. "I don't want the bitch," he said, "but I have got to have somebody."

Dinah had been a student at Wendell Phillips. She had won an amateur con-

Left to right: Lonnie Simmons; Pete (?); Dave Young; Harlan Floyd; Harry "Pee Wee" Jackson; Red Cooper; and Ocie Johnson on drums. In Pearl Harbor in 1944.

test at the Regal Theater and gigged around the country with Lionel Hampton's Orchestra for seventy-five dollars a week. Her best known record up until that time was a bold and unabashed rendition of "Evil Gal Blues," which she waxed with Lionel Hampton's orchestra for Keynote Records in 1943.

Dinah Washington was the first big time act to appear at the Ritz Lounge. Her salary was $250 per week. She had not been at the club ten days before we started having standing room only crowds in that non-air-conditioned room. On weekends, people would stand in lines extending one-half block east of Oakwood Boulevard just to hear Dinah and sweat. Mike DeLisa and his henchmen from Club DeLisa would come down almost every night trying to figure out what made this black blues singer such a sensation. The two solid months that Dinah remained at the Ritz during her first engagement, the club stayed packed as tight as a can of sardines nightly. Jimmy Cooper was so glad to get her back later that year when she returned from a road trip that he increased her salary to $750.

In 1950, we began recording with Dinah for Mercury Records. I remember that when the contract expired Dinah had been visited at the club by several recording companies. One night an executive from Mercury Records came down to the Ritz Lounge to talk to Dinah.

He said, "Dinah, I want to talk to you for a minute."

Dinah replied loudly, "Well, go ahead and talk, god-dammit. I'm not going anywhere. I'll be right here."

"Well," he said, "it's private."

"Shit!" Dinah fired back. "These are Dave Young's niggers. Go ahead. You can

Left: Dinah Washington in a mink gift from a recording company. Below: At the Ritz Lounge. Third from left is Johnny Hodges; Jimmy Cooper, owner of the lounge; Duke Ellington at mike; Eddie Plique; and at extreme right Allen Drew the comedian.

say anything in front of them that you want to. I am talking to two or three other companies because your company fucked up and I am not going to renew the contract."

The record executive had placed a large, white, tissue-covered box on top of the piano. Dinah was ranting, raving and telling the man to go straight to hell. The fellow went over to the piano and unwrapped the box and pulled out a full length white mink coat. Holding the coat up with both hands, he said, "This is a gift from the company."

Dinah's salty talk instantly turned to dripping maple syrup when she said, "Why in the hell didn't you say you wanted me to sign that god-damn contract?"

Foul-mouthed Dinah always respected me. Jimmy Cooper couldn't talk to her any kind of way. Jimmy would always come to me and say, "Man, you've got to go in and talk to her."

When he asked me to perform this task, Dinah was usually going overboard cussing somebody out. In her bitter moods, she would cuss out a room full of patrons. I would say, "Dinah, you're belittling me."

She always replied, "Professor, I'm not trying to belittle you, but this mother. . . ."

I'd say, "See what I mean? You have got to be a lady."

When she finished her last engagement at the Ritz, she pleaded with me to go on the road with her as her manager. I was tired of the road, and show business as such, and wanted out. I would not go. I decided weekend gigs around Chicago, and a day job as an advertising executive at the *Chicago Daily Defender,* would be my cup of tea.

Dinah Washington (center), relaxing with friends at the Ritz Lounge.

John Young

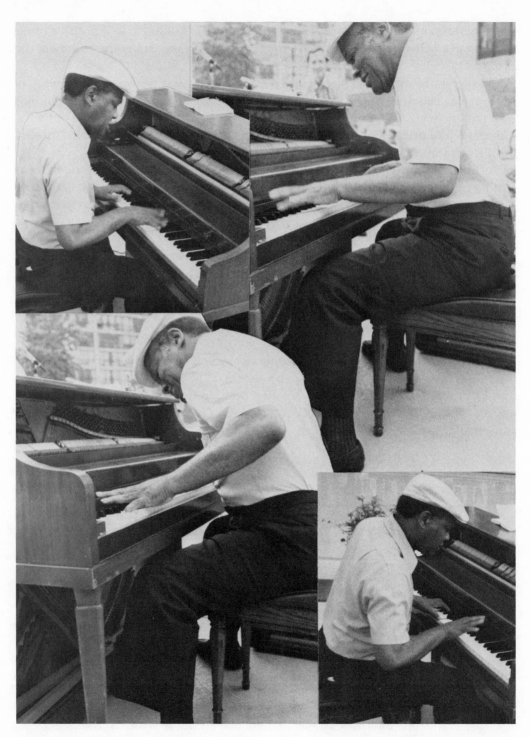

"European audiences are unique in that when you're playing, they are so quiet you can actually hear a pin drop."

John Young

BIRTHDATE: March 16, 1922
BIRTHPLACE: Little Rock, Arkansas
INSTRUMENT PLAYED: Piano
OCCUPATION: Pianist, Arranger, Band Leader
PERFORMED WITH: Andy Kirk's Orchestra, Joe Williams, Nancy Wilson, Dick Gregory, Lurlene Hunter and Redd Foxx.

My earliest recollection of piano was in my home. I had a brother named Mike who was very good at playing the blues. He was a past master at playing "How Long Blues" and all of the other blues numbers that made up the repertoire of most of the Saturday night rent party piano players. I would listen to Mike with a great deal of joy because I dug him. In fact, I used to imitate him by crawling up on the piano stool and picking out little tunes. I actually taught myself a song called "Stagger Lee." Then my brother showed me how to play the "How Long Blues." The family assumed that I was a very gifted child, but then most families feel that way about their children. My mother decided to send her little genius to study piano with Mrs. Myrtle Stuessy who had a small studio at 47th and Vincennes. Mrs. Stuessy gave me my initial formal music training.

At Willard Elementary School, located at 4915 South St. Lawrence, Dorothy Donegan played the piano when the students marched out for recess or lunch, and she often played at special school programs and assemblies. Dorothy Donegan was *the* pianist at Willard School.

By the time I reached DuSable High School in January, 1935, I had actually been studying piano at least five years. My earliest jazz influence on piano was Earl Hines. As a kid I used to listen to him play on the radio broadcasts from the old Grand Terrace. During the same period I listened to Duke Ellington broadcasting live from the Cotton Club in New York City. Earl "Fatha" Hines was really my first love on the piano. I think he influenced most of the piano players of my generation and beyond. He certainly left his stamp on Nat "King" Cole and other DuSableites like Thomas Rigsby, Rudy Martin, Martha Davis, June Evans, and a host of other piano players. Earl had that trumpet style of piano playing that we all loved to emulate because it was new and exciting. To me, it was more electrifying than the stride piano style of Fats Waller.

I never thought of Fats Waller as a piano player and yet he was a good one, as I later recognized. I always thought of him as a fat comedian who happened to play piano. He was a stride piano player who was always making jokes. I simply didn't respect him as a piano player because of the clowning. He would be beating the piano to death and saying, "Yes, yes, yes," or "Don't give your right name." That shallow, house-rent party kind of talk as he played was musically distracting and I could not pay him any really serious attention.

At DuSable High School, Captain Walter Dyett was the great band teacher and Dr. Mildred Bryant Jones, the harmony instructor, was the head of the music department. Dyett acquainted me with all types of musical terms, stock arrangements, modulations from key to key, and, of course, he was a disciplinarian of the first order. I recall an incident in the *Hi-Jinks* of 1937. The *Hi-Jinks* was an annual musical that the DuSable youngsters produced and that ran four or five consecutive nights every spring to capacity crowds. The *Hi-Jinks* was a very popular event in the years before World War II. We had a twenty-five-piece pit band playing for the show with two pianists—Dorothy Donegan and myself. I will never forget Captain Dyett's way of looking at you and talking in a way that made you feel smaller than a thumb tack. I later learned that he did that because he didn't want us to get big-headed. He was always afraid that we would get the big head and not adhere to his discipline.

He would cuss you out and do all kinds of things to humiliate you and keep you under control. I remember one night I was thrown out of the *Hi-Jinks*. I later found out he did it to shake me up. The cause of the incident was a girl on stage who was a big snickerer. Every time she snickered, her legs flew open. I was down in the pit playing a piano modulation in order to attach together two musical arrangements written in different keys when this chick snickered and threw her legs open at the wrong time.

Momentarily, I looked up from the pit and forgot what I was doing, and there were two bars of silence. Captain Dyett leaned over and looked at me with that one eye and said, "What the hell is wrong with you?" That shook me up and I was hurt. Then I missed another bar and he told me to get up and get the hell out of the band pit.

All of this took place on the second night of the *Hi-Jinks* in 1937. The first night everything was perfect and I took care of business. My friends had been there the first night and my family was coming the third night, so I was really hurt when he threw me out. Fortunately, he would not permit anyone to leave the pit because of the high steps until the lights went up, so I just sat there beside Dorothy Donegan waiting for the lights to go on. In the meantime, the band started playing "Prelude to a Kiss," to be sung by Elizabeth Hunt. Her name is now Elizabeth Moutoussamy, but we called her "Squeaky" back in those days. Dorothy said to Captain Dyett, "Can John play 'Prelude to a Kiss' because I don't know the song?"

Captain leaned over and said, "He can play it if he keeps his head."

That was all I needed. I got down on the piano stool and played "Prelude to a Kiss," and I was through looking up on that stage. Dorothy actually knew how to play the song, but she was kind enough to use that excuse to keep Captain Dyett from kicking me out of the band that night. I'll be forever grateful to her for that gesture.

In the *Hi-Jinks* at the time was Redd Foxx, but I didn't pay too much attention to him because he had what we called a "tramp" band, which I didn't consider music, and I really didn't consider him funny. In later years I worked with him and had an opportunity to learn to appreciate him as a person and a great entertainer.

I worked with Redd Foxx at Herman Roberts' 500 Room on East 63rd Street and found him to be a beautiful dude. I have played about two or three gigs with Foxx in Chicago. I also found that there was a big difference between Foxx and Dick Gregory. When you announce Foxx's name, he's right there, on stage, bam. But when you announce Dick Gregory's name, it may be anywhere from five to eight minutes before he reaches the stage. He stops and shakes hands and talks with people at the tables, and you are just vamping the piano waiting for him to arrive. But I would say that they are both great comedians and I have enjoyed working with them.

I got my big break in 1942. I was working out at Joe Hughes' DeLuxe Club at

63rd and South Parkway in Chicago with a fellow named Swingley O'Neal. We had Nick Cooper on trumpet and John Levy on bass. John Levy is now the manager of both Joe Williams and Nancy Wilson. I can't remember who was on drums, but Swingley was on saxophone. Anyway, Harry Gray, who was then the president of the musicians union, called me up one morning with his loud, booming voice. He talked in a tone that would almost scare me to death, and this time I thought perhaps his call was prompted because I hadn't paid my dues or had done something wrong. But he said, "John Young, this is Harry Gray at the union. Andy Kirk needs a piano player. Do you want the job?"

I didn't know what to say. I was only twenty years old. He told me to think about it and to call him back. I was apprehensive. I didn't know whether to go with Andy Kirk or not. I didn't know how my mother would take it or what would happen. Finally, I discussed it with my mother and we decided I should not pass up the opportunity. So I called Harry Gray and told him I would take the job. I joined Andy Kirk's band in Cleveland, Ohio. That was some experience, playing with a big name band. Andy Kirk, Count Basie, Duke Ellington and Jimmie Lunceford were the popular big bands of that period, so I was highly honored. When you saw me, Travis, in 1943, I had been with the band a year. That was in the Youngstown, Ohio, Auditorium and you were wearing a soldier's uniform. I remember how you marveled at the way I played "Boogie Woogie Cocktail."

Let me tell you how I learned that song. Actually, Andy Kirk had no piano arrangement for that tune, so I bought the record and took it home and listened to it the entire afternoon. That night I performed it, according to Kirk, as though I had been playing it for twenty years. If you listen to my rendition of "Boogie Woogie Cocktail" and the rendition of Ken Kernsey, the composer of the song, even today they sound almost identical. I, personally, cannot tell the difference.

I found Andy Kirk a very nice man to work for. However, he wasn't innovative at all, and wouldn't do anything one would consider out of the ordinary. He tried to stay within a given pattern, unlike Duke Ellington, who was always introducing new material. In fact, Kirk wouldn't select any guys for his band who he felt were controversial, militant or radical. He wanted fellows that would not cause any trouble, who were peaceful and just wanted to play. We didn't have too many dope addicts in the band, either. A few of the cats smoked pot, but none of them snorted or shot up. I recall once we were in El Paso, Texas, and I went over to Juarez, Mexico, to get a gift for my wife. When I came back across the border, some of the other dudes in the band had gotten pot by the bags full and went through the guards without any problem. But when I and Billy Sharp, who was the road manager, tried to get clearance through the border patrol, they stopped us and took us into a little room and made us strip. They went through all the linings of our clothing and belongings trying to find dope. It was fortunate

John Young with the Kirk Band at the Band Box in Chicago's Loop.

that they chose the two dudes in the band who were really square, otherwise someone would have gotten busted. That was a degrading experience.

During the war, I was introduced to white and colored drinking fountains and white and colored waiting rooms as we traveled throughout the South by train because they took the buses away from us due to gasoline shortages. All of the big bands had to travel by railroad. It was the worst thing in the world because they would put us in the front car of the train, right next to the coal car. There was no air conditioning and, if you opened the windows for air, the coal cinders would blow right in on you. Of course, the whites were sitting back in the passenger cars in air-conditioned comfort. Whenever the assistant train engineer would shovel coal, all of the coal dust and cinders would fly back on us. Of course, the irony of the thing was when we would get off the train, white folks would look at us and say, "Look at those filthy niggers." But there was no other way for us to look because we had been sweating and felt stinky and dirty from the subhuman treatment we had received on the train. We were victims of American democracy.

The train's eating facilities were also Jim Crowed. We were not permitted to sit in the dining car. A guy would come through the train periodically with sandwiches chanting: "Get yo' ham samich." We were glad to get them, otherwise we would have starved to death on the trains. Occasionally, he would bring cokes back to wash the "ham samich" down. Those experiences I will never forget, and I certainly wouldn't want to repeat them. But blacks, in or out of the music business, suffered the same humiliation of Jim Crow laws across this country.

June Richmond was the vocal star in our band. You probably remember she worked with Jimmy Dorsey as his first black singer back in 1938. She also worked with Cab Calloway and Andy Kirk in the early 1940s. I remember June as an overweight crapshooter. She would shoot dice with those cats like a natural man. She loved to play poker and was a strong woman, but a lot of fun, just as you saw her on the stage. She would gamble away her money and it was funny to me how she went about it. As soon as the bus would pull off, they started poker and June would get right up in the thick of all those guys and play poker and lose all her money. When they would get to the theater later and shoot dice in the basement after the shows, she would get down on the floor and shoot dice just like the rest of them. I loved her. She was a great entertainer.

June would often trick me. Whenever she wanted an arrangement, she would always tell me she had to have it right away and, of course, she would put on a big act. She would come to me in tears and throw fits, and I later learned why she did this. She didn't want to give me too much time to write the arrangement. She was smart because she knew if I had a lot of time, I would overload the arrangement. Most musicians, particularly piano players, like to show off their education whenever they write a musical arrangement, and she knew that. So the arrangements that I turned out for her fast were always very simple and were considered good. Everyone liked to play them because they weren't loaded. Some musicians write arrangements that are so loaded, it would take Scott Joplin or Starokadomsky to work through them.

June's favorite was "Hey Lordy, Momma." When she sang that song and did her pimp walk on the stage, it absolutely broke up the house. Incidentally, she was also quite a dancer. June couldn't have been more than five feet five inches tall at the most and had to weigh 275 pounds, but she was as agile as a butterfly. I later learned that her weight killed her. She died of a heart attack at a relatively early age on August 14, 1962. She was a great artist.

Another lady I enjoyed working with is Nancy Wilson. I worked with Nancy Wilson and Redd Foxx at the Sutherland Hotel at 46th and Drexel. I remember the manager, whom we called "The Wiggler," couldn't understand the big crowds that Nancy and Redd brought into the place the entire period they were there, so he decided to book them separately. He brought Nancy back at a later date, and also brought Redd back, and they both drew the same large crowds, individually.

The John Young Trio: Lurlene Hunter, vocalist; Leroy Jackson on bass, and Eldridge Freeman on drums.

They are two of Chicago's favorite people. John Levy, Nancy's manager, wanted me to become her pianist on a regular basis because he considered me a decent kind of fellow. I gave the idea some serious consideration and decided against it because I wanted to do something with my own band. I didn't want to go through that road work again. I have found that in traveling you usually don't make enough money to sustain yourself. There are many expenses a traveling musician has to meet while on the road, such as hotel, laundry, food and, if you have a family, you have to send funds back home to meet the same costs you have incurred on the road. A guy making $400 or $500 a week, paying those heavy double bills, could actually come out in the hole. Joe Williams has a deal here at Rick's Cafe in Chicago. Whenever he brings anyone in from out of town, rooms are automatically rent free, which permits you to send the rent money home.

I went to Europe in 1977 to play in the jazz festivals. The rent wasn't free but we received a relatively good discount. European audiences are unique in that when you're playing, they are so quiet you can actually hear a pin drop. Many times I have had to look around to see if anyone was in the house, and yet there were several thousand people out there listening intensely and waiting patiently for us to complete our rendition. Once you have completed the number they break into applause so loud that you feel like a king. They have an appreciation for American jazz that is unbelieveable, and quiet as it's kept, they know more about us than we know about ourselves. Those people who interviewed me in Europe knew when I was born, where, and how long I had played with bands. I became suspicious. I asked myself how can these people know so much about me and what were their motives. I guess it was just their love of music and musicians. To them, we are unique in our contribution to American jazz, which is now appreciated more outside the continental United States than it is within. That is a sad commentary on American culture.

In recent years I have worked with Joe Williams on a number of occasions, and I would describe him as a true jazz singer, with a great jazz background. Working around him is a pleasure. He is a singer for all seasons and a great ballad man, too, handling classics or any kind of song that a singer should handle evenhandedly. He likes for his musicians to be on the ball and does not appreciate anyone who is not disciplined. He will not tolerate slackness or laziness. We had to be on the bandstand and able to kick off on time. Joe would never want to be left standing up there to kick off a tune, looking around, feeling silly because the musicians weren't ready. He wanted the musicians to hit that first note with confidence and vitality. Joe is strictly a businessman and one of the true businesslike persons that I've had the opportunity to work with, who also happens to be a great entertainer. Don't fool around with Joe Williams because he is taking care of serious business.

I found working with Eddie Jefferson the same. It's too bad his life was snuffed out in Detroit by a crazy fan. He would take a song like "Body and Soul," and scat-sing it in such a fashion that you would think you were listening to a natural saxophonist—a fantastic talent.

Most of the singers, the better ones that I have worked with, play piano. Sarah Vaughan plays good piano and Dinah Washington and Ella Fitzgerald were also pretty good. Carmen McRae is a professional when it comes to the keyboard. I remember that on many occasions Dinah Washington would say, "Move over, let me try my part out on the piano," and she would sit down at the piano and actually play the tune as well as most piano players.

It brings to mind an interesting point Dizzy Gillespie once made: "You can mentally see the notes as you play them." Most of the better musicians that I have worked with see the notes as they play them; that is, if they know the piano keyboard. Better music schools today almost make it mandatory that singers learn to play piano as part of their vocal training in order to be fully accomplished.

In my opinion, among the younger dudes, the most important piano influence is McCoy Tyner out of Philadelphia. He plays what I call outside of school; that is, outside of chord structure where you free yourself of chords and time and everything else. Tyner's type of playing is not without discipline and it has a home base. In other words, he can always return safely to the basic chords. Sometimes, these guys will go off and they can never get back to home base, but Tyner is one of the guys we really have to watch. I think he's got a lot of talent and is a great influence on today's trends on piano.

AUTHOR'S NOTE

I went to both elementary and high schools with John Young and watched him develop as a fellow piano player. I have often wished I had his great talent. At age fifteen, he was writing Duke Ellington and Jimmie Lunceford-type arrangements. I bought many of his scores for my orchestra. I will never forget his treatment of Jimmie Lunceford's "Don't Count Me Out." It was absolutely fantastic. His work made my band sound like the real Jimmie Lunceford Orchestra.

In my opinion, John Young is one of the great Afro-American talents that never reached full potential. It is our loss.

Sources

THE INCUBATION OF JAZZ IN THE WHITE CITY
SOURCES

BOOKS:

Bancroft, Hubert Howe, *The Book of the Fair,* Vol V. Chgo and San Francisco: Bancroft Co., 1893.

Bontemps, Arna. *They Seek a City.* NY: Doubleday, 1945.

Duster, Alfreda M., ed. *Crusade for Justice: The Autobiography of Ida B. Wells.* Chgo: University of Chicago Press, 1970.

Epstein, Dena J. *Sinful Tunes and Spirituals.* Urbana: University of Illinois Press, 1977.

Evans, Mark. *Scott Joplin and the Ragtime Years.* NY: Dodd, Mead, 1976.

Hamm, Charles. *Yesterdays: Popular Song in America.* NY: W. W. Norton, 1979.

Haskins, James. *Scott Joplin: The Man Who Made Ragtime.* Garden City, NY: Doubleday, 1978.

Jasen, David A. and Trebor Jay Tichenor. *Rags and Ragtime—A Musical History.* NY: Seabury Press, 1978.

Levy, Eugene. *James Weldon Johnson: Black Leader, Black Voice.* Chgo: University of Chicago Press, 1973.

Lomax, Alan. *Mister Jelly Roll.* Berkeley, CA: University of California Press, 1950.

Lyons, Len. *The 101 Best Jazz Albums.* NY: Wm Morrow, 1980.

Pierce, Bessie Louise. *A History of Chicago. 1871–1893.* Chicago: University of Chicago Press, 1957.

Ransom, Reverdy C. *The Pilgrimage of Harriet Ransom's Son.* Nashville, TN: A.M.E. Sunday School Union, 1946.

Stearns, Marshall & Jean. *Jazz Dance.* NY: Schirmer Books, 1979.

Taylor, Billy. *Jazz Piano: A Jazz History.* Dubuque, Iowa: William C. Brown Co 1982.

Travis, Dempsey J. *An Autobiography of Black Chicago.* Chgo: Urban Research Institute, 1981.
Ulanov, Barry. *Handbook of Jazz.* NY: Viking, 1960.

NEWSPAPERS:

"World's Fair Notes," *Detroit Plaindealer,* April 8, 1893.
"Event-filled Moments at White City," *The Broadax,* May 4, 1893.
"World's Fair Open," *Washington Bee,* May 7, 1893.
"Mr Douglass a Guest," *Detroit Plaindealer,* May 12, 1893.
"'Tis Now Dedicated," *The Broadax,* May 18, 1893.
"A New World's Fair Wonder," *Washington Bee,* July 1, 1893.
"Oh, That Mister Jelly Roll," *Chicago Daily News,* Aug 3, 1974.

PAPERS:

A Bontemps, "History of Negro Music and Musicians in Chicago," Jan 4, 1938. Unpublished WPA paper.
Horace Cayton, "A Survey of Negro Music," April 11, 1940. Unpublished WPA paper.

NO SEATS ON THE MAIN FLOOR
SOURCES

BOOKS:

Duster, Alfreda M., Ed. *Crusade for Justice: The Autobiography of Ida B. Wells.* Chgo: University of Chicago Press, 1970.
Editors of Ebony. *The Ebony Handbook.* Chgo: Johnson Publishing Co, 1974.
Gosnell, Harold F. *Negro Politicians: The Rise of Negro Politics in Chicago.* Chgo: University of Chicago Press, 1935.
Hughes, Langston & Milton Meltzer. *Black Magic: A Pictorial History of the Negro in American Entertainment.* Englewood Cliffs, NJ: Prentice Hall, 1967.
Myrdal, Gunnar. *An American Dilemma.* NY: Harper & Bros, 1944.
Ransom, Reverdy C. *The Pilgrimage of Harriet Ransom's Son.* Nashville, TN: A.M.E. Sunday School Union, 1946.
Rowland, Mable. *Bert Williams, Son of Laughter.* NY: The English Crafters, 1923.
Toll, Robert C. *On With the Show: The First Century of Show Business in America.* NY: Oxford University Press, 1976.

Travis, Dempsey J. *An Autobiography of Black Chicago.* Chgo: Urban Research Institute, 1981.

Tuttle, William, Jr. et al. *A People and a Nation.* Boston: Houghton Mifflin, 1982.

NEWSPAPERS:

"Negroes Envision Theater," *Chicago Sunday InterOcean,* May 12, 1901.

Chicago Daily Defender: "Colonial Theater Refuses Colored Gentleman," June 4, 1910; "George W. Walker," Jan 14, 1911; "Globe Theater Takes Notice," Jan 6, 1912; "Grand August Carnival," June 15, 1912; "Men Who Built the South Side," May 17, 1913; "Demand to Revoke Theater Licenses," Sept 6, 1913; "Review of the Theaters," May 9, 1914; "Bert Williams," July 11, 1914; "Chateau Garden Draws Color Line," Aug 6, 1914; "Opening Day of Atlas Theater," Sept 26, 1914; "The New Owl," Feb 3, 1917.

PERIODICALS:

"The Symbolism of Bert Williams," *Crisis,* May, 1922.

INTERVIEWS:

Wm. Y. Browne, July 26, 1977, Aug 1, 1981.

Earl B. Dickerson, 1977, 1981, 1982, 1983.

Lucille Farmer: Many conversations.

Mittie Travis: Many conversations.

PAPERS:

"Papers from the files of the Carter Woodson Library, 1938." Unpublished WPA documents.

ON THE TRAIL OF CHICAGO'S BLACK BELT'S
BALLROOMS AND SALOONS
SOURCES

BOOKS:

Gosnell, Harold F. *Negro Politicians: The Rise of Negro Politics in Chicago.* Chgo: University of Chicago Press, 1935.

Griffith, Richard & Arthur Mayer. *The Movies.* NY: Simon & Schuster, 1957.

Harris, Abram L. *The Negro as Capitalist.* Philadelphia: The American Academy of Political and Social Science, 1936.

Travis, Dempsey J. *An Autobiography of Black Chicago.* Chgo: The Urban Research Institute, 1981.

Work, Monroe M. *Negro Yearbook: An Annual Encyclopedia of the Negro—1921– 22.* Tuskegee, Ala: The Negro Yearbook Publication Co., 1922.

NEWSPAPERS:

Junius Wood, " 'Colored' Chicago Bank," *Chicago Daily News,* Dec 14, 1916.

"Plan Negro Hotel," *Chicago Tribune,* Nov 12, 1922.

"Police Raids on Chicago Cabarets," *Pittsburgh Courier,* Jan 1, 1927.

"Nora Holt Opens Chicago Nightclub," *Pittsburgh Courier,* July 9, 1927.

"Sylvester Russell's Review," *Chicago Tribune,* Oct 20, 1928.

"Asks Estate to be Conserved," *Chicago Tribune,* Oct 11, 1930.

Chicago Defender: "Jesse Binga to Wed Miss Johnson," Feb 17, 1912; "Binga-Johnson Wedding," Feb 24, 1912; "Jesse Binga, Manager," July 27, 1912; "Welcome to Our Carnival," Aug 17, 1912; "Queen of State Street Carnival," Aug 31, 1912; Carl B. Lewis, "Chicago State Dope," Nov 19, 1927; "Vincennes Hotel," July 20, 1940.

PERIODICALS:

W. E. B. Du Bois, "Hopkinville, Chicago and Idlewild," *Crisis,* Aug, 1921.

RESEARCH:

Notes and letters from Overton files.

INTERVIEWS:

Wm. Y. Brown, Aug, 1981.

Anna Grinnel [Binga's first cashier], June 10, 1969.

Oscar Hill [Overton's grandson], June 10, 1969.

Richard Hill [President, Douglas Nat'l Bank], July 12, 1969.

Earl Hines, July 21, 1982.

Jewel Stradford Lafontant and Ernest Stradford, Jan 14, 1983.

Dr Julian Lewis [Overton's son-in-law], July 19, 1981.

Ripley Binga Meade [Binga's nephew], June 10, 1969.

Ida Overton, May 16, 1981.

THE JAZZ SLAVE MASTERS
SOURCES

BOOKS:

Calloway, Cab and Bryant Rollins. *Of Minnie the Moocher and Me.* NY: Thos Y. Crowell Co, 1976.

Cripps, Thomas. *Slow Fade to Black.* NY: Oxford University Press, 1977.

Dance, Stanley. *The World of Earl Hines.* NY: Chas Scribner's Sons, 1977.

Ellington, Duke. *Music is My Mistress.* NY: Doubleday & Company, Inc., 1973.

Travis, Dempsey J. *An Autobiography of Black Chicago.* Chgo: Urban Research Institute, Inc., 1981.

PERIODICALS & PAMPHLETS

"How Gangsters Ran the Band Business," *Ebony.* September, 1949.

"Why White Women Won't Let Billy Daniels Alone," *Sepia.* October, 1956.

"Goin' to Kansas City," Mid-America Arts Alliance, 1980.

INTERVIEWS:

Lefty Bates and Freddie Cole, April 7, 1982.

James DeLisa, April 1, 1982.

George Dixon, April 21, 1982.

Earl Hines, July 21, 1982.

Gordon Jones, March 30, 1982.

Dave Young, June 12, 1982.

NOTES:

Author's 1939–40 diary.

Conversation with Lucky Millinder in New York City in 1961

PIANO MAN
SOURCES

BOOKS:

Finkelstein, Sidney. *Jazz: A People's Music.* NY: DaCapo Press, 1975.

Gusnell, Harold F. *Negro Politicians: The Rise of Negro Politics in Chicago.* Chgo:

University of Chicago Press, 1935.

Hamond, John. *On Record*. NY: Summit Bks, 1977.

Hecht, Ben. *A Thousand and One Afternoons in Chicago*. Chgo: Covics-McGee Publishers, 1922.

Hoyt, Homer. *One Hundred Years of Land Values in Chicago*. Chgo: University of Chicago Press, 1933.

Jones, LeRoi. *Blues People*. NY: Wm Morrow, 1963.

Keepnews, Orrin, & Bill Graver, Jr. *A Pictorial History of Jazz*. NY: Bonanza Books, 1981.

Lieb, Sandra R. *Mother of Blues: A Study of Ma Rainey*. Amherst: University of Massachusetts Press, 1981.

Lomax, Alan. *Mister Jelly Roll*. Berkeley: University of California Press, 1950.

Oliver, Paul. *The Story of the Blues*. Radnor, PA: Chilton Book Company, 1969.

Stearns, Marshall & Jean. *Jazz Dance*. NY: Schirmer, 1979.

Sullivan, Edward Dean. *Chicago Surrenders*. NY: Vanguard, 1930.

Travis, Dempsey J. *An Autobiography of Black Chicago*. Chgo: Urban Research Institute, 1981.

NEWSPAPERS:

Chicago Daily Defender: "Booze Made Her Want Position," June 13, 1925; "Unique Ball," June 13, 1925; "Girl Taken in Raid," June 13, 1925; "Bootleggers' Profits," June 27, 1925; "Jail Woman in Raid," July 4, 1925; "Dreamland," Oct 10, 1925; "Selling Moonshine to Boys," Oct 17, 1925.

PAPERS:

"Chicago Style 1938, The Negro in Illinois"; "Native Sons of Illinois, 1939"; "Rhythm, 1940"; "Ragtime in Chicago, 1941"; "Piano, Boogie Woogie and Blues, 1940"; Unpublished WPA documents.

INTERVIEWS:

Wm. Y. Browne, July 26, 1981.

Earl B. Dickerson, 1977, 1981, 1982, 1983.

George Dixon, April 21, 1982.

Art Hodes, Mar 17, 1982.

Little Brother Montgomery, April 14, 1982.

James Pierce, June 13, 1982.

Mittie Travis, Author's mother.

Dave Young, June 2, 1982.

John Young, May 12, 1982.

NOTES:

Author's diary and scrapbook for 1940.

YOU ARE GOING TO BE MORE THAN ME
SOURCES

BOOKS:

Albertson, Chris. *Louis Armstrong: Giants of Jazz.* NY: Time-Life Books, 1978.

Chilton, John. *Who's Who of Jazz.* NY: Time-Life Records Spec Ed, 1972.

Dance, Stanley. *The World of Earl Hines.* NY: Chas Scribner's Sons, 1977.

Gilmore, Al-Tony. *Bad Nigger.* Port Washington, NY: Kennikat Press, 1975.

Hodes, Art and Charwick Hanse, eds. *Selection from the Gutter.* Berkeley, CA: University of California Press, 1978.

Hoskin, Robert. *Louis Armstrong: Biography of a Musician.* CA: Holloway House, 1979.

Lang, Ian. *Jazz in Perspective.* NY: DeCapo Press, 1976.

Lomas, Alan. *Mister Jelly Roll.* CA: University of California Press, 1950.

Louis, Joe with Edna and Art Rust, Jr. *Joe Louis: My Life.* NY: Harcourt, Brace, Jovanovich, 1978.

Lucas, Bob. *Black Gladiator.* NY: Dell, 1970.

Lyttleton, Humphrey. *The Best of Jazz: Basin Street to Harlem.* NY: Taplinger, 1979.

Mays, Benjamin E. *Born to Rebel.* NY: Chas Scribner's Sons, 1971.

Morris, Ronald L. *Wait Until Dark: Jazz and the Underworld 1880–1940.* Ohio: Bowling Green University Press, 1980.

Schaap, Dick. *Jack Johnson is a Dandy.* NY: New American Library, 1970.

Time-Life Books, eds. *This Fabulous Century 1920 to 1930,* Vol III. NY: Time-Life Books, 1969.

Travis, Dempsey J. *An Autobiography of Black Chicago.* Chgo: Urban Research Institute, 1981.

_____. *Don't Stop Me Now.* Chgo: Children's Press, 1970.

NEWSPAPERS:

Jay Robert Nash, "The Joy of Sax," *Chicago Tribune,* February 28, 1982.

INTERVIEWS:

Lil Armstrong, June 16, 1970.
Roy Butler, Mar 16, 1982.
Sy Oliver, April 30, 1982.
Mittie Travis.
Dave Young, June, 1982.

PAPERS:

Dempsey Travis, diary and scrapbooks for 1939–1940.

JUMPING AT THE SAVOY
SOURCES

BOOKS:

Chicago Commission on Race Relations. *The Negro in Chicago.* Chgo: University of Chicago Press, 1922.

Dance, Stanley. *The World of Earl Hines.* NY: Chas Scribner's Sons, 1977.

Harris, Abrams L. *The Negro as Capitalist.* Philadelphia: The American Academy of Political and Social Science, 1936.

Ottley, Roi. *The Lonely Warrior.* Chgo: Henry Regnery, 1955.

Ramsey, Frederic, Jr. *Jazzmen.* NY: Harcourt, Brace, 1940.

Rosenthal, George S. & Frank Zachary. *Jazzways.* NY: Greenberg Publisher, 1946.

Travis, Dempsey J. *An Autobiography of Black Chicago.* Chgo: Urban Research Institute, Inc., 1981.

NEWSPAPERS:

"New Savoy Ballroom," *Pittsburgh Courier,* Oct 22, 1927.

"Chicago's Million Dollar Ballroom," *Pittsburgh Courier,* Nov 12, 1927.

"Chicago Stage Dope," *Pittsburgh Courier,* Dec 3, 1927.

Chicago Defender: "Binga State Bank Victor," Dec 3, 1927; "New Building Progresses," July 23, 1927; "Savoy," Oct 29, 1927; "Savoy to Open," Nov 5, 1927; "Mayor Thompson at Savoy," Nov 12, 1927; "Plantation Frolics at Savoy," Nov 19, 1927; "Smart Set at Savoy Opening," Dec 26, 1927; "Theater Reviews," Feb 4, 1928; "Salaries and Advertisements," Feb 25, 1928; "Directors of Binga Bank Honored," Sept 1, 1928.

INTERVIEWS:

Kenneth Blewett, April 7, 1982.
Wm. Y. Browne, July 26, 1981.
Cab Calloway, Jan 14, 1983.
Carol Chilton, Jan 13, 1983.
Joe Crawford, Dec 27. 1980.
George Dixon, April 21, 1982.
Mittie Travis. Many conversations.
Dave Young, June 12, 1982.

THE MANY FACES OF LADY SAVOY: 1927–1948
SOURCES

BOOKS:

Dance, Stanley. *The World of Earl Hines.* NY: Chas Scribner's Sons, 1977.
Driggs, Frank & Harris Lewine. *Black Beauty, White Heat: A Pictorial History of Classic Jazz.* NY: Wm Morrow, 1982.
Terkel, Studs. *Giants of Jazz.* NY: Thos Y. Crowell, 1957.

MAGAZINES AND PAMPHLETS:

The Savoyager, June 16, 1928.
The Savoy News, Aug, 1940.
The Savoy Chatterbox, June, 1938.
"Parham Starving. He Only Gets 5 Meals a Day," *Downbeat,* Mar, 1939.

NEWSPAPERS:

Chicago Defender: "Defender Ball All Set for Tuesday Eve," June 22, 1928; "Savoy to Thrill Its Patrons with Circus Tent Attraction," Sept 15, 1928; "Walter Barnes Draws 5,200 Dancers to the Savoy Ballroom," Aug 16, 1930; "Erskine Tate & Dave Peyton to Hold Music Battle," April 30, 1930; "Earl Hines for Valaida Snow Back in City at Savoy," Mar 18, 1933; "Battle Expected to Draw Huge Crowd Between Ella Fitzgerald and Viola Jefferson," July 16, 1938; "Free Skating Lessons—January 27th at the Savoy," Jan 14, 1939; "Harlan Leonard to Savoy, Jan 14," Jan 6, 1940; "King Kolax Band Plays Savoy, Jan 21st," Jan 20, 1940; "Savoy to be Seen—Valentine Party February 11," Feb 10, 1940; "Oliver Bibb to Take in One-Niters," Feb 24, 1940; "Eddie Stovall's Band Plays Savoy on

Sunday," Mar 16, 1940; "Les Hite & Band to Play Savoy Here," April 6, 1940; "Jitterbugs Await the Ink Spots at Savoy," April 20, 1940; "Lunceford at Savoy, Jitterbugs all Set for Big Jamboree," May 18, 1940; "Jimmy Noone Plays Savoy Sunday Night," June 8, 1940; "Floyd Ray's Band to Play Savoy July 21st," July 20, 1940; " 'Tisket-A-Tasket' Star Plays Savoy Sunday. Crowns Beauty Queen," Aug 17, 1940; "Count Basie, Swing King, to Play Loop and Savoy," Aug 10, 1940; "Charlie Barnett's Band to Play Savoy," Nov 7, 1940; "Nat Cole Plays Return Date at Savoy Ballroom," Mar 14, 1942; "Jay McShann, Recording Sensation, Battles Kolax at Savoy Sunday," Feb 7, 1942; "Cab Calloway, Prince of Hi-de-ho, Will Play Dance Sunday," Jan 31, 1942; "Jive Cadillac Band at Savoy," Aug 10, 1942; "Louis Russell Plays Dance at Savoy Sunday," Aug 12, 1944; "Charlie Parker versus Gene Ammons at Savoy," Mar 6, 1948.

INTERVIEWS:

Eddie and Mary Etta Plique, Sept 13, 1982.

Dr Jive Cadillac, June, 1983.

Jimmy Davis, June, 1983.

Vernon Guider, June, 1983.

Harry Gray [President of Local 208, affiliate of the American Federation of Musicians], Oct, 1982.

William Samuels [Secretary of Local 208 of the American Federation of Musicians], June, 1983.

Ken Blewett, April 7, 1982.

Mittie Travis.

Willie Howard, 1962.

NOTES:

Eddie Plique's pictorial diary for the years 1931–1944.

Notes from the author's personal diary, 1936–1947.

JAZZ JOINTS ALONG EAST GARFIELD BOULEVARD
SOURCES

BOOKS:

Chilton, John. *Who's Who of Jazz.* NY: Time-Life Records Spec Ed, 1978.

Dance, Stanley. *The World of Earl Hines.* NY: Chas Scribner's Sons, 1977.

Terkel, Studs. *Giants of Jazz*. NY: Thos Y. Crowell Co, 1957.

Travis, Dempsey. *An Autobiography of Black Chicago*. Chgo: Urban Research Institute, 1981.

_____. *Don't Stop Me Now*. Chgo: Children's Press, 1970.

NEWSPAPERS:

"Ammons is Hit at DeLisa," *Pittsburgh Courier*, July 27, 1935.

"Dance Creations that Died," *Pittsburgh Courier*, Oct 21, 1929.

Chicago Defender: "El Rado Cafe," Feb 15, 1930; "Platinum Lounge," April 24, 1937; "Pops Platinum," June 5, 1937; "Grand Terrace Will Open," June 5, 1937; "Tunes at Boulevard Lounge," May 4, 1940; "308 Club's Band," Jan 11, 1941; "Chorines Feted," Jan 10, 1942; "Billy Mitchell at DeLisa," Feb 28, 1942; "The 'It' Club Entertainer," May 2, 1942.

INTERVIEWS:

Floyd Campbell, April, 1982.

Oliver Coleman, February, 1961.

Milton Hinton, February 22, 1983.

Dave Young, June 12, 1982.

PAPERS:

"The Negro in Illinois," 1938. Unpublished WPA paper.

Author's diary 1936–1938.

CLUB DELISA
SOURCES

BOOKS:

Dance, Stanley. *The World of Earl Hines*. NY: Chas Scribner's Sons, 1977.

Dexter, Dave. Jr. *The Jazz Story from the 90's to the 60's*. Englewood Cliffs, NJ: Prentice-Hall, 1964.

Hare, Maud Cuney. *Negro Musicians and Their Music*. NY: Da Capo Press, 1974.

Jones, LeRoi. *Blues People*. NY: Wm Morrow, 1963.

Keepnews, Orrin & Bill Grauer, Jr. *A Pictorial History of Jazz*. NY: Bonanza Books, 1966.

Oliver, Paul. *The Story of the Blues*. Radnor, PA: Chilton Bk, 1969.

Simon, George T. & Friends. *The Best of the Music Makers.* Garden City, NY: Doubleday, 1979.

Travis, Dempsey J. *An Autobiography of Black Chicago.* Chicago: Urban Research Institute, 1981.

Whitney, Balliet. *Night Creature: A Journal of Jazz, 1975–1980.* NY: Oxford University Press, 1981.

PERIODICALS:

"Billy Eckstine." *Ebony.* Mar, 1949.

"At DeLisa." *Flash.* June, 1951.

"George Kirby." *Ebony.* Jan, 1951.

"21 Years on Stage." *Sepia.* Jan, 1956.

"Gatemouth Moore." *Ebony.* Dec, 1949.

"The Night Club where Stars are Born." *Sepia.* 1957.

NEWSPAPERS:

Ted Watson, "Red Saunders at DeLisa," *Pittsburgh Courier,* Jan 28, 1939.

"Billy Eckstine at Club DeLisa," *Pittsburgh Courier,* Oct 14, 1939.

Chicago Defender: "Ignore Vice Drive," April 27, 1935; "Thirty-five Cent Nights at Swingland," Jan 27, 1940; "Record Crowds Expected," Mar 16, 1940; "New Show," June 1, 1940; "Three Spots Open After Hours, June 22, 1940; "Billy Mitchell at DeLisa," July 13, 1940; "Partello at DeLisa," Aug 3, 1940; "Band Popularity Poll," Dec 14, 1940; "Blaze Destroys DeLisa," Feb 15, 1941; "Probe of DeLisa Fire," Feb 15, 1941; "Stampede at Theater," April 12, 1941; "DeLisa to Re-Open," April 19, 1941; "Spots Hit Peak," April 26, 1941; "Club DeLisa," April 26, 1941; "Good Music at DeLisa," June 7, 1941; "Show at DeLisa," June 21, 1941; "Club DeLisa Show Clicks," July 15, 1941; "Billy Mitchell at DeLisa," Feb 28, 1942; "Stars at DeLisa," Mar 30, 1946.

INTERVIEWS:

Lefty Bates, March, 1982.

Freddie Cole, March, 1982

James DeLisa, April, 1982.

George Dixon, April, 1982.

Harry Gray, Oct, 1982.

Earl Hines, July, 1982.

Joe Williams, Aug, 1982.

Dave Young, June, 1982.

NOTES FROM SCRAPBOOKS AND DIARIES:

Freddie Cole, 1927 to 1940.
Mary Milton, 1914 to 1936.
Dempsey Travis, 1936 to 1942.

PAPERS:

Onah L. Spencer, *Composer and Trail Blazer*, 1938. Unpublished WPA papers.

THE REGAL THEATER THAT I REMEMBER
SOURCES

BOOKS:

Anderson, Jervis. *This Was Harlem*. NY: Ferrar Straus Giroux, 1982.
Dance, Stanley. *The World of Earl Hines*. NY: Chas Scribner's Sons, 1977.
Plackson, Sally. *American Women in Jazz*. NY: Seaview Books, 1982.
Travis, Dempsey J. *An Autobiography of Black Chicago*. Chgo: Urban Research Institute, 1981.

PERIODICALS:

"Regal Celebrates 18th Anniversary," *Sepia*. September, 1945.
"The Regal Story," *Flash Magazine*. February, 1951.
Theater Historical Society, Annual Number 7, 1980.
Balaban & Katz Magazine. August, 1928.

NEWSPAPERS:

Chicago Defender: Carrie B. Lewis, "Chicago Stage Dope," Dec 10, 1927, Mar 3, 1928; Dave Peyton, "Chicago Theatrical Notes," Jan 27, 1928, Jan 14, 1928, Jan 28, 1928; "Regal Theater Will Open," Jan 14, 1928; "Bldg Commissioner Inspects New Regal Theater," Jan 21, 1928; "Splendid New Theater," Feb 4, 1928; Dave Peyton, "The Musical Bunch," Feb 4, 1928; "Crowds Enter New Theater," Feb 11, 1928; "Great Banner Works at the Regal," Feb 25, 1928; "Great Show for Regal," Mar 3, 1928; "Death of Regal Theater," Nov 24, 1973.

INTERVIEWS:

Ken Blewett, April 7, 1982.
Wm. Y. Browne, July 26, 1981.

Floyd Campbell, Mar 16, 1983, April 13, 1983.
Joe Ducibella (Dir. Chgo. Chapter Theater Historical Society), Nov 8, 1982.
Eve Wheatley Edwards, April 18, 1982.
Dave Young, June 12, 1982.

KEN "MR. REGAL" BLEWETT
SOURCES

BOOKS:

Anderson, Jervis. *This was Harlem*. NY: Ferrar Straus Giroux, 1982.
Dance, Stanley. *The World of Swing*. NY: Chas Scribner's Sons, 1974.
_____. *The World of Earl Hines*. NY: Chas Scribner's Sons, 1977.
_____. *The World of Count Basie*. NY: Chas Scribner's Sons, 1980.
Driggs, Frank and Harris Lewine. *Black Beauty, White Heat. A Pictorial History of Classic Jazz 1920–1950*. NY: Wm Morrow, 1982.
Gillespie, Dizzy with Al Fraser. *To Be Or Not To Bop*. Garden City, NY: Doubleday, 1979.
Plackson, Sally. *American Women in Jazz*. NY: Seaview Books, 1982.
Schiffman, Jack. *Uptown: The Story of Harlem's Apollo Theater*. NY: Cowles Bks, Inc., 1971.
Travis, Dempsey J. *An Autobiography of Black Chicago*. Chgo: Urban Research Institute, Inc., 1981.

NEWSPAPERS:

Pittsburgh Courier: "Bill Bailey," May 25, 1935; "Sissle/Waters in Chgo," June 8, 1935; "Fight of Fights," Aug 10, 1935; "Big Money," Feb 4, 1939; "Stage Shows Should be Revived," Feb 18, 1939; "Fess Williams," Feb 18, 1939; "Stage Show Returns to Regal," Sept 2, 1939; "Chgo's Two Mecca Theaters," Feb 27, 1940; "Basie Gets State-Lake Booking," July 17, 1940; "Hampton's New Style," May 17, 1942; "Power Behind Hampton," April 22, 1944.
Chicago Defender: "Barthelmess Talking Film," Jan, 1929; "Bill Robinson's Charity Show," Jan 11, 1929; "Regal's Vodvil Show," July 6, 1929; "Huge Minstrel Show," July 6, 1929; "Large Crowds to Regal," July 13, 1929; "Hot Show at Regal," July 13, 1929; "The Idle Rich," July 20, 1929; "Dave Peyton in East," July 27, 1929; "Regal Offers Talkies," Aug 3, 1929; "Regal Vodvil," Aug 3, 1929; "Garbage at Regal," Aug 10, 1929; "Fox Movietone Follies at Regal," Aug 17, 1929; "Stepin Fetchit on Screen at Regal," Aug 24, 1929; "Donald King at Regal," Aug 31, 1929; "Rowdyism at Theater," Aug 31, 1929; "Banner Month at Regal," Sept

7, 1929; "Shows at the Regal," Sept 14, 1929; "Songbird at Regal," Sept 14, 1929; "Comedy and Mystery," Sept 21, 1929; "Bojangles Bill," Oct 12, 1929; "Josephine Baker at Regal," Nov 16, 1929; "New Stage Show," Nov. 23, 1929; "Burlesque at Regal," Nov 24, 1929; "Hallelujuah," Jan 25, 1930; "Public Demand Heavy for Regal," Nov 28, 1931; "Remodelled Eat Shop," Mar 14, 1936; "Andy Kirk Autographs Records," Mar 12, 1938; *"Hi-Jinks* New Crop of Stars," Mar 25, 1940; "Hawkins at Regal," Mar 22, 1941; "B & K Employees in Party," Jan 24, 1942; "Fess Williams at Regal," Jan 24, 1942; "Erskine Hawkins' Band," Feb 21, 1942; "Andy Kirk's Band," April 4, 1942; "Sadie Bruce at Regal," May 2, 1942; "Meet Lionel Hampton," Feb 13, 1943.
"Days at the Regal," *Chicago Tribune,* May 30, 1983.

MAGAZINES:

"The Chicago Regal," *Balaban and Katz Magazine,* May, 1928.
"Regal Celebrates 18th Anniversary," *Sepia,* Feb, 1945.
"Grotto and Regal," *Flash,* Feb, 1946.
"Ken Blewett—Man Behind the Regal," *Flash,* Feb/Mar, 1950.
"The Regal Story," *Flash,* 1950.
"Oldest Midnight Show," *Sepia,* Sept, 1957.
"The Apollo Story," *Apollo Magazine,* 1965.

INTERVIEWS:

Ken Blewett, April 7, 1982.
Cab Calloway, Jan 14, 1983.
Floyd Campbell, April, 1982.
George Dixon, April 21, 1982.
Dizzy Gillespie, June 2, 1982.
Franz Jackson, Jan 5, 1982.
George Kirby, June 11, 1982.
Daddy O'Daylie, Sept 17, 1982.
Eddie Plique, Sept 13, 1982.
Herman Roberts, April 8, 1982.
Joe Williams, Aug 26, 1982.
Dave Young, June, 1982.

NAT "KING" COLE REMEMBERED
SOURCES

NEWSPAPERS:

Chicago Defender: "King Cole Signs Up," Aug 26, 1944; "King Cole Sold on His Guitar," Jan 3, 1948.

"Woody Herman Guest Star on King Cole Trio Time on NBC," *New York Age,* July 12, 1947.

New York Post: "Cole Attack Empties White Council Hall," April 13, 1956; "Nat Cole: They Could Have Sold It If They Wanted To," Nov 21, 1957. "The Voice is Stilled. Nat King Cole," Feb 27, 1965.

MAGAZINES:

"Old King Cole," *The Orchestra World,* April, 1945.

Ebony Magazine: "Nat Cole May Gross $50,000 a Day from Singing One Song," Oct, 1953; "The Nat King Cole Nobody Knows," Oct 1956; "King Cole's Wife Goes Back to Work," Dec, 1955; "Death Stills Voice of World Famed Master Balladeer at Age 45," April, 1965.

"The Nat King Cole Story," *Congressional Record,* Nov 26, 1963.

"Music Get Another Cole," *Sepia,* Oct, 1957.

"The King & I," *Our World,* July, 1954.

"Press Crucifies Nat King Cole," *Sepia,* June, 1956.

INTERVIEWS:

Billy Eckstine, July, 1983.

Henry Fort, Feb 1983.

Baldwin Tavares, June, 1983.

Marty Faye, Feb, 1983.

Nancy Wilson, June, 1983.

Kenneth Blewett, April 7, 1982.

Eddie Plique, Sept 13, 1982.

NOTES:

Memorandum from Gene Howard's King Cole Trio Bio File 102347.
The author's personal diary.

ROBERTS SHOW CLUB
SOURCES

NEWSPAPERS:

Chicago Defender: "Phyllis Branch & Jackie 'Mom's' Mabley Appearing," Jan 30, 1960; "Roberts Show Club Announces No-Admission Charge for February," Feb 13, 1960; "The Next Feature at Roberts Will be Billy Eckstine," Feb 27, 1960; "Billy Eckstine Triumphed for Opening Jam at Roberts," Mar 12, 1960; "Redd Foxx Jokes His Way up to Roberts Club," April 2, 1960; "The Jewelbox Revue Starts Limited Engagement at Roberts Lounge," April 9, 1960; "Roberts Show Club Presents the Rhythm Kings," May 14, 1960; "Roberts Show Club Presents Milt Buckner & His All-Star Revue," May 21, 1960; "Roberts Show Club Presents Red Saunders & JoAnn Henderson," June 18, 1960; "Duke Ellington & Count Basie's Orchestra to Arrive in Fall," July 30, 1960; "Johnny Hartman Held Over At Roberts," Sept 10, 1960; "Ray Charles Revue Held over Another Week," Sept 24, 1960.

MAGAZINES:

"New Home for Happy Feet," *Ebony*, June, 1956.

INTERVIEWS:

Herman Roberts, owner of Roberts Show Club, April 8, 1982.
Dick Gregory, comedian.
George Kirby, comedian.
Billy Eckstine, singer.
Dorothy Donegan, pianist.
Marty Faye, radio & TV personality.

NOTES:

Memorandum from files of Herman Roberts.
 Herman Roberts, April 8, 1982.
 Dick Gregory, July, 1982.
 George Kirby, June, 1983.
 Billy Eckstine, July, 1983.
 Dorothy Donegan, June, 1983.
 Marty Faye, Feb, 1983

 Cole: They Could Have Sold It If They Wanted To," Nov 21, 1957. "The Voice is Stilled. Nat King Cole," Feb 27, 1965.

Index